T0389270

Photography and History in Colonial Southern Africa

This book studies the relationship between photography and history in colonial Southern Africa, using a series of encounters with Southern African photographic archives to reflect on photography as a distinct historical form.

Through the use of private and public archives, images produced by African itinerant photographers, white settlers, and colonial state institutions, this book explores the relationship between photography and history in colonial Southern Africa. Late nineteenth century Cape Colonial prison albums, police photographs from German South West Africa, African studio portraits, identity documents, travel permits and passports from the 1920s and 1930s, visual studies of whiteness and blackness authored by settler photographers, South African *dompas* photographs from the 1950s and 1960s, and aerial photography from the Eastern Cape in the mid-twentieth century are examined to highlight the ways in which photographic images cut across conventional institutional boundaries and complicate rigid distinctions between the private and the public, the political and the aesthetic, the colonial and the vernacular, or the subject and the object. *Photography and History in Colonial Southern Africa* argues that rather than understanding photographs as a means of preserving and recreating the past in the present, we can value them for how they evoke at once the need for and the limits of historical reconstruction.

This book will be of interest to students and scholars of colonial history, photographic history, visual media, and African studies.

Lorena Rizzo is a historian at the University of Basel, Switzerland. She has taught in universities in Switzerland, Germany, Namibia, South Africa and the USA, curated photographic exhibitions, and organised public history projects across Europe and Southern Africa.

Routledge Studies in the Modern History of Africa

This series includes in-depth research on aspects of economic, political, cultural, and social history of individual countries, as well as broad-reaching analyses of regional issues.

Themes include social and economic change, colonial experiences, independence movements, post-independence governments, globalisation in Africa, nationalism, gender histories, conflict, the Atlantic Slave trade, the environment, health and medicine, ethnicity, urbanisation, and neo-colonialism and aid.

Forthcoming titles:

Human Rights in Sierra Leone, 1787–2016
The Long Struggle from the Transatlantic Slave Trade to the Present
John Idriss Lahai

Miscegenation, Identity and Status in Colonial Africa
Intimate Colonial Encounters
Lawrence Mbogoni

Displaced Mozambicans in Postcolonial Tanzania
Refugee Power, Mobility, Education, and Rural Development
Joanna T. Tague

Africans and the Holocaust
Perceptions and Responses of Colonized and Sovereign Peoples
Edward Kissi

Photography and History in Colonial Southern Africa
Shades of Empire
Lorena Rizzo

Photography and History in Colonial Southern Africa
Shades of Empire

Lorena Rizzo

Routledge
Taylor & Francis Group

LONDON AND NEW YORK

First published 2020
by Routledge
2 Park Square, Milton Park, Abingdon, Oxon OX14 4RN

and by Routledge
52 Vanderbilt Avenue, New York, NY 10017

Routledge is an imprint of the Taylor & Francis Group, an informa business

British Library Cataloguing-in-Publication Data
A catalogue record for this book is available from the British Library

Library of Congress Cataloging-in-Publication Data
A catalog record has been requested for this book

ISBN: 978-1-138-34301-6 (hbk)
ISBN: 978-0-429-43945-2 (ebk)

Typeset in Bembo
by Lumina Datamatics Limited

Contents

Acknowledgements

There are a number of institutions and people without whom this book would not have been possible. I began working on this project as a fellow in the Department of Africanamerican and African Studies at the University of Michigan in 2010. I would like to thank Derek Peterson for hosting me, and David William Cohen for the many conversations, early morning neighbourhood breakfasts, and walks around Ann Arbor. Helmut Puff and Kathryn Babayan were lovely friends and colleagues with whom to share the joys and sorrows of diasporic lives. Claire Zimmerman, Christopher Ratté, and their two children, Helena and Leo, hosted me and made me feel welcome and at home. Between 2011 and 2013 I was a research fellow in the Centre for Humanities Research (CHR) at the University of the Western Cape (UWC) in Bellville, South Africa. These were the formative years for this project, since I could do extensive archival research, interviews, and oral history. Premesh Lalu and Suren Pillay were generous hosts at the CHR, and every conversation with them was exciting, instructive, and critical for refining my understanding of South African history and critical theory. Ciraj Rassool and Lelie Witz at the History Department of UWC have been colleagues and friends for many years. I value their ongoing interest in my work, their intellectual generosity, and their exceptional knowledge of South African pasts and presents. Ciraj, Leslie and Gary Minkley, at the University of Fort Hare, Alice, Eastern Cape, South Africa, have been critical in transforming South African history, and they have been an inspiration for those of us who wish to push the boundaries of the discipline and write imaginative histories that speak to audiences within and beyond the academy in meaningful ways. While at UWC, I was privileged to meet a group of exceptional co-fellows and members of faculty, among them Phindezwa Mnyaka, Nina Sylvanus, Ruchi Chaturvedi, Jane Taylor, Noeleen Murray, Brian Raftopoulos, Maurits van Bever Donker, Janeke Thumbran, Bianca van Laun, and Anna Selmeczi, all of whom made the CHR a place of scholarly rigour, and social and personal well-being. Lameez Lalkhen was a remarkable and friendly administrator, who made the lives of international visitors as comfortable as possible. The summer schools organised by Premesh Lalu, Gary Minkley and Helena Pohlandt-McCormick were great opportunities for intense discussion and for strengthening our ties across disciplinary fields and geographical regions. I continue to value the colleagues I met on these occasions and the friendships forged. Archival research in Cape Town was critical for some of the key arguments developed in the book. Erika Le Roux and staff at the Western Cape Archives and Records Service were incredibly helpful and supportive in accessing the photographic collections and granting permission to reproduce and publish photographs. Collections at the South African National Archives and the Ditsong Museum of Cultural History in Pretoria, the Museum Africa in Johannesburg, and the National Geospatial Information in the Department of Rural Development and Land Reform in Cape Town were all easily accessible, and the archivists most helpful in securing high-quality reproductions of photographs. I am particularly indebted to Elize Schneigansz for her research assistance. Tina Smith, head curator at the District Six Museum, and Paul Grendon, independent photographer in Cape Town, have become dear friends and family, critical interlocutors, and generous colleagues, who introduced me to the thriving world of Cape Town's museums, festivals, and creative and visual arts, and have refined my understanding of diverse cultures and practices of knowledge production. I am grateful to Paul Grendon for allowing me to use some of his photographs in the book. Research for the book also included regular visits to Namibia, where I worked in various archives and collections. My thanks go to the National Archives of Namibia and to their retired head archivist Werner Hillebrecht, who continues to be generous and helpful whenever I need advice in locating photographs and contextualising them in a history of archival acquisition, conservation, and classification that remains, at times, nebulous. My Namibian colleagues have always been supportive of my work and have made the many visits and research initiatives over the past two decades always pleasurable and successful. My thanks go to Martha Akawa and Godman Gwasira at the University of Namibia, Saara Ilovu at the Usakos Museum, and last but not least to Jeremy Silvester at the Museums Association of Namibia. In 2013 I returned to Europe and took up a post in the History Department at the University of Bielefeld, Germany. My thanks go to Angelika Epple for her commitment to make African history part of the curriculum there. I enjoyed two years of teaching, and the possibility to think about my work in Southern Africa within the framework of transnational and global history. Between 2015 and 2017 I had the privilege to spend two years at Harvard University, first as a visiting scholar at the Center for African Studies and later as the Oppenheimer fellow at the Hutchins Center for African and African American Research. The years spent at Harvard provided the perfect academic environment for writing the book, and many colleagues there have shared ideas and made critical comments on earlier drafts of chapters. My gratitude and thanks go to Jean and John Comaroff, who have been mentors and friends for many years. Their scholarly creativity and rigour, and their intellectual generosity are exceptional; the many conversations in Cambridge, Basel, and Cape Town were simply wonderful.

Henry Louis Gates Jr. was a generous host at the Hutchins Center, and I am grateful to him for creating a fellowship programme that enables scholars from across the world and the disciplines to meet and engage with each other's work. Christian Crouch and Gaiutra Bahadur have been wonderful co-fellows; my thinking and writing on history and photography has benefited enormously from our exchanges and conversations during the Hutchins Center Fellows Colloquium. My sincere thanks go to Krishna Lewis and to her colleagues, all of whom have made the fellows feel at home.

Writing this book would never have been possible without my closest colleagues in Basel, Dag Henrichsen at the Basler Afrika Bibliographien (BAB) and Giorgio Miescher at the University of Basel. They are outstanding scholars of Namibia and Southern Africa, with whom I share a very long intellectual relationship and a passion for Namibian history. Dag Henrichsen and his colleagues at the BAB have made my work in their archives and library always pleasant, and particular thanks go to Susanne Hubler for helping with locating photographs and securing permission to publish. Giorgio Miescher has read all the chapters and made critical comments throughout. Many more colleagues have read earlier versions and have critically engaged the arguments proposed in the book whenever I presented them in colloquia, seminars, and lectures. My thanks go to Jean and John Comaroff, Geoff Eley, Julia Thomas, William Beinart, James Merron, Luregn Lenggenhager, and Zeynep Gürsel. Finally, I remain deeply thankful to the late Patrick Harries, whose passion for Southern African pasts and presents and curiosity for ways of writing history that were not his made him an exceptional mentor and friend.

Basel, January 2019

Introduction
Shades of empire

My interest in writing a book on photography and history in colonial Southern Africa has come from different directions and was inspired by a variety of research questions. Some of the original concerns have survived the unforeseen twists and turns of the writing process, and they therefore deserve mention. Obvious, perhaps, is the initial charm of the Southern African collections of historical photographs themselves: their intricate visuality, materiality, and sensuality; their troubling appearance but ultimate aesthetic appeal; their privileged status in the archive; and their unsettling ability to literally bring the past before our eyes all held the promise of an opening towards writing history of a different kind.[1]

Certainly, historians have long shown curiosity about photographs as historical sources – not just since the visual turn – and by the late 1990s, visual history began to flourish in Southern African academic research and writing.[2] More specifically in South Africa and Namibia, this shift in intellectual discourse concurred with a critical revision of academic history articulated under the auspices of public history, museum and heritage, and memory studies.[3] Here, historical photographs featured prominently, since they strongly resonated with the desire to recover people, places, and times lost to the physical and social ruination brought about by colonialism, segregation, and apartheid.[4] There is no doubt that across an increasingly diverse range of articulations of historical consciousness, photography has been considered particularly appealing because of the tangible and visceral encounter with people's history that it offers, and its conduciveness to a more subjective reframing of the past and an imaginative conception of the future.[5] In the past 25 years, historical photographs have, in short, invigorated and enriched the production of Southern African historical narratives that strove to speak to the present in more pertinent and meaningful ways.[6]

The revision of Southern African history in the post-apartheid era and the accompanying critical role of visual history formed the framework within which *Photography and History in Colonial Southern Africa* came into being. However, my primary interest in this project arose from a theoretical probing of the historical status of photography, on the basis of which one would have to ask a set of specific questions: How do photographs become historical evidence? How do they acquire historical meaning? What do photographs tell us about the past? How and why would one propose an account of Southern African pasts that is based primarily on historical photographs? What does it mean to write not a history *of* photography, but one made *by* photographs?[7] And how and why, finally, would we narrate an allusive, incomplete, contingent, scrappy kind of history that arises from photographic images?[8] These questions have been addressed from different scholarly perspectives, in and beyond the discipline of history, and, as will become clear throughout the book, they all reflect an interest in unsettling the certainties of historical method and interpretation, especially once photography helps reveal the partial nature of any historical inscription and understanding.[9]

Underlying most contemporary theorising are, more or less explicitly, the works of Walter Benjamin, Siegfried Kracauer, and Roland Barthes, and their deliberations on photography and history remain critical to the arguments proposed here. Those arguments will especially be concerned with the ways in which these authors reflected on analogies between thinking of history and thinking of photography, pointing to their shared ontological, conceptual, and epistemological grounds. Dismissing what Benjamin and Kracauer in particular saw as the delusive historicist belief in holistic recuperation and cognition, they all fostered an understanding of the past as a series of fleeting moments and fragmented images, and of the assemblage of those moments and images as history as a mere act of mimetic inscription and citation, reproduction, and repetition.[10] If anything, photographic reality and historical reality were, to all of them, inherently instable, incoherent, and discontinuous.[11] The language is conducive for assessing how they conceived of the photographic image, medium, and technology as a useful metaphor for understanding not only the concept of history, but also, and especially, the reconfiguration of the relationship between history and memory, a mediation that they all deemed to be a key feature of modern experience and thought.[12]

Notwithstanding the current enthusiasm for these "classics", there is, I believe, a need for a word of caution. As much as Benjamin and his peers have pushed us onto new, if sometimes uncertain theoretical terrain, it is important to keep in mind that their interest was more in the philosophy of history and the politics of aesthetics than in doing and writing history *per se*. Therefore, remaining solely in their company would lead down the garden path, especially if we sail in the misty lee of nostalgia, loss, and death.[13] More importantly, perhaps, these particular thinkers do not resolve methodological and analytical problems that arise once we attempt to explain how specific photographs distinguish themselves from any other historical form in a given context, and how they might have become meaningful in the different institutional and discursive realms in which they were produced, circulated, and viewed.[14] Caution is not dismissal, though, and there are reasons to continue to interrogate Benjamin, Kracauer, and Barthes – and obviously the rich literature that draws on their work – while concurrently keeping theory on the ground and remaining committed to probing philosophical abstraction against the contingencies and distinctions of historical specificity.

Obviously, this is where historical inquiries are most promising and confident. But there are further reasons for placing historical photographs in particular cultural, institutional, or visual contexts, without assuming these to be given, fixed, unified, or coherent.[15] We shall do so especially because contextualising helps counter the tendency and temptation to understand photographs as signature images that stand in for ideas, ideologies, disciplines, and politics, or modes of vision assumed to be characteristic of certain periods and localities.[16] The category of "colonialist photography" is just one expression of the described tendency, but clearly one amongst those that needs critical revision in a book on photography in colonial Southern Africa.

I have adopted a few strategies throughout this work that helped to "keep theory on the ground". However, if readers expect a history of photography *per se* in Southern Africa – one that moves from the introduction of the medium in South Africa in the mid-1840s to its spread across the subcontinent and use by European missionaries and colonial bureaucrats; white amateur and professional photographers, adventurers, explorers, scientists, and settlers; and, finally, possibly since the interwar period but certainly after World War II, Africans themselves – they will be disappointed.[17] Rather, the main interest that was and remains formative for *Photography and History in Colonial Southern Africa* was in exploring how the region's history could be narrated on the basis of historical photographs, and if such a project would differ from accounts that privilege the written record. The geographical focus is on South Africa and Namibia, the pairing arising from South African colonial rule in Namibia, which began after the German defeat in 1915 and ended with Namibian independence in 1990. As a result, Namibia was incorporated into an expanding and thickening territorial and social landscape marked by racial segregation and apartheid, within which the colony and its inhabitants were relegated to the backwaters of a fraught and foul modernity.[18] However, this embroiled history and its repercussions, which explain at least part of the enduring condition of coloniality in both countries, remain strangely ignored, especially in South African history.

Scholarly shyness of more integrated understandings of the South African-Namibian intertwining has been explained by the failure to recognise the intricacy of empire, colonialism, and nation in the sub-region, which can hardly be reconciled with imperial histories drafted on metropolitan, that is to say British and French, models.[19] This critique has not merely been a nod towards the fashionable paradigms of transnational or entangled history.[20] What is at stake, rather, is an attempt to overcome the teleological understanding of South Africa's gradual disengagement from the British Empire, and to reckon its emergence and consolidation as a modern nation-state (though tainted by internal colonisation) precisely in the light of Namibia's complicated trajectories through German and South African colonialisms, and the latter's entanglement with multiple South African and European metropoles.[21] This line of argument was expected to enable a more dynamic approach, which understands empire and nation not as abstracted categories, but as variable historical manifestations and emerging properties of power and sovereignty, marked by the uneven spread of capitalism and colonialism throughout the Southern African region, expanding external and internal frontiers, shifting territorialities, and ever-changing regimes of difference.[22]

Photography and History in Colonial Southern Africa builds on these earlier attempts to rethink history in the region, especially where these have opened ways of thinking about empire in terms of networks and circuits along which things and ideas moved – within and between nations and colonies, metropoles and peripheries. This is empire as a way of knowing and being, a constellation of power and authority that engendered how people and things were continuously made and unmade, assembled and dispersed. It is, essentially, along these lines that we can explore what we gain from unearthing the layers of South African-Namibian historical entanglement *through* photography. Such an approach involves asking a number of questions that aim at explaining how empire and colonialism conditioned the spread of photography in the region, and how, conversely, photographs projected and mediated, represented and moulded, and scrutinised and contested the idea and experience of the colonial endeavour and its modernising claims. How did colonial power relations and administrative structures imposed by the colonial, segregationist, and apartheid states shape the production, circulation, and consumption of photographs? What kind of visual economies emerged in the wake of colonial and capitalist penetration in the region in this period? What readings did disciplinary regimes and discourses of race and ethnicity, imposed by science and modernising state institutions, encourage or enforce?[23]

Scholars of visual history have explained how German and South African colonial occupation determined and, ultimately, obstructed the emergence of a strong and diverse photographic culture in Namibia up until the 1960s.[24] The plurality of colonialisms engendered complex visual and knowledge economies – be it as part of South Africa's efforts to substantiate its claim to the Namibian territory vis-à-vis the international community, German photographic production that continued after Germany's defeat and loss of the colony in 1915, or importantly, if harder to retrace, African engagements with the medium since the mid-nineteenth century. Yet, the relationship between photography and colonialism, and image and power remain historically and theoretically complicated.[25] Also, as the editors of *Colonising Camera* have argued, the Namibian case illustrates how much the circuits of power and knowledge can run on different courses. The trajectories of photographs into the archive indeed proved complicated, and their accumulation and preservation in various collections was often haphazard, uneven, and anonymous.[26] This "messiness" of the Namibian photographic archive is in part to be explained by its status as a peripheral entity, constituted in defining ways in the shadow of South African institutional and knowledge hegemony. Similar inquiries into the significance of photographies produced on the margins, Namibian and other, within the South African visual landscape remain, unfortunately, much less pursued.[27]

However, *Photography and History in Colonial Southern Africa* is not just an attempt to write Namibian visual history into an alleged South African photographic canon. Instead, I am interested in intersections, not only the ones that point to entangled histories, but also those that enable us to rethink the categories, chronologies, and scales that shape historical thinking and writing. As suggested earlier, such rethinking will be based on considering historical photographs as images and objects; it will evolve once we linger on their visuality and materiality, before retracing their trajectories within and beyond institutional and discursive domains, through geographical space and historical time. It will also emerge from the clusters in which photographs assembled with other images, texts, objects, and bodies, and acquired meaning within multiple material constellations while moving from one context of viewing to another. Finally, the possibility of historical revision will accrue from configuring photography not as a set of images and material objects alone, but as a field of *practices*, which includes placing oneself in front of a camera as much as producing photographs; collecting, curating, and displaying photographic images; and reactivating them in different forms of historical inquiry and representation.[28]

Such an approach will require us to remain close and attentive to the visual archives of South Africa and Namibia and to move to the foreground particular photographs preserved within these archives. The point of departure for each of the following chapters is a specific photographic collection; what links them conceptually throughout the book is a continuous concern with how the archive shaped photographic production in the region. Here, *Photography and History in Colonial Southern Africa* builds on a consolidated critique of the colonial archive, now conceived as less of a material repository of historical data and more of a process, discursive framework, and a set of relations within which historical evidence and "hierarchies of credibility" are produced.[29] Mining content has given way to paying attention to archival placement and form.[30] Furthermore, as an expression of a deep scepticism of colonial knowledge production tout court, scholars have increasingly argued that what constitutes the archive, the form it takes, and the systems of classification and epistemology it engenders essentially reflect critical features of colonial politics and state power.[31] In light of such justified suspicion of colonial knowledge production, including in its postcolonial formulation, exposing the problems of "colonial photographs" as historical sources seems pertinent.[32] What enables them to constitute truthful representations of reality? In what way does their realist and evidentiary claim depend on the material effects of a unifying archive? As is well-known, nineteenth-century regimes of truth, optical empiricism, *and* systems of record-keeping were constitutive of and constituted by photography's deployment in scientific knowledge production and as part of the (Colonial) state's surveillance apparatus.[33] But nineteenth-century photographic realism and instrumentality alone cannot serve as ground on which to sound photography's status as an historical and archival object. Rather, we need to explain what the specific requirements of evidence are in a given context, at a given moment, and ask what status, *other than evidence*, photographs have as historical form, both within the constraints of the colonial archive and, crucially, beyond it.[34]

The critical revision of the archive will remain essential throughout the following chapters, all of which highlight the ways in which historical photographs constitute a series of micro-intentions rather than reflections of universalising desires.[35] Still, *Photography and History in Colonial Southern Africa* continues to analyse photographic archives precisely regarding the desires, intentions, hopes, and expectations that the archive attributes to the visual, without assuming photographs to function – inevitably, let alone effectively – as vehicles of cultural meaning or instruments of colonial power.[36] But why should we emphasise the need for a careful, ethnographic reading of the archive, and why do this in the context of Southern African visual history? As suggested earlier, there continues to be a tendency to understand South African and Namibian history within the teleological framework of colonial penetration and the consolidation of first the segregationist and then the apartheid state, with their ultimate dismantlement by nationalist resistance and emancipation.[37] Photographic archives simultaneously sediment and disrupt this narrative of the rise and fall of colonial state power and apartheid; they validate and belie the solidity of colonial epistemology and rationality; and they assert and question what is retrievable and knowable. The aim here, therefore, is to refine and complicate our understanding of photography's ambiguous effects on Southern African history and its archival mediation. And yet, there might be, once again, the need to keep our feet on the ground. This book clearly wishes to push the limits of archival credibility. As others have done, it argues that in some instances it proves more productive not to reduce archival narratives to fiction, but to understand them as institutional formations and mechanisms that had real effects, since they imposed some readings over others and foreclosed some interpretations while encouraging others.[38] Rather than trapping ourselves in an intractable split between construction and deconstruction, it seems more important not to fetishise photographic archives but to keep an eye on both the capabilities *and* limits of archival authority. Finally, we need to remind ourselves that there is a world of images and visual practices that never left a trace in the archive, as much as there are myriads of photographs that, once they entered archival collections, lay dormant for an indefinite time.

It is clear by now that *Photography and History in Colonial Southern Africa* will follow a rather circular line of thinking. Historians of photography are familiar with moments at which it looks as if photographs raise more questions than provide answers to what happened in the past.[39] The more we devote ourselves to photographic images, the more they seem enigmatic, vague, and contradictory. The desire to understand Southern African history through the lens of photography takes us onto slippery paths, and it remains a challenge to decide how to shore up an emerging historical interpretation, which refuses to write off uncertainty, ambiguity, and conjecture. But the leap into the unknown releases forms of creativity and enables a "combing" of history and theory, which commits itself to thinking and writing about collections of historical photographs in a productive and refined way, rather than to any particular disciplinary convention or canon – historical or other.[40] This is, however, less an argument in favour of the interdisciplinarity engraved in visual studies, than an interest in *indiscipline*.[41] My main concern is in describing a problem – the relationship between photography and history – and to find historical and theoretical avenues through which to propose a careful discussion of particular Southern African photographs. The result is a book structured less chronologically – as historians might still find preferable – but more along a visual thread specified by a selection of photographic collections and woven into a broad-meshed theoretical fabric. The photographs themselves, the kinds of questions they raise, the kinds of structures of viewing and knowing they enact, and the kinds of interpretations they induce, thence, determine the methodology. However, I am not suggesting a prescribed path of inquiry, an interrogatory space defined by particular photographs. Rather, I am describing a series of archival encounters that generated a range of analytical possibilities and encouraged a particular theoretical interrogation.[42] Thus, while the chapter titles might appear to go adrift, each pursuing its own idiosyncratic interest, they simply delineate the book's different entry points to an entangled photographic landscape. Still, readers might value more detailed explanations of the historical, visual, and analytical connections at work.

Chapter 1 – *Assemblage: Photography and colonial policing in German South West Africa 1910–1913* – looks at a collection of police and prison photographs and its affiliated textual archive from Namibia under German colonial rule. It pays careful attention to the ways in which we encounter these photographs in the archive – their placement, visuality, and materiality – and explains the specific contexts in which the images were produced. Based on a meticulous archival probing, the chapter argues that while the main photographic project pursued by the German colonial administration was originally coined as an exercise in modern criminalistics, it ultimately failed to yield most of the desired results. The photographs, registers of prisoners, lists of escaped convicts, fingerprints, and anthropometric measurements did not allow for the systematic identification of African subjects or the control of their movement, residence, and employment histories. In other words, while we encounter a copious pool of archival documents, the material defies a consistent and unified historical account of a modernising state bureaucracy and its surveillance apparatus. In view of this interpretative impasse, but assuming that the administrative endeavour did have effects, if unanticipated ones, the chapter considers the collection of police and prison photographs within the framework of assemblage theory.[43] Thereby, it succeeds in explaining how the visual work done by the police and penal system in the German colony spilled out of its institutional and discursive bounds and reassembled in new material and virtual formations. Three instances of such dispersals are discussed in depth: settler photography and the conflation of surveillance and desire; physical anthropology and counterinsurgency; and fingerprinting and racial science.

Chapter 2 – *Bodies and things: Photography and the person in Southern Africa, 1920s–1960s* – continues along similar lines, though it shifts attention from the institutional to the individual level by discussing the role of photography for the classification and identification of bodies along the lines of race, gender, and citizenship more systematically.[44] Photography – as one of the indexical modalities of the visual (fingerprinting being the other one) – was an important domain in which citizens and subjects negotiated state imposed epistemologies of the body. The chapter draws on two theoretical propositions in order to frame the discussion: Roberto Esposito's "Dispositif of the Person", and Thomas Lemke's expanded understanding of Foucault's notion of governmentality that considers the multiple *conjunctions between bodies and things*.[45] Using a large archive of identity documents, travel certificates, permits, labour recruitment passes, and passports produced between the 1920s and 1960s, the chapter explores how photographs were harnessed for classification and typology, reification, and abstraction. But likewise, we'll explain how every photograph swayed between serving as a visual synecdoche of race, tribe, ethnicity, or nationality on the one hand, and disclosing the partiality and fragmentation, specificity, and contingency of all these categories on the other hand. The issuing of identity documents is usually understood within the domain of state action that generally produced repressive visual forms, such as in the case of the South African enforcement of the *dompas* system. Still, even within bureaucratic registration, we find a remarkable diversity in aesthetic language and visual practice that made space for African agencies, self-articulations, and critiques of the hegemonic claims enforced by racial projects under segregation and apartheid. Some of these contestations come into view once we pay attention to African photographers' involvement in government schemes, and the photographic subjects' efforts to draft subaltern notions of personhood, individual positionality, and embodied experiences of belonging. In a more theoretical gesture, finally, the chapter explains how various bureaucratic projects assumed that the body, the person, and the photographic image conditioned and constituted each other, and concurrently, how by placing the making of visual bodies at the centre of historical narration we can transform our understanding of colonial state formation and the constitution of a modern nation in the region.

Chapter 3 – *Augenblick: The moment in Namibian photography, 1930s–1960s* – is, at first sight, a caesura, since it moves more explicitly than the two preceding ones to the question of photography and history. It does so by focusing on one of the key problems in the theory of photography, namely "the burden of the moment".[46] Photographs are understood to either capture a moment, a mere fragment of time, an elusive, accidental or even trivial instant, or to freeze time by extracting a particular moment and turning it into something significant, momentous, and something that resonates with what philosophers call the *Augenblick*. It is this tension between the transient and the persistent, between the arbitrary and the essential that complicates photography's relationship to time, history, and memory, and conditions the way we correlate the photographic and the historical event. The chapter explores what particular historical photographs from Southern Africa tell us about this relationship by investigating the kind of analytical work moment and Augenblick do once we think about these concepts not as abstractions alone, but within a specific historical situation. The first part considers the work of "white" photographers in Namibia. Settler photography was fundamental in shaping the colonial Southern African aesthetic order, and throughout most of the twentieth century, numerous settlers became amateur or professional photographers in Namibia and were deeply troubled by the question of race.[47] By investigating how settler photography oscillated between the moment and the momentous, the first part of the chapter retraces "white" photographers' attempts to enforce and stabilise particular notions of racialised subjectivity. This concerned the articulation of both whiteness and blackness, or the representation of landscape, and it essentially turned race into a matter and modality of seeing.[48] The second part of the chapter moves on to the contemporaneous work of African itinerant photographers and present-day women collectors of historical photographs in Usakos, a central Namibian town, in order to investigate if and how the moment and Augenblick of photography in the aesthetic encounter between Africans differed from the one in settler photography. It offers a discussion of private photographic collections from a former African location and argues that the photographs assembled here give way to important contestations of the hegemonic visual order. These contestations concern, on the one hand, the temporality of Augenblick, which explicitly depends on the photographs' movements in and out of history, memory, and at times nostalgia; on the other hand, they speak more explicitly to Augenblick's spatial connotations, i.e. its philosophical conception as both an instant *and* a site of historical awareness and transformation.

Chapter 4 – *Heterotopia: Aerial photography and mapping in the Eastern Cape, 1930s–1960s* – invites readers, once again, to adjust to a significant shift in scale and embark on a vertiginous transition to a peculiar space-time configuration: aerial photography in the Eastern Cape in the period between the 1930s and 1960s. The chapter investigates what this specific form of visualisation and the terrains it produced tell us about the relationship between photography and history. Aerial photographs are commonly associated with military intelligence and surveillance, in Southern Africa and beyond; but they also became a favoured visual means in the everyday civilian, bureaucratic, and technocratic understanding and management of both the physical and social landscapes across the region.[49] Thus, aerial photography was crucial for the modernist projects in the late segregationist and apartheid periods. They are evidence of a strong interest in developing a distinct aesthetic language for landscape, which would help substantiate the preoccupation with a residential racial order. Theoretically, aerial photography has long been understood in terms of the Foucauldian model of panoptic vision and the idea of an omniscient gaze; yet, more recent debates have noted how the general monolith of visual panopticism tends to swallow the histories of diverse archives and specific localities. In line with this critique, formulated for example in the work of Paula Amad, the chapter explores how the extensive purview of aerial photography relates to the enclosed, small-scale, but no less totalising world of the archive.[50] In other words, the chapter investigates how aerial photographs provided the means to perceive the world as an expressive, skin-like surface and, thereby, encouraged an understanding of the surface as an event, a readable text, and living archive. Presuming that aerial photography constituted a distinct view – rather than a mere mimetic reproduction of reality – which countered everyday perception and brought together seemingly incompatible sites, the chapter finally explores how the collections of photographs discussed here took on heterotopian qualities: as visual emplacements that seemed untrue to, but were still based in everyday reality; and as flattened and geometricised imag(in)ings, which replicated, exaggerated, reduced, or transformed a particular place – the Eastern Cape – into a representational space in which temporal juxtapositions, ambiguities, and contradictions would be intensely felt.[51]

Finally, and in line with the book's circling form of reasoning, Chapter 5 – *Presence: The Breakwater prison albums, Cape Town, 1890s–1990s* – takes us back to the beginning and even beyond. The chapter considers a series of photographic albums produced at the Breakwater Convict Station in Cape Town in the late nineteenth and early twentieth centuries. It examines the extent to which this photographic project resonated with the global proliferation of Bertillonage and was part of an attempt to professionalise the penal system at the Cape.[52] Yet, the photographs were also the product of a distinct local and historically contingent negotiation of how the medium would help constitute a particular subject of rule: the modern prisoner. The first part of the chapter revises some of the standard arguments in the literature and offers an analysis of the albums' complicated position in the archive that circumvents an easy blending of the image/object into the narrative of a colonial disciplinary, let alone a panoptic regime of vision. Instead, it pays attention to the archival, semantic, and aesthetic ambiguities of the photographs and the ways in which colonial prison and police institutions attempted to contain these. Exploring Susan Buck-Morss' idea of (an) aesthetics in the prison context, one of the main concerns in this first part is to highlight the intricacy of the imprisoned subject's growing exposure to an environment marked by a set of technologies, including photography, which regulated time, space, and the body.[53] Obviously, this discussion resonates with the one proposed in Chapter 1, though the grounds shared between the two parts of the book are historical as much as analytical. But the affinity is partial, and it comes to an end in Chapter 5's second part, which looks at contemporary readings of this body of historical prison photographs within the framework of genealogical and memory studies in contemporary South Africa. Here, we explore yet another instance of photography's role in mediating the past through readings that seek to address one of the critical concerns of historical narrative: the tension between representation, i.e. the preoccupation with historical meaning, and *presence*, i.e. the movement away from a constructed past to a past that actually existed and speaks to us in a presumably unmediated way through things that we can feel, touch, and see.[54] Portraits of African historical subjects that survive in photographic collections prove to be, as the chapter shows, particularly pertinent to the desire for a return to the presence of the past.

Photography and History in Colonial Southern Africa, in sum, delves into a specific selection of photographic collections, and in each case, it does so through the lens of a particular theoretical problem. However, there are lines of thought that run through all the chapters. As discussed earlier, reflecting on the colonial archive is one of them. The preceding outline of the book's structure makes it clear that a further inquiry pursued consistently is the problem of time and space, and their respective configuration in photography and history. Here, discourse on photography has emphasised the ways in which the photographic image complicates the clear distinction between past, present, and future, defying, as it were, the continuous flow of historical time. Photographs constitute fragments of both time *and* space, yet they have an unsettling ability to fix and recreate – re-present – the object they extract from a "there and then" in the "here and now".[55] Distance to history is reduced, reality freed from the conditions of time and space, and the past's presence in the image conflated into the image itself.[56] Though we might raise strong objections against such reasoning, at least photographic fragmentation remains critical for questioning the idea of temporal continuity and spatial homogeneity.[57] It is at this point where photography highlights a tension within the discipline of history: the questioning of unified categories of time and space – so intrinsic to theories of modernisation – versus the preference for a notion of multiple temporalities and spatialities, and their mutual conditioning.[58] This tension resonates, again, with the writings of Benjamin, Kracauer, and Barthes, who, as we noted earlier, had long taken note of analogies between photographic image and medium and the making of history. I would like to close this introduction by briefly resuming the line of thought from a slightly different angle, one that helps us conceive of photography and history more explicitly as two modalities of mediating and conceptualising space–time constellations. This is not to say that photography and history are or do the same, notwithstanding occasional, almost bizarre overstatements in the form of – "there can be no thinking of history that is not at the same time a thinking of photography".[59] Such reductions and generalisations are not for those who wish to understand their relationship by explaining what specific photographic archives and collections tell us about the ways in which time and space are thought of in a particular historical context. The moment has come, therefore, to turn to Southern Africa.

Notes

1 See Eduardo Cadava, *Words of Light: Theses on the Photography of History*. Princeton, 1997, p. xvii.

2 For a discussion of the place of photography in historical writing see Jennifer Tucker in collaboration with Tina Campt, Entwined Practices. Engagements with Photography in Historical Inquiry. *History and Theory*, Theme Issue 48, 2009: 1–8. On the visual or pictorial turn see W.J.T. Mitchell, *Picture Theory. Essays on Verbal and Visual Communication*. Chicago and London, 1995, p. 11. For writings on photography in Southern Africa, especially South Africa and Namibia, see Patricia Hayes, Jeremy Silvester and Wolfram Hartmann, Photography, History and Memory, in Wolfram Hartmann, Jeremy Silvester, and Patricia Hayes (eds.), *The Colonising Camera. Photographs in the Making of Namibian History*. Cape Town, Windhoek, Athens, 1998, pp. 2–9.

3 Leslie Witz, Gary Minkley and Ciraj Rassool, South Africa and the Unsettling of History, in ibid., *Unsettled History. Making South African Public Pasts*. Ann Arbor, 2017, pp. 1–26.

4 See e.g. Darren Newbury, 'Lest We Forget': Photography and the Presentation of History at the Apartheid Museum, Gold Reef City, and the Hector Pieterson Museum, Soweto. *Visual Communication*, 4, 3, 2005: 259–295.

5 See Elizabeth Edwards, *The Camera as Historian. Amateur Photographers and Historical Imagination, 1885–1918*. Durham, 2012, p. 7. This resonates with what Batchen called the "future anterior of presence", see Geoffrey Batchen, *Burning with Desire. The Conception of Photography*. Cambridge (MA), 1997, p. 213.

6 Annie E. Coombes, *History After Apartheid: Visual Culture and Public Memory in a Democratic South Africa*. Durham, 2003.

7 Patricia Hayes, Introduction: Visual Genders. *Gender & History*, 17, 3, 2005: 519–37, here p. 520. Hayes makes this argument based on Christopher Pinney, *"Photos of the Gods": The Printed Image and Political Struggle in India*. London, 2004, p. 9; Hayden White in conversation with Ethan Kleinberg, Center for the Humanities, Wesleyan University, published online in October 2013 [https://www.youtube.com/watch?v=ViG30Fkz2cI].

8 Patricia Spyer, Photography's Framings and Unframings: A Review Article. *Society for Comparative Study of Society and History*, 43, 1, 2001: 181–92, here p. 189.

9 Elizabeth Edwards, *Raw Histories. Photographs, Anthropology and Museums*. Oxford, New York, 2001, p. 10; see also Jean and John L. Comaroff, Introduction: The Portraits of an Ethnographer as a Young Man, in John L. Comaroff, Jean Comaroff, and Deborah James (eds.), *Picturing a Colonial Past. The African Photographs of Isaac Schapera*. Chicago, London, 2007, pp. 1–18.

10 Gregory Paschalidis, Images of History and the Optical Unconscious. *Historein* 4, 2003: 33–44; Christine Mehring, Siegfried Kracauer's Theories of Photography: From Weimar to New York. *History of Photography*, 21, 2, 1997: 129–36.

11 Inka Mülder-Bach, The Exile of Modernity. Kracauer's Figurations of the Stranger, in Johannes von Moltke and Gerd Gmünden (eds.), *Culture in the Anteroom: The Legacies of Siegfried Kracauer*. Ann Arbor, 2012, pp. 276–292, here p. 290.

12 Cadava, *Words of Light*, pp. xviii–xix; Tim Dant and Graeme Willoch, Pictures of the Past. Benjamin and Barthes on Photography and History. *European Journal of Cultural Studies*, 5, 1, 2002: 5–23.

13 Edwards, *Raw Histories*, p. 11.

14 Poole, An Excess of Description: Ethnography, Race, and Visual Technologies. *Annual Review of Anthropology*, 34, 2005: 159–179, here p. 162.

15 See Dominick LaCapra, Rethinking Intellectual History and Reading Texts. *History and Theory*, 19, 3, 1980: 245–76, here p. 247.

16 Elizabeth Edwards, Photographic Uncertainties: Between Evidence and Reassurance. *History and Anthropology*, 25, 2, 2014: 171–88.

17 But see Patricia Hayes, Power, Secrecy, Proximity: A Short History of South African Photography. *Kronos*, 33, 2007: 139–62.

18 Jeremy Silvester, Marion Wallace and Patricia Hayes, "Trees Never Meet". in Patricia Hayes, Jeremy Silvester, Marion Wallace, and Wolfram Hartmann (eds.), *Namibia under South African Rule: Mobility & Containment 1915–1946*. Oxford, Windhoek, Athens, 1998, pp. 3–48; and more generally Saurabh Dube and Ishita Banerjee-Dube, Introduction: Critical Questions of Colonial Modernities, in ibid. (eds.), *Unbecoming Modern. Colonialism, Modernity, Colonial Modernities*. New Delhi, 2006, pp. 1–31.

19 Dag Henrichsen, Giorgio Miescher, Ciraj Rassool and Lorena Rizzo, Rethinking Empire in Southern Africa. *Journal of Southern African Studies*, 41, 3, 2015: 431–5.

20 See David Simon (ed.), *South Africa in Southern Africa: Reconfiguring the Region*. Oxford, 1998. For a more general reflection on transnational history, including its possible entanglements with imperialism, see Michael McGerr, The Price of the "New Transnational History". *The American Historical Review*, 96, 4, 1991: 1056–67.

21 Henrichsen et al., Rethinking Empire, p. 433.

22 See Ann L. Stoler and Frederick Cooper, Between Metropole and Colony: Rethinking a Research Agenda, in A.L. Stoler and F. Cooper (eds.), *Tensions of Empire: Colonial Cultures in a Bourgeois World*. Berkeley, Los Angeles, 1997, pp. 1–41; Frederick Cooper, Introduction: Colonial Questions, Historical Trajectories, in ibid., *Colonialism in Question. Theory, Knowledge, History*. Berkeley, Los Angeles, London, 2005, pp. 3–32.

23 Deborah Poole, An Excess of Description, pp. 160–1.

24 Hayes et al., Photography, history, and memory, pp. 2–9.

25 Ibid., p. 4; also Elizabeth Edwards, Thinking Photography beyond the Visual?, in J.J. Long, Andrea Noble and Edward Welch, *Photography. Theoretical Snapshots*. Abingdon, New York, 2009, pp. 31–48, here p. 41.

26 Hayes et al., Photography, History, Memory, p. 7.

27 But see for example John Liebenberg and Patricia Hayes, *Bush of Ghosts: Life and War in Namibia, 1986–1990*. Cape Town, 2010.

28 See on the "practice turn" in visual studies and other fields Asko Lehmuskallio and Edgar Gomez Cruz, Why Material Visual Practices?, in Edgar Gomez Cruz and Asko Lehmuskallio (eds.), *Digital Photography and Everyday Life*. Abingdon, New York, 2016, pp. 1–16.

29 Ann Laura Stoler, "In Cold Blood": Hierarchies of Credibility and the Politics of Colonial Narratives. *Representations*, 37, 1992: 151–89.

30 Ann Laura Stoler, Colonial Archives and the Arts of Governance. *Archival Science*, 2, 2002: 87–109, here p. 90.

31 Stoler, Colonial Archives, p. 87.

32 Critical for the postcolonial critique of the colonial archive is Gayatri Chakravorty Spivak's Can the Subaltern Speak?, in Cary Nelson and Lawrence Grossberg (eds.), *Marxism and the Interpretation of Culture*. Urbana, 1988, pp. 271–313. For an elaborated discussion of postcolonial thinking about the archive see Sandhya Shetty and Elizabeth Jane Bellamy, Postcolonialism's Archive Fever. *Diacritics*, 30, 1, 2000: 25–48.

33 Allan Sekula, The Body and the Archive. *October*, 39, 1986: 3–64, John Tagg, *The Burden of Representation. Essays on Photographies and Histories*. Minneapolis, 1993, pp. 60–4; Elizabeth Edwards, Ordering Others: Photographies, Anthropologies, Taxonomies, in Chrissie Iles and Russel Roberts (eds.), *In Visible Light. Photography and Classification in Art, Science and The Everyday*. Oxford, 1997, pp. 54–68.

34 Edwards, *Raw Histories*, pp. 12–13. The discussion anticipated here concerns the ways in which *Photography and History*, and especially Chapter 3, reflect on thinking about photographs as "historical evidence" or, alternatively, of "photographic events". See more generally Linda Hutcheon, *A Poetics of Postmodernism. History, Theory, Fiction*. New York and London, 2004, p. 122.

35 Poole, An Excess of Description, p. 162.

36 W.T.J. Mitchell, What Do Pictures "Really" Want? *October*, 77, 1996: 71–82.

37 See e.g. William Beinart and Saul Dubow, Introduction: The Historiography of Segregation and Apartheid, in ibid. (eds.), *Segregation and Apartheid in Twentieth Century South Africa*. London, New York, 1995, pp. 1–24.

38 Stoler, In Cold Blood, p. 183; Stoler, Colonial Archives, p. 91.

39 Edwards, Photographic Uncertainties, p. 176.

40 The term "combing history" is borrowed from David William Cohen, who understands combing as "representing simultaneously the power to cover and veil knowledge from inspection, but also the power to restore it in practice". See David William Cohen, *The Combing of History*. Chicago and London, 1994, p. 246.

41 See on indiscipline W.T.J. Mitchell, Interdisciplinarity and Visual Culture. *Art Bulletin*, 77, 4, 1995: 540–4, here p. 541.

42 See the introduction to Tina M. Campt, *Listening to Images*. Durham and London, 2017, pp. 3–11.

43 The chapter opens with Rosanne Kennedy, Jonathon Zapasnik, Hannah McCann and Miranda Bruce, All Those Little Machines: Assemblage as Transformative Theory. *Australian Humanities Review*, 55, 2013: 45–66.

44 This is one of the key concerns in Namibian and South African historical and sociological research. See for an overview of ongoing academic and public debates Jeremy Seekings, The Continuing Salience of Race: Discrimination and Diversity in South Africa. *Journal of Contemporary African Studies*, 26, 1, 2008: 1–25.

45 Roberto Esposito, The *Dispositif* of the Person. *Law, Culture and The Humanities*, 8, 1, 2012: 17–30; Thomas Lemke, New Materialisms: Foucault and the "Government of Things". *Theory, Culture & Society*, 32, 4, 2015: 3–25.

46 Peter Burleigh, The Burden of the Moment: Photography's Inherent Monumentalizing Effect, in Ladina Bezzola Lambert and Andrea Ochsner (eds.), *Moment to Monument. The Making and Unmaking of Cultural Significance*. Bielefeld, 2009, pp. 185–195.

47 See Wolfram Hartmann (ed.), *Hues between Black and White. Historical photography from colonial Namibia, 1860s to 1915*. Windhoek, 2004.

48 See the Preface to W.T.J. Mitchell, *Seeing Through Race*. Cambridge (MA), 2012; and the introduction to George Yancy, *Black Bodies, White Gazes. The Continuing Significance of Race in America*. Lanham, Boulder, New York, London, 2016.

49 For a general introduction see Denis Cosgrove and William L. Fox, *Photography and Flight*. London, 2010.

50 Paula Amad, from God's-eye to Camera-eye: Aerial Photography's Posthumanist and Neo-humanist Visions of the World. *History of Photography*, 36, 1, 2012: 66–86.

51 See e.g. Peter Johnson, The Geographies of Heterotopia. *Geography Compass*, 7, 11, 2013: 790–803.

52 See Keith Breckenridge, Introduction: The Global Biometric Arena, in ibid., *Biometric State. The Global Politics of Identification and Surveillance in South Africa, 1850 to the Present*. Cambridge, 2014, pp. 1–26.

53 Susan Buck-Morss, Aesthetics and Anaesthetics: Walter Benjamin's Artwork Essay Reconsidered. *October*, 62, 1992: 3–41.

54 Ranjan Ghosh and Ethan Kleinberg (eds.), *Presence. Philosophy, History, and Cultural Theory for the Twenty-First Century*. Ithaca and London, 2013.

55 André Bazin and Hugh Gray, The Ontology of the Photographic Image. *Film Quarterly*, 13, 4, 1960: 4–9, here p. 8; Roland Barthes, The Rhetoric of the Image, in ibid., *Image, Music, Text*. New York, 1977, pp. 152–63, here pp. 158–9; Edwards, *Raw Histories*, p. 8.
56 Cadava, *Words of Light*, p. xxiv.
57 Tim Dant and Graeme Gilloch, Pictures of the Past. Benjamin and Barthes on Photography and History. *European Journal of Cultural Studies*, 5, 1, 2002: 5–25.
58 See e.g. Lynn Hunt, *Measuring Time, Making History*. Budapest, New York, 2008; Charles W.J. Withers, Place and the "Spatial Turn" in Geography and in History. *Journal of the History of Ideas*, 70, 4, 2009: 637–58.
59 Cadava, *Words of Light*, p. xviii.

1 Assemblage

Photography and colonial
policing in German South
West Africa, 1910–1913

Horizon

Whenever police photographs from the period of German colonial rule in Namibia come into view, they are, almost inevitably, outlined against the horizon of the South West African War of 1904–1908. Widely understood as the first genocide of the twentieth century, the war has figured as one of the key subject matters of Namibian, and to a lesser extent German, historiography.[1] On the sidelines of a predominant preoccupation with questions of violence, catastrophe, annihilation, and trauma – habitually substantiated with illustrating images of captivity, mutilation, starvation, and death – there have been occasional attempts to understand and study the visual economy of the war and its afterlife as a historical problem in its own right.[2] While there was no official, systematic visual propaganda that came along with the war, thousands of illustrations, postcards, and photographs – all authored by the colonial rulers – circulated widely in contemporary German magazines, colonial literature, and coffee-table books. Images of German colonial soldiers and their heroic deeds on battlefields stylised as sites of technological and industrial achievement were expected to fuel public support and enthusiasm for the war in the metropole. Photographs of imprisoned African men, women, and children herded together in concentration camps or public executions and hangings of demonised foes conjured the triumph and legitimacy of a brutal but fateful battle fought by civilised soldiery against a barbarian race. Depictions of African men and women, spared from death and deportation but coerced into captivity and forced labour, claimed to evidence the just punishment inflicted on those who had dared to revolt.[3]

A more recent and sustained interest in the colonial war as genocide, and its imagery – including sensitive photographs that display the limit of historical retrospection's voyeurism[4] – finds expression in a number of historiographical reaches, among them the (post-colonial) engagement with Germany's violent colonial past, and the preoccupation with anticolonial and resistance histories cultivated in Namibian academic and public debates to this day.[5] Photographs have crowded scholarly and public representations of the war in various ways, whereby there has been a disconcerting willingness to deploy photographic images as evidence underscoring the discourses of both genocide and resistance.[6] In doing so, the present debates have sometimes provided, unintentionally perhaps, older tendentious usage of photographs with a problematic resonance chamber, in particular those images that were published in the context of First World War British colonial propaganda aimed at decrying German imperialism, as much as abetting its own interests.[7] In addition to these unquestioned continuities of the visual evidentiary, there are deeper difficulties that concern the terms and categories on which one grounds historical understandings of the South West African war, and the photographs that are brought into its orbit.[8]

In her critique of the "scholarly fashion" to read imperial violence as genocide, Nancy Rose Hunt has recently pointed to a set of problems in producing simple narratives that congeal spectacular violence as *event* and wedge historical imagination into a dualism between horror and humanitarianism.[9] The South West African War and its lasting perceptual salience in academic and public consciousness is as much a case in point as Hunt's area of interest, Colonial Congo.[10] In both cases, photography played a significant role in mediating atrocity, death, and trauma.[11] Hence, moving away from the spectacular visual dispositive of the war – and the iconography of concentration camps – towards the less exceptional and ordinary, from the singular to the plural, repetitive, and everyday, will help attenuate the sharp contours of a circumscribed event that has neatly been differentiated from a single *before* and *aftermath*. This is not to say that tremendous violence was not part of German colonialism in Namibia before, during, and after the war of 1904–1908. But the historical iterations and trajectories of persecution, violence, and death might be less linear or resolved. Indeed, police photographs from German South West Africa chart a situation and milieu that troubles the epistemological clarity of war – as for example in *war photography*.[12] Images produced in contexts of surveillance and imprisonment, albeit or precisely because they pertain to structurally repressive realms, point to the intricacy and multiplicity of historical terrains on which colonised subjects experienced forms of persecution, wrongdoing, and violation. For them, one is tempted to say, the distinction between war and peace was likely to be less effective or pertinent.

Vignette

In early August 1911, the central government in Windhoek announced the imminent establishment of a police records department. As Governor Theodor Seitz, who authored the instruction, noted, the new department accounted for the government's intent to consolidate the main "auxiliary sciences" in criminalistics – identification and crime scene photography, dactyloscopy (i.e. the registration of fingerprints), and a book of mug shots, or – as contemporaries would have called it – a rogues gallery.[13] The governor's advice was not articulated out of thin air, but actually arose from prior efforts undertaken across the colonial bureaucracy in the field of policing and criminal identification, as much as these efforts had remained haphazard and unsystematic. A first demand for action had emerged as early as 1906, when Governor Friedrich von Lindequist – Seitz's predecessor – bemoaned the intrusion of what he called "criminal gangs" from the Cape, who were said to exploit chaotic conditions caused by the war ravaging German South West Africa at the time. Von Lindequist suspected delinquents of all sorts of rapidly expanding activities across the territory and of being, as he suggested, up to "serious mischief" in and around the coastal town of Swakopmund.[14] In view of these alarming trends, he hoped to close ranks in relation to the matter and persuade the Cape Town authorities to provide Windhoek with photographs of and personal information about the brigands, whom he expected to have entered police records as a matter of course. In exchange, von Lindequist held out the prospect of ceding photographs taken of detainees in the German colony to the Cape police forces. But the German consul in Cape Town curbed the governor's enthusiasm, and von Lindequist's initiative was set aside – allegedly, to support more temperate, diplomatic procedure; but the initiative probably failed because of the immediate and urgent demands of an ongoing war.[15]

Still, while transnational policing proved utopian, the domestic ignorance of investigative work, the governor noted, would not remain unchanged for much longer. Tentative beginnings could indeed be identified: firstly, the Windhoek police had explored modern methodologies – notably fingerprinting and sim-plified measurement à la Bertillonage – in 1906 and in Swakopmund in 1908, possibly by those detective constables from Germany and the Cape who had just been relocated to the South West African colony.[16] In addition, in 1907 the central government launched a training course in criminalistics, out of which six locally trained police officers came off with tested honour.[17] As a result, by 1908 the district offices in Windhoek, Swakopmund, and Lüderitzbucht had at least one detective at their command, i.e. a person who had acquired some knowledge of criminal identification – if at first theoretical rather than practical.[18] Yet, von Lindequist's offer to provide the Cape authorities with *photographs* of detainees was undoubtedly pretentious and expressed wishful thinking more than real circumstances. In fact, first attempts to introduce photography to police work were not made until 1909 and were restricted to individual police and district officers trying their hand at basic camera work under preposterous technical, financial, and institutional conditions.[19] Overall, in the second decade of German colonial rule, and certainly until after the end of the war, modern forensic methodology remained a delicate plant of sorts.

Material sprout – the photographic album

The 1911 announcement of a police records department is captivating, in its tone more than in its textual craftsmanship. Governor Seitz's language reads well in its effort to conjure a moment of inauguration, a foundational act that anticipates its future assessment as origin. Yet, 1911 did not mark the beginnings of South West African modern investigative and identification practices. As it often does, the promises of colonial discourse diverged from actuality, and the expected harvest – a consolidation of criminalistics – failed to materialise. Still, there were some efforts here and there: soon after proclaiming the new departmental initiative, the government published a mandatory injunction to produce personal descriptions of prisoners and take their fingerprints.[20] A 12-page document specified the procedures to be adopted in all major prisons across the colony and required the penal institutions to release the collected data to the police records department in Windhoek and the district authorities in Lüderitzbucht. The envisaged system set its sight on men with "dubious reputation", "professional gangsters", criminals who were meant to be deported from the colony, vagrants and professional beggars, and "shady immigrants and other suspects". Women of comparable savour were likewise brought into focus, and – as was eventually specified – "coloured people" (*Farbige*) as well. To produce valuable descriptions of those criminalised, prison and police officers were urged to adhere closely to Bertillon's anthropometric description (the measurements and *signalement*), which included body height and shape, facial characteristics, hair, gait and posture, and striking features such as scars or tattoos.[21] Additionally, officers were encouraged to register the person's language, his or her clothing and profession, and any other information considered useful for the purpose of identification. Similarly, fingerprints were to be recorded on pre-printed cards, whereby the prescription determined meticulously how to proceed. In March 1912, these regulations were extended to the district offices, all of which were equipped with the necessary materials, i.e. fingerprint cards and ink.[22] While the forms for the measurements and *signalement* provided space for an image as well, requests to take photographs of detainees remained exceptional and a theory more than practice – at least once we cast a glance beyond the central government. Generally, the 1911 instructions seem to have produced meagre yields. A report to the Windhoek authorities authored by the police records department drew sober conclusions:

> The orders given by the government on the 22nd of April 1912 concerning the registration and submission of fingerprint cards with personal description and photograph seem to have attracted little interest from the district offices. Fingerprint cards were hitherto submitted by the offices in Lüderitzbucht, Swakopmund and Gibeon, with photographs only Lüderitzbucht and Swakopmund; they concern whites and coloureds. With the exception of Lüderitzbucht and Gibeon, fingerprint cards are only submitted occasionally, which makes one believe that Swakopmund does not apply the procedure entirely, and all other district offices don't apply it at all.[23]

Notwithstanding the evident disappointment, the report pinned all its hopes on photography, while simultaneously finding fault with the fact that – besides Windhoek and Lüderitzbucht – no district office in the colony owned an official photographic camera. In fact, police officers and detectives repeatedly pointed out the shortage of material resources and deficiency of photographic equipment. Their reports are particularly revealing, as they evidence how official shortcomings gave way to remarkable individual creativity. We read this account of a sergeant based at Swakopmund in 1911:

> The lack of a photographic apparatus, which is indispensable for documenting states of affairs, makes itself felt greatly. The official apparatus 4½ × 6 at our disposal is insufficient, and the undersigned bought an apparatus 13 × 18. With this one we have taken the required images throughout last year. Also, there are a number of dangerous coloured criminals (burglars, cattle thieves), and a number of Bushmen are about to be sent here from Grootfontein district. 3 of them just arrived. In my view it is essential to photograph them and to produce exact personal descriptions of them. I have already started to do so, and I attach a copy, which should meet the requirements. I kindly ask to return it. However, the value of this record will not show until later, once it will be necessary to identify criminals after they've committed a crime anew.[24]

For now, the story runs aground. Governor Seitz's "General regulations concerning the use of photographic apparatuses employed by the judicial police" issued in 1914 awkwardly confined themselves to pecuniary matters.[25] The verbosely technocratic document dovetails with a fragmented corpus of archival papers, and there is no discernible narrative. We are almost tempted to say that German colonial criminalistics in South West Africa died before it began, and the whole issue did not lead anywhere. And yet, it did – not in terms of historical progress, but as material densification. The principal form it assumed was a photographic album – hardly the desired outcome or final product of the preceding story so rudely interrupted. At this point in time, while admittedly a notable object, the album – surrounded, as we shall see, by a porous archive – can be no more than the sprout of a material and visual assemblage.

Here we turn to an unusual artefact, the *Fotografie Album 1b Farbige*.[26] Measuring 40 × 33 centimetres, it has to date been kept in the blue cover characteristic of German colonial archival holdings of the time. Fading colour and traces of past handlings convey a textured sense of the album's increasing age. It contains 40 white pages with prefabricated incisions for mounting eight to twelve (and occasionally more) single photographs by their corners on each page. While there is no author and date given, this photographic assemblage's beginnings undoubtedly go back to Governor Seitz's 1911 instructions and his specific mention of a book of mugshots.

The few illegible scribblings on the front and back covers provide little evidence for further clarification; but the "mug shots" are there – in large numbers, lined up one after the other, page after page (Figure 1.1).

Conveniently, the material and visual characteristics of the album are telling – we are obviously concerned here with a particular kind of police

(a)

(b)

Figure 1.1 (a & b) Fotografie Album 1b, Farbige.

photography; one that pointedly obeyed an inner logic and epistemology, if not always in its execution, then at least in its ambition and orientation. Rogues galleries as a photographic genre emerged in the second half of the nineteenth century in the context of profound social concerns with crime, in general, and with recidivism in particular.[27] They became popular in police work across the metropoles and colonies, and while von Lindequist's fear of intruding criminal gangs might have expressed nervousness of war in 1906, it also invoked this tale of modern visual forensics. Yet, every beginning is difficult, more so perhaps on the periphery, and as police and prison authorities in South West Africa began to take photographs of those they termed criminals, their images were initially stubborn and erratic (Figure 1.2).

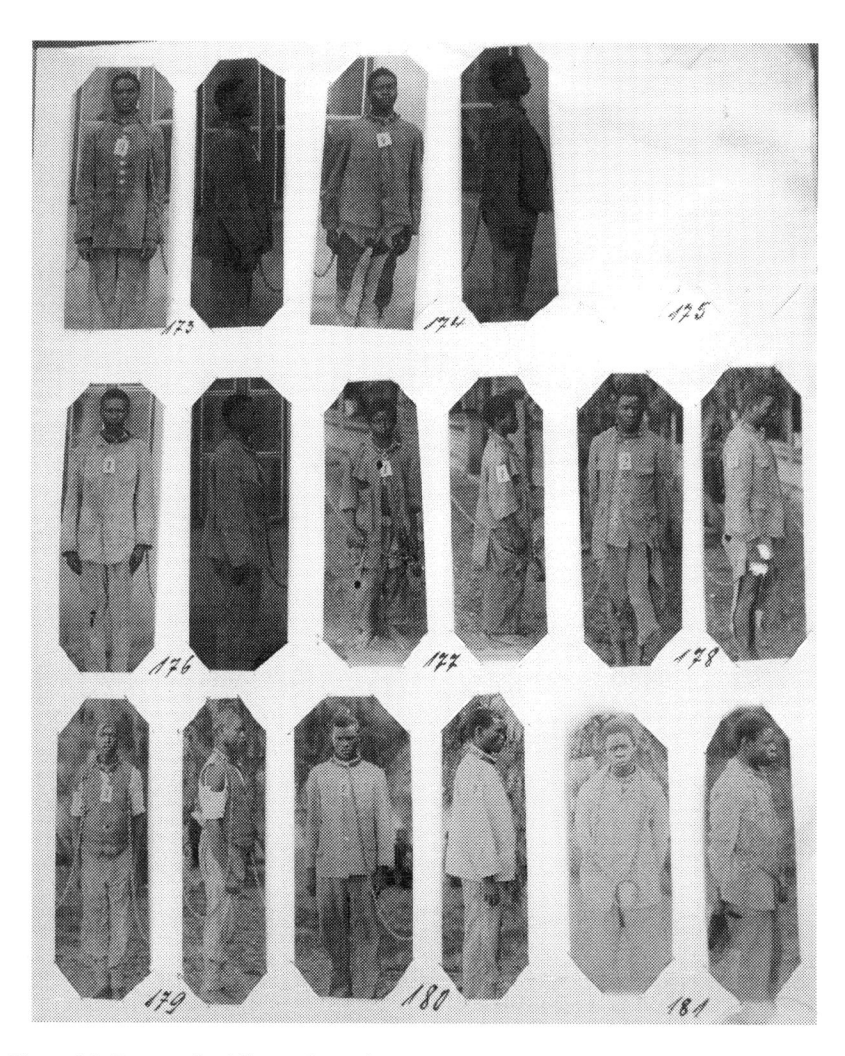

Figure 1.2 Fotografie Album 1b, Farbige.

This image illustrates the general pattern adopted throughout most pages in the album, where the photo mount determined the arrangement of the single photographs lined up in regular rows. At first sight, the viewer receives the impression of order and uniformity. The single images, cropped to identical size and shape, become comparable and analogous, merging into a repetitive seriality that solidifies from one page through the next one. The visual equality seems to find its equivalence in the compulsiveness of the photographic situation, in which men were placed before the camera, and full-length front and profile views alternate and repeat themselves. Further coherence and connectivity are given by the chains that mark the men's status as captives and extend continuity from one man to the other and beyond the single photographic frame. This is indeed a finely executed example of panoptic vision, in which a visual representation becomes the substitute for a material structure – the prison – and, as John Tagg noted long ago, the photograph stands in for the cell.[28]

However, upon closer examination, the visual refinement crumbles. We begin to notice differences at the level of image content, deviations from an implicit model, singularities that point to the specificity of each and every photograph, veiled clues to the uniqueness of every moment and individuality of the photographic subjects. Bare walls used as backdrops sometimes neutralise the setting, but more often windows, porches, and even trees mark diverse outdoor venues, just as varying clothes, civilian and uniformed, suggest different institutional sites. Likewise, there is aesthetic variation, and with every page, partial views along a faltering search for a coherent photographic language drift past. The heterogeneity is, though, no news to histories of forensic photography; rather the album constitutes a validation of the general farrago of photographic practices, styles, and conventions that continued to exist in the early decades of the twentieth century (Figure 1.3).[29]

There is cause for curiosity as we move towards the album's closing pages, where things disintegrate rapidly. At this point, the photographs are arranged unsystematically, and there are substantial differences in image style, quality, and material condition. Loose images placed between album pages, photographs stapled together into image samples, and an erratic entanglement of tattered and faded copies completes the visual hotchpotch. We have dropped out of a semblance of order, whereupon we encounter a jumbled assemblage of images that resemble residues of unmethodical handling, gathering and discarding, care and neglect.[30] We should bring to mind the situation described by officers of the police records department in 1911. Here, they bemoaned the chaotic conditions that prevailed in the district departments charged with photographic documentation, the failed attempt to implement a centralised image repository in Windhoek, and the lack of financial resources and photographic equipment that came along with individual solutions to the problem of photographic registration of detainees. Nevertheless, there were occasional attempts at methodological perfection (Figure 1.4).

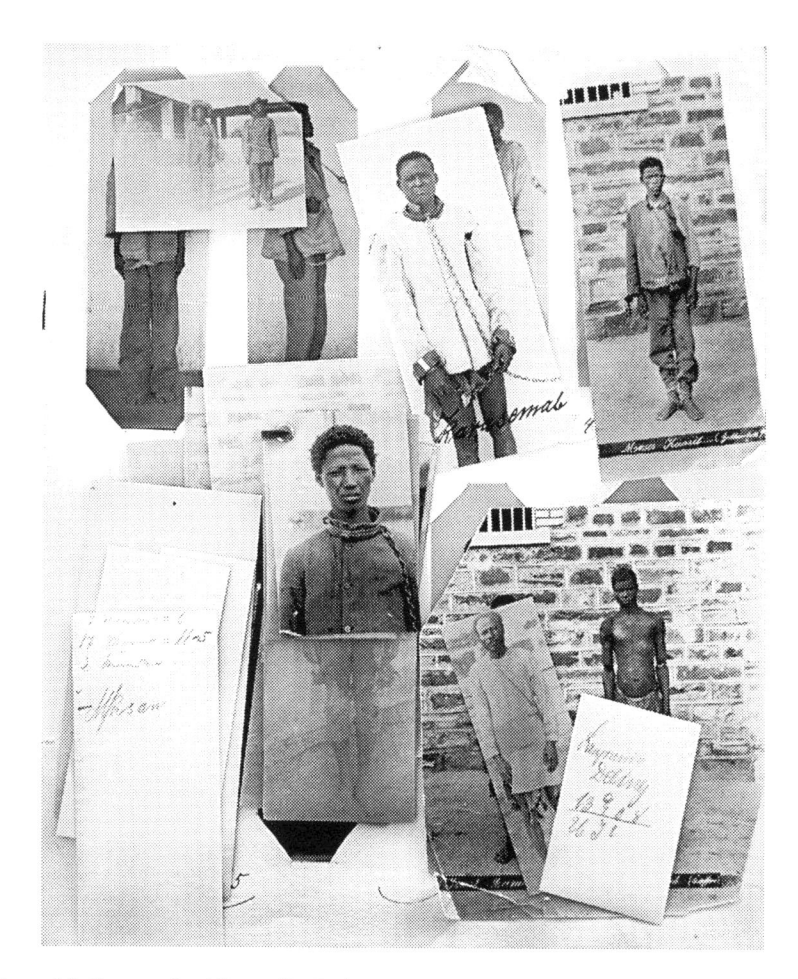

Figure 1.3 Fotografie Album 1b, Farbige.

Figure 1.4 Fotografie Album 1b, Farbige.

These three images are among the few examples of photographs in which the person portrayed was placed in front of a neutral backdrop (probably a white sheet or canvas) and on a recurring wooden stool. We are presumably either encountering the work of a single prison officer or entering the venue of a particular police station furnished according to the requirements of more professional forensic photography. In any case, it appears that efforts were made here to bring photographic practice in line with the standards set by Bertillonage, an interpretation supported by the fact that detainees were asked to place their hands visibly on their chest, enabling the practice of photography to speak to one of its criminological counterparts – physiognomy.[31] Ultimately, though, these images remained exceptional in the Windhoek album, and their visual ambitiousness makes them appear somewhat misplaced. Their inclusion remains a puzzle, and they fail to be indicative of a systematic order of any kind.

Nevertheless, once we depart from a detailed view of single photographs and pages, and take into account the album as an entity, some elements of overall concept and design become visible. Let us recall, for example, the album's title – *Fotografie Album 1b Farbige*, a formulation, which is suggestive of the presence of further albums, such as a volume 1a, which would have possibly included photographs of malefactors and felons of European descent. It is indeed remarkable that here the German colonial government remained strikingly silent on matters of convict classification and segregation common in the penal system at the time.[32] Their focus was notably on recidivism, i.e. on recurrent, or what they would call habitual criminal activity by the same individuals (Figure 1.5).[33]

Similar uncertainty applies to the inclusion in the album of only two images in which the photographic subject is a woman, identified as *Tabakaus Eikas*.[34] In a photographic compendium that otherwise showed exclusively men – though of different age – the inclusion of a female detainee is at least unexpected. The album does not allow drawing any conclusion beyond speculation, conjectures of bureaucratic flaw, or operational inattentiveness that suited the messiness and disorder of image piles and samples described before and compromised the factitiousness of photography as a documentary methodology. Or perhaps the woman's photographic presence is a mere case of historical contingency. We are left, for now, with yet another unspecific would-be clarification by Governor Seitz, offered again in 1911:

> For the rogues gallery the administrative offices will only send in photographs of persons who have either been previously convicted or who have proved to be part of the world of professional criminality through their current felonies. The inclusion of the photograph in the album is decided upon by the government.[35]

There are important addenda to review, a few material ramifications in a loose archival assemblage, though they gradually lead us away from the album as such.

Figure 1.5 Fotografie Album 1b, Farbige.

The first document associated with the photographs in the album is the *Register of detainees placed in convict stations* kept in the files of the district office in Windhoek. (Figure 1.6)[36]

The register listed 51 individuals, who had been imprisoned in the period between June 1910 and December 1913. The information given included their names, nationality (ethnicity), the crimes committed, the sentences passed, their employers (public and private ones), the time period spent in prison, and remarks on admissions, possibly transfers to different prisons, police stations, and sickbays.[37] There were four women listed, who had been charged with assault and cattle theft. Ethnic classification distinguished between 15 Kaffirs (a derogative term for blacks), 2 Kru-Negroes (blacks of

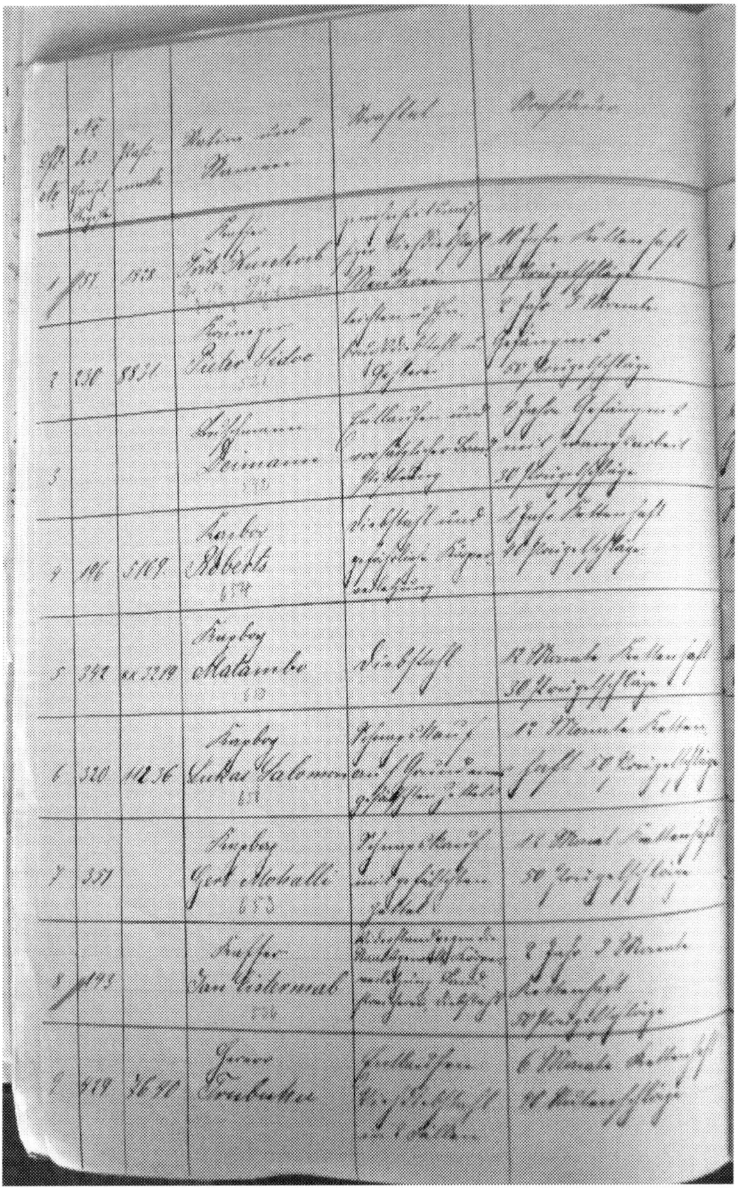

(a)

Figure 1.6 (a & b) Register of imprisoned captives. *(Continued)*

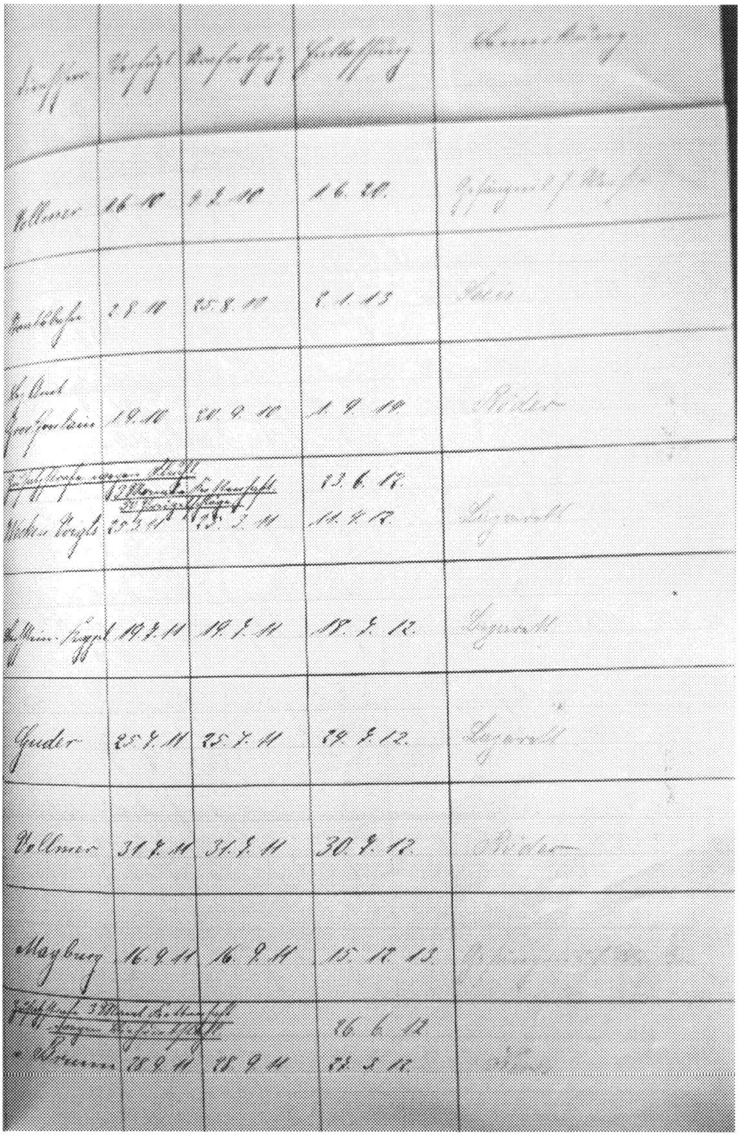

(b)

Figure 1.6 (Continued)

West African descent), 10 Bushmen (San), 6 Cape Boys (i.e. male contract workers originating from the Cape Colony), 5 Herero, 6 Hottentotts (Nama), and 7 Bergdamara. They were prosecuted for cattle theft (12 times), theft (10 times), assault (9 times), burglary (4 times), escape, i.e. desertion (4 times), illegal trade (3 times), forgery, rape, drunkenness, mutiny, and incendiary (1 time each), and habitual crime was noted in several instances. Taken together, these men and women were sentenced to 43 years and 11 months in prison, often kept in chains and forced into hard labour, while receiving 1255 lashes. Once convicted, most of them (25) were sent to the "prisons for whites" in Windhoek, to Rehoboth, or Lüderitzbucht; 16 were distributed to police stations around Windhoek, such as the ones at Seeis and Keres. In six cases, imprisonment led to referrals to sickbays (though it is not clear if as patients or as labourers), and in one case the person, a man called *Obib*, died while in custody in Rehoboth.

We have a register at hand, which was initially kept in a careful, almost pedantic manner, whereby each table column was completed with appropriate information. Towards the end, though, most data is missing, except for the names and places of incarceration. While in its initial claim the list promised to provide a comprehensive documentation of all persons imprisoned between mid-1910 and late 1913, the 40 fully registered men and women constitute a ridiculously small group if considered against the backdrop of systematic prosecution, deportation, and detention that continued to characterise, as we shall see, the decade after the war.[38] The various numbers — serial, indexical, and those pertaining to the pass tags — suggest a complex system of registration, which had been initiated in the wake of a series of "native ordinances" passed in 1907.[39] Yet, while colonial government officials made occasional reference to the comprehensive registration of Africans in the colony, the panoptic project remained obsolete, and it never materialised as part of a centralised archive of criminal identification.[40] Moreover, once we compare the register with the photographic album, expectations of numerical correspondence and order must be abandoned, given that the numbers marked on prison uniforms and clothes and those written on plates held by the photographic subjects do not coincide with any of those recorded in the register. In sum, there seems to be no obvious system of numeric coding, and thus no obvious path for decoding.

Yet some things do match; there are points at which the album and the register do concur, and archival serendipity seems to produce some kind of systemisation (Figure 1.7).

The relationships that can be established relate to detainees' names, or, more generally, to naming — a practice deeply compromised in the context of colonial surveillance and recordkeeping.[41] We would be well advised to resist the temptation to read the correspondence between names given to photographic subjects in the album and those recorded in the register as an actual correlation with the identities of the persons concerned.

(a)

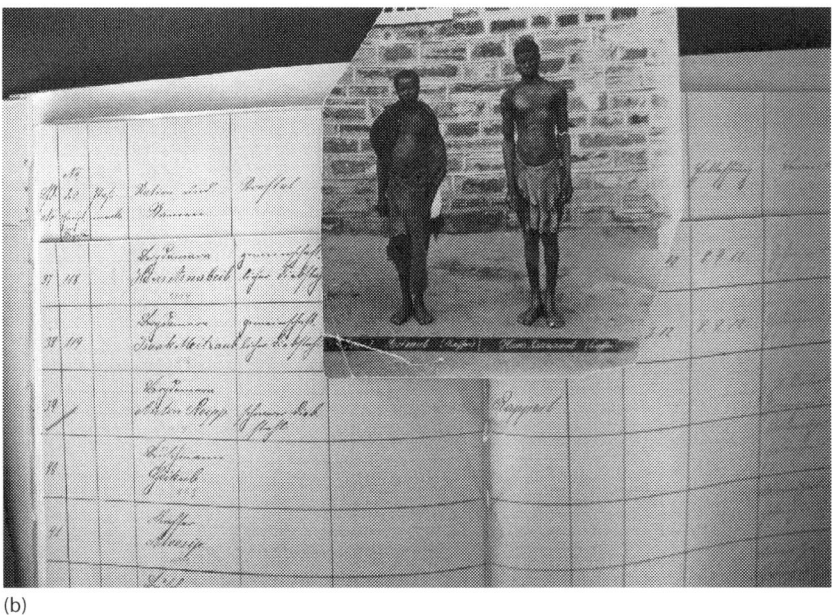

(b)

Figure 1.7 (a & b[42]) Register of imprisoned captives.

What we perceive here is, first and foremost, the connectivity of micro-practices of rule produced and mediated by a bureaucratic system through which the effect of merging is made possible in the first place. However, the composition's appeal is hard to deny, especially once a seemingly arbitrary name, as much as it might be misspelt or contrived, is given a face. In a few instances – six to be precise – this is indeed the case. Two examples shall do: firstly, *Klein Jan*, detainee No 12, classified as "Hottentott", accused of cattle theft, sentenced to three months with hard labour, later recharged with aggravated theft and punished with additional time in prison and 25 lashes, former employee of Wecke and Voigts – a prominent trading company at the time[43] – and sent to the "prison for whites" in August 1912. Jan was photographed in front of a brick building, most probably in a prison courtyard, wearing shirt, trousers, and heavy chains around his bandaged ankles. And secondly, *Hans Asnabeib* (Asanaweib) and *Isaak Meitzaub* (Meizaub), No 37 and 38, two men classified as "Bergdamara" (Kaffer), accused of collaborative cattle theft, sentenced to six months of enchained detention and 25 lashes, employed by one Heusis, detained at the "prison for whites" between March and September 1912, photographed in the same prison courtyard, their names again written on a beam placed in front of them, injuries and bandages in visible evidence. As much as we might be drawn to these material and visual condensations, and the desire to discern the contours of recognisable historical subjects, we are eventually still left only with fragments, snatches of a simple-minded criminological registration, and amputated life histories. This is likewise the case once we turn to a further archival ramification – search warrants.

By the mid-nineteenth century, search warrants had become a common genre in police communication practices globally. Warrants were published in various formats, posted in public venues and printed in mass circulation media, such as police gazettes and daily newspapers. From the 1870s onwards, they increasingly included photographs of wanted perpetrators and criminals.[44] Compared to the sophistication of police gazettes in Berlin, London, Cape Town, or Johannesburg, comparable media in German South West Africa appear modest, and the recurrence of warrants in the archive remains eclectic.[45] We are indeed faced with a riddle and tempted to say that, for mysterious reasons, yet another venture in the domain of colonial policing lacked the promised success. In fact, only the documents submitted by the district offices in Rehoboth and Keetmanshoop include search warrants, and up until the mid-1910s, only a miniscule minority – the ones that circulated between the colonial capital of Windhoek and Rehoboth – featured photographs (Figure 1.8).[46]

We find, then, a case of apparent unusual documentary integrity in relation to a young man named *Fatzke Heiob*, alias *Namakomeib*, in whose case we encounter another correspondence between the album and its archival environment: while Namakomeib's portrait merged into the seriality of image rows in the case-bound photographic compendium, it also appears as an enlarged, loose attachment to a search warrant circulated between police and prison institutions in 1914. There, we learn that

Bergdamara Fritz (Honereb, Nunerib), without a pass tag, approximately 25 years old, 1 m 62 cm tall, thickset, beginnings of a moustache and full beard, phalanx of left auricular finger is missing, born in Hoachanas, last

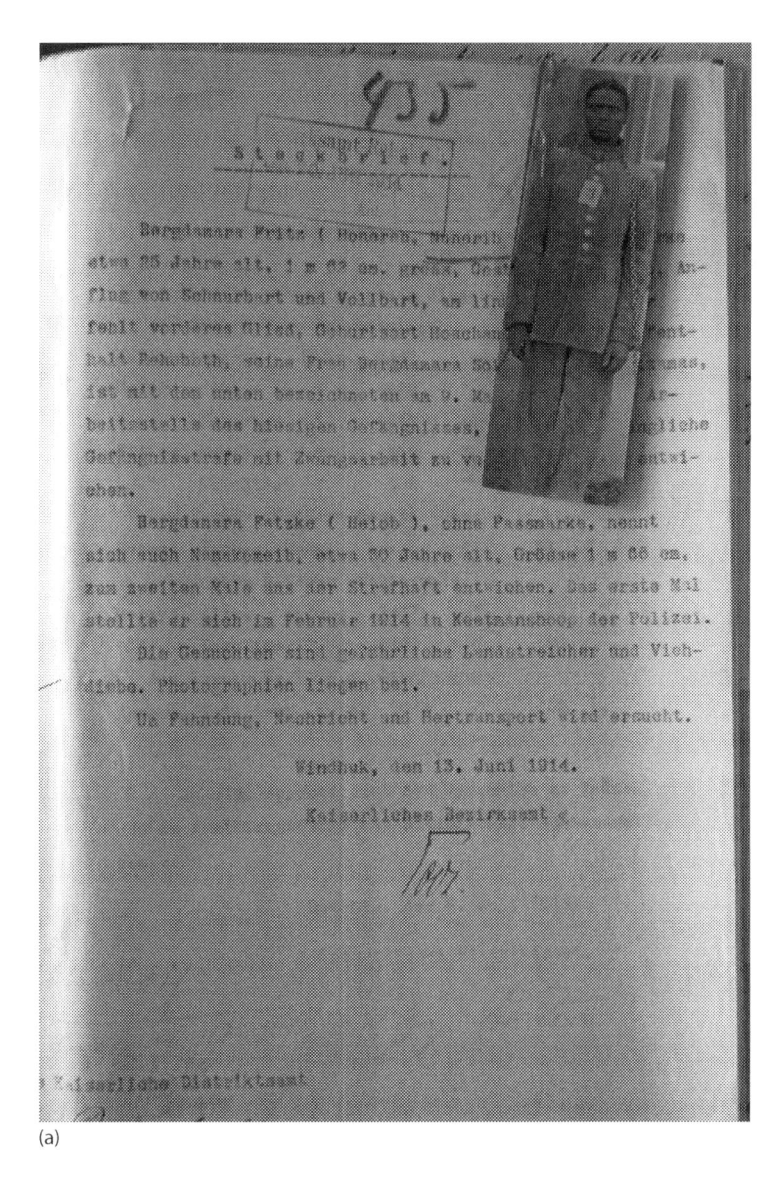

(a)

Figure 1.8 (a[47] & b[48]) Fotografie Album 1b, Farbige (b). (*Continued*)

(b)

Figure 1.8 (Continued)

whereabouts in Rehoboth, his wife Bergdamara Sofie lives in Hatzamas, escaped from his post at the local prison, where he served a lifelong sentence with hard labour, with below mentioned person on the 9th of May 1914.

Bergdamara Fatzke (Heiob), without pass tag, also calls himself Namakomeib, approximately 30 years old, 1 m 66 cm tall, escaped from imprisonment for the second time. The first time he handed himself in to the police at Keetmanshoop.

The wanted men are dangerous vagrants and cattle thieves. Photographs are attached. We appeal for search, notice and handing over.[49]

But once again, Namakomeib's traces are lost abruptly, and so are the fortunes of his companion. We do not know if the men were seen, identified, and handed over to the colonial authorities. One wonders if a fruitless man-hunt would have come as a surprise considering the lack of care in handling the photographs – one image went lost – and the inaccuracy and eclecticism of personal description. In evidencing these shortcomings, the case seems quite typical, as many warrants from this period read like bizarre and hyper-subjective displays of perceptual randomness.[50] We do come across a third brief reference to Namakomeib, Fritz, and Fritz's wife, Sofie, in the warrant issued against them with the *Registry of Native Runaways* for 1910–1915.[51] Their case seems almost an archival cast of fortune, the sole instance in which there is a correspondence between the photographic album and the various convict registers. There will be more to say about these registers later on, but for now, there is a third and final archival addendum we should briefly attend to – the *signalements* and fingerprints (Figure 1.9).

Again, the lack of correlation proves frustrating: it remains exceptional and verifiable for only a small group of fingerprint cards and personal descriptions explicitly linked to the photographs.[52]

At this point, after we have cumbersomely reviewed the inventory, one might have to propose an indulgent assessment that would attribute to the German colonial administration a kind of methodological eclecticism quite common at the time. As a matter of fact, many police and criminal investiga-tion departments across the colonial and metropolitan worlds simultaneously pursued adapted variants of Bertillonage – usually depending on resources in personnel and funds – and dactyloscopy, whereby technical sophistication and, most importantly, systematic registry were often out of reach.[53] That being said, there was nevertheless a particular amateurishness, a malfunc-tion immanent to the state of the German colonial administrative system of criminal identification, one that revealed itself, for example, in the before-mentioned inertia of police and district officers charged with identification in 1912.[54] Likewise, the meagre material results submitted to the main depart-ments in Windhoek during this period left much to be desired – or, at least, they do today in their archival manifestation.

As suggested before, the photographs, numbers, personal descriptions, mea-surements, and other information compiled by administrative institutions such as the police, prisons, and district offices across the South West African terri-tory after 1911 do not evidence – by any stretch of the imagination – any com-prehensive system. The quantitative mismatch, for example, is telling: while the photographs of 192 individuals were included in the album (or ca. 220 if we include the loose images), only 51 people were recorded in the *Register of Detainees* for 1911–1913, and there were more than 500 African men, women, and children listed in the *Registry of Escaped Natives* for 1910–1915. Given the exceptional nature of any correspondence between the set pieces, the linkages remain nebulous at best, and the archival assemblage as a whole weakens as a historical record. Ultimately, the standardisation of personal descriptions and fingerprinting – established materially by pre-printed, serial forms – constituted but a desired foil to the generality of rational disarray.

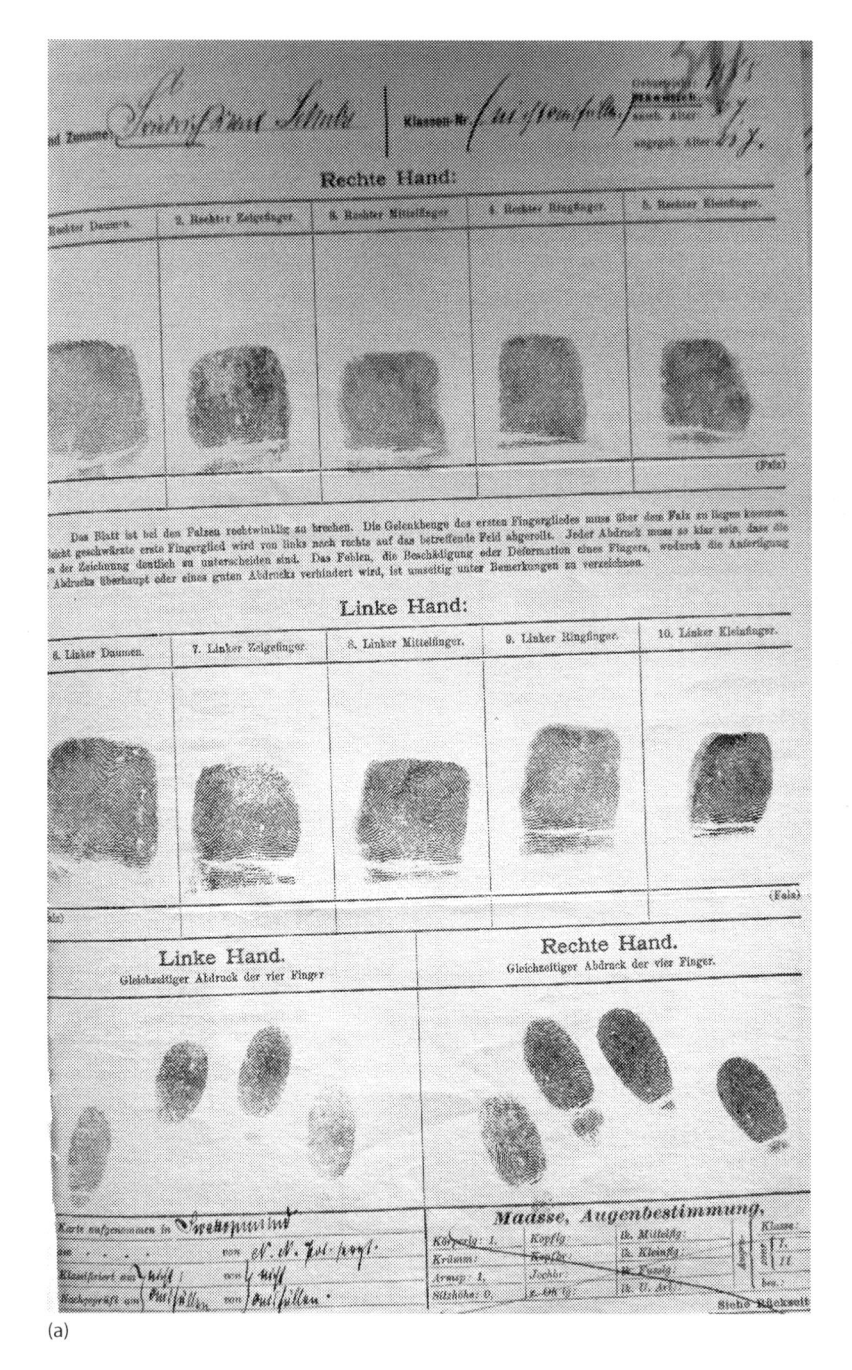

(a)

Figure 1.9 (a & b[55]) Dactyloscopy. (*Continued*)

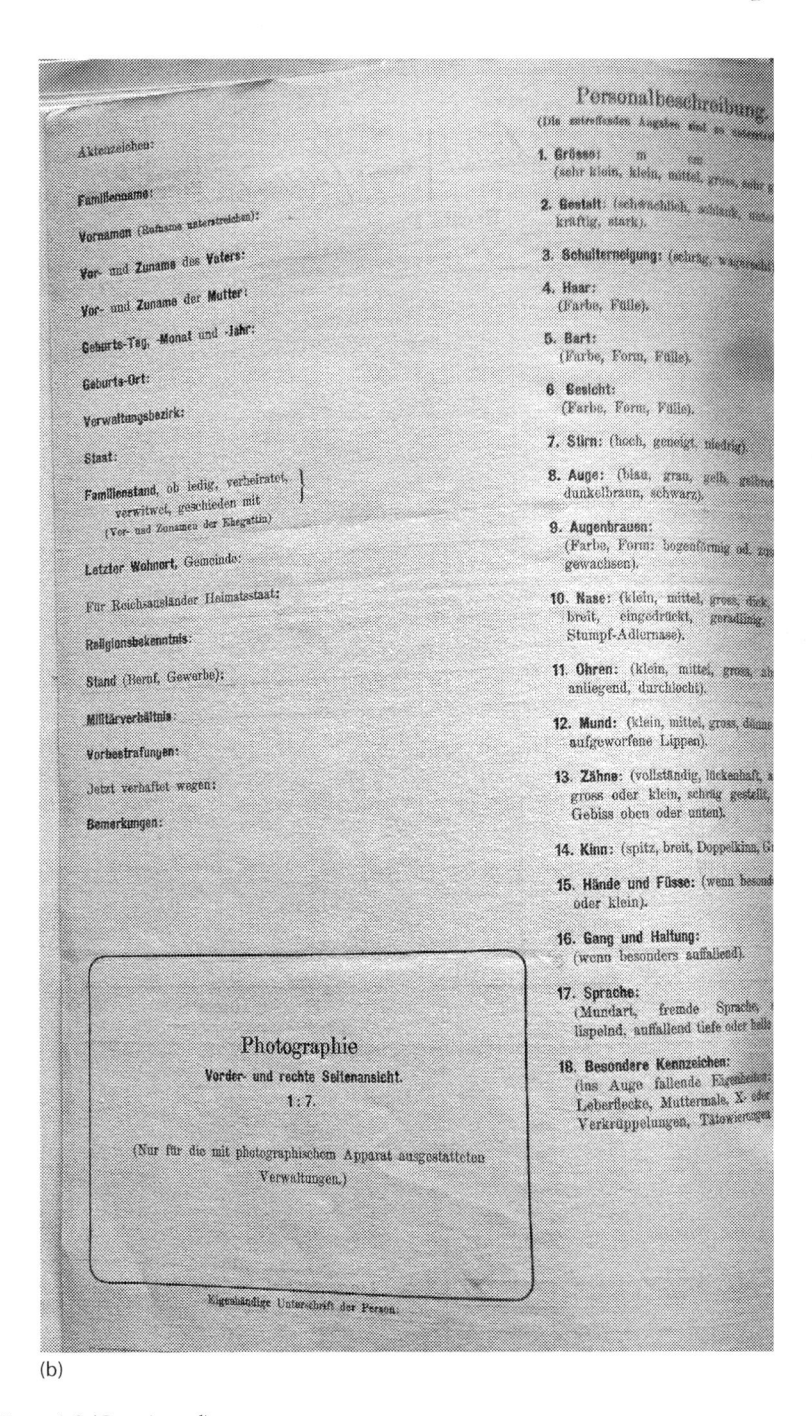

(b)

Figure 1.9 (Continued)

All of this raises the question of how we can make sense of the photographic album and its flimsy archival ramifications; how we understand what served as the historical breeding ground, in which these visual and material sprouts grew, if only in an embryonic form; and how we can understand this material – the photographs, the registers, the warrants, the *signalements*, and the fingerprints – if it effectively evidences a failing system of German colonial criminalistics.

Breeding ground – policing in German South West Africa

The 1910s, i.e. the period in which the photographic album was produced, were undoubtedly shaped by the war's catastrophic repercussions for African political, social, and economic life, and by a gradual post-war colonial reconstruction process marked by endemic repression and the prevalence of everyday forms of violence. A significant part of the indigenous population in central and southern Namibia had been killed, and thousands had been driven away, deported, or arrested.[56] Socio-political forms had by and large collapsed, and most political leaders were dead, in prison, or in exile. People had lost their homes, their cattle, their fields and gardens, and their land.[57] Yet, notwithstanding the disastrous situation, those who had survived slowly began to rebuild their lives and find ways of securing physical recovery and work towards social reconstruction. Mobility was high, as men and women, individuals and groups, moved around to find work, rebuild herds, or simply tried to survive in the *veld* by means of collecting field crops and hunting.[58] However, in a situation of mayhem and disorder, socio-economic recuperation can be prone to more forcible means: raids on people, goods, and chattels, but especially on cattle herds were common. These small and larger incursions produced an ongoing climate of deep anxiety and insecurity, among Africans as much as among colonial officials and European settlers.[59] In view of this post-belligerent dispensation, the German colonial government embarked on a socio-economic rearrangement project, which saw the implementation of a series of restrictive measures aimed at stabilising the colonial economy and forcing the African subject population into a tightly restricted system of wage labour.[60] First, labour was required in the commercial farming sector, i.e. on white-owned farms in central and southern Namibia, the number of which increased significantly after 1908.[61] Secondly, additional labour was needed in a rapidly growing mining industry, particularly when diamonds were discovered in the area around the coastal town of Lüderitzbucht in the south in 1908, and copper mining thrived more north around Tsumeb. And thirdly, the government began to invest substantially in infrastructure, such as dams and boreholes, harbours, roads, and most importantly railways – large-scale projects, all of which required a significant and continuous supply of labour.[62] Governance was based on a more differentiated administration: the territorial division was refined, and districts were extended gradually and increased from three in the early 1900s to 11 until 1915.[63] Immediately after the war, the central administration was reorganised into four departments – for internal administration, transport, legal matters, and military security, and in 1910, further units for native affairs and public works were added.[64] In addition, the colonial government massively reduced the military forces (the *Schutztruppe*) to a permanent strength of 1967 German soldiers and 600 African auxiliaries,[65] and the establishment of a civilian police force began.[66]

The profound transformation of the colony, the domination of which the German colonial empire henceforth understood as a mandatory commitment, required the thorough entrenchment of control over land and people. The centrepiece of securing the envisioned configuration was laid down in three native ordinances (*Eingeborenenverordnungen*) in as early as 1907, which put the relationship between white and black on a new legal basis by means of a systematic registration of all Africans, the introduction of a compulsory pass regime, and the regulation of work contracts.[67] From the colonial government's point of view, these new provisions were considered key to the post-war transformation, as it meant to ensure a modern and efficient social structure and secure law and order. The native ordinances would in fact enable the authorities to determine how many people and who stayed in each district at any given time, where individuals lived, and where they worked.

In order to do so, district officers were urged to register all Africans who lived in the South West African colony. Every black person's identification was to be guaranteed by the introduction of a pass system, under the terms of which every African above the age of seven had to carry a numbered pass tag to be produced on demand to the police, or to any white person, for control purposes. Passes henceforth regulated African mobility: they needed to be renewed in case of changing residence and complemented by travel permits once people desired to move between districts.[68] The native registers and the pass laws were meant to level the distribution of labourers across the colonial territory and the different economic sectors, and while the government supervised African residents in locations close to urban centres and towns, their abidance on private land, i.e. on commercial farms, was sweepingly limited to a maximum of ten families per employer. Population control brought along some additional duties for employers, who were all requested to register their workers and regularly report on their numbers and identity to the regional authorities. More importantly, though, the native ordinances laid down the legal framework for labour relations and work contracts, and African unemployment – henceforth called vagrancy – became a de facto offence. Service books, issued by police and district officers, were compulsory and included personal information – name, ethnicity, pass number, date and duration of employment, terms of notice, and salary – which was squared with official registers and records. Subjecting labour contracts to official regulation and control did entail some basic protection of workers – such as food provision and health care – but its main purpose was ultimately to curtail flowering illegal employment in a context of growing structural labour shortage.[69]

Administrative effort and expenditure grew significantly because of the native ordinances, but it was only in 1911 that beginnings of a more thoughtful native administration began to show.[70] Gradually, native commissioners were appointed to those districts regarded by officials to be particularly overstretched: Windhoek, Lüderitzbucht, Keetmanshoop, and – subject to specific provisions – Swakopmund, where individual commissioners were deployed to control labour relations, mediate conflicts between farmers and farm workers, supervise African residence, and keep record of criminal affairs for the attention of the central government. Officially, the native commissioners were regarded as intermediaries and "advocates of the natives" – and this is how they had been promoted to the African subject population. Yet, ultimately, they served as agents of more effective and successful surveillance and control, of residents, labourers, *and* regional government bodies – the district offices, above all. Still, taking into consideration the entire post-war period and keeping an eye on conditions prevailing across the colony, the native commissioner's impact remained – relative to the authority and leeway of district officers – restricted.

In a nutshell, the native ordinances of 1907 produced a situation in which the de facto legal status of African subjects became a matter of their integration into the colonial economy.[71] Contemporary public debate in the colony left no doubt about it, as we read in a local newspaper:

> The native must be made aware that he has a right to exist only in direct dependence on the territorial authorities; without this, he is in a certain sense an outlaw; a livelihood outside of working for whites is not available to him.[72]

The regime entrenched in these regulations, henceforth, governed and shaped everyday confrontations between Africans and the state, whereby structural problems characteristic of German colonial rule in the post-war period would become evident. Colonial jurisdiction over African men and women was never codified; since the early 1900s, it had been grounded in regulations issued by the governor alone, and applied not by attorneys or judges, but by district officers in charge.[73] While this amounted to a conflation of the judiciary and administration and fostered a level of autotelic arbitrariness hard to assess, sentences passed against Africans were initially for the most part related to offences against property and usually punished with short imprisonment and flogging.[74] Colonial warfare changed the course of things dramatically, and harsh punishment, including grave abuses and killings, became common for even the tiniest trespassing, evermore bizarrely classified and extended to broadly defined notions of insolence, disobedience, or even lying. The native ordinances tied in perfectly with post-war white-supremacist understandings of repressive subjugation, notwithstanding their *prima facie* legalism. The administration's idea of a pacified colony and its main interests were couched imperiously in terms of "law and order", political stability, economic viability, and administrative regularity and efficiency. They were less geared towards constitutionality and justice,[75] and state reform – as it appeared on the contemporary political agenda across the German empire – left much to be desired in South West Africa, particularly once we look at the police and penal system.[76]

A civilian police force was officially established in 1905, but it became de facto operational only in 1907.[77] While it was in theory modelled on metropolitan gendarmeries in Germany, in the South West African context, the police kept an affinity with the *Schutztruppe* – out of which it partly emerged – and hence remained affected by military style and logic.[78] By 1908, 160 white policemen and 350 African auxiliaries were mandated to implement administrative regulations across a territory that extended over more than 800,000 square kilometres divided up into four districts. While in 1909 there were 69 police stations in South West Africa, most of them were staffed with one or two policemen (52), and only some had reasonable units at their command.[79] Police duties comprised border and farm protection, the maintenance of law and order, surveillance and detection of criminal activities, and – most importantly – the enforcement of the native ordinances. In the execution of all these duties, police stations were first answerable to the district offices and then to the governor directly. As we saw earlier on, the central government had high hopes of the police controlling the colony and putting an end to rampant theft and assault on people's lives and property. But limited funding and the consequent lack of sufficient personnel and equipment made the task a matter of sheer impossibility.[80] It was therefore considered necessary to limit policing to territorial zones of key interest: the stretches of land along main roads and railway lines (100 km on each side), the mining districts, infrastructural facilities, and towns and villages.[81] Likewise, the central government's priorities favoured a predominant focus on crime, the prevention of which required both the control of the African population *and* the surveillance of the settler community.

Let us recall von Lindequist's nervousness in his report on the intrusion of "criminal gangs" into the South West African territory in 1906; at that point, the governor had no call to differentiate malefactors along racial lines, as there were renowned bandits from all walks of life entering the colony.[82] But moods changed quickly, and attention shifted towards the African population, whose criminalisation grew exponentially once the native ordinances were adopted. The prosecution of thieves, vagrants, and criminal gangs became a clear focus of policing, and regular punitive expeditions against people who tried to make a living outside the wage labour economy – on minimal small-stock husbandry, hunting, gathering, and small-scale trade – took root by 1908.[83] One macabre showpiece of police patrolling was the systematic coursings against so-called Bushmen, who were said to commit regular stock thefts and armed attacks on commercial farms and on parties of northern migrant workers on their way to the German colonial heartland. Between 1911 and 1912, 400 such patrols were sent out to the

Grootfontein, Outjo, Rehoboth, and Maltahöhe districts.[84] Those captured were either imprisoned or coerced into forced labour on farms, mines, and diamond fields, and once Governor Seitz authorised police and the military to shoot people on the run, many were killed.[85] Once more, state violence against African subjects reached terrifying levels, calling to mind atrocities committed during the 1904–1908 war. It thus seems reasonable to suggest that, once the war was over, what made everyday terror into policing was less a matter of scale, let alone of ethics, morale, or humanitarianism, but simply one of bureaucratisation and rationalisation.[86] The punitive economy made space for the settlers as well, even though relationships between white farmers and the colonial administration continued to be marked by mistrust and conflict.[87] In the domain of policing and surveillance, especially once it served labour recruitment, they could act in concert. Interests converged, *nota bene*, despite significant but largely undocumented violence from farmers against farm workers – a fact that required repeated intervention from the authorities, but was often tolerated and legitimised as an expression of the "right of paternal chastisement" applied by superior masters towards infantilised servants.[88]

The persecution of Bushmen – an endeavour referred to, at the time, as the elimination of the so-called "Bushman plague" – and the violent besetment of those who escaped the clutches of the state, evidence the structural amalgamation of surveillance and the labour economy. The countless arrests and imprisonments lead us, without detour nor relief, into the abyss of the German colonial penitentiary – the sombre arena, we will recall, of photographic trial and assemblage.[89] The penal system in post-war German South West Africa constituted an institutional form of punishment situated in a broader landscape of formal and informal penalisation, prosecution, and correction. As the case might be, African men and women could be alternately judged and convicted by local chiefs and headmen under customary law, or by farmers, policemen, or district officers, and at times by more high-ranking government officials under colonial jurisdiction.[90] In the last case, sentences included fines and floggings – often executed on the spot and without hearing – deportation, forced labour, imprisonment, or any combination of these.

Unlike in the metropolitan situation, the number of those convicted and imprisoned in South West Africa grew steadily after 1908.[91] A closer look at official statistics is revealing regarding both quantitative growth and classification of offences. During the reporting year of 1908–1909, for example, crimes and offences committed by Africans against property, which included theft, embezzlement, robbery, blackmailing, and forgery, produced the following figures: (a) 15 terms of imprisonment of more than one year, (b) 32 sentences of six months to one year, (c) 169 imprisonments up to six months, (d) 11 punitive fines, and (e) 169 corporal punishments. In 1910–1911, the respective numbers doubled, then again in 1911–1912, a year in which out of a total of 3252 convictions, 1222 lead to imprisonment.[92] Taken together and considered over the period between 1900 and 1913, 39% of the punishments handed out to Africans entailed imprisonment, and within these, 45% came along with corporal punishments.[93]

Accommodating the growing numbers of detainees was another matter altogether, as infrastructure and buildings left much to be desired. Since the 1890s, district offices, as well as military and police stations, had been equipped with cells for captives. Most of these facilities remained provisional and consisted of small rooms, separate huts, or wooden sheds, a situation that persisted, in most areas beyond the urban centres, far into the twentieth century.[94] The government only began building actual prison facilities for Europeans in 1905 and for African convicts after the war, whereby the question of segregation of inmates along racial lines soon emerged as a main concern.[95] But implementing any classification and separation of prisoners, which might have also begun to address some of the standards defined in prison reforms in the German empire in the mid- and late nineteenth century, would hopelessly lag behind in the South West African context.[96] In 1908, most prisons in the colony did not have the infrastructural resources and premises to separate Africans from Europeans, and the chronology of segregation according to classes of prisoners, age, and gender remains unclear.[97] A rare archival reference points to the difficult conditions that prevailed in prisons in the early 1900s and to the particular vulnerability of female detainees:

> There is unfortunately reason to believe that coloured women were used by male convicts in exchange for money [...] The assistant district officer immediately walled up the door between the women's room and the interior of the prison [...] Currently there is still a suckling child in the prison, whose mother, a prostitute, is a convict. Admittedly, the sanitary conditions are untenable; under the corrugated iron roofs the temperature rose lately up to 37 degrees Celsius during the day, and putrid smell emanated from the native cells [...] There's an attempt to cover the iron roofs with grass, and two new cells are being built in the courtyard.[98]

At this stage, only Windhoek and Lüderitzbucht possessed penal institutions that allowed for the separation of male and female or black and white prisoners.[99] But further structural efforts were discernible in 1910, when Swakopmund built a separate prison for "native convicts", and the Omaruru prison extended its premises accordingly.[100] Notwithstanding the modest architectural improvements, in most penal facilities, and certainly in the sordid cells provided by district offices, as well as police and military posts across the territory, the conditions of imprisonment were disastrous – for women, children, and men. Contemporary debate, both among colonial officials and in the broader settler society, included at times peculiar arguments about the pros and cons of "native incarceration", and presumptions about Africans "relishing" their stay in prison – as it offered board and lodge for free – enjoyed great popularity.[101] Power and privilege often speak arrogantly, and the ludicrousness of such contention is beyond any doubt. But the notion of "prison as convalescence" helped legitimise the claim that, unlike in Germany, in the colony corporal punishment was a *sine qua non* of a successful penitentiary system that would ultimately turn savages – men, women and youth alike – into civilised, if subordinate, members of society.[102] And, as we saw earlier on, there is statistical evidence for sentencing regularly including flogging and whipping. Physical mistreatment and abuse were some of the reasons that mortality rates in German South West African prisons were very high; malnutrition, lack of hygiene, and chronic disease were others. When C. Wandres, missionary of the Rhenish Mission Society, visited the prison in Windhoek in 1908, he was deeply shocked by the darkness, squalor, and lack of air in cells, where vermin infested prisoners' bodies, everything smelled of faeces, and there was no provisioning for the sick and dying.[103] Actually, missionaries were recurrent critics of conditions of imprisonment, and even within the colonial administration disapproving voices could occasionally be heard, especially so when Berlin took notice.[104] But by and large dissent failed, and given that, unlike e.g. in the neighbouring Cape Colony, there were no external inspections that would have increased pressure on prison authorities, conditions did not improve for years to come.[105]

Deprivation and grievance persisted in regard to prison labour as well, given that economic valorisation of convicts and the production of a cheap workforce remained the *raison d'être* of the penal system between 1908 and 1914. The post-war economic recovery and the growing shortage of labour on farms, mines and diamond fields, railway and road construction, and even within the various state departments favoured a political climate in which declaring forced labour to be both a desirable disciplinary tool (*Erziehung durch Arbeit*) and an effective form of punishment seemed more than appropriate.[106] Indeed, the standardisation of prison labour in 1909 made no secret of the economic rationale at work, and in view of chronic financial shortage, prison labour helped lower the net costs of rations and general sustenance of convicts.[107] Here and there, the central government felt qualms about the system's purposiveness, as expressed in a report Governor Seitz submitted to the German Colonial Office in 1909:

> I have felt for a long time – and it has now become a certainty – that a large part of the district officers and head of stations have gone astray in regard to native jurisdiction [...] Often sentences are imposed that are much too long, simply to have as many prisoners as possible to be made available for labour.[108]

The public did not share Seitz's concern. Their main preoccupation seemed to be that, in several instances and readily on public works, black and white convicts were seen to perform labour jointly. This kind of public exposure of white convicts was considered inappropriate and detrimental to white reputation, and this type of common work likely to foster racial mixture.[109] To soothe the waters, it was henceforth avoided whenever possible. Still, the central government continued to be nervous about excesses within the penal system, and several admonitions sent to various district offices in 1912 urged the local authorities to secure minimal provision and care for imprisoned forced labourers, and to make sure that treatment of women and children be subjected to appropriate diligence. Eventually, statutory regulations were issued that were meant to remedy the worst abuses, afford protection against maltreatment, and make sure that timely discharge was observed.[110]

Criminalised, detained, and imprisoned Africans defied the brutality of colonial policing and punishment, using the structural weaknesses of the police and penal systems whenever possible. Let us recall the case of Fatzke Heiob, alias Namakomeib, and the search warrant issued against him in 1914 by the Windhoek authorities – just one example of the hundreds of recorded escapes that troubled the German colonial authorities and alarmed farmers and urban dwellers alike.[111] And indeed, there were many opportunities for breakouts, as a local newspaper reported in 1913:

> Like on most police stations, there is no prison cell at Seeis. The cells that have been gradually built from stones and clay are not necessarily escape-proof. Prisoners have therefore been chained to each other but could still escape.[112]

However, similar problems were also encountered in the big prisons, e.g. in 1905 in Swakopmund when three inmates escaped within a period of five weeks; or in Windhoek, where first six and later four convicts managed to break out the same year. The most common method for evading confinement, though, was outdoor labour, such as in railway and road construction or on remote infrastructural sites, since work gangs comprised of up to 60 convicts were often supervised by only three to four police men, who were obviously overburdened.[113] Police patrols were sent out regularly to recapture escaped prisoners, and warrants issued against those on the run circulated between district offices, police, military posts, and the central authorities in Windhoek, if somewhat unsystematically. To what extent these measures were successful remains unclear, but in any event, the persistence of official fear of prison escapes raises questions about the limits and shortcomings of colonial policing, surveillance, and confinement in the 1910s.[114]

As suggested earlier on, while reading the colonial archive we are well advised to keep in mind that German colonial ideas and hopes of total conquest and control of the African population remained a fantasy. The South West African territory was simply too extensive, and the government lacked the resources in funds and personnel to achieve its proclaimed aims. Likewise, colonised subjects – while undoubtedly suffering under a repressive regime – kept finding ways of resisting and evading the grip of the state and its executive institutions, such as the police. Destroying or manipulating identity documents and using various names were the practices that threatened to unhinge colonial surveillance most. Breach of contract was very common as well.[115] And as a last resort, those who were persecuted might attempt to leave the territory, for a time or for good – be it northwards beyond the Police Zone, where German colonial rule was never directly implemented, or southwards into the Cape Colony, trusting, perhaps, that conditions beyond the German sphere of interest might be less malevolent.

Assemblage

As described before, the situation in the early 1910s provided the fertile ground on which the photographic album and the affiliated archival materials emerged and thrived. But it is worth asking in more detail about the *kind* and *quality* of the relationship between historical objects and images and the worlds from which they originate. Historical causality is barely a matter of course and even less one of unclouded transparency. As much as we understand early twentieth-century German colonial policing and confinement in South West Africa as giving meaning to the album – and we do so with good reason – there are further inquiries that prove valuable once they take us beyond meaning-making and representation alone. The album's materiality and visuality tell us something about the problem of historical genre and medium that condition the way in which we encounter historical artefacts in the archive, and in doing so, complicate the question of how we might proceed in inserting them into historical narration.[116]

The complex relationship between the visual and narration makes itself felt once we reconsider the photographic album from German South West Africa. The photographs, as much as the fingerprints and personal descriptions associated with them, somehow *resist* – echoing W. T. J. Mitchell's phrasing – a smooth blending into the historical teleology of modern criminalistics.[117] To wedge these archival materials, fragmented as they are, into the bodice of a progressing history of colonial surveillance and policing, in which the rogues gallery becomes the ultimate fruit of success, feels problematic, as it closes down interpretative avenues that prefer to nourish and cherish the humours and contingency of the past. This is why I have thus far, occasionally and not inadvertently, referred to the album and the archival files that relate to it as *assemblage* – a term that needs further explanation.

Kennedy et al. provide a useful formulation of assemblage, a concept derived from the work of Giles Deleuze and Félix Guattari, which can serve as a point of departure for the subsequent discussion of the photographic album and its affiliated archive.[118] Across its various appropriations and evocations, assemblage has generally come to designate "an ongoing process of arranging, organising or congealing" in order to understand how "heterogeneous bodies, things or concepts come in connection with one another".[119] Highlighting connectivity and valuing dynamic arrangements, assemblage clears a space in which to map material and semiotic relations and directs attention towards the transient and the continuous process of making and remaking. Importantly, and with an interest in asking what assemblages do, rather than defining and establishing what they are, Deleuze and Guattari make a conceptual distinction between horizontal and vertical axes, which constitute the temporal and spatial elements of an assemblage. While the horizontal axis describes the emergent properties, content, and expression of an assemblage – i.e. the incorporation of words, meaning, material, and substance in a temporary cluster – the vertical axis refers to the creation of a territory and involves a distinction between being made (territorialisation) and becoming unmade (deterritorialisation) as bodies, things, and concepts come together and disperse.[120] Assemblages are, thus, never still, and as unstable configurations, they are infused with and depend upon their ever-changing composition and articulation.[121] Deleuze's and Guattari's concept clearly moves away from questions of signification to the question of capacity, from meaning-making to what exceeds representation. Described as temporally and spatially contingent, assemblages are not components bound together through a lineage of shared descent; what they reveal above all are nonlinear and nonpermanent connections and, in their "rhizomatic" composition, they have no beginning or end, but instead multiple entry points.[122] While Kennedy et al do not make this explicit, their formulation of assemblage has significant bearing on received understandings of historical linearity and progression. Given that "assemblages do not arise from linear genealogical roots to be traced, but rather are heterogeneous multiplicities that evolve with ever-increasing connections", they trouble rather than undergird simplistic understandings that attempt to causally link sequential, detached historical events or episodes.[123]

This notion of assemblage suggests, then, laying to rest the above-mentioned classification of the South West African photographic album as the material result of a progressive history of modernising colonial policing and surveillance. At the very least, assemblage invites us to pause and consider the album as a puzzle, in view of both its material and semiotic relationships – to other objects and images – and the question of historical process. Let us be more specific about the concept's appeal and potential value for the following discussion. Firstly, the notion of assemblage helps scrutinise the real and virtual, social and conceptual unity of the album and associated archival materials, and bring into question if and how the single components – photographs, fingerprints, names, numbers, measurements, and personal descriptions – relate to each other by virtue of an intrinsic interiority to a whole, however described. Secondly, assemblage disturbs a powerful archival effect, through which the album emerges as a privileged object – what we are left with, as it were. It is this temptation to conflate the album's material and visual persistence, assumed to be constitutive, one way or the other, of historical meaning that needs to be unhinged. Thirdly, and with an eye on the specificities of time and locality, assemblage and its forces of territorialisation and deterritorialisation open up the possibility of spatial and temporal deferrals, giving rise to doubts about an inevitable congruence between a territory mapped by the photographic album and its surrounding archive on the one hand, and a territory charted by colonial institutions such as the police on the other hand. What if the album proved, ultimately, a failure within the logics of policing and surveillance, but its scions would nevertheless thrive elsewhere and at another time? What if, in other words, police photography spilled out of its own temporal and spatial bounds?[124]

Territorialisation

Rethinking the photographic album and its surrounding archive first through the lens of territorialisation requires us to disregard, for a moment, the limitations and shortcomings highlighted hitherto, and reconsider if and how this particular visual and material assemblage was indeed productive – in short: what it *did* in the context of German colonial policing.

We now return to the registers of convicts and "escaped natives" referred to earlier in the chapter. Records of detained Africans go back to the early years of German colonial presence. By 1898, the few military posts scattered across the central and southern parts of the territory, most notably the detachments in Warmbad and Keetmnashoop, had begun to submit quarterly reports to the central government in Windhoek. These reports were intermittently synthesised into a centralised register of convicts, an eclectic compilation of 148 individuals sentenced to imprisonment within a period of nine years, i.e. up to 1907, when the register ended.[125] The early recordings were kept simple; they featured names of detainees (all of them male), date and place of arrest, offence and sentence passed, former employers, and tribal membership (*Stammeszugehörigkeit*), though at times noted simply as "African". The listings, particularly the ones sent in from the military posts, and later the police and district offices, seem to have been composed diligently, and there is no sign of abrupt bureaucratic lapse or documentary negligence. But, the records are clearly marked by the specificity and confinement of small-scale locality and less by classification and abstraction, given that, upon closer inspection, names of individual convicts and employers (exclusively farmers) prove recurrent, as do offences, many of which consist of farm workers deserting their workplace. At this level, the lists of detention simply mirror the micro-dynamics of a small, local farming economy and its conflictual nature. Likewise, notable here is the attention paid to place-names and the properties of the country, often described in the language of military patrolling and policing, as if documenting and recording arrests served geographical reconnaissance rather than criminal identification. Yet interestingly, the mundane empiricism of these early records changed, and by 1910, it gave way to a different rationale, as we see reflected in later registers of convicts and runaways and in the photographic album, all of which had been brought more in line (as we saw) with the requirements of modern criminalistics.

In terms of territorialisation, the rationale of criminal documentation, as flawed as it might have been in detail, was – in its aggregation, as an assemblage – productive in at least two ways. Policing and imprisonment aimed at capture, both literally and metaphorically – at arresting moving bodies, confining them to the partitioned and segregated space of the prison, and connecting them into larger functional ensembles. But, in view of an elusive and unintelligible African subject population, an inept police force, and the deplorable state of the colonial penal system, there was a need for more efforts, effects at the level of statement and enunciation. It was at this point that photography, anthropometric measurement and description, and fingerprinting were meant to do their work: as a methodological ensemble aimed at smoothing and rendering variety uniform; attaching discernible properties to bounded bodies; recording, naming, identifying, and classifying individuals, and inserting them into the discourse of criminalisation – a misanthropic system of knowledge production and judgement.[126] But there is also a less conspicuous effect of territorialisation: recording meant verification and reassurance; its effects were constitutive, once the archive of images, measurements, and fingerprints put meat on the bones of a weak bureaucracy, and their circulation routinely marked the chains of command thereby enshrining institutional connectivity. In a context of post-war reconstruction, and in a situation characterised by district offices and police posts that were poles apart from the central government in Windhoek, where staff often carved out a miserable existence in isolation on the colony's peripheries, entrenching the topography and topology of colonial policing was crucial. Also, the registers of convicts point to territorialisation in a sense more literal than assemblage theory might have it, as they disclose the ways in which policing and imprisonment, and the registration and classification of individuals, became a function of and tributary to the geography and temporality of the colonial economy. There is in fact a disturbing correlation between the constitution of nodes of labour recruitment – the flourishing of diamond mining at Lüderitzbucht, the expansion of railway construction across the colony, and the building of harbour infrastructure at Walvisbay – and the concentration of convict populations at Keetmanshoop in the south or Swakopmund on the coast.[127] Consequently, and unintentionally perhaps, the album, the fingerprints, and the registers, all of which drew upon the classification of convicts along racial and ethnic lines, ultimately amounted to an exercise in spatial reshuffling and racial mapping. If this was mapping of a special kind, it was nonetheless one that evolved on the sidelines, or rather, as we shall see, in the abyss of more reputable attempts to map the colony's ethnographic and racial landscape.[128]

Deterritorialisation

Placed against the labour, time, personnel, and financial resources deployed in the production of the album, fingerprints, personal descriptions and measurements, and the hopes and desires attached to them, the bureaucratic yields of the surveillance assemblage remained small. It seems natural, then, to direct attention towards instances of deterritorialisation, moments at which components of the archival assemblage dispersed beyond the domain of the police and penitentiary, and leaked into new constellations, where they were, however, stabilised and reterritorialised.[129] We shall explore three such instances, regarding which an important specification seems necessary. What will be of primary concern is less the pursuit of particular images, and less a retracing in terms of the social biography of a specific photograph.[130] Rather, the focus will be on the moments and points at which images, objects, and concepts constituted in the one assemblage – the *Fotografie Album 1a Farbige* and its affiliated body of texts – resurface in a different one, whereby the movement of merging and borrowing, exchange and interaction between different assemblages was primarily given expression and form at the level of the material and visual. If we keep an eye on the instability of the assemblage, its dependence on ongoing processes of making and remaking, we will find a good opportunity to observe that the dispersal and leakage had transformative effects, by which means the materialities and iconographies of policing and imprisonment began to *be* and *do* something else.[131]

Deterritorialisation 1 – memorial mosaic

The first instance of leakage or dispersal is a group of prison photographs included in a private photographic album from German South West Africa, presumably assembled between 1909 and 1915.[132] Kept in a rust brown linen cover and with a consistent internal layout that makes space for four images on each page, it contains 210 mounted black and white photographs, many of which were taken in urban settings, usually in Windhoek, Swakopmund, or Keetmanshop. In terms of image genres and subjects, the album covers landscapes, and individual and group portraits that eclectically map the physical and social environment of the colony and provide casual, almost innocuous glances at buildings and infrastructure, and at moments of work, leisure, or family life. At a quick glance, the mundane visual mosaic appears quite characteristic of the numerous memorial albums produced by policemen, soldiers, and civilian members of the settler community during the German colonial period.[133] But looking more closely, we come across substantial groups of photographs in the album that prove eminently sensitive, since they include nude portraits of African women, many of which lean towards problematic modalities of seeing and should, at best, be classified as pornographic.[134] The extent of objectification and exposure is aggrieving, given that the album's material and visual organisation leaves little room for subjectivity. While all photographs are consecutively numbered – an archival procedure with a touch of rationality that seems odd for a private collection – there are only occasional specifications of dates and locations, and in some cases, the names of photographic studios, subjects depicted in the images, or addressees of photographic prints are noted on the back and front sides.[135] Browsing through the album, the encounter with prison images – whose irreverence is in no way inferior to the pornographic ones – seems at first sight somewhat unexpected, a puzzle (Figure 1.10).

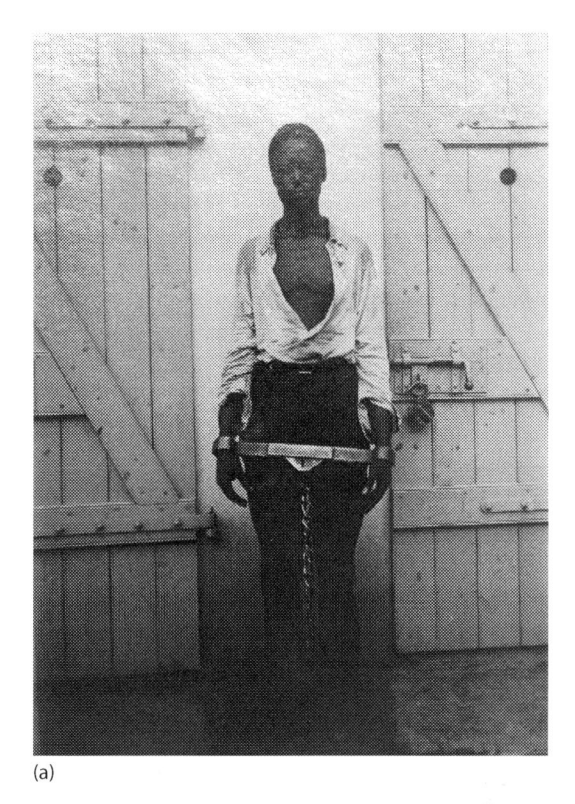

(a)

(b)

Figure 1.10 (a) Portrait of an unidentified man in prison, n.d. (b) Shower in prison courtyard, n.d.

We are on uncharted terrain here, where there are but a few notes of guidance. As suggested at the outset of this chapter, the circulation of images of captives and detainees had become an uncanny occurrence in the German colonial visual economy during the period of the South West African War. Militarism as a characteristic feature and cultural disposition of colonial society endured into the post-war period, especially in the domain of photographic production and consumption.[136] But this album diverts us from the theatre of war and its public spectacle of almost boundless brutality into the domain of less vociferous private collections, as much as we continue to wade through the cesspool of wretched and unfettered masculinity.[137] It remains to be clarified how and why, after 1907–1908, prison and police images continued to make their way into the private domain and into this particular album.

Answering the question will remain speculative and conjectural; we do not know the author or collector, nor do we know the specificities of the album's trajectory from the German colony to the metropole and its ultimate storage in the archive.[138] Is the inclusion of the two photographs reproduced here a mere caprice of the past, or a conundrum proposed by a visual history that remains, in many ways, unexplained? We will puzzle over their presence in the album. Let us take time to look at these images more carefully, not least because the generic category of "prison photographs" runs the risk of glossing over their dissimilarity. Image number A03_0060 is a full-length frontal view of an unidentified man in what seems to be a prison courtyard. There is no date nor place given. He wears civilian clothes, and while they look worn-out by the time of the man's captivity, his white shirt, black trousers, and belt with buckle remain intriguing if frail indications of lost social standing. The quality and elegance of his attire is barely perceivable and recedes from the visual dominance of the chains on his hands and feet. The imposing prison structure marked by the cell wall and concrete floor suggests that the image was taken in one of the larger prisons at the time, i.e. in Windhoek, Lüderitzbucht, or Swakopmund. While this photograph would indeed go well with the German colonial police album we have been concerned with earlier on, this is clearly not the case for the second image, numbered A03_0187.[139]

Here the scene is a different one, though we remain in the prison space. We see a group of young men, many of them juveniles, while they are probably forced to have a shower. The *mise-en-scène* seems deliberate in emphasising the scale of the wall and the cold materiality of the courtyard against which the men appear small, fragile, and exposed, disoriented in their gathering under the metal construction of the shower. Concrete and iron give an edge to the nakedness of their bodies. We witness a moment of transition and transformation, as if all reference to life in freedom still clinging to the body needed to be washed away in order to yield the purified, bare body of the detainee.[140] The transformation occurs under the supervision of a uniformed African policeman, who attentively watches what is going on. Visually he acts as *repoussoir*, guiding our eye and thereby conditioning our entanglement in a perpetual act of surveillance.[141] This photograph reminds us, indeed, of how coloniality draws on the naturalisation of a privileged and often voyeuristic gaze that likes to enter spaces of seclusion, where it forces subjects into unsparing exposure, but likewise establishes forms and relations of pleasure and intimacy, as challenged and fraught as they might be.[142] The photographic camera as inquisitive peephole plays an important role here in revealing a key productive effect of this album as photographic assemblage, in which the surveillance and erotic economies overlap.[143] Both economies cherish seeing as the object of desire, and both depend on a distinction and tension between visibility and invisibility, such that in the prison space vision meanders larcenously along the shielding of detainees behind prison walls, eager to second the camera in finding its longed-for loopholes. Once we raise the question about these two photographs' presence in the album through the lens of assemblage, we direct attention away from image content and style alone towards mechanisms of remaking and rearrangement in new constellations of visual connectivity. And we discover an ambivalence inherent in surveillance assemblages, in which images retain their capacity to move and disperse, although, or precisely because, they originate from contexts marked by an intense preoccupation with containing and arresting movements, flows, and volatilities.[144]

How can we, though, put more flesh on the bone and ground the dynamics of visual containment and dispersal in the specificity of the German colonial police and penitentiary in South West Africa in the 1910s? How do we understand the particular assemblage of images, objects, sites, agencies, and forces? There is reason to believe that accessibility of police-posts and prisons was important, as much as the availability and circulation of photographic equipment, as we saw earlier on. Likewise, forms of image reproduction and consumption would have had an effect on image circulation and dispersal. And indeed, we are lead back, once again, to our conversation with Governor Seitz, who proved well and truly farsighted – not just that he made significant efforts in regulating the photographic process in police and prison work, but also that he strove to control the circulation of images. His response to the fact that policemen had begun to use their private photographic cameras was ambivalent, and he anticipated their desire to harness the photographs for private purposes. In addition, he took up a restrictive position towards the work of professional photographers, both in taking photographs and in reproducing and publishing them.[145] His scepticism was, as we saw, justified, and several avenues opened up for the leakage of prison and police photographs into the private domain. Album A03, *Foto-Album Südwestafrika*, is a case in point, since here prison photographs became components of a memorial mosaic that ultimately served a problematic entanglement of surveillance and desire.

Deterritorialisation 2 – physical anthropology

A second, different instance of deterritorialisation shows itself once the photographic camera is pointed at imprisoned individuals not by policemen or prison wardens, but by physical anthropologists. We enter this problematic domain of colonial scientific practice in late 1912, when an Austrian geographer, publicist, would-be ethnographer, and physical anthropologist – Franz Seiner – wrote to the Colonial Secretary in Berlin, after he had taken several photographs of "Bushmen" prisoners in Grootfontein and Swakopmund. His letter is worth quoting at length:

> Your excellency! Most humbly I allow myself to write to you regarding the following matter of general interest: The Bushmen are highly sensitive of any change of climate and way of life; I've been recently able to assure myself of this fact in the prisons in Grootfontein and Swakopmund in the years of 1910–1912. In Grootfontein, which is located on the margin of the Kalahari and has a climate very much comparable to the one prevalent across the Kalahari landscapes, many detained Bushmen die after just six months of imprisonment due to exhaustion. Images 1 and 2 show such emaciated Bushmen.
>
> Now all Bushmen, who have been convicted to sentences of more than one year, are taken from the inland to the prisons in Lüderitzbucht and Swakopmund, and this removal amounts to a death sentence given the harshness of the coastal climate. In the prison at Swakopmund I did not only find 10-year-old boys, but also women with babies; all of them obviously perished, and three boys were ill after spending one week in Swakopmund.[…][146]

What seemed ostensibly motivated by a humanitarian concern with prison conditions and the human consequences of a ruthless penitentiary was, as we shall see, more likely an expression of Seiner's hypocrisy and ultimately driven by his ambition to secure the undisturbed unfolding of a career in the making. His letter did, admittedly, cause a bit of a stir, and the district officers as well as the prison surgeons at Swakopmund and Grootfontein had to submit reports to the authorities in Windhoek accordingly.[147] They were all apologetic, accusing Seiner of distortion of facts, and one of them even included photographs as evidence for proving Seiner's account wrong.[148] Governor Seitz must have appreciated the visual refutation, as he seemed alarmed about the political agitation Seiner's photographs might have possibly triggered if circulated. Answering the colonial secretary's request for clarification, the most powerful man in the colony eventually defended the harshness required on the administration's side. The critical argument was the alleged havoc caused by criminal gangs and, in particular, the so-called "Bushmen plague" mentioned earlier on, although Seitz conceded that African insurgency was in essence the response to an advancing colonial frontier in the north.[149] Seitz' assessment would have come as no surprise to Seiner, who had himself by then spent a substantial amount of time in South West Africa and acquired first-rate knowledge of the workings and functioning of German colonial policing, prosecution, and detention – of which we will see more later. For now, it is Seiner's contention that it was the Bushmen's distinctive disposition, sensitivity to climate, and dependence on a particular way of life for survival, which shall concern us for a moment. These pronouncements struck the note of science, and his words evidenced an academic parvenu's aspiration to join the ranks of a renowned group of scholars, most of them German geographers and zoologists, who had a sense of urgency of the impending "extinction of human species" and puzzled over the racial classification and distinction of what they termed *Hottentotts* and *Bushmen*.[150] The men of science were thus anxious to find pertinent evidence for their adventurous theories by means of anthropometric and anthropological research, and to do so, nothing seemed better suited than a German colony in which the African population had been brutally subjected.

The beginnings of this line of research fell during the period of the war and clustered around the writings of one of the leading scholars in the field at the time, Leonhard Schultze, whose work left deep imprints on a wide range of disciplines including zoology, geography, linguistics, and physical anthropology.[151] Schultze travelled extensively across Southern Africa between early 1903 and late 1905. Deeply marked by war-related events, his journey took him first, in April 1903, from the areas around Lüderitzbucht and Walvisbay up to Swakopmund along the South West African coast, where he pursued research on fisheries on behalf of the German imperial government. Later that year, he ventured through southern *Damaraland*, namely the region between Swakopmund and Windhoek, and eventually returned to Lüderitzbucht. A short stay at the Cape in early 1904 made him conclude his research on the coastal economy. In 1904, Schultze also travelled in southern Namibia and the Northern Cape (in what was then called *Gross-* and *Klein Namaland*) to British Bechuanaland and the southern Kalahari. In 1905, Schultze returned to Swakopmund, where he spent several months doing research on the so-called *Topnaar Nama* people in the area around Walvisbay. Reaching southern Namibia in August, his research was increasingly overshadowed by military surveillance and action. Not that he was bothered too much by this; on the contrary, meeting the commanding officer of the German troops, Lieutenant General von Trotha in Keetmanshoop, who invited him to join the military campaign against the rebellious Witbooi units in October 1905, was a thrilling experience that Schultze valued as an encouragement of his studies and as auspicious opportunity to return to the Kalahari from the West. Subsequent to these increasingly adventurous endeavours, the scientist-made-war-correspondent returned to Cape Town and eventually left Southern Africa for Germany in November 1905.[152]

The research trips across Namibia, South Africa, and Botswana were crucial for Schultze's academic career, and he was widely celebrated as a prolific writer who published in the most renowned German anthropological and ethnographic journals and series of the time.[153] Schultze's study *Aus Namaland und Kalahari* (1907) and his *Zur Kenntnis des Körpers der Hottentotten und Buschmänner* (1928) were considered seminal in the racial classification and anthropometric description of a population he proposed to henceforth call *Koisan*, a term that combined "Koi" (Nama) and "San" (Bushmen).[154] Yet what is of greater concern here is Schultze's embeddedness in what can only be assessed as a highly problematic predatory economy of German research and collecting institutions, which subsisted on an almost unlimited grip on the lives and bodies of interned and incarcerated African men, women, and children during and – in an almost unfettered way – after the war.[155] As we shall see, the anthropometric measurements and photographs Schultze took of a small group of people in the vicinity of Walvisbay and of prisoners in Keetmanshoop were part and parcel of this repressive system of knowledge extraction.[156]

Just a few more words about Seiner, who was anxious to follow in Schultze's footsteps, even though as contemporary academia might have considered him not to be worthy enough.[157] Franz Seiner had visited the South West African colony in as early as 1902–1903, but his most intense travel period began three years later. Between 1906 and 1912, he managed to go on several research expeditions that took him across central Namibia, to the Caprivi and Sambesi (where he made extensive cartographic recordings), to the central Kalahari, and to the Omatako valley around Tsumkwe in the northeast. Seiner was a zealous collector of botanical, zoological, ethnographic, and anthropological specimen and artefacts, many of which he supplied to German and Austrian botanical and ethnographic museums and university collections.[158] Notwithstanding incessant conflicts over ownership and use of research results with the German Colonial Office, which paid for most of his expeditions, Seiner published a series of pseudo-ethnographic articles and bold theoretical essays on an increasingly popular concern in German racial science in the 1910s – the question of miscegenation. The titles of his anthropological publications, most of which underscored his bizarre notion of a distinctive *Bastard-Bushman* – evidence how the preoccupation with race had gone astray.[159] But it was indeed through his publication work and especially his emphasis on photography as evidence for racial theory that Seiner succeeded in gaining grounds in a competitive scholarly domain. Very much in line with the Schultzian tradition, Seiner didn't shy away from measuring and photographing prisoners, and it was indeed this body of photographic work that attracted wide interest among metropolitan collecting institutions, publishers, and scholars alike, since the prison photographs constituted an increasingly sought-after scientific commodity.[160]

In 1906, a few requests for prison photographs sent from the Ethnographic Museum in Berlin to the Cape authorities met with outright disapproval, as it was felt (at least officially) that free-handed dealings with such images would "hurt the feelings of imprisoned native criminals".[161] Such norms were less fastidiously observed in the German colony, as is well known. Schultze's and Seiner's camera work in various South West African prisons takes us back to the question of prison photography's leakage beyond its bureaucratic enclosure. It is therefore worth revisiting the images they produced – less as illustrations in the context of racial science, but as an instance of dispersal and reterritorialisation in a wider assemblage of police and prison photography.

Chronology and seniority require us to start with Leonhard Schultze. In his introduction to the first volume of a monumental zoological and anthropological report on "Western and central South Africa", Schultze noted that the war had earned him numerous "fresh native corpses, which he was able to dissect on the spot." These remains had been, he continued, convenient additions to the study of living bodies often conducted on "imprisoned Hottentotts at his disposal".[162] And indeed, numerous photographs are scattered across his publications, although Schultze never specified which images precisely had been taken in prisons, police stations, or prisoner camps. He claimed that brute force was not inevitable, and Bushmen and Hottentotts could usually be convinced to allow measurements and nude photography if offered small presents.[163] Yet, often the photographs themselves, i.e. their framing and image content – the visible backdrops, uniforms, and sometimes injuries – are in fact highly suggestive of their production in sites of surveillance and detention. This is particularly true for those images taken in the prison in Keetmanshoop in 1905, where Schultze's camera displayed an almost unbearable indecency and seemingly could not get enough nudity and close-ups of male and female genitalia. The level of exposure and infringement upon people's physical and personal integrity cannot be written off and needs to be kept in mind, especially once we try to understand what these reterritorialised photographs become and do in a project of physical anthropology and racial science (Figure 1.11).

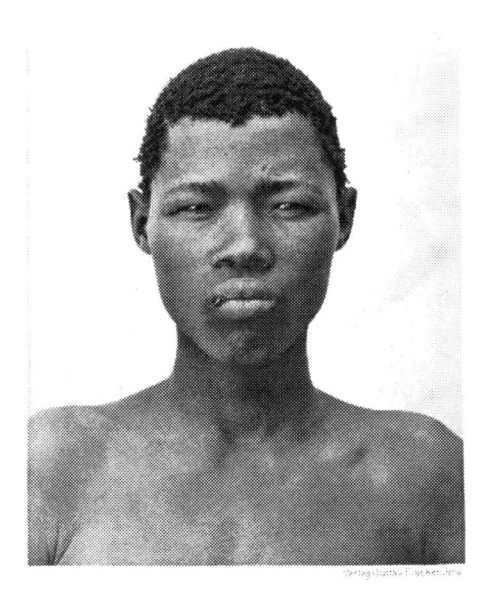

Figure 1.11 Schultze Jena, *Zur Kenntnis*, 1928: Plate number VII, photograph number 45, *O:sob*, Keetmanshoop in 1905.

Schultze never cared to explain or analyse his photographs properly. The images seem, at first sight, to be used as mere pedagogical illustrations that evidence the significance attributed to visualisation in the various strands of anthropological research. However, it is also Schultze the zoologist at work here, inviting readers and viewers to contemplate not individual people, but *species*, whose status of idiosyncrasy and alterity is evidenced and mediated through detailed visual information. Still, the illustrative concealed a normative framework of an entirely different kind. A closer look at one of Schultze's seminal works – *Zur Kenntnis des Körpers der Hottentotten und Buschmänner* – will underscore this position.[164] It is time to speak to the photograph reproduced here: the image was part of a series of 18 plates published in the said study, which consisted of one, two, or up to four photographs each. Included in plate number VII, photograph number 45 was said to depict a 20 year-old man named *O:sob*, born at *!Garitsama!ga:os* [sic] on the Fish River, member of the *!Kxaro!o:an* [sic] tribe (Hottentott) and photographed by Schultze in Keetmanshoop in 1905.

The captions and numbers added to the images correlated with two tables, one for Hottentotts and one for Bushmen, which regrouped the photographic subjects according to racial and tribal affiliation and summarised information on names, age, place of birth, and site of photographic recording (see Table 1.1). Yet, another group of tables finally listed the details on anthropometric measurements taken and linked these, to bring the method full circle, to the numbering of the photographic plates.

As a critical reader, one is inevitably incited to do the appropriate detective work and verify if the suggested correlation between the assembled components – anthropometric measurements, names, numbers, and photographs – is in fact accomplished. Once this work has been done, the verdict is indisputably unfavourable, as there is remarkable confusion and mismatch between the data presented; the sheer volume of information generated seems to have been a significant obstacle to systematisation and ultimately a source of error. We could concede that systematisation and consistency might have been the Achilles tendon of early twentieth-century German colonial endeavour, whether in science or in policing. Yet, it still comes as a surprise that a renowned scholar and proven researcher in Jena, Germany, would exercise as little care as would the officers in the criminal records department in Windhoek, South West Africa, once they composed the photographic album and its associated list of prisoners. Nevertheless, or precisely because of this common if unintentional methodological weakness, the messiness of information and recording ultimately unearths something else. What presents itself as a methodologically substantiated clarification of the alleged racial difference between Hottentotts and Bushmen (and this is what Schultze's scholarship and photography was essentially about) was at its heart nothing else than an exercise in colonial forensics – in Bertillonage, if you like, in which anthropometric measurements, photographs, and even samples of hair mimicked the prison photographs, signalements, and fingerprints.[165] The *crème de la crème* of German physical anthropology would

Table 1.1

A. Verzeichnis der untersuchten Personen.

Ueber die Schreibweise hottentottischer Wörter siehe die Bemerkungen in der Erläuterung zu Tafel I.

Laufende Nummer	Eigenname	Alter (Jahre)	Geburtsort	Ort der Beobachtung	Abbildung
	Stamm der *t-Amin* oder *Gomen* sie selbst nennen sich auch *Mü-ʻʻei-n*), Topnaars.				
1	*ǀNu-mabeb*	50	—	Rooibank im Hinter- land der Walfischbai	Taf. VI oben rechts, Lit.- Verz. No. 81, Taf. XV
2	*Kǀu-mi*	50	*Hʻrovas,* aber alle Vor- fahren in Rooibank	Rooibank	—
3	*t Na-revab*	60	Rooibank	Rooibank	Taf. VIII oben rechts
4	—	20	Rooibank	Rooibank	Taf. VI oben links, Lit.- Verz. No. 81, S. 176, 177
5	*Ga-rolab*	20	Rooibank	Rooibank	Taf. VIII oben links
6	*Kǀu-ri-hai-b*	30	Rooibank	Rooibank	Taf. VIII unten links
7	—	20	Rooibank	Rooibank	
8	*ǀ Gai-eb*	40	—	Rooibank	Taf. XI unten rechts
9	*So-deb*	20	*ǁNa-os gama-b* Kuiseb- gebiet	Rooibank	Taf. X, der Jüngere
10	*t Niseb*	20	Rooibank	Rooibank	—
11	*Da-seb*	25	Rooibank	Rooibank	—
12	*Bu-sab*	20	Rooibank	Rooibank	—
13	*Ga-meb*	45	Rooibank	Walfischbai	Taf. XI oben u. links unten
14	*ǀA-baseb*	30	Rooibank	Walfischbai	—
15	*ǁHa-ot-ei-b*	30	Rooibank	Walfischbai	—
16	*So-ndab*	25	*ǂHau-vas* in Damara- land	Walfischbai	—
17	*ǀ U-ibeb*	35	bei Windhuk	Walfischbai	—
18	—	45	bei Rooibank	Walfischbai	—
19	*Ga-oseb*	30	bei Zandfontein	Walfischbai	—
20	*t Ga-bagab*	25	Zandfontein bei Wal- fischbai	Walfischbai	—
21	*ǀGa-raseb*	25	Narafeld bei Rooibank	Walfischbai	—
22	*A-m na-b*	35	—	Rooibank	Taf. X, der Aeltere
23	*ǂHo-bevab*	40	Rooibank	Rooibank	—
	Stamm der *ǀKu-ragui-kʼom,* Fransman-Hottentotten				
24	*So-ndab*	25	*Ha-ruvas* bei Auob	Keetmanshoop	—
	Stamm der *ǀ Ha-bobe-n,* Velschoendragers.				
25	*ǀGo-hoseb*	25	Sandfeld, östlich von Keetmanshoop	Keetmanshoop	—
26	*ǁGa-niʻʻgo-rob*	50	*ǂ ös* im südlichen Namaland	Keetmanshoop	Taf. IX unten rechts
27	*Go-gob*	20	Slangkop	Keetmanshoop	—
28	—	20	*ǀHeis*	Keetmanshoop	—
29	*Dyu-ndab*	22	*Kǀo-es*	Keetmanshoop	—

have staged protests against such comparison. But it was, in fact, Schultze himself who invited the proposed analogy. At one point in *Zur Kenntnis*, he conceded – as if in doubt of the spirit and purpose of his effort – that local opinion had its own theory. It framed the problem of racial classification grittily and sarcastically as one of surveillance: "What is a Bushman can be discerned as much in the prisons of the cities in British South Africa as in the wild, where all cattle thieves, who refuse to be settled and are of any descent, Hottentott or other, count as Bushmen".[166]

Franz Seiner tells us even more about this conflation of science and polic- ing, this new assemblage, one that ultimately amounted to the constitution of criminal races. Unlike Schultze, Seiner – a daredevil and loudmouth com- pared to his colleagues, who usually abstained from political opinion making in their academic writings – left no doubt about the constitutive entanglement of colonial and anthropological interest in Hottentotts and Bushmen in German South West Africa, and his forensic methodology was in no way inferior to Schultze's.[167] But Seiner's stronger interest in miscegenation took him to the northeastern area of the territory, where, conveniently, there was an important prison in Grootfontein. The coincidence was indeed productive, and Seiner was quite honest about it, such as in his *Beobachtungen und Messungen an Buschleuten* published in 1912, where his formulations swayed back and forth between policing and researching, and more often read like crime reports rather than scientific accounts. Introducing the sample of measurements and observations evaluated for his article, Seiner described the subjects of research as follows:

> Measurements and observations were made of a group of Kung (subgroup unknown) captured at Nurugas, who – after they had stolen police owned cattle, threatened police officers and resisted arrest – were taken to the prison at Grootfontein, except for two Bushmen who were shot. Two men confessed the theft and were taken to the district officer, who sentenced them to several years of hard labour and deportation to Swakopmund prison. The rest, nine men, was released after a few days.[168]

His comments regarding the seven women arrested at Nurugas are almost bio-political in tone:

> While the men are in prison in Grootfontein, the women are employed at the police station in Nurugas, where they cohabit with single Bergdamara men. Bastards born from these relations make for useful farmworkers.[169]

Furthermore, collaboration with police opened up productive avenues that transcended practical matters and questions of access to research subjects and moved towards collective knowledge production. Seiner valued the experience of men on the ground, who spent extended periods observing and scrutinising the character, behaviour, and whereabouts of a colonised population that was seen as particularly volatile and inconceivable. He hence recorded that

> the Hei//kum [sic] are, according to reports from military and police patrols, physically identical with the Kung, while we have no knowledge of those seemingly weak Bushmen, who have been forced back by the Hei//kum and now sit in Owamboland, where they are probably tributaries to the Owambo.[170]

Yet, Seiner's affinity towards the police and penal system was by no means just a matter of scientific and/or colonial rationale; it was, instead, as much the result of his own angst. Every time he had distanced himself from the nodal points of surveillance and incarceration and ventured into the open *veld* in search of "Bastard Bushmen", his life was threatened – by his guides and carriers, his translators, and mostly by those whom he intended to measure and photograph. It is indeed telling and almost ironic – were it not for the viciousness of the general situation – that in the course of an attack on Seiner by "a horde of criminals and thieves," his assailants took his botanical and ethnographic collections and destroyed his photographic equipment.[171] This might explain why, in view of his impending bankruptcy and departure from South West Africa, we rediscover Seiner's words quoted earlier on, *then* used as part of his complaint to the colonial secretary and couched in an alleged concern about Bushman sensitivity to imprisonment, climate, and nutrition, *now* as part of the uncanny *jumelage* of science and surveillance:

> [...] Years ago, a small number of Bushmen was taken to London, where they soon perished. I nevertheless do not consider it to be impossible to take Bushmen to Europe and to keep them alive for a couple of months, provided one takes precautions (such as taking along Feldkost). In any case, and considered from the perspective of anthropological research, it would be much more convenient to deport the dangerous criminals to Hamburg and Berlin, rather than just to Swakopmund.[172]

Deterritorialisation 3 – criminology

The "native body" had been placed at the core of the project of colonial policing and recording. Bodies were the linchpin of the surveillance assemblage, and they moved along its vectors and circuits of dispersal. The third and final instance of deterritorialisation we shall explore takes us to the outermost margins of the physical and archival corpus and a distinct modality of visualisation – fingerprints. Our entry point is yet another request – this time a metropolitan one – which reached the central government in the South West African colony in 1906, and was authored by the director of police in Hamburg Gustav Roscher. Once Roscher had extensively praised the benefits and importance of dactyloscopy for modern police work and specified his interest in improving the system of fingerprint registration and classification, he explained the nature of his request:

> As it is of vital importance for the improvement of the system to understand how the four accepted patterns – loops, whorls, arches, composites – are distributed among the different races (*Völker*) and tribes, I permit myself to ask the colonial government to collaborate in trying to solve this question of utmost scientific and practical importance. I am asking to use the enclosed fingerprint cards for the recording of 100 fingerprints of local natives, and to return these cards to me. It should be kept in mind to select as many individuals as possible for each race and tribe. In case there would be a large amount of human material [sic] and the number of cards would not be enough, I would kindly ask to record the fingerprints on simple paper.[173]

Roscher was no stranger to police institutions across the German empire. He was at the forefront of attempts to modernise criminalistics and had stood out in his conception of police work as a scientifically and almost intellectually grounded endeavour.[174] He was also the initiator and founder of the Criminological Museum in Hamburg in 1893, an institution he understood to be crucial for the education of police officers and the general public alike.[175] Furthermore, his request was in no way unusual, as contemporary interest in fingerprinting was strong, from both criminologists and scientists across the world.[176] As an individual who moved with ease in both domains, Roscher perfectly embodied the scientification of metropolitan and colonial state administrations, in general, and the police in particular.[177] It comes as no surprise, then, that Windhoek responded positively, and eventually, in late May 1907, Roscher gave his thanks for a "substantial amount of fingerprints" received from South West Africa (Figure 1.12).[178]

It is worthwhile dwelling in the colony for a moment and reconsidering what the roots and aims of fingerprinting were here. The establishment of the criminal records department in Windhoek in 1911 had raised some dust about the systematic recording of fingerprints, but the practice had already begun to proliferate across diverse contexts that were not bound to police work alone, even if they preserved, obviously perhaps, an aura of

(a)

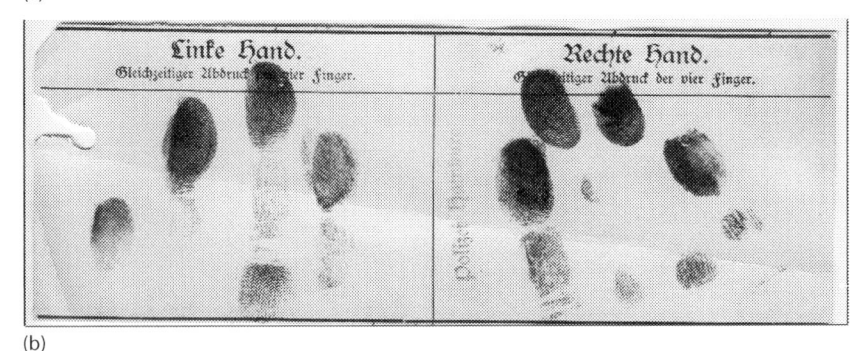

(b)

Figure 1.12 (a & b[179]) Fingerprints from German South West Africa, n.d.

identification and surveillance.[180] Like in its neighbouring South African territory, the South West African administration encouraged the use of fingerprints as a substitute for "unreliable native signatures", which more often than not consisted of a trivial cross placed under statements, contracts, permits, or certificates; but even after 1911, the various modalities of signing remained in use.[181] The domain in which fingerprinting was imposed most consistently, though, was labour recruitment, and prints flourished particularly as a means of control of those who might have broken contract.[182] It is perhaps due to the conflation of the police, penal, and labour systems described earlier that fingerprints became the most important and everyday visual marker of an overarching colonial rationale. But there were further reasons for this.

As is well known, the key figure in generalising and popularising fingerprinting as a means of fixing identity was Francis Galton, whose late nineteenth-century writings had helped underscore bureaucratic enthusiasm for dactyloscopy across the empire.[183] Galton combined an interest in developing a method of collecting, reading (i.e. classifying and codifying), and registering fingerprints, which would be cheap and simple enough for metropolitan and imperial bureaucrats, with a commitment to use fingerprints as the basis for scientific statements about social and racial types and the hereditary nature of deviance.[184] What proved to be a key advantage of fingerprints was that, unlike photographs, personal descriptions, and even anthropometric measurements, they were linked to a person's body as an unchanging, permanent physical characteristic.[185] And because fingerprints were seen as thoroughly indexical, their recording less susceptible to error, and their organisation, classification, and quantification amenable to systematic order and the archive, fingerprinting gave the appearance of being both a particularly effective bureaucratic method, as well as a scientifically grounded and hence superior form of representation.[186]

Notwithstanding the alleged methodological impeccability and pecuniary quality of fingerprinting, forensic practice in German South West Africa in the first two decades of the twentieth century evidences, as we have seen, the intricacy and simultaneity of different methods, all of which harboured their own illusions and hollow promises. And indeed, as much as fingerprinting began to establish itself in the colony as an everyday institutional procedure, in policing and beyond, its value for criminal identification remained contested, presumably because actual police work was never in a position to examine and assess its viability.[187] It seems as if the German colonial administration would never witness a conviction of a felon based on fingerprinting, as the official chronicles of criminal identification in South West Africa date first achievements of this sort to the period after the First World War, and hence give credit to its South African rival and successor.[188] Irrespective of bureaucratic procrastination, though, fingerprinting – like photography – made it into the domain of German racial science, as Roscher's letter and request bring to our knowledge.

But what was it that ultimately made fingerprints of interest to him? Roscher was obviously trying to follow in the steps of Galton, who had advocated for the statistical comparison of fingerprints in order to classify racial groups. His request for 100 prints from the German colony might not have satisfied the quantitative requirements of contemporary scientific sampling but given that the South West African authorities had just begun to introduce fingerprinting to police work, the number seems substantial. What revealed Roscher's scientific predilection more particularly, though, was a handwritten note he added to his letter, in which he specified his priority interest – how could it be otherwise? – in fingerprints of Hottentotts and Bushmen. Ironically, Galton had soon given up on finding evidence for racial difference in fingerprint patterns, but this seemed to have little effect on Roscher, perhaps because he remained a man of practice with a vested interest in the method's success and reputation.[189]

The *Fingerprints of a Hottentott Woman from Lüderitzbucht* are the sole, fragile trace of fingerprinting by the colonial authorities that remains in the Hamburg archives today. But the dispersal of fingerprints and its reterritorialisation in German criminology and racial science was sturdier, and it persisted far into the twentieth century.[190] We can hardly imagine what the level of objectification, and the experience of one's body being ripped of any sign of sociocultural belonging and turned into a bare physical entity that could be disassembled and broken down into abstract components (photographs, fingerprints, measurements), meant to those who were exposed to the forensic eye of policemen and scientists alike. However, in one instance there is exceptional evidence. We are taken back to a familiar site, the police station in Keetmanshoop in southern Namibia, which, as one of the nodal points in the topography of colonial policing, reopened its doors to anthropometric research in 1931. It is here that we get a sense of how well the subjects of scrutiny understood the merging of criminalistics and science for which fingerprinting had become iconic.

> Of all measures (photography, anthropometric measurements, voice recordings, and life-casts) the taking of dactyloscopic prints were liked the least by the natives. The police does [sic] the same and I had to declare each time that the prints were only for me. Still, one could tell the crimination of their records by the trembling of hands.[191]

Afterlives

Our point of entry has been an image and object, a photographic police album produced by the criminal records department in Windhoek, German South West Africa, between 1911 and 1913. Today, we encounter this album in the archive as part of a fragmented, loosely associated corpus of texts and images. Some of these invited us to gradually leave this notable object and the centre of colonial power and move towards its margins, in order to sight ephemeral materials produced by peripheral district offices, prisons, and police posts. Placing this assemblage of images and texts in relation to a history of colonial policing and surveillance in the Namibian colony has helped to chart a landscape in which attempts at introducing modern technologies – photography, anthropometry, and dactyloscopy – to police and prison work delineated the institutional and topographical skeleton of post-war colonial state reconstruction. Still, the relationship between this history and the material and visual traces it left to posterity might be less evident than we tend to assume, particularly if we keep in mind the archive's role in precisely inscribing photographic images as unique and privileged documentary evidence.[192] Raising the question about the album's presence in the archive and casting doubts on its historically continuous material, visual and discursive unity has informed the analytical move to think about these archival materials in terms of assemblage. The aim was to transcend the conventional framework of visual representation and historical meaning-making, and move towards processes of arranging, relating and connecting, making and unmaking; in short, from the firmness of signification to the flexibility of capacity.

In line with assemblage theory, the concern has been with forms of territorialisation, i.e. with what the album and its surrounding archive tell us about how images, words, bodies, and concepts came together and were being made within the policing assemblage. Keeping in mind the limits and weaknesses of the visual and material yields of German colonial criminalistics, there were nevertheless productive effects that concerned the production of particular subjects and bodies, their confinement into the segregated space of the prison, and their insertion into a discourse of deviance and criminality. Territorialisation has also been thought of more literally, in order to unearth the ways in which "knowledge" produced by the police in the course of identifying, measuring, describing, and classifying African men, women, and youth constituted an important, if fraught form of racial mapping. Yet, delineating the contours of colonial criminalistics and weighing its material fruits as part of an exercise in recording, integrating, and merging has conveyed a sense of meagreness and failure – at least as long as one remains within the material margins of the surveillance assemblage and the notion of a delimited institutional domain of policing. Deterritorialisation, therefore, served to open up paths into exploring instances in which the visual products of police work spilled beyond its own boundaries and dispersed and reassembled in new sets of relations – in a private collection; in physical anthropology; and finally, in criminology.

The processes of assemblage, territorialisation, and deterritorialisation discussed throughout this chapter unfolded in a context, we might recall, in which the German colonial administration strove to impose a regime of repressive legislation that aimed at controlling and regulating African political, social, and economic life. The underlying rationale was a radical transformation that would bring post-war colonial society in line with a rapidly expanding farming and mining economy in need of ever-increasing numbers of cheap labourers. The constitution of a modern police and penitentiary system after 1908 was undoubtedly geared to the political economy of settler colonialism and the predatory logics of land appropriation and resource extraction.[193] Policing, as much as or precisely because it was meant to secure the imposition of colonial policy and regulation on Africans, was indeed the domain in which the clash between the state and its subject population was, obviously perhaps, chronic and most acute. Yet, the police and the penitentiary are also a domain in which we can discern, in a Foucauldian vein, the productivity of power[194] and understand how the crises created by colonialism – large scale impoverishment, displacement and deportation, persecution and death, and African responses to all of them – conditioned what Hunt has called "state nervousness". Read within this framework of power's agitation, restlessness, tension, and at times even paranoia, the photographic album, registers of prisoners, anthropometric measurements, and fingerprints evidence how the police and penal system laboured to counter African defiance – in a double move that resulted in what was claimed to constitute knowledge production but ultimately served to impose expedient sociocultural "facts".[195] For those exposed to the surveillance and criminological experiment, we must not forget, policing and surveillance more often than not amounted to a horrifying manifestation of what Georges Balandier called "a grotesque sociological experience".[196]

Retracing the ways in which police and prison photography (and fingerprinting) moved into the domain of private collections, physical anthropology and criminology has unearthed ways in which the forensic coupled with economies of erotic and scientific desire. This sort of reciprocal fecundation is not new to histories of photography across the colonial world, and it has recurrently been addressed in studies of colonial science in general, and anthropology in particular.[197] But there is more to say here, more threads to add to the fabric of colonial vision as it spread out in German South West Africa and obtrusively engulfed, like a glutinous foil, the "native body". The expansion of surveillance and the carceral via photography or indexical modalities of the visual makes the argument proposed in this chapter resonate with Paul Virilio's "logistics of the image", or "logistics of perception". These terms denote an "operational agenda according to which perception is appropriated, delimited, and further produced by means of (visual) technologies", and through which the body is given particular shape, less in visual representation than in a diverse range of institutional practices in which photographic images partake.[198]

It is precisely on the grounds of practices that take place outside of the police and penal system – in science, in private collecting – that a particular modality of *state seeing* – what we have called forensic vision – is generalised and normalised, with eyes inquisitively and invariably laid on the subjected body. However, there are likewise forms of *state readings* that came to the fore, once we considered the conjunction of surveillance and science. When photographs (and other information) produced in service of physical anthropology and criminology prove to be deeply embedded in and facilitated by the colonial police and penitentiary system – as was the case in Schultze's, Seiners's, and Roscher's work – science becomes an uncanny accomplice, ready to join into the language of racial alterity as counterinsurgency.[199] It is precisely this expansion of state seeing and state reading that, eventually, afforded the imagery of German colonial policing an adamant afterlife; we have come across one moment of reactivation in the early 1930s, but many more would come.

Notes

1 The literature is extensive, but see *inter alia* Horst Drechsler, *Aufstände in Südwestafrika. Der Kampf der Herero und Nama 1904 bis 1907 gegen die deutsche Kolonialherrschaft*. Berlin, 1984; Jan Bart Gewald, *Herero Heroes. A Socio-political History of the Herero in Namibia 1890–1923*. Oxford, Cape Town, Athens, 1999; Jürgen Zimmerer, *Deutsche Herrschaft über Afrikaner. Staatlicher Machtanspruch und Wirklichkeit im kolonialen Namibia*. Hamburg, 2001; David Olusoga and Casper W. Erichsen, *The Kaiser's Holocaust. Germany's Forgotten Genocide and the Colonial Roots of Nazism*. London, 2010; and with a more general focus on colonialism and German history Sara Friedrichsmeyer, Sara Lennox, and Susanne Zantop (eds.), *The Imperialist Imagination: German Colonialism and Its Legacies*. Ann Arbor, 1998.

2 Joachim Zeller, "Wie Vieh wurden hunderte zu Tode getrieben und wie Vieh begraben". Fotodokumente aus dem deutschen Konzentrationslager in Swakopmund/Namibia 1904–1908. *Zeitschrift für Geschichtswissenschaft*, 3, 2001: 226–43; ibid., Oorlog in Deutsch-Südwestafrika. Fotografien aus dem Kolonialkrieg 1904 bis 1907. *Fotogeschichte*, 85/86, 2002: 31–44; ibid., "Images of the South West African War": Reflections of the 1904–1907 Colonial War in Contemporary Photo Reportage and Book Illustration, in Wolfram Hartmann (ed.), *Hues between Black and White: Historical Photography from Colonial Namibia 1860s–1915*. Windhoek, 2004, pp. 309–23; George Steinmetz and Julia Hell, The Visual Archive of Colonialism: Germany and Namibia. *Public Culture*, 18, 1, 2005: 147–84.

3 Helmut Bley and Leonhard Harding (eds.), *Namibia under German Rule*. Münster, 1996, pp. 164–5; Zeller, Oorlog, p. 36.

4 Susan Sontag's *Regarding the Pain of Others*. New York, 2003, and Georges Didi-Huberman's *Images in Spite of All*. Chicago and London, 2008, remain crucial here.

5 See in particular Larissa Förster, Dag Henrichsen, and Michael Bollig (eds.), *Namibia-Deutschland. Eine geteilte Geschichte*. Köln, 2004; Marion Wallace, *A History of Namibia. From the beginning to 1990*. London, 2011, pp. 177–82.

6 Seen most clearly in Olusoga and Erichsen, *The Kaiser's Holocaust*, 2010.

7 See Jeremy Silvester and Jan Bart Gewald, *Words Cannot Be Found. German Colonial Rule in Namibia: An Annotated Reprint of the 1918 Blue Book*. Leiden, 2003.

8 For a critical discussion see Birthe Kundrus, From Herero to Holocaust? Some Remarks on the Current Debate. *Africa Spectrum*, 40, 2, 2005: 299–308.

9 Nancy Rose Hunt, *A Nervous State. Violence, Remedies, and Reverie in Colonial Congo*. Durham and London, 2016, p. 3.

10 Robert Gordon's critique of the concept of "Herero genocide" has pointed in a similar direction. See Robert J. Gordon, Hiding in Full View. The "Forgotten" Bushman Genocides in Namibia. *Genocide Studies and Prevention*, 4, 1, 2009: 29–57.

11 For the Congo see e.g. Christina Twomey, Framing Atrocity: Photography and Humanitarianism. *History of Photography*, 26, 3, 2012: 255–64.

12 Zeller, Oorlog, p. 36.

13 NAN BLU 265, Das Kaiserliche Gouvernement an das Bezirksamt Lüderitzbucht, Windhoek, 3. August 1911.

14 NAN ZBU 751 II a 4, Verbrecheralbum, Fingerabdrücke, Bd 1. Kaiserliches Bezirksgericht Swakopmund, von Lindequist an das Konsulat in Kapstadt, 10. Februar, 1906. See also Jürgen Zimmerer, *Deutsche Herrschaft.*, pp. 149–50.

15 NAN ZBU 751 II a 4, Verbrecheralbum, Fingerabdrücke, Bd 1. General-Konsul Kapstadt an den Kaiserlichen Gouverneur von Lindequist, 5. Juni, 1906.

16 NAN ZBU 751 G II a 4, Verbrecheralbum, Fingerabdrücke, Bd 1. Der Polizeidirektor, Gustav Roscher, Polizeibehörde Hamburg, an das Kaiserliche Gouvernement von Deutsch Südwest Afrika, 22.Mai.1907. The early experiments with fingerprinting were initiated by police institutions in Germany. We'll come back to these later.

17 Sven Schepp, *Unter dem Kreuz des Südens. Auf Spuren der Kaiserlichen Landespolizei von Deutsch Südwestafrika.* Schriftenreihe der Deutschen Gesellschaft für Polizeigeschichte Bd. 8. Frankfurt, 2009, p. 158; NAN ZBU 751 G II a 4, Verbrecheralbum, Fingerabdrücke, Bd 1. Das Kaiserliche Gouvernement, Seitz, an das Kaiserliche Bezirksamt Windhoek, 3.8.1911.

18 Schepp, *Unter dem Kreuz*, p. 160.

19 Ibid., pp. 163–4.

20 NAN ZBU 751 G II a 4, Verbrecheralbum, Fingerabdrücke, Bd 1. Der Kaiserliche Gouverneur Seitz an das Bezirksamt Windhoek, Anschluss an die Verfügung vom 3.8.1911.

21 On Bertillonage and the categories for personal descriptions see Josh Ellenbogen, *Reasoned and Unreasoned Images. The Photography of Bertillon, Galton, and Marey.* Pennsylvania, 2008, pp. 29–54.

22 NAN BWI 254, Kaiserliches Gouvernement, Hintrager, an das Bezirksamt Windhoek, 25. Juni 1912.

23 NAN ZBU 751 G II a 4, Verbrecheralbum, Fingerabdrücke, Bd 1. Kriminalpolizei an das Kaiserliche Gouvernement, Windhoek, 16. Juli 1913. The original text is in German, the translation is mine.

24 Detective Springborn, district office Swakopmund, 8.7.1911, quoted in Schepp, *Unter dem Krenz*, pp. 163–4. Original in German, my translation.

25 NAN ZBU 751 G II a 4, Verbrecheralbum, Fingerabdrücke, Bd 1. Das Kaiserliche Gouvernement, Seitz, an alle Bezirks- und Distriktämter, Windhoek, 1. April 1914.

26 NAN ZBU Pol/A. 737.

27 See Alan Sekula, The Body and the Archive; Peter Hamilton and Roger Hargreaves, *The Beautiful and the Damned. The Creation of Identity in 19th Century Photography.* London, 2001, pp. 57ff.; Jens Jäger, Erkennungsdienstliche Behandlung. Zur Inszenierung polizeilicher Identifikationsmethoden um 1900, in Jürgen Martschukat and Steffen Patzold (eds.), *Geschichtswissenschaft und performativer turn. Ritual, Inszenierung und Performanz vom Mittelalter bis zur Neuzeit.* Köln, 2003, pp. 207–28.

28 John Tagg, Evidence, Truth, Order: A Means of Surveillance, in Jessica Evans and Stuart Hall (eds.), *Visual Culture: The Reader.* London, Thousand Oaks, New Delhi, 1999, pp. 244–73.

29 Susanne Regener, *Fotografische Erfassung.* München, 1999, p. 104. Regener sees in these aesthetic variations in police photography an expression of pre-Bertillon forensic documentation practices that tend to disappear towards the mid-twentieth century.

30 Elizabeth Edwards and Janice Hart, Introduction. Photographs as Objects, in Edwards and Hart (eds.), *Photographs Objects Histories: On the Materiality of Images*. New York and Oxford, 2004, pp. 1–15.

31 On Bertillonage see Regener, *op. cit.*, pp. 113 and 148, and John Tagg, *The Burden of Representation*, pp. 87–8.

32 NAN BSW 29, Gefängnissachen, Das Kaiserliche Bezirksamt Swakopmund an das kaiserliche Gouvernement in Windhoek, Swakopmund, 25. November 1908, contains some information regarding Swakopmund in 1908, when two racially segregated prisons were made available. The new one, for "white" convicts only, contained cells for 27 men, out of which 24 were meant to host one prisoner only. No further information is given; also NAN ZBU 637 F III e 2, Kaiserliches Bezirksamt Windhoek an das Kaiserliche Gouvernement, 5.12.1901. See more generally Jakob Zollmann, *Koloniale Herrschaft und ihre Grenzen. Die Kolonialpolizei in Deutsch Südwest Afrika, 1894–1915*. Göttingen, 2010, p. 126; for a more general discussion of racial segregation in the penal system in the German colonies in Africa see Rolf Schlottau, *Deutsche Kolonialrechtspflege. Strafrecht und Strafmacht in den deutschen Schutzgebieten 1884 bis 1914*. Frankfurt, 2007; for South Africa see S. Singh, The Historical Development of Prisons in South Africa: A penological perspective. *New Contree*, 50, 2005: 15–28; for Africa more generally Florence Bernault and Janet L. Roitman (eds.), *A History of Prison and Confinement in Africa*. Portsmouth, 2003.

33 See e.g. Robert Gaupp, Über den heutigen Stand der Lehre vom "geborenen Verbrecher". *Monatsschrift für Kriminalpsychologie und Strafrechtsreform*, 1, 1904/05: 25–42; but see more generally Martin Chanock, Criminological Science and Criminal Law on the Colonial Periphery: Perception, Fantasy and Reality in South Africa, 1900–1930. *Law and Social Inquiry*, 20, 4, 1995: 911–39.

34 The name and its spelling need to be seen as part of an identification procedure in police and penal institutions, it might not be the woman's actual name.

35 NAN BWI 254, Kaiserlicher Gouverneur von Deutsch Südwestafrika, Theodor Seitz, an das kaiserliche Bezirksamt Windhuk, Sicherheitspolizei und Erkennungsdienst, Windhuk, 3. August 1911. Original in German, my translation.

36 NAN BWI 254 S 8 q, Kaiserliches Bezirksamt Windhoek, Sicherheitspolizei und Erkennungsdienst Band 1, 1.1.1911, Verzeichnis der im Gefängnis befindlichen Gefangenen [n.d.] The images reproduced here show the first two pages of the register, while the table reproduces this part in an English translation.

37 For the last 12 individuals (No 40 to 51) the list only provides information on names, nationality, and place of imprisonment.

38 See Zollmann, *Koloniale Herrschaft*, p. 188ff; Zimmerer, *Deutsche Herrschaft*, pp. 127ff.; Jürgen Zimmerling, *Die Entwicklung der Strafrechtspflege für Afrikaner in Deutsch-Südwest Afrika 1884–1914*. Eine juristisch/historische Untersuchung. Bochum 1995. Zimmerling (pp. 140–1) provides the following figures: for 1910/11: 2370 sentences, out of which 542 involved imprisonment (the balance being corporal punishments and punitive fines); for 1911/12: 3252 sentences, out of which 1222 involved imprisonment. The number of sentences passed against Africans in 1912/13 – 3194 in total – is given by Udo Kaulich, *Die Geschichte der ehemaligen Kolonie Deutsch-Südwestafrika (1884–1914). Eine Gesamtdarstellung*. Frankfurt, 2001, p. 134. Both authors refer to the statistics attached to the annual reports published by the German administration and submitted to the German Colonial Office.

39 See Wallace, *A History*, pp. 184–5; Helmut Bley, *Kolonialherrschaft und Sozialstruktur in Deutsch-Südwestafrika 1894–1914*. Hamburg, 1968, p. 208.

40 Bley, *Kolonialherrschaft*, p. 286; Wallace, *A History*, p. 187; Zimmerer, *Deutsche Herrschaft*, p. 127.

41 Ellen Ndeshi Namhila, *Recordkeeping and Missing, "Native Estate" Records in Namibia. An Investigation of Colonial Gaps in a Post-colonial National Archive.* Tampere, 2015, p. 46.

42 These two photographs depict a situation that is not given per se in the archive, but resulted from an authorised, temporary joining of photographs taken from the album (NAN ZBU Pol/A. 737) and the register (NAN BWI 254 S 8 q).

43 Wecke and Voigts was founded in 1892 in Okahandja, but in 1912 the trading company had opened branches in Windhoek, Swakopmund, and Grootfontein. See Daniel Joseph Walther, *Creating Germans Abroad: Cultural Policies and National Identities in Namibia.* Athens, 2002, p. 30.

44 Peter Becker, The Standardized Gaze: The Standardization of the Search Warrant in Nineteenth-Century Germany, in Jane Caplan and John Torpey (eds.), *Documenting Individual Identity: The Development of State Practices in the Modern World.* Princeton and Oxford, 2001, pp. 139–63; Regener, *Fotografische Erfassung*, pp. 87–101. The posting of warrants in public seems to have been encouraged by the central government in Windhoek in 1912; see NAN BKE 62, Fahndungssachen, Der Kaiserliche Gouverneur, stellv. Hintrager, an das Bezirksamt Keetmanshoop, Windhoek, 28 October 1912.

45 There are files that relate to the so-called *Fahndungsblatt*, a monthly bulletin published by the central government between 1908 and 1910. The Fahndungsblatt included very short search warrants, but these concerned criminalised individuals of European descent only. No photographs were included. See NAN ZBU 751 G IIa 3, Fahndungsblätter.

46 NAN BRE 27 contains 2 cases in which warrants came along with photographs.

47 NAN BRE 27, Das Kaiserliche Bezirksamt Windhuk an das Kaiserliche Bezirksamt Rehoboth, 13, Juni 1914.

48 Detail from a page in the photographic album NAN ZBU Pol/A. 737.

49 NAN BRE 27, Das Kaiserliche Bezirksamt Windhuk an das Kaiserliche Bezirksamt Rehoboth, 13, Juni 1914. Original in German, my translation.

50 See also Zollmann, *Koloniale Herrschaft*, p. 144.

51 NAN BKE 237, UA 12/6, Suchregister für entlaufene Eingeborene, 1910–1915.

52 These documents are all filed under NAN ZBU 751 II a 4, Verbrecheralbum, Fingerabdrücke, Bd 1.

53 See Regener, *Fotografische Erfassung*; Tagg, *The Burden of Representation*; Becker, The Standardized Gaze, pp. 148ff.

54 See footnote 23.

55 NAN ZBU 751 G II a 4, Verbrecheralbum, Fingerabdrücke, Bd 1. Der Kaiserliche Gouverneur Seitz an das Bezirksamt Windhoek, Anschluss an die Verfügung vom 3.8.1911.

56 Northern Namibia, i.e. the kingdoms of Owambo and various societies in the northwestern and northeastern parts of the territory had not been drawn into the orbit of German colonial rule and remained beyond the colonial territory, namely the Police Zone.

57 Wallace, *A History,* pp. 183–4. There were a few exceptions, among them the Bondeslwarts, people at Berseba and Rehoboth, who had been *nolens volens* loyal to the Germans and were allowed to keep parts of their land and stock. See Reinhart Kössler, *In Search of Survival and Dignity: Two Traditional Communities in Southern Namibia under South African Rule.* Windhoek, 2007, pp. 43–5.

58 Wallace, *A History,* pp. 183 and 189; Jan-Bart Gewald, *Herero Heroes: A Sociopolitical History of the Herero of Namibia, 1890–1923.* Oxford, Cape Town, Athens, 1999, pp. 192ff.

59 Zollmann, *Koloniale Herrschaft*, p. 132; Gordon, "Hiding", p. 38. The literature tends to read social disorder prevalent after the war along racial lines, highlighting social banditry as a survival strategy for Africans, while noting anxieties and paranoia on the side of white settlers and colonial officials.

60 See e.g. Zimmerer, *op.cit.*, pp. 176ff.

61 Christo Botha, The Politics of land settlement in Namibia, 1890–1960. *South African Historical Journal*, 42, 2000: 232–76; and Gordon, "Hiding"; land placed under settlers' control increased from 4.4% in 1903 to 13% in 1910, i.e. to 1331 farms totalling 13.4 million ha in 1913.

62 Ulrike Lindner, *Koloniale Begegnungen. Deutschland und Grossbritannien als Imperialmächte in Afrika 1880–1914.* Frankfurt, New York, 2011, pp. 377ff.

63 Northern Namibia, i.e. the areas north of the so-called police zone, remained beyond German colonial rule. See Harri Siiskonen, *Trade and Socioeconomic Change in Ovamboland, 1850–1906.* Helsinki, 1990; and Patricia Heayes, Jeremy Silvester, Marion Wallace, and Wolfram Hartmann (eds.), *Namibia under South African Rule: Mobility and Containment, 1915–1946.* Oxford, Windhoek, Athens, 1998, p. 3.

64 Udo Kaulich, *Die Geschichte der ehemaligen Kolonie Deutsch-Südwestafrika*, p. 97ff.; Wallace, *A History*, p. 198.

65 Zimmerer, *Deutsche Herrschaft*, p. 116; Kaulich, *Die Geschichte der ehemaligen Kolonie Deutsch-Südwestafrika*, notes that the number of Schutztruppe soldiers had reached 14'500 men in 1906.

66 Zollmann, *Koloniale Herrschaft*, p. 43.

67 Zimmerer, *Deutsche Herrschaft*, p. 77; Wallace, *A History*, p. 183.

68 Ibid.

69 Zimmerer, *Deutsche Herrschaft*, p. 80.

70 Ibid., p. 118;

71 Zollmann, *Koloniale Herrschaft*, p. 100.

72 *Windhuker Nachrichten*, 19. September 1907; quoted and translated in Gordon, "Hiding", p. 33.

73 There was a fundamental distinction between jurisdiction over natives and Europeans. By 1906 South West Africa's white population was tried by professional judges in district courts in Windhoek, Omaruru, Swakopmund, Lüderitzbucht, and Keetmanshoop, and a high court in Windhoek established in 1903 (Bley, *Kolonialherrschaft*, p. 71).

74 Kaulich, *Die Geschichte der ehemaligen Kolonie Deutsch-Südwestafrika*, p. 132. Concerning the structural tension between law and order, the judiciary and the administration, see Martin Chanock, *The Making of South African Legal Culture 1902–1936: Fear, Favour and Prejudice.* Cambridge, 2001.

75 A rough translation of the German *Rechtsstaatlichkeit*.

76 For a more detailed discussion of the debates on state reform in Germany and its colonies at the time see Zollmann, *Koloniale Herrschaft*, pp. 50–53.

77 Zimmerer, *Deutsche Herrschaft*, p. 112ff.; Zollmann, *Koloniale Herrschaft*, p. 38; Kaulich, *Die Geschichte der ehemaligen Kolonie Deutsch-Südwestafrika*, p. 159.

78 Marie Muschalek, Honourable Soldier-Bureaucrats: Formations of Violent Identities in the Colonial Police Force of German South West Africa, 1908–18. *The Journal of Imperial and Commonwealth History*, 41, 4, 2013: 584–99.

79 Zimmerer, *Deutsche Herrschaft*, p. 117.

80 Zollmann notes that in 1907 the budget for police in South West Africa amounted to 1.7 million and in 1912 to 2.5 million – i.e. remarkably low compared to expenditures in contemporary French and British colonies. See Zollmann, *Koloniale Herrschaft*, p. 46. Also Mathieu Deflem, Law Enforcement in British Colonial Africa: A Comparative Analysis of Imperial Policing in Nyasaland, the Gold Coast, and Kenya. *Police Studies* 17, 1, 1994: 45–68; E. Frankema and M. van Waijenburg, Metropolitan Blueprints of Colonial Taxation? Lessons from Fiscal Capacity Building in British and French Africa, c. 1880–1940. *The Journal of African History*, 55, 3, 2014: 371–400.

81 Giorgio Miescher, *Namibia's Red Line: the History of a Veterinary and Settlement Border.* New York, 2012, p. 44.

82 See Charles van Onselen, *The Fox and the Flies. The Secret Life of a Grotesque Master Criminal.* New York, 2007. Joseph Silver, van Onselen's main character, reached Swakopmund in 1905, where he is said to have continued his lowlife activities, including prostitution, burglaries, and illegal alcohol sales (pp. 270ff).

83 Wallace, *A History*, p. 187; Zollmann, *Koloniale Herrschaft*, p. 54.

84 Gordon, "Hiding", p. 35.

85 Wallace, *A History*, p. 187. Seitz's orders were given in ordinance number 26883/5391 on the 24 October 1911. See Gordon, "Hiding", footnote 41 for archival references.

86 Muschalek, Honourable Soldier-Bureaucrats, p. 592; also Gordon, "Hiding", p. 41.

87 Zollmann, *Koloniale Herrschaft*, p. 19 and pp. 301/02; Bley, *Kolonialherrschaft*, pp. 270–2.

88 Martin Schröder, *Prügelstrafe und Züchtigungsrecht in den deutschen Schutzgebieten Schwarzafrikas.* Münster, 1997.

89 The literature on the German colonial penal system in Namibia is very limited. A chapter in Zollmann, *Koloniale Herrschaft*, remains the only scholarly treatment up to date. Kathleen Rahn, Die Geburt des Gefängnisses in Deutsch-Südwestafrika. Freiheitsstrafe und Strafvollzug von 1884 bis 1914. *Jahrbuch für Überseeische Geschichte*, 14, 2014: 243–54, is a research report on an ongoing PhD project, which contains references to archival sources and preliminary hypotheses.

90 Officially and since 1896, criminal jurisdiction in relation to Africans was part of the district officer's duty and authority, yet jurisdiction under "customary law" and its social institutions continued, albeit in a way formally unrecognised by the German colonial legal system. See Harald Sippel, Rechtspolitische Ansätze zur Vermeidung einer Mischlingsbevölkerung in Deutsch-Südwestafrika, in Frank Beker (ed.), *Rassenmischehen, Mischlinge, Rassentrennung. Zur Politik der Rasse im deutschen Kolonialreich.* Stuttgart, 2004, pp. 138–64, here p. 143.

91 Rahn, Die Geburt des Gefängnisses, p. 245.

92 Jürgen Zimmerling, *Die Entwicklung der Strafrechtspfleg.* There were 4 groups of offences: one that included crimes against the state and public order (treason and obstructing an officer in the performance of duty); crimes against persons (morality, bodily harm, and assault, unlawful detention); property (theft, embezzlement, robbery, blackmailing, and forgery); and a last group with unspecified crimes (other). Needless to say, and in contradiction to Zimmerling, these statistics need to be read critically, and they remain silent on dark figures. Still, Rahn, Die Geburt des Gefängnisses, confirms the figures for 1911/12. Both authors use statistical sources kept at the federal archives in Berlin, Germany.

93 Rahn, Die Geburt des Gefängnisses, p. 245.

94 Rahn, Die Geburt des Gefängnisses, p. 247; Zollmann, *Koloniale Herrschaft*, p. 126.

95 Kaulich, *Die Geschichte der ehemaligen Kolonie Deutsch-Südwestafrika*, p. 130. See also footnote 33.

96 See e.g. Thomas Nutz, *Strafanstalt als Besserungsmaschine: Reformdiskurs und Gefängniswissenschaft 1775–1848.* Munich, 2001; For comparative debates in the British empire see W. J. Forsythe, *The Reform of Prisoners 1830–1900.* London, 1986.

97 BArch R 1001/5119, Das Kaiserliche Gouvernement von Deutsch-Südwestafrika, Hintrager, an das Reichskolonialamt Berlin, Windhoek, 11.4.1910. Zollmann, *Koloniale Herrschaft*, p. 216. Zollmann says nothing about prisoner classification in general and separation of detainees along gender lines.

98 BArch 1001/5119, Kaiserlicher Bezirksamtmann von Eschruth an den Gouverneur, Keetmanshoop, 22.11.1908: von Eschruth is also quoted in Rahn, Die Geburt des Gefängnisses, p. 249. The translation of the German original is mine.

99 Rahn, Die Geburt des Gefängnisses, p. 250.

100 BArch R 1001/5119, Das Kaiserliche Gouvernement von Deutsch-Südwestafrika, Hintrager, an das Reichskolonialamt Berlin, Windhoek, 11.4.1910. Zollmann, *Koloniale Herrschaft*, p. 127.

101 Zollmann, *Koloniale Herrschaft*, p. 132; Kaulich, *Die Geschichte der ehemaligen Kolonie Deutsch-Südwestafrika*, p. 134.

102 Schröder, *op.cit.*, p. 52.

103 Zollmann, *Koloniale Herrschaft*, p. 132.

104 Gordon, "Hiding", footnote 5, quotes from a report by the Anglican reverend W.A. Norton, who visited the prison in Grootfontein sometime in the 1910s, and had been upset by the "Bushman" prisoners' fears and anxieties; see for critical voices in South West Africa Zollmann, *Koloniale Herrschaft*, p. 133.

105 See for prison inspections in the Cape Colony Harriet Deacon (ed.), *The Island: A History of Robben Island, 1488–1990*. Cape Town, 1996, pp. 33ff.

106 Zimmerer, *Deutsche Herrschaft*, pp. 110–11.

107 NAN ZBU 637 F III d, Arbeitsordnung in den Gefängnissen des Schutzgebietes Deutsch-Südwestafrika, 16.2.1914, which eventually formalised the regulations on prison labour.

108 Governor Seitz to the German Colonial Office, 28.1.1909, quoted in Rahn, Die Geburt des Gefängnisses, p. 253. My translation.

109 NAN ZBU 637 F III e 2, Gefängniswesen Specialia, Kaiserliches Bezirksamt Windhuk, Brill, an das Kaiserliche Gouvernement, 5.12.1910. Rahn, Die Geburt des Gefängnisses, p. 251; Zollmann, *Koloniale Herrschaft*, p. 141.

110 Zollmann, *Koloniale Herrschaft*, p. 136.

111 NAN BKE 237, UA 12/6, Suchregister für Eingeborene, 1910–1915, listed – as mentioned earlier on – more than 500 jailbreaks.

112 The *Südwestbote* based its article on a report authored by the Windhoek district officer in 1913, quoted in Zollmann, *Koloniale Herrschaft*, p. 142. The translation of the German original is mine.

113 Zollmann, *Koloniale Herrschaft*, pp. 142/43.

114 Among the 530 recorded cases of escaped prisoners in the period between 1910 and 1915, 83 cases are marked as "resolved", though it's not clear if this meant recapture, death or permanent disappearance. NAN BKE 237, UA 12/6, Suchregister für Eingeborene, 1910–1915.

115 See Wallace, *A History*, p. 188.

116 See W. J. T. Mitchell, *Picture Theory*, pp. 281–85; Mitchell sees the relationship between photography and language as a "site of resistance", pointing to how readings of photographs are partly narrative and contextual, but how, at the same time, the medium circumvents narration.

117 W. J. T. Mitchell, *Picture Theory*, p. 281.

118 Rosanne Kennedy, Jonathon Zapasnik, Hannah McCann and Miranda Bruce, All Those Little Machines: Assemblage as Transformative Theory. *Australian Humanities Review*, 55, 2013: 45–66. The main reference for their discussion is Gilles Deleuze and Félix Guattari, *A Thousand Plateaus. Capitalism and Schizophrenia*. Minneapolis and London, 1987.

119 Kennedy et al., *op.cit.*, p. 45; also George E. Marcus and Erkan Saka, Assemblage. *Theory, Culture & Society*, 23, 2–3, 2006: 101–9, here pp. 102–3.

120 See in more detail Paul Patton, *Deleuzian Concepts: Philosophy, Colonization, Politics*. Stanford, 2010, p. 52.

121 Kennedy et al., All Those Little Machines; Marcus and Saka, Assemblage, p. 102.

122 Tony Bennett, Anthropological Assemblages: Producing Culture as a Surface of Government. *CRESC Working Paper Series*, 52, 2008: 2–16, here p. 4.

123 Kennedy et al., All Those Little Machines, p. 57.

124 See Hunt, *A Nervous State*, p. 9.

125 The quarterly reports are filed under NAN BKE 212 B II 66.0 1–3, Gefangenen Register, Auszüge 1898–1912, and the central register of convicts under NAN BWI 435, Eingeborenen Strafregister 1895–1907.

126 This is obviously a reading along the lines of the Foucauldian understanding of prisons as disciplinary machines and panoptic institutions. For a reading of Foucault's model alongside assemblage theory see William Bogard, Surveillance Assemblages and Lines of Flight, in David Lyon (ed.), *Theorising Surveillance: The Panopticon and Beyond.* New York, 2006, pp. 97–122, here pp. 104–5.

127 See in particular NAN BKE 237, UA 12/6, Suchregister für entlaufene Eingeborene, 1910–1915, which specifies convict's origin and place of arrest and allows for point by point retracements and temporal shifts of spatial clusters of arrest and detention, many of which seem very much in line with the architecture of the colonial economy.

128 See for policing and racial mapping John Noyes, *Colonial Space. Spatiality in the Discourse of German Southwest-Africa, 1884–1915.* Chur, 1992, p. 274.

129 If one wishes to remain within the framework of assemblage theory, Deleuze's and Guattari's notion of "molecular line" as the force capable of destabilising or deterritorialising assemblages, but with the effect of restabilization, comes closest to what we are about to retrace. For sure, the processes to be described are less transformative than those released by "lines of flight". See Renée C. Hoogland, *A Violent Embrace: Art and Aesthetics after Representation.* Lebanon NH, 2014, p. 60.

130 Elizabeth Edwards*, Raw Histories*, pp. 13–16.

131 See the introduction to Philip Carabot, Yannis Hamilakis, and Eleni Papargyriou (eds.), *Camera Graeca: Photographs, Narratives, Materialities.* London, 2016.

132 Basler Afrika Bibliographien, Archival Collection, Album A03, Foto-Album Südwestafrika.

133 Dag Henrichsen, Ozombambuse and Ovasolondate: Everyday Military Life and African Service Personnel in German South West Africa, in Wolfram Hartmann (ed.), *Hues between Black and White*, pp. 161–84, here p. 162.

134 Jeremy Silvester, Patricia Hayes, Wolfram Hartmann, "This Ideal Conquest": Photography and Colonialism in Namibian History, in Wolfram Hartmann, Jeremy Silvester, and Patricia Hayes (eds.), *The Colonising Camera*, pp. 10–19, here p. 13.

135 Some of the female photographic subjects have been identified thanks to the "Picturing the Past" series authored by Jeremy Silvester for *The Namibian Weekender* in October 1997. See on this initiative Patricia Hayes, Jeremy Silvester and Wolfram Hartmann, "Picturing the Past": The Visual Archive and Its Energies, in Carolyn Hamilton, Verne Harris, Jane Taylor, Michele Pickover, Graeme Reid, and Razia Saleh (eds.), *Refiguring the Archive.* Dordrecht, 2002, pp. 103–33.

136 Henrichsen, Ozombambuse.

137 John Phillip Short, Novelty and Repetition: Photographs of South West Africa in German Visual Culture, 1890–1914. In Hartmann (ed.), *Hues Between Black and White*, pp. 211–28, here p. 212.

138 The catalogue entry for the album notes that it was acquired in an auction as an image collection assumed to have been compiled by a German farmer in Namibia between 1909 and 1915. The album is today kept in the archives of the Basler Afrika Bibliographien, a research institution and library focused on Namibia.

139 This photograph is one in a pair of images depicting the same situation.

140 Admittedly the performance and photographic recording of detainees having a shower could as well be read as an indication of modern hygiene in the penal system.

141 See for *repoussoir* W.T.J. Mitchell, *Landscape and Power.* Chicago and London, 2002 (2nd edition), p. 25.

142 Homi K Bhabha, The Other Question…Homi K Bhabha Reconsiders the Stereotype and Colonial Discourse. *Screen*, 24, 6, 1983: 18–36, here pp. 24–5.

143 Zeller, "Wie Vieh", p. 236; Hartmann, *Hues*, p. 73, where a few images from the album are reproduced.

144 See Bogard, Surveillance assemblages, p. 101.

145 NAN BLU 265, Das Kaiserliche Gouvernement, Gouverneur Seitz, an die Kaiserlichen Bezirks (Distrikt) Ämter, Windhuk, 1 April 1914.

146 BArch R1001/5119, Letter from Franz Seiner to the Colonial Secretary, Graz, 30 November 1912. The letter has been published in F.D. Mueller, *Kolonien unter der Peitsche*. Berlin, 1962, pp. 167–68. Seiner enclosed five photographs showing two completely emaciated men, two women with babies, and three boys, all of them naked, the men kept in chains. Because of their sensitive nature, I prefer not to reproduce the photographs here. The photographs have not been removed from the file. The translation of the German original is mine.

147 NAN ZBU 2043 W II o 2, Bezirksamtmann Grootfontein, i.V. Link, an den Kaiserlichen Gouverneur in Windhuk, Grootfontein, 6.8.1913; BArch R1001/5119, Dr. Zacheler an das Kaiserliche Bezirksamt Grootfontein, 6 August 1913.

148 BArch R1001/5119, Dr. Brenner an das Kaiserliche Bezirksamt Swakopmund, 29 August 1913. Brenner claimed to have photographed the same men, women, and children depicted in Seiner's photographs, pointing to the ways in which imprisonment had helped them recover physically. He remains silent on how these individuals might have felt about the repeated exposure to the camera while in prison. The photographs are included in the file.

149 BArch R1001/5119, Bericht des Kaiserlichen Gouverneurs von Deutsch-Südwestafrika, Seitz, an den Staatssekretär des Reichskolonialamtes. Windhuk, 13. September 1913. Published in Müller, *op.cit.*, p. 169.

150 See on fears of vanishing peoples and salvage discourse in the German colonial empire George Steinmetz, The uncontrollable afterlives of ethnography. Lessons from "salvage colonialism" in the German overseas empire. *Ethnography*, 5, 3, 2004: 251–88.

151 Larissa Förster und Holger Stoecker, *Haut, Haar und Knochen. Koloniale Spuren in naturkundlichen Sammlungen der Universität Jena*. Weimar, 2016, p. 50.

152 Leonhardt Schultze Jena, *Aus Namaland und Kalahari. Bericht an die Kaiserliche Preussische Akademie der Wissenschaften zu Berlin über eine Forschungsreise im westlichen und zentralen Südafrika, ausgeführt in den Jahren 1903–1905*. Jena, 1907, pp. vi–vii; Förster et al., *Haut und Haar*, pp. 53–7.

153 Among them the *Zeitschrift für Ethnologie* and the *Denkschriften der medizinisch-naturwissenschaftlichen Gesellschaft*. For a ccomprehensive list of his publications see Förster et al., *Haut und Haar*, pp. 119–20. For a contemporary appraisal of Schultze's scholarship see Isaac Shapera, Review: Zur Kenntnis des Körpers der Hottentotten und Buschmänner (Zoologische und anthropologische Ergebnisse einer Forschungsreise im westlichen und zentralen Südafrika. Bd. V, Lfg. III) by Leonhard Schultze. *Africa: Journal of the International African Institute*, 2, 4, 1929: 433–4.

154 Robert Gordon's work on German physical anthropology and their preoccupation with Bushmen is crucial here. See Gordon, "Hiding", pp. 44–6, and R. J. Gordon, The Rise of the Bushman Penis: Germans, Genitalia, and Genocide. *African Studies*, 57, 1, 1998: 27–54.

155 Holger Stoecker, Thomas Schnalke, and Andreas Winkelmann (eds.), *Sammeln, Erforschen, Zurückgeben? Menschliche Gebeine aus der Kolonialzeit in akademischen und musealen Sammlungen*. Berlin, 2013. There is evidence that Schultze collected human remains and the dead bodies of Bushmen, Nama, and Herero in South West Africa during his journey and later sent them to Germany. See Förster et al., *Haut und Haar*, p. 59.

156 Gordon, "Hidden", p. 45.

157 The only available study of Seiner's life and work is a shockingly apologetic volume edited by Helga Kostka, entitled *SeinerZeit. Redakteur Franz Seiner und seine Zeit*. Graz, 2007. On doubts about Seiner's qualification see Kostka, *SeinerZeit*, p. 144.

158 Kostka, *SeinerZeit*, p. 196.

159 The relevant publications are Franz Seiner, Die Buschmänner des Okawango- und Sambesigebietes der Nord-Kalahari. *Globus. Illustrierte Zeitschrift für Länder- und Völkerkunde*, 1910; Franz Seiner, Beobachtungen und Messungen an Buschleuten. *Zeitschrift für Ethnologie, Sonderdruck aus Band 3, Heft 2*, 1912; Franz Seiner, Beobachtungen an den Bastard-Buschleuten der Nord-Kalahari. *Mitteilungen der Anthropologischen Gesellschaft*, 1913.

160 Among the scholars keen to use Seiner's and Schultze's photographs was the renowned geographer Siegfried Passarge, professor at the Colonial Institute in Hamburg, who used them e.g. in his Grundlinien im ethnographischen Bilde der Kalahari-Region. *Zeitschrift der Gesellschaft für Erdkunde*, 1905: 68–88; and in the volume edited by Hans Meyer, *Das deutsche Kolonialreich; eine Länderkunde der deutschen Schutzgebiete. Unter Mitarbeit von Professor Dr Siegfried Passarge und Professor Dr Leonhard Schultze*. Band 2, Leipzig 1910/1911. See more generally Udo Krautwurst, The Joy of Looking. Early German Anthropology, Photography and Audience Formation. *Visual Anthropology Review*, 18, 1–2, 2002: 55–79.

161 NAN ZBU 751 Verbrecheralbum, Der Kaiserliche Generalkonsul, Gumboldt, an den Kaiserlichen Gouverneur in Windhuk, von Lindequist, Kapstadt, 5. Juni 1906.

162 Leonhard Schultze, *Zoologische und anthropologische Ergebnisse einer Forschungsreise im westlichen und zentralen Südafrika ausgeführt in den Jahren 1903–1905 mit Unterstützung der Kgl. Preussischen Akademie der Wissenschaften zu Berlin*. Bd. 1: Systematik und Tiergeografie. Jena 1908, p. v–viii, here p. viii.

163 Schultze, *Aus Namaland und Kalahari*, p. 100.

164 Leonhard Schultze, Zur Kenntnis des Körpers der Hottentotten und Buschmänner. In ibid., *Zoologische und anthropologische Ergebnisse einer Forschungsreise im westlichen und zentralen Südafrika ausgeführt in den Jahren 1903–1905 mit Unterstützung der Kgl. Preussischen Akademie der Wissenschaften zu Berlin*. Bd. 5: Systematik, Tiergeographie und Anthropologie. Jena, 1928, pp. 127–45.

165 See Anette Hofmann, Widerspenstige Stimmen – Unruly Voices. Gespenster – Spectres, in ibid. (ed.), *What We See: Reconsidering an Anthropometrical Collection from Southern Africa – Images, Voices, and Versioning*. Basel, 2009, pp. 23–57, here p. 31.

166 Schultze, "Zur Kenntnis", p. 161. The original reads: "Und was ein Buschmann sei, liesse sich in den Gefängnissen der Städte Britisch-Südafrikas ebenso klar ausmachen wie in der Wildnis, wo alle siedlungsscheuen Viehdiebe hottentottischer oder sonstiger Abstammung als Buschmänner gälten".

167 Franz Seiner, Ergebnisse einer Bereisung der Omaheke in den Jahren 1910–1912. *Mitteilungen aus den deutschen Schutzgebieten*, 26, 3, 1912: 227–316, here p. 282. Hofmann, Widerspenstige Stimmen, pp. 35–6, makes a similar argument about the conflation of science and police work in an anthropometric project pursued in the early 1930s in southern Namibia, though no prisoners were involved in that case.

168 Franz Seiner, Beobachtungen und Messungen an Buschleuten. *Zeitschrift für Ethnologie*, 1912: 275–88, here p. 280. All translations of Seiner's texts are mine.

169 Seiner, "Beobachtungen", p. 283. Seiner's biopolitical vision was rather contested among colonial officials stationed at Grootfontein, see e.g. BArch R1001/5119, Dr. Zachlehner an den Kaiserlichen Bezirksamtmann Grootfontein, 1. Mai 1913.

170 Fanz Seiner, "Ergebnisse", p. 284.

171 Franz Seiner, "Ergebnisse", pp. 301ff.

172 Seiner, "Ergebnisse", p. 293.

173 NAN ZBU 751, Polizeidirektor Dr. Roscher, Hamburg, an das Kaiserliche Deutsche Gouvernement in Windhuk 30 April 1906. The translation of the German original is mine.

174 See Gustav Roscher, Bedürfnisse der modernen Kriminal-Polizei. *Archiv für Kriminalanthropologie und Kriminalistik*, 1899: 244–58, where he declared substantial libraries that included criminological, anthropological, psychological, and medical scholarship as much as crime novels, to be a *sine qua non* requirement for at least medium-sized police stations; and ibid, Die daktyloskopische Registratur. *Archiv für Kriminalanthropologie und Kriminalistik*, 1904: 129–41. Roscher most important publication was *Grossstadtpolizei. Ein praktisches Handbuch der deutschen Polizei*. Hamburg, 1912. See on Roscher as a key figure in early twentieth century German policing Jens Jäger, Photography: A Means of Surveillance? Judicial Photography, 1850–1900. *Crime, History & Society*, 5, 1, 2009: 1–25, here p. 13.

175 Susanne Regener, Criminological Museums and the Visualisation of Evil. *Crime, History, Society*, 7, 1, 2003: 43–56.

176 Simon Cole, *A History of Fingerprinting and Criminal Identification*. Cambridge (MA), 2001.

177 For the German context see the introduction to Jens Ruppenthal, *Kolonialismus als Wissenschaft und Technik. Das Hamburgische Kolonialinstitut 1908 bis 1919*. Stuttgart 2007.

178 NAN ZBU 751, Der Polizeidirektor Gustav Roscher an das Kaiserliche Gouvernement in Windhuk, Hamburg 22. Mai 1907.

179 Police Museum Hamburg, 8G/III, Fingerprints of a Hottentott woman in Lüderitzbucht, n.d.

180 Zimmerer, *Deutsche Herrschaft*, p. 125; and more generally Cole, *A History of Fingerprinting*, p. 60.

181 NAN BWI 254, Sicherheitspolizei und Erkennungsdienst. Kaiserliches Gouvernement an das Kaiserliche Bezirksamt Windhuk, 26 June 1912; for neighbouring South Africa see Keith Breckenridge, Flesh Made Words: Fingerprinting and the Fantasy of Documentary Panopticism, 1900–1930. *History and African Studies Seminar*, 2, 2001: 76–96, here p. 78.

182 Zimmerer, *Deutsche Herrschaft*, pp. 124ff.

183 The literature on Galton and fingerprinting is extensive, but see for Africa in general Daniel Brückenhaus, Identifying Colonial Subjects. Fingerprinting in British Kenya, 1900–1960. *Geschichte und Gesellschaft*, 42, 2016: 60–85; and for South Africa Breckenridge, Flesh Made Words, pp. 78–9.

184 Brückenhaus, *op.cit.*, p. 63.

185 Mira Rai Waits, The Indexical Trace: A Visual Interpretation of the History of Fingerprinting in Colonial India. *Visual Culture in Britain*, 17 January 2016: 18–46, here p. 43.

186 Sekula, *op.cit.*, p. 57.

187 See for skepticisms of dactyloscopy and Galton's system that persisted into the early twentieth century Milos Vec, Die Spur des Täters. Bertillonage, Daktyloskopie und Jodogramm: Fortschritte und Versprechungen der naturwissenschaftlichen Kriminalistik um 1900. *Juridikum*, 2, 2001: 89–94, here p. 91.

188 Oskar T. Berner, *Die Schweizer in Südwestafrika*. Windhoek, 1998, p. 43. The first detective to have identified a perpetrator thanks to fingerprinting is said to have been Franz Karl Dettling in Windhoek in 1918. Dettling had moved from Ceylon (Sri Lanka) to Johannesburg in 1900 and, in 1916, he became head of the criminal investigation department in Windhoek.

189 See Breckenridge, Flesh Made Words, p. 86 for a similar persisting interest in the South African colonies.

190 A notable case is the research of Pastor Martin Gusinde, who in 1950/1951 recorded 1500 hand- and fingerprints of Bushmen in the southern Etosha and Okavango areas in northern Namibia. He later ceded parts of the prints to German racial scientist and eugenicist Eugen Fischer. See Adelheid Wessler, Von Lebendabgüssen, Heimatmuseen und Cultural Villages. Museale Repräsentationen des Selbst und des Anderen im (De)Kolonisierungsprozess Namibias. Unpublished PhD thesis, Köln, 2007, p. 89, fn 70.

191 The quote originates from the diary of artist Hans Lichtenecker and refers to his study of Bushmen undertaken in Namibia in 1931. The quote is reproduced and translated from the German original in the introduction to Hoffmann, *What We See*, p. 9.

192 See e.g. Okwui Enwezor, Archive Fever: Photography between History and the Monument. In Enwezor, Okwui (ed.), *Archive Fever: Uses of the Document in Contemporary Art*. New York, 2008, pp. 11–51, here p. 12.

193 See for colonial Africa more generally Florence Bernault, The Politics of enclosure in Colonial and Postcolonial Africa, in Florence Bernault and Janet L. Roitman (eds.), *A History of Prison and Confinement in Africa*. Portsmouth, 2003, pp. 1–54.

194 Michel Foucault, The Subject and Power. *Critical Inquiry*, 8, 4, 1982: 777–95, here p. 791.

195 Hunt, *A Nervous State*, pp. 8 and 17.

196 The reference to Balandier's work is taken from Hunt, *A Nervous State*, p. 17, where the English translation published in 1961 is used. See Georges Balandier, The Colonial Situation: A Theoretical Approach, in Immanuel Wallerstein (ed.), *Social Change and Colonial Situation*. New York, 1966, pp. 34–61, here p. 38. For the original see Georges Balandier, La situation coloniale: approche théorique. *Cahiers Internationaux de Sociologie*, 11, 1951: 44–79, here p. 10, which reads: "en faisant le tableau des réactions diverses à la situation coloniale, elle nous montre combien cette dernière peut jouer le rôle d'un véritable révélateur; et la colonisation apparaît comme une épreuve imposée à certaines sociétés ou, si l'on peut risquer l'expression, comme une expérience sociologique grossière".

197 See Elizabeth Edwards, Professor Huxley's "Well-Considered Plan", in Edwards, *Raw Histories*, pp. 131–56; Christopher Pinney, *The Coming of Photography in India*. London, 2008.

198 Virilio is discussed in these terms in John Johnston, Machinic Vision. *Critical Inquiry*, 26, 199: 27–48, here pp. 30–1; see Paul Virilio, *The Vision Machine*. Bloomington, 1994, p. 63.

199 Hunt, *A Nervous State*, p. 11. Hunt speaks of primitivism as counter-insurgency.

2 Bodies and things

Photography and the person in
South Africa, 1920s–1960s

Introduction

Photographs do not evenly track the regular course of time, quietly lining the paths of history like docile illustrations waiting to be blended into narratives of chronological unfolding. Photographs are, rather, a recalcitrant, unpredictable historical form; they confuse our sense of linear temporality as they surface unexpectedly, proliferate at one time and place while being absent at others. As ostensible windows onto a reality lost, they are particularly appealing to those who wish to recover the past, yet they often remain obscure, swaying between the promise of revealing everything and the refusal to disclose anything.[1] Keeping an eye on photographic discontinuity, dissipation, and impenetrability, we leave the German colony of South West Africa, and its assemblage of surveillance photography, and move on to a different place and time. We shall immerse ourselves in two archival collections produced on two different occasions, by first adopting the broader perspective of the emerging South African nation after Union in 1910, only to zoom in and explore the terrain of a peripheral, if critical, region within the political geography of apartheid: the Eastern Cape in the 1950s and 1960s.[2] Both archives emerged in the context of determining and documenting individual identity, though in different keys; the interwar period of South African nation-building brought to the fore modern notions of citizenship and nationality – deeply intertwined with and complicated by imperial economies of migration and racism – while the apartheid period highlighted the constitution of subjects as part of a process of internal colonisation and racial mapping. Thinking about these archives and the documentary regimes they stem from requires, as a first move, approaching them as epistemological projects, in the course of which the South African state strove to define and enact a reified system of classification along the lines of citizenship and nationality, race and ethnicity, class, and gender. Against the backdrop of political and ideological consolidation, these documentary regimes charted an administrative space in which particular technologies of power helped constitute bodies as fixed, closed, and legible entities to be inserted into efficient and rationalised forms of governance.

We will come across a set of objects and images by now familiar to us – photographs, fingerprints, and physiognomic descriptions, and their various forms of materialisation and visualisation. These images and texts provide the basis for a number of questions: What do these materials and their implication in documenting and defining subjects reveal about the dynamic relations between bodies and things? What, more specifically, do the case studies we will consider evince about photography's productive effects on bodies? How are photographic images implicated here in practices that constitute bodies? Bureaucratic identification practices in the 1920s and 1930s, and also the 1950s and 1960s, evolved against the backdrop of defining the body politic and articulating the inclusion of individuals into or their exclusion from the South African nation-state; keeping this in mind, how did bodies and things come to define and mediate forms and conditions of political, moral, and legal being, i.e. of personhood, and concurrently of non-being, of mere physicality – in short: of matter? And vice versa: How are body and person involved in constituting images, objects or things, among them photography? Finally, to dwell on the varieties of this questioning a bit longer, what are the practices through which the boundary between photography, body, and person emerge and are stabilised?

These questions point towards the specific analytical path this chapter attempts to pursue. It proceeds from the assumption that documentary projects at the behest of the South African state administrations in the interwar and apartheid periods can be understood as biopolitical, in Foucauldian terms, in which *both* people and things were made up, and in which the interaction between bodies and photographs was not one between stable entities, but rather a relational matter, in which one conditioned the other.[3] Two texts provide the theoretical thread along which the following discussion combs through these archival collections. One of them is Roberto Esposito's essay "Dispositif of the Person", in which he retraces how the category of person, in its iterations through Christian dogma, Roman juridical codification, and the modern process of subjection/subjectivisation described by Michel Foucault, establishes the distinction of person from the living being on which it is grafted (the body) and thereby comes to function as "the crucial passage through which a biological material lacking in meaning becomes something intangible".[4] The deeper paradigmatic continuity that links these diverse and historically distant attempts at systematising a metaphysics of person, Esposito tells us, is that while it provides a language that unifies human beings, it only does so through the differential logic of the category of person, in order to establish a hierarchical typology of different statuses and intermediate stages of personhood over time – producing full persons, semi-persons, those who can enjoy the title of person only if and once certain conditions have been met, non-persons, and even what is otherwise considered to be a thing, namely slaves. The implication here, noted almost with *Schadenfreude*, is that while one might see in "person" an idea that protects and preserves the sanctity of life, it comes along with its lower and negative counterparts and essentially serves as "the backdrop against which looms", inevitably and always, "the figure of the thing".[5] It is at this point that Esposito's language, and his deliberate choice of a theatrical metaphor, reminds us of the performativity of the category of person, particularly if we keep in mind that, ultimately, bodies become persons *de iure*, i.e. staged before the law and hence – arguably in the modern period – from the perspective of the state.

The second text that will inform the arguments made in this chapter is a reading of Foucault's work on governmentality proposed by Thomas Lemke, because it speaks to our concern here, more specifically, and enables us to extend Esposito's analysis towards a framework that pays attention to the role played by artefacts and images in constituting body and person and establishing the distinction between them.[6] Lemke investigates Foucault's lectures at the Collège de France in order to flesh out what they might offer for a reconsideration of material things and technical artefacts – and we should add visual objects as well – not as mere resources or raw material, but as active forces participating in processes of materialisation and the production of bodies. His point of departure, which is of interest to us here, is Foucault's reading of Guillaume de la Perrière's conception of the art of government, conceived as the "right disposition of things", rather than sovereignty over a territory and the subjects that inhabit it, and therefore proposes an understanding of government that relies on a "complex of men and things", without distinguishing or juxtaposing the one mode of power to the other.[7] From this perspective, as Lemke continues to explain, the *government of things* ceases to rely on a foundational sorting between subjects and objects, but consists as much in establishing the distinction between them as in enacting "the boundaries between socially relevant and politically recognised existence and 'pure matter', something that does not possess legal-moral protection and is 'reduced' to 'things'".[8] Foucault's later writings seem to offer, if we follow Lemke's reading, an expanded understanding of power's productive effects on bodies that moves beyond the conventional idea of bio-politics, being predominantly preoccupied with physical and biological existence, and shifts attention towards the multiple conjunctions between bodies and things, the material and the non-material, the physical and the moral, matter and meaning.[9] In short, while Foucault's lectures on governmentality help address, as both Esposito and Lemke recall, the modern process of subject-formation through various forms of subjugation and discipline, it likewise targets procedures of defining moral and political existence.

With these readings in mind, it is now time to move back to the South African context and to briefly specify how we might put to work the theoretical and analytical propositions only just outlined. What the case studies ask for is not an exercise in theoretical abstraction and generalisation. The archives of individual identification produced in the interwar and apartheid periods delineate a particular historical terrain, enabling us to investigate what the *specificity* of bodies and things at hand tells us about the material, visual, and technical conditions that produced them. But the case studies also require us to keep an eye on spatial and temporal contingency, in order to understand how photography, body, and person proved to condition each other at these particular historical conjunctures.

Moving bodies, moving images in the 1920s and 1930s

Exploring photography's insertion into the framing of body and person takes us first to a moment in time when the question of determining an individual's identity became a matter of central concern in South Africa's nation-building project. We begin in the period after South African Union in 1910, when state policy and governance aimed at controlling and managing the disposition and mobility of differentiated subject populations more systematically, while simultaneously defining people's inclusion in or exclusion from the national body politic along the lines of race, gender, and nationality.[10] As a consequence thereof, the state bureaucracy produced an extensive, intricate archive that comprises textual and visual records documenting the registration and identification of African, Asian, and European men and women, who moved in and beyond the reach of South Africa's expanding political and economic dominion throughout the 1920s and 1930s.

Figure 2.1 was part of a passport application submitted on 20 September 1934 by James Dzoye to the magistrate in Windhoek, the capital city of South Africa's northern colony South West Africa.[11] The application included, beside the image, an official declaration compiled by the magistrate and specifying information about the applicant. Based on the data recorded, Dzoye was an "Angoni" originating from Blantyre, British Nyasaland, a British subject by birth, and at the time a resident of Windhoek.[12] He was born in 1892, unmarried, and employed in a local shop. In a separate row on the declaration's right-hand side, the magistrate added the required, brief physiognomic description of Dzoye, which included his height, the colour of his eyes and hair, and reference to outstanding physical markers. In the left-hand bottom corner, finally, Dzoye signed the declaration with his name and fingerprint. The application had been submitted for an intended journey to Luanda, and on 26 September 1934, Dzoye was indeed issued a passport numbered W2254.

James Dzoye's application is kept in a file entitled *Native Affairs Passports for Natives* in the National Archives of Namibia in Windhoek, along with those of six other men and one woman, who originated from South Africa, Malawi, Angola, Namibia, Ghana, and Liberia, and who applied for travel documents during the 1920s and 1930s. The small collection stands out as a singular fragment, and it remains difficult to make sense of its position within the archive. Placed among the Native Affairs Department's copious documentary production, the materials contained in the file resonated with native administration's idiosyncratic concern with racial and ethnic classification.[13] Yet upon closer examination, there are pointers to intricate composition and wider circulation in a documentary network that span diverse administrative

Figure 2.1 James Dzoye, 1934.

entities, such as the magistrates' courts, the immigration department, or the police, and accordingly moved across bureaucratic categories and terminology. As an assemblage of texts and images, the file thus proves complicated. Three of the applications resemble the one submitted by James Dzoye and include the formal declaration as well as certified black and white photographs. One comprises personal letters and correspondence between various state departments, while the remaining three cases merely consist of brief informative messages and notations.[14] Dzoye's application is interesting in many ways, but here I would like to use its undetermined archival position and narrative framing to dwell upon the kinds of questions we might raise in thinking about the texts and photographs kept in this file.

James Dzoye's photograph is an interruption of an archival flow otherwise determined by the logics of bureaucratic narration and temporality; it invites us to pause and open ourselves to the ways in which the image speaks to the senses. Portrait photographs trigger personal responses, and they have an unsettling ability to recreate the subject in the present.[15] Who was this man? What kind of socio-economic position did his elegant attire reference – was he a member of a transnational economic or educational elite, drawing from sophisticated cultural repertoires of self-fashioning?

The quality and beauty of the image is compelling, and the portrait as a visual genre honours its subject by shedding light on his individuality and social standing.[16] Still, the photograph is fragmentary, elusive; it frames but a moment in time and its material presence remains somewhat cryptic.

How do we make sense of the recurrence of studio and portrait photographs in a colonial archive of administrative registration and identification – of photography's *honorific* function inserted into a mundane but *repressive* bureaucratic context that rested upon hierarchies of social and racial difference?[17] Portrait photographs rely on representation as a given set of signifiers associated with the personal and social life of its subject, inviting us to ask if this portrait was not part of a different cultural practice, intended perhaps for personal use in a family album, for framing and display, or as an intimate addition to personal correspondence. Given the diversity of images included even in a file as small as the one we have at hand, why were portrait photographs acceptable for some applications, while others featured more standardised images?[18] And finally, what does this photograph tell us about the bureaucratic fabrication of body and person in colonial Southern Africa in the interwar period?

Scholars of photography have repeatedly reminded us to be wary of documentary readings of historical photographs that focus on image content alone and to likewise pay attention to the materiality of images in order to retrieve the ways in which they might become meaningful.[19] But the question of materiality concerns all historical sources, texts as much as photographs.[20] The files considered here merely contain the prescribed forms and correspondence related to the application process, and they usually do not, alas, provide us with the actual documents eventually issued to applicants, a material fact that importantly determines our engagement with them. The forms compiled by the magistrates and officers of the Native Affairs Department were based on specific epistemological registers, and they drew from a bureaucratic rationality that combined biographical information and physiognomic description with photographs and fingerprints. Taken together, these various registers constituted, it seems, a pragmatic and easy-to-handle, soft version of Bertillonage.[21] But while institutional practices of identification account, at least partly, for the presence of photographs in the file, the question of how we think about them historically might have to be pushed a little further. Photographs constitute a particular representational form, and the ways in which their presence in the archive evokes or performs the presence of the person in the photograph is compelling and, as Roland Barthes has so suggestively described, deceitful at the same time.[22] This is why, when looking at James Dzoye's photograph taken in 1934, we face a tension between, on the one hand, a sense of suspension and freezing of the subject, of time and space within the photographic frame, and, on the other hand, a sense of transcendence triggered by the photograph's intrinsic reference beyond its frame, towards the indeterminacy of body and person through time and space.[23]

James Dzoye remains nebulous, a fragment of himself.[24] This archive does not enable us to recover him, nor his male and female fellow applicants, in terms of a social history that asks about their biographies and social and cultural worlds.[25] What we encounter here instead is a conglomerate of written and visual documents, a paper regime engendered by the bureaucratic practices of identification and regulation. Throughout this process, the body – in its function as the object of administration – was subjected to an incisive fragmentation into a set of physically, socially, and racially defined categories that would determine its place within the colonial hierarchy and, in moral and legal terms, the subject's status as a person.[26] In James Dzoye's case, the categories at work would hence inevitably classify him first as "Native" (race), then as "Angoni" (tribe/ethnicity), male (gender), unmarried (marital status), wage labourer (class), and from Nyasaland and British subject by birth (citizenship) – the last category eventually entitling him to the right to be issued a passport.[27] The described itemisation and classification resonated into larger semantic spaces – those of an early twentieth-century South African nation in the making and its fragments and fringes.[28] Saul Dubow's retracing of South Africa's ideological constitution as a nation-state after Union in 1910 rightfully points to its racial disposition based on the notion of a "white man's land" and, accordingly, the political disenfranchisement of its African and Asian subject populations.[29] Yet, while Dubow's argument continues to rest within historical narration determined by the category of the nation, critical scholarship has proposed inquiries into the modern nation-state that attend to its formation in the global context of imperialism and racism.[30] Therein, modern economies of migration have been considered constitutive of the nation's concern to control the mobility of populations increasingly classified in terms of nationality and citizenship.[31] This line of argument helps to refigure some of the conventional assumptions about South African nation building and reposition its consolidation within a transnational framework.[32] While the historiography has extensively considered processes of South African internal colonisation – and we will speak to this in more detail in the second part of this chapter – imperial dimensions engendering these processes have widely been blended out.[33]

The presence of James Dzoye and a small group of "natives" applying for passports in Namibia in the 1920s and 1930s reference transnational entanglement and integration in intriguing ways. Indeed, by the mid-1930s, South Africa's political geography in the region was firmly established, and the Namibian colony was but one, albeit the outstanding, constituent of an expanding politico-economic sphere profoundly marked by industrial capitalism and African and Asian migrant labour.[34] Yet, while these men and women and their histories and trajectories mirror, in some sense, the political and economic conditions imposed by South Africa's imperial project, they more importantly point to how this emergent nation-state operated discursively, by means of inscriptions and reifications of body and person. These were in turn refracted through manipulations of race, ethnicity, class, and gender.[35]

It is these inscriptions of difference that the following pages seek to attend to, and it will be of particular interest to explore how photographs came to inhabit these spaces of difference, and how they might have helped to disrupt if not transcend them.[36]

Framing person

The post-1910 South African nation was based on a notion of "white" citizenship as much as it aimed at relegating Africans and Asians to political minority.[37] Still, as a dominion within the British Empire, South Africa remained subject to British imperial legislation, which granted political rights by birth or naturalisation and merely varied in terms of age and gender.[38] Hence, the registers and practices applied by the segregationist state in order to ensure the production and maintenance of differential hierarchies of person had to be grounded in the conjunction of circumscribed political and racial categories with the control and registration of mobility, both within and beyond its territorial borders.[39] As we shall see, between the 1910s and 1930s, the classification and control of citizens and subjects proved to be, in many ways, a matter of applying and implementing incoherent legislation, and as a consequence, it was characterised by unclear administrative practice.[40] This favoured conditions in which determining an individual's identity and status in terms of nationality, citizenship, class, or race would produce diverse material and discursive forms that engendered cumbersome bureaucratic action.

Figure 2.2 is a photograph submitted by Marie Schiffer Lafite, who in 1914 applied for an identity certificate that enabled her to travel to Mauritius in order to visit her relatives.[41] The file compiled by the immigration officer in Cape Town, similarly to Dzoye's case, contains only fragments of information. It tells us that Schiffer Lafite, a shop assistant by profession, originated from Mauritius and had lived for 12 years in the coastal city of Port Elizabeth. She moved to Cape Town in 1902, after her first husband left her, and later remarried a French hairdresser called Lafite.[42] In view of the affidavits she produced as part of her application, the immigration office eventually granted Schiffer Lafite a certificate that approved of her journey and, more importantly, her right to return to the Cape after a year of absence.[43]

The file of Marie Schiffer Lafite illustrates how, in the 1920s and 1930s, the person was conceived of in terms of a set of thresholds, and how in turn, race and gender complicated the making and positioning of the body within South African social and legal hierarchies.[44] As mentioned earlier on, applying for a document of passage that sanctioned an individual's transnational mobility entailed his or her reconstitution within the framework and idiom of the racialised nation. Schiffer Lafite was thus declared to be a "creole"/"coloured" woman from Mauritius; but while her Mauritian background entitled her to the common status of a British subject, it also provided the grounds on which the state fixed her condition of extraterritoriality and homelessness by ultimately forcing Schiffer Lafite into the category of alien.[45]

Figure 2.2 Photograph on certificate issued to Marie Schiffer Lafite, 1914.

There is further ambiguity in this archive, and the narrative of the file, as fragmentary as it was, produced flaws in the administrative containment of the subject. The dissonance emerged at those points where Marie Schiffer Lafite used the narrow spaces at her disposal to perform her sense of body and person and to determine how she would come into view.[46] One of the realms providing for such spaces was marital status, and in Lafite's case, the disrupted narration of marriage and separation. Any application for documents certifying individual identity and sanctioning mobility implied, at the time, the provision of information regarding marriage, through which both South African and British imperial citizenship and nationality legally codified men as standard and women as derivative categories.[47] Read against the official framework in place, Schiffer Lafite's recounting of the fleetingness of her civil commitments might have appeared problematic in terms of the established moral regime, and the affidavits attesting to her impeccable reputation suggest an astute anticipation of possible bureaucratic query.[48]

Still, the strategic narration of parts of her biography might likewise have drawn from other registers, in which the sequence of marriage was less a question of hampered administrative clarification, let alone of moral decay, than of her intricately gendered socialisation, intimacy, and desire. The trajectories, circuits, and circulations delineated in Schiffer Lafite's narrative, as much as they were interrupted by the logic of bureaucratic registration, hinted at how her social and cultural worlds were framed by the dynamics and frailties of female diasporic belonging, domicile, and migrancy in early twentieth-century Southern Africa.[49] Rather than following the linear mode of documentary narration, her presence in the archive emerges through selective performances that contextualise Schiffer Lafite in a complex field of non-racial socialisation in the urban milieus of Cape Town and Port Elizabeth in the early 1900s and link her to African cultures of voyage.[50] Likewise, her intended journey to Mauritius, which entailed a long absence from the Cape and an extended visit to family, anchored her in a sociocultural space that transcended the territoriality of the South African nation, countered the disposition of long-distance labour migration, and complicated categories of racial classification.[51]

It is at this point, in the disruption of linear narration, where the photograph might have indeed tipped the scale.[52] Since the beginning of the twentieth century and increasingly so after the First World War, photographs had become a requirement for official travel documents, both in the colonies and the metropoles.[53] In the South African context, this kind of administrative photography operated within cultural registers used by colonial subjects to articulate their notions of embodied personhood and raise claims to sociopolitical recognition. Applying for official documents of voyage was a difficult undertaking in the first place, and most Africans remained confined to paper regimes that routinely used fingerprinting but would deny visual documentation as sophisticated as photography.[54] Marie Schiffer Lafite was among a privileged group of African women that was literate, multilingual, and had access to studio photography, and she harnessed all of these in pursuing an official sanctioning of her journey.[55] The interwar period was still marked by the lack of formal requirements regarding photographic images considered acceptable for a permit or passport application, and the photograph used in Schiffer Lafite's case was in fact an original studio portrait and persuasive in its deployment of Victorian codes of embodied gender rationality, which drew from distinct iconographic conventions and imaginaries of class mobility marked by the studio space, impeccable attire, and visual conceptions of respectability.[56] In view of the immigration officer's prompt and positive response to Schiffer Lafite's request, the careful and strategic composition of her appearance and performance of person had, eventually, paid off.

Genealogical clusters

Figure 2.3 shows a graphic composition produced by the immigration department in Cape Town in 1922. It is part of a file on Eva and Lai Wing and their seven children.[57] According to the compiled forms and attached correspondence, Eva Wing applied for an identity certificate for herself and her children in order to accompany her husband on an extended journey to China and return after a period of three years. For this purpose, she

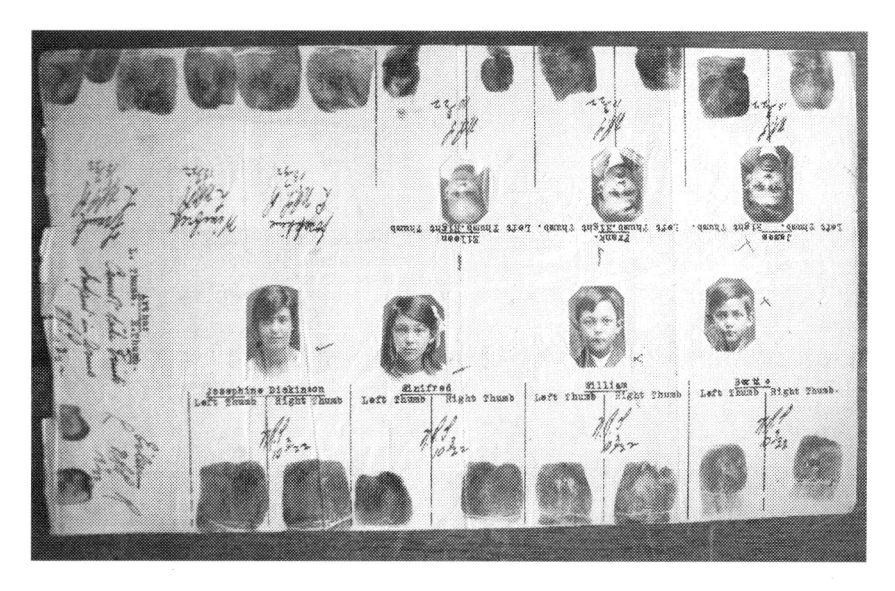

Figure 2.3 Genealogical arrangement of the Wing family, 1922.

submitted a series of photographs produced two years earlier in a studio in Port Elizabeth, where the family resided. Among these, we come across a family photograph of careful composition in an elegant studio setting, where Eva Wing and her husband Lai were surrounded by their children and a young woman, Josephine Dickinson, possibly a distant relative employed as *gouvernante* or nanny, who joined the group in the portrait. Along with the family photograph came individual portraits of the children, as well as Dickinson, where the impeccable appearance and costly attire of every young person came into close view.[58] Again, information on the family's history and living environment is scant. Lai Wing was said to be a trader of Chinese descent and, if judged by the sophisticated photography produced, of a certain economic standing and possibly part of a cosmopolitan milieu of aspiring African and Asian entrepreneurs, craftsmen, and traders based in the major cities and towns of the Cape.[59] Marriage and birth certificates attested to the duration of the conjugal union and the children's ages, and copies of immigration permits retraced Lai Wing's history of domicile and occupation in the Cape Colony since the early twentieth century. The file marked the family as "Asiatic", though Eva Wing's application for the certificate specified her local origins and her racial classification as "coloured".

As suggested before, this archive does not necessarily lend itself to a recuperative project but becomes revealing here in what it tells us about the constitution of the family, or rather genealogy, as an element of colonial governance, and the ways in which this constitution was discursively and visually articulated.[60] Uma Dhupelia-Mesthrie has carefully retraced how the personal files of Indian men residing in the Cape began to swell in the 1920s and 1930s, once bureaucratic interest in the documentation and verification of the identity and domicile of wives and children became more meticulous.[61] And indeed, there seems to have been a narrative shift that saw the supersession and eventual replacement of a diverse range of statements and affidavits, such as the ones submitted by Schiffer Lafite, by a growing bureaucratic reliance on rationalised forms of genealogical recording in numerical listings and iconographic diagrams that determined the identity of each individual in terms of his or her position within a family and social group.[62] The graphic composition shown in Figure 2.3 illustrates how the administrative bricolage of biographical information and indexical representation became complicated, and how it affected male and female adults as much as children and infants. But how can we make sense of this bureaucratic attention, and the time and, one is almost tempted to say, care applied to making bodies and persons into stable and legible entities?

The historical conditions that account for the file on the Wing family concern the unresolved and often precarious situation of those classified as "Asiatic" in early twentieth-century South Africa. These images and texts resonated with longer trajectories of economic exploitation, colonial state supervision, and political marginalisation, and they referenced both the imaginaries and realities of indentured and forced labour that had shaped the lives of many Chinese and Indian immigrants to South Africa in the early 1900s.[63] After Union, the presence of these people remained an issue of concern, and it was increasingly read through the lens of a desired racial disposition of the emerging South African nation.[64] In line with the notion of a "white man's land", the Indian and Chinese population became a problem of demography and of numerical proportion and, accordingly, a potential threat to European or "white" predominance.[65] This became increasingly true in view of a growing preoccupation with social disorder, poverty, urbanisation, and "racial mixing", and the official inflation of the ideologically charged debate on "poor white-ism" in the mid- and late 1920s.[66] Yet, this archive also invites us to consider the ways in which genealogy served broader social imaginaries, and how the family became the subject of bureaucratic practices underscoring processes of state formation and nation building.[67] As Elizabeth Povinelli argues, by the second half of the nineteenth century, theorists had refined the political elaboration of a specific notion of the family as the core institution of the modern nation-state that would enforce a dichotomous division between the domestic and private spheres, and would be modelled on two principle divisions, between woman/mother and man/father, and between parent and child.[68] Thus the heterosexual family became the social nucleus out of which all other differences – class, race, ethnicity, or nationality – could be derived.[69] The archives considered here mirror these ideological formations in many ways, and the files highlight how the administrative integration of individual men and women into the normative space of the family, enmeshed with a set of assumptions about genealogy and biology, underpinned categories of South African racial classification.[70]

The ways in which the bureaucracy handled the Wing family is, again, telling at this point. We could interpret the graphic elaboration of the familial relations, the verification of Eva and Lai's parental status, and the registration of each and every child's age as clues to rationality and administrative accuracy. Yet, these laborious documentary practices that concerned all those classified as "non-white" were likewise entrenched with racist assumptions about promiscuity and uncurbed reproduction, which fostered a lack of clarity concerning the identity of African, Chinese, Indian and "coloured" children.[71] Furthermore, the determination of genealogical relations was meaningful for social classification – particularly when, as the Wing family's case seemed to suggest, promiscuity and miscegenation complicated questions of race, belonging, and nationality.[72] In theory and by law, the hierarchical inscription of gender relations in both the familial and the national would have privileged the man as the standard for classification, and Eva Wing's position in the midst of an archive of "Asiatics" confirmed this practice.[73] It was indeed precisely the category of "Asiatic" that infused the genealogical graphic of the Wing family, which in turn constituted the visual idiom through which bodies could be conceived and inserted into administrative procedures that determined their condition of being and denied South African citizenship and nationality.[74]

But the Wing family's application and their sophisticated photographic representation unsettle the inevitability of an administrative reading. As in Marie Schiffer Lafite's case, the genre of portrait photography had crucial material effects on how colonised subjects would embody and perform their own narratives of sociality and belonging.[75] As argued above, the Wing's careful staging in the portraits referenced nuanced hierarchies and relations within the family, as much as it constituted the familial as the location of emotional and social security, of respectability and socio-economic well-being.[76] It is through the strategic deployment of photographic objects and the visual idiom that they were allowed to interrupt the teleological narration and categorical abstraction of the racialised person – by focusing on the particular rather than the generic, and on the individual rather than the collective – and to counter the exclusionary practices of the segregationist order.[77] This is not to say that Eva Wing's understandings of family and the gender relations it produced were necessarily different from an official moral order of domesticity and social respectability; but, it is an attempt to pay attention to the use of images and objects that shaped her intervention in the formation of these social categories and values and thus to delineate how photography conditioned them.

Transgressions of whiteness

The question of respectability was, as several scholars of Southern African social history have shown, by no means limited to African, Indian, or Chinese men and women, but likewise concerned those classified as European or "white", particularly during the interwar period, in which the category of whiteness remained an unstable one.[78] Moving back into the Namibian archives, we can retrace some of the more submerged trajectories of white racialisation and their bearing on body and person. The occupation of Namibia in 1915 by South African military troops, and the subsequent integration of the territory as a League of Nations Mandate from 1921 onwards, changed the parameters of whiteness in important ways.[79] While throughout the first two decades of the twentieth century the debate was framed in terms of British-Boer antagonism and focused on attempts to constitute a unified white identity within an integrated South African nation-state, the occupation of the former German colony of South West Africa posed new challenges caused by the repudiation and suspiciousness of a hostile German settler population.[80]

Figures 2.4 and 2.5 are two portrait photographs taken from the passports issued to Augusta and Ella Dietrich by the German General Consul in Pretoria in 1924.[81] We will briefly dwell on these documents of passage as objects and images.[82] Both passports were printed on patterned paper, and a brown cardboard cover enclosed thirty-two pages, the first of which recorded the name of the (male) person, the names of the wife and children, and the nationality of the bearer. On the next two pages were the photograph and name of the person and a certification of identity by a state official – in this case, the German consul. The passport furthermore provided brief physiognomic description and the record of basic biographical data. While it did not specify the details of the intended journey, the booklet indicated the period of validity and left space for a series of extensions.[83] Read in documentary terms,

Figure 2.4 Passport photograph of Augusta Dietrich, 1924.

Figure 2.5 Passport photograph of Ella Dietrich, 1924.

the two women, a mother and her daughter, were of German nationality by birth; they resided in the coastal town of Swakopmund in central Namibia; and neither of them bore any unusual physical marks. The passport certified their identity and nationality within South West Africa and Germany, and its validity covered a period of two years, to expire on 1 February 1926.

These passports are marked by a specific historical moment, when the question of the German settler community's nationality, and by implication, political loyalty came under scrutiny by the South African administration in Namibia. Namibian historiography has retraced the social and ideological frameworks that informed the complicated process of integrating this specific section of the population up to 1924, when Germans residing in the territory were naturalised as British subjects; an issue we will have to discuss more later on.[84] But this voluminous archive, which consists of hundreds of applications, marks the importance of "white" identity politics in the 1920s in distinct ways, as it is set apart from earlier, more dispersed histories of European immigration to the region.[85] While these interlaced trajectories remain important, I am interested here in paying attention to a particular line of rupture that ran through the process of white integration and manifested itself in specific articulations of the racialised female body.[86]

The scarce information we have on Augusta and Ella Dietrich provides glimpses at how the negotiation of gendered body and person became problematic for the articulation of whiteness. Alongside the passports, the women's file included reports by the South African police in Swakopmund, which recorded their involvement in illegal business and earlier convictions of Augusta Dietrich for "illicit alcohol sales to natives".[87] Once the women applied for international travel documents, surveillance began anew and produced astounding accounts:

> Miss Dietrich was used as the outside watchman when liquor was sold to natives. In this case Police had to do with two very cute characters, and that is why Mrs Dietrich was arrested only once. Miss Dietrich was as well as her mother under Police observation. Some years before her mother was arrested, it was already known to Police that she started to be out with men at night and in 1917 she was seen sleeping with a man named Thiel in one room. This was when she was a girl of seventeen years of age. In another occasion she was found at three o'clock in the morning with a man named Thiel (same as above) both drunk in the street; she was taken home by Police and thereafter Thiel was taken home. Thiel was the lawful husband of a Prostitute named Hedwig Schutt (Schutz?) married at Swakopmund.[88]

The police report contrasted with the message of the portrait photographs, in which the two Dietrich women aimed at presenting themselves in the best light possible. This was marked materially by submitting professionally produced studio photographs, as much as it drew from sophisticated iconographies of bourgeois portraiture.[89] The careful selection of attire, conventional in Augusta's and fashionable in Ella's case, palpably strove to articulate claims to respectability and reference imaginaries of entrepreneurship associated with the coastal towns of central Namibia. And finally, the ownership of a passport linked the women to a culture of voyage popular among those sections of the "white community" with strong ties to the German and, more generally, the European metropoles.[90] In the official reading, the photographs might have spoken, therefore, to the women's "very cute character" apologetically referred to in the report. Yet, more importantly, the tension that emerged between the photographs and the police's account echoed cultural anxieties among the male colonial elite, in which female moral integrity (or decay) became constitutive of the construction and conservation of racial categories.[91]

Within such preoccupations with gender disorder, both illicit liquor trade and prostitution had long been core concerns, particularly if they entailed transgressions of gender roles and violations of racial boundaries.[92] And it is precisely against this racialised assessment of danger that the archive of German naturalisation in the 1920s destabilised and denaturalised the category of whiteness.[93] As visual inscriptions, Augusta and Ella Dietrich's photographs operated in a representational field that produced particular imaginaries of female bodies within the German settler community, ideally associated with domesticity and with sexual and moral integrity.[94] On this point, they echoed equivalences with larger notions of "white" gender norms and sustainably nurtured symbolisms of South African integration.[95] Yet, on the other hand, the naturalisation process and its documentary regime inevitably unearthed ruptures and unintentionally exposed important layers of social stratification among German settler women. Indeed, the diversity of photographs assembled in the archive spelled out the divisions between bourgeois women – representing the cosmopolitan world of wealthy traders, entrepreneurs, and estate owners, usually based in the major Namibian towns or in possession of valuable commercial farmland – and rural women, who lived in modest farming communities in the vicinity of small towns or in remoter areas of the colony. It was within this dissonant visual field that Ella and Augusta Dietrich came to embody the worlds of bodily deviance and diversity of "white" female experience that continued to trouble the foundations of racial segregation and undermined an unambiguous category of whiteness.

To recall some of the key points made so far before we move on to a later moment and the second part of this chapter: The files documenting James Dzoye's, Marie Schiffer Lafite's, Eva and Lai Wing's, and Augusta and Ella Dietrich's applications for passports and travel certificates are part of a larger paper regime produced as the result of an administrative attempt to develop an epistemology of body and person in line with the ideological formation of an emerging South African nation after 1910 that would entrench particular notions of racial difference and gender hierarchy. Given the political disenfranchisement of a majority of the African and Asian population in South Africa and the Namibian colony at the time, and an administrative practice that preferred to use fingerprinting and physiognomic description for the bureaucratic representation and mediation of the racial other's body, the mere fact that African, Indian, and Chinese men and women managed to apply for and secure authorised international travel documents that included photographs is remarkable in the first place. Against this backdrop, one wonders if bureaucrats in the immigration and native affairs departments sensed the complications that could possibly emerge once people would make use of private photographs and insert personal images/objects into the bureaucratic process, thereby undermining the stability and clarity of racial, gender, and social categories. As a matter of fact, the intricacy and quality of studio portraiture complicated, as we saw, reified notions of embodied personhood, and because of the richness and density of the social imaginaries these photographs spoke to and the openings towards life-worlds they offered, these images constituted a powerful visual idiom through which Africans and Asians, men and women (including "white" women) could articulate their claims to be placed and *seen* within a political formation that, in the 1920s and 1930s, was still in the making – South African citizenship and its parameters of inclusion and exclusion.

In what follows, we will in part continue to walk on the grounds of defining the body politic and the South African state's attempt to determine the criteria for political and social participation, whereby epistemologies of body and person remain crucial. But moving into the post-Second World War and apartheid eras will entail, as we shall see in a moment, a significant shift with regard to photography's material and visual effects, in a new administrative regime of identification and surveillance that would mark a process of exacerbated internal colonisation.[96]

Population registration, 1950s–1960s

In the early 1950s, the South African government, by now bound to the project of apartheid, embarked on one of its most ambitious and extensive schemes directed at the registration, identification, and control of its subject population. Two pieces of legislation, the Population Registration Act No. 30 of 1950 and the Natives (Abolition of Passes and Co-ordination of Documents) Act No. 67 of 1952 laid the groundwork for the administrative re-articulation and implementation of control policies and practices prescribing and curtailing people's rights of residence, mobility, and work (Figure 2.6).[97]

While the population registration scheme made provisions for every South African above the age of 16 years (regardless of race) to be issued an identity number and document, the Natives (Abolition of Passes and Co-ordination of Documents) Act concerned only those classified as "native", and required them henceforth to permanently carry a "reference book". The reference book – or *dompas*, as it was popularly known among those who had to carry it – was an elaborate object.[98] Usually kept in a brown cover, it was made up of two parts. First, it contained a laminated identity card that featured the

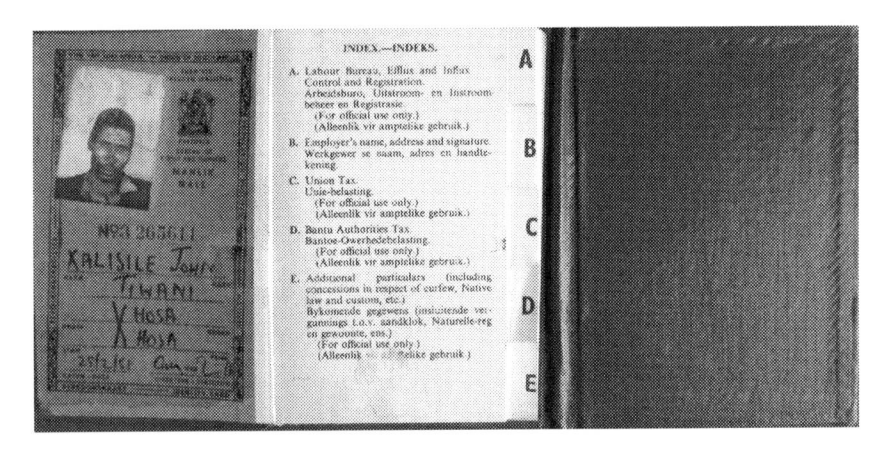

Figure 2.6 Dompas issued to Xalisile John Tiwani.

name of the bearer, his or her ethnic affiliation, the date on which the card was issued, the signature of an official, and a black-and-white portrait photograph. Second, the book included five consecutive documentary sections (A–E) that listed information on permissions to enter urban areas, record of required medical examinations, names and addresses of employers, work status, and receipts for tax payments.[99] The reference book replaced a plethora of permits, passes, tax receipts, and identity certificates that had been in use since the early twentieth century. While the apartheid government praised the new system as a modern, rational, and efficient form of registration, the book first and foremost marked the advent of a panoptic form of policing envisioned by the notorious regime.[100]

The registration of men classified as "native" and the issuing of reference books to them began in March 1953.[101] Mobile teams of the Native Affairs Department chose the main industrial employers around Pretoria, the Witwatersrand, and the Vaal Triangle for a first round of registration that lasted six months, in which more than 400,000 industrial workers were issued reference books. The main institutional body responsible for the process was the Central Reference Bureau in Pretoria, and it was here where fingerprints taken were classified, associated with a national identification number, and a set of photographs, ordered, and filed in a cabinet. Once registration was underway in the main urban and industrial centres, the process was extended to the rural areas of Natal and the Transvaal, and by 1958, the scheme began to target women as well.

As Keith Breckenridge has rightfully argued, the reference book system began to crumble at a very early stage in its implementation. Although being registered and issued a *dompas* required every individual to have an impeccable record of tax payments – a prerequisite that caused problems to many – the overwhelming number of people who applied for reference books, and accordingly submitted fingerprints and photographs to be processed, caused long delays in the work of the Reference Bureau. Additionally, applications for duplicate books due to theft or loss of originals reached an average of 3000 per month as early as 1954 and added to increasingly chaotic conditions. If nothing else, the recurrent mix-up of fingerprints, identity numbers, and photographs eventually induced the Bureau to introduce filing cabinets and microfilms in the late 1950s, but by then, massive resistance to the reference books and systematic acts of forgery brought the entire scheme to a near collapse.[102] The state responded to these acts of defiance with increased policing and large scale arrests of offenders that reached a monthly average of 49,000 in 1962.

Because the *dompas* signified the coercive nature of the apartheid state, it has ever since captured popular and political imaginaries – prominently so, for example, in Athol Fugard's *Sizwe Bansi is Dead*[103] – and has accordingly played an important role in historical writing.[104] Within these imaginaries and scholarly debates, the focus has been on how the reference book system led to a deterioration of the lives and working conditions of men and women classified as "native" or Bantu; how the book served and perhaps even fuelled the racial politics of a totalitarian regime; and how, accordingly, it provoked immense daily and organised resistance by those placed under its rule.[105]

Dompas

Here we pursue a slightly different entrance into the theme, again shifting attention to the visual and material, and proposing an analysis of the *dompas* as an object and image. Because state authorities praised the reference book as an icon of a rationalisation process, one aimed at synthesising earlier forms of documentation of an individual's life, provenance, residence, and labour relations, it is worth unravelling how this sophisticated and complex object was materially constituted, what it was made of, and from what kinds of discursive registers it drew. The population registration scheme was the first occasion on which the South African state systematically required every adult citizen and subject to be photographed. We are thus entering a context and moment in time in which photography was applied on a large scale and affected vast sections of the subject population. Because the photographic medium came to occupy such a distinctively important place in the scheme, the population registration and introduction of reference books throughout the 1950s and 1960s constitutes an exceptional case study that enables us to inquire what kind of photographs it yielded, how these images were used, what they were meant to do, and how the photographs took part in a range of material and social practices producing body and person.

The reference book became the new blueprint for the classification and identification of "native" bodies, and it drew from a combination of indexical registers and an elaborate bureaucratic taxonomy and nomenclature. Yet to become operational, i.e. a useful means of control and surveillance, and meaningful in terms of the information it enclosed, the reference book required an adequate institutional and semantic backdrop. It was the function of the Central Reference Bureau to provide this framework of legibility, and most of the work done by its employees consisted of inserting the information gathered in a rapidly expanding system of registers and filing cabinets, and to guarantee the comparability and verifiability of visual and written data. As we shall see, while the Bureau focused on fingerprints as the modern form of biometric identification, everyday control and surveillance of men and women required by police, magistrates, and employers to carry the book would rest, however, on the material and visual integrity of the photograph and the book as a whole.

The following discussion draws on research conducted in the Western Cape Archives and Record Service in Cape Town; the documents on file there actually concern the implementation of the scheme in both the Western and Eastern Cape and occasionally include materials related to a number of towns in the Northern Cape as well. The archival composition and classification mirrors the logics and workings of the apartheid administration at the time, as well as the chronologies and geographies of the registration scheme. The archive's centrepiece is made up of files produced in the magistrates' offices throughout the Cape regions, who had been commissioned with executing the registration and issuing reference books. While browsing through these archives, one comes across a file entitled *Itinerant Photographer 1962–1963*, which is of special interest to the questions that concern us here.[106] The file contains fragments of correspondence between the magistrate in Kentani, the chief native commissioner/magistrate in Umtata, and the director of the Reference Bureau in Pretoria composed in 1963. The examination and reading of the rest of the archives follows the narrative threads proposed by the documents kept in this particular file, which provide the entrance into a retracement of the scheme's implementation in the Eastern Cape, and more precisely in the former Transkei, where population registration and the issuing of reference books began around mid-1955.[107] Again, we will approach the introduction of the *dompas* first, with a particular interest in photography, body, and person, and then look at the scheme within a regional and local context.

The files in the magistrate's archives of the Transkei contain correspondence among the officers stationed in the smaller towns and villages throughout the region; letters and minutes between the magistrate and chief native commissioner in Umtata, the administrative centre at the time, and the Central Reference Bureau in Pretoria; the communication with the mobile teams that travelled throughout the area and registered men, and later women, during a period of almost ten years; and finally, letters and notices exchanged between the magistrates and local residents, missionaries, teachers and church elders, photographers, and others on issues relating to the population registration and the reference books. Most importantly for our purpose, these files contain a large number of applications for *dompases*.

Before we move to a closer reading of these images and texts, there is a need to point to some material absences in these archives. With one exception – the reference book issued to Xalisile John Tiwani in 1958 – there are no reference books as such kept in the magistrates' files, although the textual documents provide a tangible sense of how the books were produced and circulated between Pretoria, Umtata, and the respective towns and villages in the Transkei until they were eventually delivered to their owners. Generally speaking, this archive conjures and enforces a narrative of undisturbed and untroubled rationality, effectiveness, and functionality of a bureaucratic system and scheme, administered uniformly and effectively even by those state officials stationed on the most remote internal frontiers. This narrative of modern rationality stifles any reference to contestation, inquiry, and resistance, urging us towards a reading of the archive *along the grain*.[108] Yet, we shall also explore, of course, how a careful inquiry into the photography produced in the course of the population registration and issuing of reference books in the Transkei might provide directions for reading against the grain, for unhinging the described narrative and questioning the self-description of one of the most notorious apartheid schemes.

Itineraries

As mentioned above, the archive suggests that the systematic registration of individuals applying for reference books in the Eastern Cape was up and running in 1955.[109] Here as anywhere else, the economic rationale behind the scheme was more than obvious, and indeed the authorities left no doubt that the significance of the region for industrial and agricultural labour recruitment made the formal registration of men in the Transkei an urgent priority.[110] Although the Native Affairs Department in Pretoria had provided regional offices throughout the country with so-called *Consolidated Standing Circular Instructions*, regarding what was by then commonly referred to as "the population registration of natives" immediately after the Act of 1952 had been passed,[111] it was only in April 1955 that the Chief Magistrate requested the commencement of operations in and around the Transkeian administrative centre.[112] Two months later, the first round of registration materialised: a mobile unit, consisting of twelve men, namely "a team leader, one official photographer, one fingerprint assistant, one embosser, six temporary native clerks, one temporary native recorder and one camera assistant" was said to be visiting Umtata in June, and the local magistrate was required to inform residents accordingly, who would be then asked to report at the designated registration centres and bring along their tax identity numbers.[113] In theory, this procedure was meant to be repeated throughout the Transkei by two mobile units, and Pretoria expected all men above the age of 16 and residing in the region to be issued reference books by the beginning of February 1958.[114]

But on the ground, this template soon proved to be unsustainable, particularly so once the registration of women began in 1957 and increased the demands on the mobile teams.[115] The Transkeian authorities had indeed reckoned at an early stage that procedures needed to be further adjusted to local conditions, and as early as April 1956, the magistrate in Umtata had asked his fellow officers throughout the region to report on the number of people that needed to be registered in their relative districts, assess the availability of photographers on the spot, and make suggestions for the location of registration centres and suitable itineraries.[116] As we shall see, the magistrates' response was quite revealing, and the archives provide a vivid picture of a complex visual economy and diverse visual practices in the region at the time.

First, though, we will go back to the registration process *per se* and take a closer look at the work the mobile teams performed once they registered individuals.

Figure 2.7 shows the application forms attributed to a 16-year-old youth called Andile Pinkerton Booi, who applied for a reference book in Engcobo in 1961.[117] At the time, this assemblage of documents constituted a characteristic, if not model application insofar as it included the C. 25 form (the yellow card with personal information on the applicant including a space for the photograph), the B.A. 147 form (the dactyloscopy, i.e. the set of fingerprints),

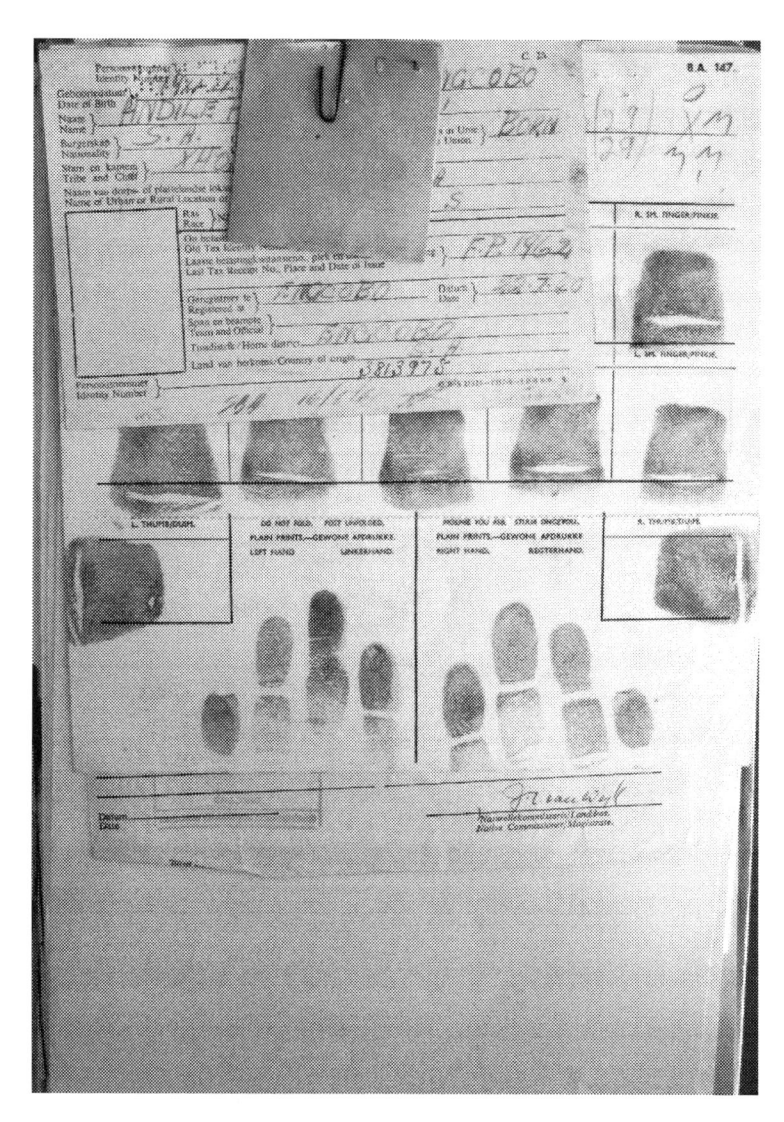

Figure 2.7 Application for reference book submitted by Andile Pinkerton Booi, 1961.

and a brown E5 envelope with two black and white photographs enclosed. It is at this point at which the files provide a tangible sense of the bureaucratic backdrop to the population registration and the growing degree of administrative centralisation. Indeed, once the application process was concluded, all the information produced was supposed to have been sent by the magistrate to the Central Reference Bureau in Pretoria, where, as mentioned before, it would be processed and archived and, eventually, the applicant would be issued a reference book. The book was then sent back to the local magistrate who would finally instruct the person concerned to collect it. All in all, the entire procedure would require a period of at least one month.

But the course of action summed up here flattens the configuration of the application process in many ways and suggests a material and administrative clarity and purposefulness that belies one that was in practice much more erratic, chaotic, and – to say the least – contested. Although the scheme was meant to simplify and standardise the documents in use, applying for an identity document continued to mean very different things in terms of its material outcome: brown or green reference book, exemption certificate, temporary identification certificate – or no book at all.[118] Moreover, the fact that Andile Pinkerton Booi's completed application was kept in the Engcobo magistrate's files provides an important example of bureaucratic disruption; the questions of why his application was not forwarded to Pretoria and whether he ever received a *dompas* remain unanswered.

What does this particular conglomerate of cards, forms, and photographs, one example of many kept in the files of the various magistrates in the Transkei, tell us about the "population registration of natives"? And what can we say about the role photography played therein? The application forms provided a particular kind of information on the subjects applying for reference books. In Andile Pinkerton Booi's case, the C. 25 card stated that he was born in Engcobo in 1944, and therefore was 16 years of age and a South African national by birth; he was single, male, Xhosa Zibi, and at the time of registration resided at Tora, a village about 50 km south of Engcobo. The card furthermore listed Pinkerton Booi's old tax identity number, added his new national identity number, and recorded the date of his last tax payment. Lastly, it noted precisely when and where the registration had been done. A dactyloscopy featuring the young man's entire fingerprints and a set of two black-and-white portrait photographs, certified by a government official, completed the application.

The application process described above reflects the continuities of bureaucratic rationality that link the interwar period paper regimes with those in apartheid South Africa. For those men and women classified as "native", registration under the population registration scheme entailed, once again, a fragmentation that required them to represent themselves according to more than familiar administrative categories, including age, provenance, marital status, racial and ethnic classification, and gender. These categories served, as noted earlier, as the invisible backdrop against which bodies would be made into legible and manageable entities in a register that attempted to reconstitute subjects furnished with a number (the National Identification Number), recorded statistically (according to the tax records), identified biometrically (based on the fingerprints), and classified (along social, ethnic, and racial lines).[119] It was eventually this classificatory framework that defined the space in which the photograph would act, responding as it were to the ways in which the bureaucratically recomposed person eventually came into view.[120]

Photographs

The way that photographs are kept in the population registration archive makes their position ephemeral. Some of them are attached to the corresponding application and kept in the brown envelope, but many of them are loosely placed between documents, slipping between papers. They are often small, hardly larger than a stamp, and hence always at risk of being lost or mixed up, both in the past, when they were produced and included in an application, and the present, within the archive.[121] Their ephemerality is likewise apparent in their dwindling image quality, as most of the photographs have begun to fade, whereby some of their subjects have by now become almost unrecognisable. This material and visual volatility in the archive undermines unambiguous interpretation and threatens attempts at biographical recovery.

Still, these images evoke a powerful presence. As suggested earlier, while contemplating James Dzoye's portrait, we noticed that there is, indeed, an unsettling ability of the photographic image to (seemingly) recreate its subject in the present. Scholars of visuality have addressed this effect in different ways, often through an engagement with Walter Benjamin's concept of aura in relation to photography. Miriam Bratu-Hansen, for example, begins her seminal essay on Benjamin with a reflection on a common understanding of aura as "an elusive phenomenal substance [...] that surrounds a person or object of perception, encapsulating their individuality and authenticity".[122] Aura, it seems, participates in and instantiates the logic of the trace or the indexical dimension in photographic signification. Here, Benjamin conceived of aura less in terms of an inherent property of persons or objects, as Bratu-Hansen continues to explain, but as something that pertains to perception and becomes visible only on the basis of technological reproduction. In other words, it is not the presence of the photographic subject itself, but the particular condition of exposure and the kind of looking (or gaze) it anticipates and responds to that at once threatens and inscribes the body's authenticity and individuality.[123]

How does this contestation of the body's presence in the photograph and the structure of vision resonate in the Eastern Cape magistrate's archives? Figure 2.8 takes us back to Andile Pinkerton Booi's application for a reference book in Enqcobo in 1961 and to its particular kind of photographic framing.[124] The enclosed photograph relied, as we shall see in a moment, on established visual conventions in which the camera focused on particular body parts, on the head and face placed against a neutralised backdrop. Arjun Appadurai has called these photographs on official documents "face prints", images that claim to capture the subject's individuality – his or her aura – not through any documentary technique but rather by echoing their indexical companions, fingerprints.[125] The terminology is powerful, and the rhetorical move highlights the ways in which these photographs "imprison the body in visual realism" and semiotic standardisation. Yet, the framing

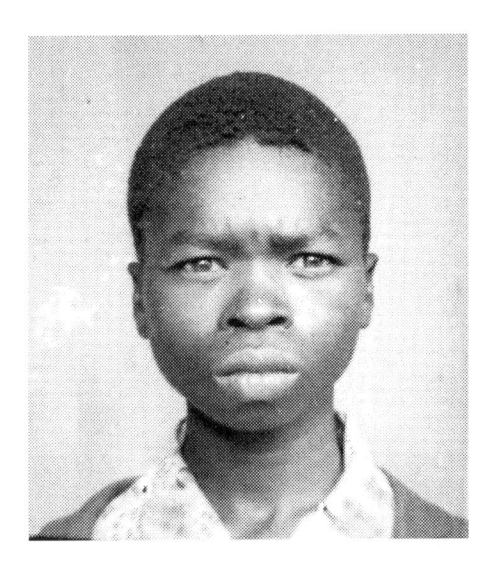

Figure 2.8 Photograph of Andile Pinkerton Booi, 1961.

nevertheless remains epistemologically ambivalent, as it was precisely the undefined backdrop that marked the uncertainty about what these photographs were asked to represent.[126] The population registration scheme, then, raises the problem of body and person in particular ways. It requires, if we continue to follow Appadurai's argument, an assessment of wider discursive framings – frames and practices that helped contain photographic meaning and determined the ways in which the photographs would be perceived. And it is, ultimately, the question of framing and perception that takes us back, once again, to the work of the mobile registration units.[127]

As mentioned earlier on, the registration of men, and later women, in the Transkei was meant to be done by an official mobile team, which included one photographer and a number of auxiliary clerks.[128] Yet, as a result of the rapidly growing numbers of people who needed to be registered, local magistrates decided to make use of photographers available on the ground. The articulation of their desire to use local resources fell on sympathetic ears. In fact, a number of labour recruitment agencies, among them the Natal Sugar Planters, the Native Recruiting Corporation Ltd., and the Illovo Sugar Estates Ltd., immediately offered to register and photograph labourers by themselves, claiming that they had actually always done so.[129] Obviously, this proposal helped maintain some of their freedom of scope in the organisation of labour recruitment, and though the Transkeian authorities resented the persistence of commercial recruiters' market autonomy, the scheme's immediate requirements forced them to give in.

The magistrates' search for a sustainable registration method identified further practitioners in a quite sophisticated, local photographic culture.

A few commercial photographers, such as F.L. Simpson and Raymond Lee, had photo studios in and around Umtata and East London; in some of the smaller towns and villages, members of the tiny settler community, who usually engaged in amateur landscape photography and portraiture, likewise agreed to produce appropriate registration photographs.[130] Most importantly though, and to the administration's astonishment, the most noticeable initiative came from local black photographers, who proactively approached the magistrates and offered their services. Between 1958 and 1962, seven independent photographers, namely W.B. Diko and Edward B. Ntsane in Mount Frere, S.M. Mabude in Bizana, Nelson Manxiwa in Willowvale, Isaak Keswa in Umzimkulu, Elliot Sixabayi in Cofimvaba, and James Mpuku in Ngqeleni, applied for permission to participate in the registration scheme, arguing that their knowledge of the area, their experience in "servicing their own communities", and the quality of their photographic work made them genuine candidates (Figure 2.9).[131]

Noting the diversity of photographic practices, yet reluctantly conceding the necessity to use all services available in the Transkei for the registration scheme, the Reference Bureau in Pretoria approved the involvement of private photographers, while at the same time trying to control the heterogeneous visual economy. The prescription of technical equipment to be used

Figure 2.9 Unidentified, 1960.

and the standardisation of the photographic images themselves became the means by which they managed to do so. In an annexure regularly attached to the circulars sent out by the magistrate in Umtata over a period of several years, the format, style, and materiality of the photographs were meticulously determined. According to the guidelines, every photographer had to produce two separate photographs of each individual, 1⁹⁄₁₆ inches in height, 1⅛ inches in width (corresponds ca. 4 × 2.85 cm), with no white margins; the frame of the image was to include head and shoulders, with "the size of the head not less than ⅞ of an inch and not more than 1 inch".[132] The person was to be photographed without a hat, turban, veil, eye glasses, spectacles, or any other addition to the face that would "alter the natural likeness". No shadow of the person was to be visible, and no part of the face or the shoulders blended to the background. Full face visibility, including the ears, was required, and the photographers had to advise those in front of the camera to refrain from tilting their head. Likewise, photographers were asked to use good quality negative and printing paper, panchromatic emulsion of reputable brand, and negatives of normal contrast to be printed on suitable grade of single weight glossy paper with full tonal range and without loss of detail. Finally, every photographer was invited to adopt a system by which he would be able to trace particulars of the photograph of any person taken by him, if, when necessary, either the photograph or the registration form was handed to him by any state official. Based on these instructions, the Central Reference Bureau reserved its right to reject any photograph considered to be insufficient.[133]

The prescription of technical equipment was as significant. The population registration scheme became the occasion on which the apartheid state facilitated the mass introduction of Polaroid cameras throughout South Africa and into the most remote areas of the country. In the early phase of the scheme, photographers in the Transkei used different cameras, but by the early 1960s, the Polaroid became a requirement for any professional involvement.[134] While this technical shift facilitated the work of photographers to some extent, as it reduced delays and made their equipment lighter,[135] it nevertheless transformed their interaction with clients substantially. The local culture of portraiture had thitherto taken place in the context of personal encounters between photographers and photographed, either in spaces provided by the cameramen or in people's homes;[136] but producing portraits for registration changed the quality of the interaction, as it became part of a rationalised, accelerated, and palpable technological operation.[137] L.J. Lemmer, chief clerk of the Reference Bureau, had indeed anticipated these operational effects.[138] During an official conference held in Pretoria in 1953, Lemmer had envisioned the required rationality and its purpose as follows:

> When the Native presents himself, his photograph is taken by a special camera. Within a minute two photographs of each Native would be ready. It has been tested and found that between 600–700 Natives

can be photographed in a working day. After the photographs are taken the Native goes to the section where his fingerprints are taken, and his name and particulars obtained. By that time his photograph is ready. From there he is taken to a Native clerk where the identification card is completed. It will then be pasted into a book and sealed by a special stamp. This cannot be removed without damage to the book.[139]

The implementation of the population registration scheme in the Transkei in the late 1950s and early 1960s, with its focus on two powerful indexical registers – photography and fingerprinting – and a prescribed administrative structure that gravitated around the Central Reference Bureau in Pretoria, shaped the mediation between bodies classified as "native" and apartheid state authorities as an increasingly technological matter. Requests and complaints from residents in the region are consistently marginalised in the archive, and if they received attention at all, the defiance was neutralised and blended into a narrative of harmless negotiation that concerned questions of organisation and rationality of registration. This was the case, e.g. when the magistrate in Umtata received a letter of complaint by a group of women in Mputi, a village 35 km east of Engcobo, in 1957, who asked the official to "appoint the date and come and explain to us all about this photographing",[140] or when individuals wrote letters and complained about mismanagement and corruption among headmen and clerks, who used the registration scheme as a means of political tutelage or personal gain.[141] But what these interventions likewise indicate is a growing concern of men and women in the light of a panoptic regime imposed by technocrats, and the production of standardised photographs, which – unlike studio portraiture and its variegated imagery – were brought in line with a classificatory, bureaucratic language. As we shall see, it was precisely the photographic standardisation that came to occupy a pivotal place within the apartheid state's population scheme. Standardisation was likewise key in defining the relationship between image, body, and person.

Semblance

Photographs were meant to serve the desire to fix and classify bodies. Yet sure enough, population registration remained a material and discursive space in which the intricacy and reliability of "photographic likeness" or "semblance", as contemporaries would call it, surfaced as an unresolved issue many a time. Indeed, by the late 1950s, the bureaucratic question of identification had increasingly been grounded in fingerprinting and a complex system of numerical registration and archival order,[142] both considered complementary means by which the instability and uncertainty of photographic meaning could be contained.[143] Yet, we might arguably propose, the two indexical registers were, while they shared discursive ground, deployed here within different practices of representation and perception, an instance that precisely invites us to think about the photographs beyond the problem of identification alone.

The magistrates' archives are suggestive here because they reveal deep scepticism towards the photographic medium, among the magistrates themselves, as much as local headmen and residents.[144] Remarkably, their anxiety, mistrust, and at times outright rejection resonate with some of the arguments developed by Walter Benjamin in his seminal essay *The Work of Art in the Age of its Technological Reproducibility*.[145] It is worth recalling his propositions and their consequences for thinking with care about photography as a form of technological mediation.

Benjamin's reflections on technology are based on a fundamental distinction. First, he identifies a primeval technology, which in its origins constituted a counterpart to nature and served man to shape and master natural forces (and magic). What marks the modern, mechanical age, in contrast, is the emergence of a second technology, one that would differ in orientation and aim at the interplay between nature and humanity, thereby operating by means of experiments and varied test procedures:

> The origin of the second technology lies at the point where, by an unconscious ruse, human beings first began to distance themselves from nature. It lies, in other words, in play.[146]

Further on in his essay, it is the notion of play that serves as an entrance into the discussion of technological mediation and perception. In an extended footnote, Benjamin retraces the origins of artistic activity in mimesis, where he locates two polar aspects of art: semblance and play, semblance being key to auratic perception. What makes the polarity between semblance and play significant, in dialectical terms, is that it is precisely determined by the distinct intentions of the first and second technology; while the former continues to be motivated by the logics of semblance, the latter accrues from an inexhaustible reservoir of experimenting procedures, from play, imitation, or re-semblance.[147] Benjamin's concern was primarily with film, a medium in which he believed the element of semblance had entirely been displaced by the element of play and therefore embodied technology's revolutionary potential.[148] Photography, he believed in contrast, continued to be haunted by an unresolved tension between semblance and play. His awareness of photography's undetermined position as a form of technological mediation takes us back to the population registration, as it helps explain the medium's ambiguous effects therein, its unresolved position between "semblance and play". While it may seem a stretch to read this tension in the Eastern Cape archives as having a revolutionary potential, retrieving the ways in which these materials reference different forms of technological adaptation could disclose some of the contestations that otherwise remain submerged in and marginalised by the colonial archive's hegemonic gesture.[149]

As argued on several occasions throughout this chapter, the photographs produced for the reference books functioned within a specific classificatory framework, which helped constitute the "native body" in terms of a set of prescribed categories that conditioned, almost in the fashion of captioning, the images' reception, and thereby helped contain the instability of photographic meaning.[150] Still, administrative practice could never fully control the effects of photographs within the registration scheme. Ironically it was, as we shall see, precisely the desire for controlling photographic representation, and the wish to use photographic technology in mediating an unambiguous relationship between subjects marked by race and their sovereign, the apartheid state, which became a source of contestation and arbitrariness.

The *dompas* came to embody this idiosyncratic redefinition of body and person, while concurrently denoting the new quality and scale of the state's intended hold on its subjects, given that it constituted the material and visual instantiation of everyone's condition of containment, outside of which there would be no acceptable, legitimate, or perceivable form of existence.[151] Conceived of as an all-encompassing, if not panoptic form of surveillance, and alimented by the multiplication and repetitiveness of its material objects and visual codes, the scheme strove to remap each and every place and location in the South African landscape within a grid of racially homogeneous, but separate areas, and to control and channel the movement of things and bodies between them.[152] This delusion of grandeur had to founder, although less at the core of its spheres of activity – the mines on the Witwatersrand, the large cities of Cape Town, Durban or Johannesburg, and the areas of labour recruitment such as the Eastern Cape – than on its racial frontiers. But the Eastern Cape archives show how the fault lines cut across the entire project, which constantly threatened to undermine its own epistemological foundations.

There is one category of person in particular – the coloured – that uncovered how the question of semblance and photographic mediation marked flaws in the scheme's implementation, and it confronted the magistrates and registration teams in the Eastern Cape, it seems, rather unexpectedly.[153] The presence of people in an area otherwise classified as "native" (i.e. black, and more specifically "Xhosa" in ethnic/tribal terms), who claimed mixed descent and hybrid cultural heritage complicated notions of racial homogeneity expected to translate into a stable spatial configuration. The issue was uncomfortably dragged along for a while, until in June 1960, the authorities in Pretoria decided to send two official photographers, H.L.G. Botes and J. Verhoeven, to the Transkei and the Ciskei (the neighbouring homeland), with the aim of photographing "coloureds" and facilitating applications for identity cards.[154] A month later, the Reference Bureau additionally commissioned N.S. Harrison to travel through the region and extend the photographic recording to "all Whites, Coloureds and Asiatics".[155] But because local magistrates confirmed that there would ultimately be "white" and "coloured" pockets in but a few villages in the Transkei, Pretoria did not ruffle itself and remained pragmatic, eventually deciding that in the few cases that might come up, racial classification should have been based simply on residence and the particulars of tax payment.[156] But, alas, the problem could not be disposed of readily, and in fact, it grew once the registration teams moved north into the Northern Cape.[157]

Figure 2.10 was taken in 1956 and attributed to Martha Swarts van Wyk, who applied for an identity card (*persoonskarte*) in Kuruman in March of that year and used the registration form N.V.R. 7 prescribed for "Cape Malays, Cape Coloureds and other coloured persons" over the age of 16.[158] As in this image, many of the Kuruman photographs featured a number plate held by the person portrayed, though it remains unclear if the numbers referenced bureaucratic systems such as taxation, or if they were part of an indexical register used by the photographer in order to retrieve copies of images.[159] As suggested before, van Wyk's application and those of her fellow applicants kept in these files had given cause for concern. They were all accompanied by a formal request issued in the office of the Population Registrar, which invited the magistrate or native commissioner on the ground to re-evaluate the person's racial classification. The form phrased the registrar's doubts as follows:

> As there exists a measure of doubt as to the racial group to which he/she belongs, I shall be glad if you will kindly complete the attached questionnaire in respect of him/her and return it to me.[160]

Figure 2.10 Photograph of Martha Swarts van Wyk, 1956.

Once such a standardised request from Pretoria was sent in, the magistrates or native commissioners would have usually invited the respective person into their office, where he or she would have been required to provide specification for the completion of the said questionnaire. The interrogations were declared to be innocent bureaucratic inspections and verifications of information related to familial status and history of residence. But what they actually served as was a re-evaluation of the photographs and a reassessment of the photographic mediation of a bureaucratically contained body. This is why the Registrar in Pretoria always included photographs in his requests, which were envisaged as visual templates for the respective officers on the ground, and were believed to help them in reconsidering if the image at hand conveyed the applicant's racial affiliation in an appropriate way.[161] The result of this idiosyncratic exercise caused an intricate debate throughout the files, on image quality, appropriateness of cameras used, and the technological skills of semi-professional and amateur photographers.[162] In Martha Swarts van Wyk's case, who had indicated that she originated from the Kuruman area, and both her parents had been classified as "coloureds", as was her husband, the reassessment of photographic semblance was nevertheless requested, and once the magistrate evaluated her case, by placing the woman's "mere physicality" against the photograph, he decided to reclassify her as "native".[163]

But the problem of semblance proved a cause for persistent worry, and one of the most interesting forms it took was a phenomenon called "impersonation".[164] This was a well-established legal term, which the magistrates and native commissioners, men of justice, used to describe cases in which an individual had assumed another person's identity and had thereby, obviously perhaps, committed an offence. Actual cases of impersonation strengthened the administration's stated aim of detecting, identifying, and prosecuting all those who would not align themselves with the prescriptions of the law.[165] But there was, more importantly, an imaginary, fictional, almost poetic element to the bureaucratic concern with impersonation, which disclosed doubts and anxieties that clustered around the photographs and threatened to undermine the systemic reliance on the photographic medium and technology from within. Inevitably perhaps, the fantasy of a panoptic system of individual identification produced intrinsic loopholes, and it invited a plethora of counteracts and – to echo Benjamin's propositions – play as a modality of responding to the *dompas* system.

Here we read from one case of impersonation, which might help substantiate the assumption of an element of play:

> On 15th July, 1960 a Bantu purporting to be abovenamed, approached the Registering Officer at Langa [a black township of Cape Town] and produced reference book N. 2246319 with a view to renewing his employment permit. On being scrutinised it became apparent that there had been some tampering with the photograph in the book. The Bantu in question was referred to me for investigation. The man whose photo

appears in the reference book now, claimed to be Mlungu John Philip and was able to answer all questions in connection with the entries in the book perfectly satisfactorily. He was also able to answer questions about Kentani and Butterworth, which fact leads me to believe that he comes from the Kentani District.

The one fact that aroused great suspicion, however, was that according to the records at kept at Langa, Mlungu John Philip was a man of 55 years of age, whereas the subject of the photograph and the person interviewed were considered to be not more than 23–25 years old.

> The suspected impersonator was thereupon charged with being in this area illegally and also with mutilating or altering a reference book. He was admitted to bail in the sum of £10 while further investigation was carried out. A Photostat copy of the C. 26 Card of N.I.N. 2246319 reveals that the reference book has been tampered with. The impersonator has, however, now disappeared from Cape Town and cannot be traced by the Police. His £10 bail has been retained and, as he cannot be found, the charges against him have been withdrawn. As far as can be ascertained, the correct John Philip is at home in your District.[166]

As with many others, the advancement of this case dissolved among the conglomerate of correspondence on other issues, and the response from Kentani was not preserved in the file. Such a response would probably have rendered an account of the Kentani magistrate's interrogation of local headmen and members of the community, and possible responses to the photograph of the alleged impostor. Whatever the forms of verification might have been, the text quoted already provides insights into the bureaucracy's desire for the technological containment of the body, and the importance of the integrity of the *dompas* as an object and image mentioned earlier on. Suspicion of impersonation and the related narratives authored and mediated by state bureaucrats tell us most about the sensitivities of those who had to operate within the logics of identification, i.e. magistrates, policemen, and native commissioners. But they likewise reveal, if unintentionally, that for those forced into the reference book system, one of the most promising ways of escaping the rationale of semblance was, to recall once again Benjamin's distinction, an appropriation of technological mediation as an "inexhaustible reservoir of experimenting procedures" provided, most productively, by the photographic medium.

This is precisely why the material, visual, and semantic stability of the reference book, the *dompas*, constantly threatened to mutate into other things, other images, and other persons. Some of these mutations were caused by deliberate acts of defiance, and it therefore comes as no surprise that bureaucrats would view impersonation in terms of forgery and crime.[167] Yet, the charge of insubordination laid against those suspected of impersonation made sense only in conjunction with a category that was an administrative fiction in the first place – the "Native" or "Bantu". This is why the cases of impersonation make clear how, beyond the rationale of state administration, both categories could hardly have been considered to be attached or belonging to a particular person; in addition, their abstracted and reified definition could do nothing else than favour and facilitate the fabrication of multiple bodies and mimetic subjectivities.[168] This might, ultimately, open up alternative readings of Andile Pinkerton Booi's application, which, as we saw, was never sent from the magistrates' offices in the Eastern Cape to the Central Reference Bureau in Pretoria. The persistent presence of this material in the magistrate's archives leaves many questions open, among them if Pinkerton Booi reapplied for another reference book, or if he simply emerged as a different person, at a later stage, and somewhere else.

Conclusion

What do these case studies tell us about the relationship and distinction made between things, body, and person, once these become embedded in specific practices, discourses, and meanings? Going back, first to the interwar period and to the files produced on James Dzoye, Marie Schiffer Lafite, and Eva and Lai Wing, reveals the diversity of possible forms of arrangement and combination and the varying degrees of relationality they produced. The material and visual intricacy of the photographic image form and medium conditions the ways in which these objects surface in the archive, and the place they occupy within a heterogeneous assemblage of texts and images. But if we reconsider the photographs' effects – how they acted within administrative practices of producing bodies and persons – we encounter a constitutive tension. On the one hand, we have the bureaucratic desire to use photographic realism as a means of defining and entrenching what Esposito calls the differential logic of person and the category's typological and temporal derivatives, in order to insert these into the representational regime and racial foundations of the South African nation-state; on the other hand, we have the material and visual instability of the photographs that inevitably evoked the singularity, multiplicity, and diversity of bodies that came into view. It is precisely the fact that these archival files constitute but "fragments of life" that points to the ways photography destabilised the fixity of administrative categorisation and confused clear-cut distinctions between body, person, and the materiality of bureaucratic mediation. Dzoye's, Schiffer Lafite's, and the Wing family's successful applications for documents of voyage evidence the possibilities that emerged from these material and visual instabilities, even as the archive reminds us that their cases, once placed against the politically disenfranchised majority and those forced into the iconography of fingerprinting, remained exceptional. The archival effect is indeed powerful and complicated, creating the impression that all those bodies that remain unseen would be unseen within the political and social body; that those who "remained beneath the threshold of vision were, paradoxically, brought into view only to be made to disappear into the archive in what was an act of representational liquidation".[169] Portrait photographs and their capacity to honour the individual in his or her subjectivity and personhood remained haunted by the material and visual crudeness of thousands and thousands of work permits and labour recruitment certificates issued to Africans and Asians, who were never considered as full persons in the first place.

Things looked different, literally, in the context of population registration in the 1950s and 1960s, once much more standardised forms and means of documentation attempted to force black South Africans into an almost panoptic regime of visual surveillance. Here, we seem to encounter a situation in which the sheer scale of apartheid's core biometric project facilitated a previously unknown proliferation and multiplication of images and objects – photographs and reference books – that became the hegemonic modality through which a particular form of producing and perceiving body and person was expanded and generalised. Martha Swart van Wyk's reclassification as "native", in the course of which her body was reduced to "mere physicality" and her claim to a particular status of person (coloured) crumbled against the authority of the photographic image, provides a sense of the real consequences of photography's repressive function. But at other moments, it seems as if the bureaucratic scaffold was caused to sway, and yet again by means of the material and visual instability of the photograph and the *dompas*. As Benjamin's discussion of photography and technological mediation suggests, the medium proved deceptive, such as in Andile Pinkerton Booi's application. Here, rather than stabilising body and person, the photograph and its position among a conglomerate of indexical signs and textual fragments elucidates how the auratic effect is diverted from the body itself to the act of rationalised seeing and perceiving and hence constantly undermines any attempt to recuperate the presence of the subject.

There are, nevertheless, a few instances in which the archive speaks more directly to the complicated relationship between person and image, body and thing, namely through the category and practice of impersonation. While impersonation evidenced how, for the apartheid state, the status of person was simply a matter of the law (which *nota bene* continued to deny the status of full person to the black majority by means of a plethora of racist legislation), the ways in which population registration had grounded the category of person in the photograph and the *dompas*, i.e. in an image/object, entailed, inevitably and ironically perhaps, the possibility of inverting and disrupting the scheme's very own differential logic. We recall here Esposito's reminder that what loomed behind the category of person was the figure of the thing, precisely because, as he vividly describes, "the person doesn't coincide with the body in which it inheres, just as the mask is never completely one with the actor's face".[170] If we read his explications against the backdrop of the apartheid state's biometric project, we are ultimately taken to the clarity of population registration's dehumanising function: "once the mask is made safe, it doesn't matter what happens to the face upon which it rests and even less to the faces that do not own masks; to those who still aren't persons, or who are no longer persons, or those who were never declared to be persons".[171] Those subjected to apartheid would most likely have understood this all too well.

Notes

1 We will discuss these issues more systematically in Chapter 5.
2 See on the Eastern Cape as an important locality constitutive of the political geography of industrial capitalism and labour recruitment in twentieth century South Africa Colin Bundy, *The Rise and Fall of the South African Peasantry.* Berkeley, Los Angeles, 1979; and William Beinart and Colin Bundy, *Hidden Struggles in Rural South Africa. Politics and Popular Movements in the Transkei and Eastern Cape 1890–1930.* Berkeley, Los Angeles, 1987. For a critique and important shift in writing Eastern Cape history see Gary Minkley and Helena Pohlandt-McCormick, The Speaking Crow or 'On a clear day you can see the class struggle from here'? (Career Girls 1997). *Parallax,* 22, 2, 2016: 183–202.
3 See for careful derivation of Foucault's extended notion of biopolitics Sven-Olof Wallenstein, Introduction: Foucault, Biopolitics, and Governmentality, in Jakob Nilsson and Sven-Olof Wallenstein (eds.), *Foucault, Biopolitics, and Governmentality.* Stockholm, 2013, pp. 7–34, here p. 13.
4 Roberto Esposito, The *Dispositif* of the Person. The quote is on p. 18.
5 Roberto Esposito, The *Dispositif* of the Person, p. 24.
6 Thomas Lemke, New Materialisms. The main reference works discussed by Lemke are Michel Foucault, *Security, Territory, Population: Lectures at the Collège de France, 1977–8.* New York, 2007; and Michel Foucault, *The Birth of Biopolitics: Lectures at the Collège de France, 1978–9.* New York, 2008.
7 Lemke, *New Materialisms,* pp. 8–9.
8 Ibid., p. 9.
9 Ibid., p. 13.
10 See Saul Dubow, South Africa and South Africans: Nationality, Belonging, Citizenship, in Robert Ross, Anne Kelk Mager, and Bill Nasson (eds.), *The Cambridge History of South Africa.* Cambridge, 2011, pp. 17–65, here p. 34; and more generally Caplan and Torpey, *Documenting Individual Identity.*
11 National Archives of Namibia (NAN), SWAA 422 A 50/34, Native Affairs. Passports for Natives. Magistrate Windhoek, Declaration to be made by Applicant for Passport, Windhoek, 20 September 1934.
12 "Angoni" was the contemporary term used in colonial Southern Africa to denote Nguni speakers, and it administratively received a strong ethnic connotation. Nyasaland (sometimes spelt as Nyassaland in the Namibian archives) was at the time a British Protectorate and became independent Malawi in 1964.
13 Ivan Evans, *Bureaucracy and Race: Native Administration in South Africa.* Berkeley, 1997.
14 I have discussed another case from this file, the application submitted by David Chidanda in Lorena Rizzo, Visual Aperture: Bureaucratic Systems of Identification, Photography and Personhood in Colonial Southern Africa. *History of Photography* 37, 2013: 263–82.
15 For an extended discussion of this see again Chapter 5.
16 See, for example, John Tagg, A Democracy of the Image: Photographic Portraiture and Commodity Production, in John Tagg, *The Burden of Representation,* pp. 34–59.
17 The distinction between photography's honorific and repressive functions goes back to Alan Sekula, The Body and the Archive.

18 In the same file there is, for example, the application for a passport by Peter Dennison submitted in 1937 to the acting native commissioner in Lüderitz in southern Namibia, which included a more standardised photograph produced by commercial photographers in the main Namibian towns, such as Nitzsche-Reiter in Windhoek. See NAN SWAA 422 A 50/34, Native Affairs. Passports for Natives, Passport Application Peter Dennison, Lüderitz, 29 April 1937. State-prescribed standardisation of photographs for identity documents in South Africa and Namibia only began, as we shall see later on, in the 1950s.

19 Elizabeth Edwards and Janice Hart, Introduction. Photographs as Objects, in Edwards and Hart (eds.), *Photographs Objects Histories: On the Materiality of Images.* New York, 2004, pp. 1–15.

20 Matthew Hull, *Government of Paper: The Materiality of Bureaucracy in Urban Pakistan.* Berkeley, 2012; and Matthew Hull, Book symposium. The Materiality of indeterminacy … on paper, at least. *HAU: Journal of Ethnographic Theory*, 3, 3, 2013: 441–7.

21 On Bertillonage see Chapter 1. Also Ellenbogen, *Reasoned and Unreasoned Images*; and Sekula, The Body and the Archive.

22 See Barthes, *Camera Lucida*. On photography and performativity see Edwards, *Raw Histories*, pp. 5–6, and Elizabeth Edwards, Photography and the Material Performance of the Past. *History and Theory* 48, 2009: 130–50.

23 Marcus Banks and Richard Vokes, Introduction: Anthropology, Photography, and the Archive. *History and Anthropology*, 21, 2010: 337–49, here p. 341; Edwards, *Raw Histories*, chapter 5, pp. 107–29; George Baker, Photography between Narrativity and Stasis: August Sander, Degeneration, and the Decay of the Portrait. October, 76, 1996: 72–113.

24 Achille Mbembe, The Power of the Archive and Its Limits, in Hamilton et al., *Refiguring the Archive*, pp. 19–26.

25 Premesh Lalu, The Grammar of Domination and the Subjection of Agency: Colonial Texts and Modes of Evidence. *History and Theory*, 39, 4, Theme Issue "Not Telling": Secrecy, Lies, and History, 39, 2000: 45–68, here p. 68; Linzi Manicom, Ruling Relations: Rethinking State and Gender in South African History. *Journal of African History*, 33, 1992: 441–65.

26 Esposito, The *Dispositif* of the Person; for Southern Africa and the legal creation of the category of person see Martin Chanock, *The Making of South African Legal Culture*, pp. 225–6.

27 See for example, Richard W. Flournoy, The New British Imperial Law of Nationality. *American Journal of International Law*, 9, 1915: 870–82; Rieko Karatani, *Defining British Citizenship: Empire, Commonwealth and Modern Britain.* London, 2003.

28 My phrasing only echoes Partha Chatterjee's *The Nation and Its Fragments: Colonial and Postcolonial Histories.* Princeton, 1993, and does not, at this stage, draw systematically from his arguments.

29 Dubow, South Africa and South Africans.

30 I am using in particular Radhika Viyas Mongia, Race, Nationality, Mobility: A History of the Passport. *Public Culture*, 11, 1999: 527–56.

31 For a general discussion, see John Torpey, The Great War and the Birth of the Modern Passport System, in Caplan and Torpey (eds.), *Documenting Individual Identity*, pp. 256–70.

32 Dag Henrichsen, Donal Lowry, Giorgio Miescher, Ciraj Rassool, and Lorena Rizzo (eds.), The South African Empire. *Journal of Southern African Studies*, 41, 3, 2015. David Simon's edited volume, *South Africa in Southern Africa. Reconfiguring the Region.* Oxford, Athens, Cape Town, 1998, did not engage a historical framework, but rather focused on contemporary issues.

33 For an overview and introduction see Beinart and Dubow, *Segregation and Apartheid.*

34   See, for example, Jonathan Crush, Alan Jeeves, and David Yudelman, *South Africa's Labour Empire: A History of Black Migrancy to the Gold Mines*. Cape Town, 1991; and Charles H. Feinstein, *An Economic History of South Africa: Conquest, Discrimination and Development*. Cambridge, 2005.

35   Nicola Foote, Rethinking Race, Gender and Citizenship: Black West Indian Women in Costa Rica, c.1920–1940. *Bulletin of Latin American Research*, 23, 2004: 198–212, here p. 207; Ruth Roach Pierson, Nations: Gendered, Racialised, Crossed with Empire, in Ida Blom, Karen Hagemann, and Catherine Hall (eds.), *Gendered Nations: Nationalisms and Gender Order in the Long Nineteenth Century*. Oxford, 2000, pp. 41–62; Manicom, Ruling Relations, p. 444.

36   See Zahid R. Chaudhary, Subjects in Difference: Walter Benjamin, Frantz Fanon and Postcolonial Theory. *Differences*, 23, 2012: 151–83.

37   See Dubow, South Africa and South Africans, p. 34; Sally Peberdy, *Selecting Immigrants: National Identity and South Africa's Immigration Policies 1910–2008*. Johannesburg, 2009, chapter 3, pp. 31–55.

38   Peberdy, *Selecting Immigrants*, p. 32; K. Steinberg, *Das Staatsangehörigkeitsrecht der Südafrikanischen Union (einschliesslich Südwest-Afrika)*. Frankfurt am Main, 1955, pp. 13–16. The situation remained widely unchanged after 1927 when a separate Union nationality was introduced, but the common status of British subjects was preserved. See T. E. Dönges, *The New South African Citizenship*. London, 1949, p. 3.

39   The crucial piece of legislation in this context was the Immigrants Regulation Act of 1913, which de facto turned Asian (Chinese and Indian) and African immigrants into undesirables. See Peberdy, *Selecting Immigrants*; and Dubow, South Africa and South Africans.

40   I use Mahmood Mamdani's conceptual distinction between citizens and subjects, and while his argument has been criticised in recent years, I consider it still very appropriate for the discussion of citizenship in early twentieth century South Africa. See Mahmood Mamdani, *Citizen and Subject: Contemporary Africa and the Legacy of Late Colonialism*. Princeton, 1996.

41   Western Cape Archives and Records Service (KAB) PIO 1 – 147 E, File on Marie Schiffer Lafite.

42   The information on her first husband is as limited and only includes his surname Schiffer.

43   KAB PIO 1 – 147 E, Principal Immigration Officer, Application by Marie Schiffer Lafite, Cape Town, 1914.

44   The notion of threshold is taken from Esposito, *op.cit.*, p. 24. For a discussion that extends the argument to race and gender see Nancy Leys Stepan, Race, Gender, Science and Citizenship, in Catherine Hall (ed.), *Cultures of Empire: Colonizers in Britain and the Empire in the 19th and 20th Centuries*. Manchester, 2000, pp. 61–86, here p. 64.

45   Viyas Mongia, Race, Nationality, Mobility, p. 528. See also Leela Gandhi, *Postcolonial Theory. A Critical Introduction*. New York, 1998, p. 132.

46   Michael Goodrich, The Theatre of Emblems: On the Optical Apparatus and the Investiture of the Person. *Law, Culture and the Humanities*, 8, 2012: 47–67, here pp. 56–7.

47   See Steinberg, *Das Staatsangehörigkeitsrecht*; also Vertrees C. Malherbe, Family Law and the "Great Moral Public Interests" in Victorian Cape Town, ca. 1850–1902. *Kronos*, 36, 2010: 7–27. Most forms to be compiled for applications for identity certificates, travel permits, and passports in the interwar period, such as the one used by James Dzoye, privileged men as main applicants, and always added space for information related to their wives. Accordingly, men could apply for documents that would extend their rights of citizenship and mobility to their wives by virtue of marriage. In other cases, though, the forms provided

gender-neutral categories for spouses and hence allowed for the registration of men or women as main applicants.

48　See, for example, Timothy Keegan, Gender, Degeneration and Sexual Danger: Imagining Race and Class in South Africa, *c.*1912. *Journal of Southern African Studies* Special Issue for Shula Marks, 27, 2001: 459–77; and more generally, Ann L. Stoler, Making Empire Respectable: The Politics of Race and Sexual Morality in twentieth Century Colonial Cultures. *American Ethnologist*, 16, 1989: 634–60.

49　Schiffer Lafite's reference to her first husband "deserting" her in Port Elizabeth in the early 1900s might be read against the backdrop of the South African War and its aftermath. While there has been a growing scholarly concern with the war's impact on the African population, questions of gender remain largely unexplored. But see, for example, Greg Cuthbertson, Albert Grundlingh, and Mary-Lynn Suttie (eds.), *Writing a Wider War: Rethinking Gender, Race and Identity in the South African War, 1899–1902.* Athens, 2002.

50　Gandhi, *Postcolonial Theory*, p. 112; Uma Dhupelia-Mesthrie, The Form, the Permit and the Photograph: An Archive of Mobility between South Africa and India. *Journal of Asian and African Studies*, 46, 2011: 650–62.

51　Schiffer Lafite's simultaneous classification as "creole" and "coloured" referenced the ambiguity of both categories within racial classification in the interwar period. See Beinart and Dubow, *Segregation and Apartheid*, pp. 2–3. On Mauritius' position within a Southern African political geography and imaginary of slavery and indentured labour see Nigel Worden, Review of *Creating the Creole Island: Slavery in Eighteenth-Century Mauritius* by Megan Vaughan. *Journal of African History*, 47, 2006: 332–3.

52　Edwards, *Raw Histories*, p. 8; and more generally Hayden White, The Question of Narrative in Contemporary Historical Theory. *History and Theory*, 23, 1984: 1–33.

53　Torpey, The Great War.

54　Keith Breckenridge, Flesh Made Words; Rizzo, Visual Aperture.

55　Literacy and the knowledge of at least one European language had been made a compulsory requirement for immigrants in 1902. See Dhupelia-Mesthrie, The Form, the Permit and the Photograph, p. 655. On histories of African portraiture in South Africa see Karel Schoeman, *The Face of the Country: A South African Family Album 1860–1910.* Cape Town, 1996; Santu Mofokeng, The Black Photo Album, in Pascal Martin Saint Leon, N'Goné Fall, and Jean Loup Pivin (eds.), *Anthology of African and Indian Ocean Photography.* Paris, 1998, pp. 68–75.

56　See Richard Vokes, Introduction, in Richard Vokes (ed.), *Photography in Africa*, p. 9; Amar Wahab, Race, Gender, and Visuality: Regulating Indian Women Subjects in the Colonial Caribbean. *Caribbean Review of Gender Studies*, 2, 2008: 1–23, here p. 7. For a broader discussion of respectability in South Africa in the interwar period see Lynn Thomas, The Modern Girl and Racial Respectability in 1930s South Africa. *Journal of African History*, 47, 2006: 461–90. It is at this point where Shiffer Lafite's photograph echoes James Dzoye's portrait.

57　KAB IRC 1/2/4 73C Lai Wing.

58　These portraits, submitted in multiple copies, served as visual templates for the graphic composition shown above. Josephine Dickinson's status within the family remains, as suggested, unclear; she is sometimes counted as a daughter and in other cases, she is left out without further explanation. She might also have been a daughter of Eva from an earlier relationship.

59　See Dhupelia-Mesthrie, The Form, the Permit and the Photograph; Yoon Jung Park, Sojourners to Settlers: Early Constructions of Chinese Identity in South Africa. *African Studies*, 65, 2006: 201–23.

60 See the introduction to Wendy Woodward, Patricia Hayes, and Gary Minkley (eds.), *Deep Histories: Gender and Colonialism in Southern Africa*. Amsterdam, 2002, pp. xxi–xlvi, here p. xxiv. See Elizabeth A. Povinelli, Notes on the Gridlock. Genealogy, Intimacy, Sexuality. *Public Culture*, 14, 2002: 215–38; Malcolm Thompson, Foucault, Fields of Governability, and the Population-Family-Economy Nexus in China. *History and Theory*, 51, 2012: 42–62. Povinelli and Thompson draw from Michel Foucault's writings on governmentality.

61 Dhupelia-Mesthrie, The Form, the Permit and the Photograph, pp. 657–8; and Dhupelia-Mesthrie, Producing Biographical Knowledge about Indians in the Cape: the State, the Archives and the Historian, unpublished Inaugural Lecture, Department of History, Faculty of Arts, University of the Western Cape. Cape Town, 2009, pp. 9–10. For a more general discussion of state routine and rule that regulates and reproduces gender through marriage and family registration see Manicom, Ruling Relations, p. 452.

62 Povinelli, Notes on the Gridlock, p. 215; Dhupelia-Mesthrie, The Form, the Permit and the Photograph.

63 See Gary Kynoch, Controlling the Coolies: Chinese Mine Workers and the Struggle for Labour in South Africa, 1904–10. *International Journal of African Historical Studies*, 36, 2002: 309–29; and Park, Sojourners to Settlers. For Indian indentured labour see Uma Dhupelia-Mesthrie, *From Cane Fields to Freedom: A Chronicle of Indian South African* Life. Cape Town, 2000.

64 Peberdy, *Selecting Immigrants*; Dubow, South Africa and South Africans.

65 Peberdy, *Selecting Immigrants*, p. 33; and A. J. Christopher, "To Define the Indefinable": Population Classification and the Census in South Africa. *Area*, 34, 2002: 401–8.

66 Jeremy Seekings, "Not a Single White Person Should Be Allowed to Go Under": *Swartgevaar* and the Origins of South Africa's Welfare State. *Journal of African History*, 48, 2007: 375–94; see also Chapter 4.

67 Thompson, Foucault, Fields of Governability, p. 51.

68 Povinelli, Notes on the Gridlock, p. 224.

69 Povinelli, Notes on the Gridlock, p. 223. Also Belinda Bozzoli, Marxism, Feminism, and South African Studies, in Beinart and Dubow (eds.), *Segregation and Apartheid*, pp. 118–44, here p. 139.

70 See Saul Dubow, *Scientific Racism in Modern South Africa*. Cambridge, 1995, pp. 12–15. For a reading of racial segregation in terms of gender, see Manicom, Ruling Relations, p. 459.

71 Thompson, Foucault, Fields of Governability, p. 48. For an early discussion of these assumptions in the South African context, see Pierre L. van den Berghe, Miscegenation in South Africa. *Cahiers d'E'tudes Africaines*, 1, 1960: 68–84.

72 Dhupelia-Mesthrie, The Form, the Permit and the Photograph, p. 654; Christopher, To Define the Indefinable; and Vivian Bickford-Smith, South African Urban History, Racial Segregation and the Unique Case of Cape Town? *Journal of Southern African Studies*, 21, 1995: 53–78.

73 Negotiating racial classification remained complicated. All cases considered here concerned women originating from the Cape and classified as "coloured", whose racial classification would change because of their marriage to Indian or Chinese men.

74 Povinelli, "Notes on the Gridlock", p. 219.

75 See Mofokeng, The Black Photo Album; and more recently Erin Haney, Portraits in the World, in her *Photography and Africa*. London, 2010, pp. 57–89.

76 Gilian Rose, Family Photographs and Domestic Spacings: A Case Study. *Transactions of the Institute of British Geographers*, 28, 2003: 5–18.

77 Rizzo, Visual Aperture, p. 29.

78 Stoler, Making Empire Respectable; Thomas, The Modern Girl; Chipo Hungwe, Putting Them in Their Place: "Respectable" and "Unrespectable" Women in

Zimbabwean Gender Struggles. *Feminist Africa*, Issue on Subaltern Sexualities, 6, 2006: 33–46; Saul Dubow, Afrikaner Nationalism, Apartheid and the Conceptualization of "Race". *Journal of African History*, 33, 1992: 209–37.

79   See Marion Wallace, *A History*, p. 205.

80   Brigitta Schmidt-Lauber, *Die abhängigen Herren: Deutsche Identität in Namibia.* Münster and Hamburg, 1993, pp. 72–3.

81   NAN SWAA 1855 A 406 2.

82   See Edwards and Hart, Introduction: Photographs as Objects, p. 2.

83   This differed from British (imperial) subjects' passports, which at the time would have specified the trajectory and destination of the journey in the document.

84   See Schmidt-Lauber, *Die abhängigen Herren*; also Chapter 4.

85   Most importantly the immigration of Eastern European Jews to South Africa since the mid-nineteenth century. For a detailed discussion, see Sally Peberdy, *Selecting Immigrants*, pp. 57–83.

86   Timothy Keegan, Gender, Degeneration and Sexual Danger; Sarah Nuttall, Subjectivities of Whiteness. *African Studies Review*, 44, 2001: 115–40.

87   NAN SWAA 1855 A 406 2, Magistrate's office Swakopmund, Extract from the criminal records book, 22 February 1924.

88   NAN SWAA 1855 A 406 2, South West African Police, Passports: Mrs Dietrich and Miss Ella Dietrich, Swakopmund, 31 October 1924. This report appears substantial if compared to the usual style of police statements that, if at all requested by the magistrate or immigration offices, were often limited to one or two short sentences.

89   Most working-class and rural applicants from the German community submitted privately produced photographs and often cuttings from group portraits. See Rizzo, "Visual Aperture".

90   Rizzo, "Visual Aperture".

91   See Stephan F. Miescher, Takyiwaa Manuh and Catherine M. Cole, When Was Gender?, in Catherine M. Cole, Takyiwaa Manuh, and Stephan F. Miescher (eds.), *Africa After Gender?* Bloomington, 2007, pp. 1–15, here p. 11.

92   See Keegan, Gender, Degeneration and Sexual Danger; and Phil Bonner, Desirable or Undesirable Sotho Women? Liquor, Prostitution and the Migration of Sotho Women, in Cheryl Walker (ed.), *Women and Gender in Southern Africa to 1945*. London 1990, pp. 221–51.

93   Ann Laura Stoler, *Carnal Knowledge and Imperial Power: Race and the Intimate in Colonial Rule.* Berkeley, 2002, p. 58; Wahab, Race, Gender and Visuality.

94   See, for example, Nancy Reagin, The Imagined *Hausfrau*: National Identity, Domesticity, and Colonialism in Imperial Germany, *Journal of Modern History* 73 (2001), pp. 54–86.

95   Marijke Du Toit, Blank Verbeeld, or the Incredible Whiteness of Being: Amateur Photography and Afrikaner Nationalist Historical Narrative. *Kronos*, 27, 2001: 77–113; Philippa Levine, Sexuality, Gender, and Empire, in Phillipa Levine (ed.), *Gender and Empire*. Oxford, 2004, pp. 134–55; Joseph K. Adjaye, Review of *Bringing the Empire Home: Race, Class, and Gender in Britain and Colonial South Africa* by Zine Magubane. *Comparative Studies of South Asia, Africa, and the Middle East*, 26, 2006: 523–4.

96   The concept of internal colonialism goes back to Harold Wolpe, The Theory of Internal Colonisation: The South African Case. *Collected Seminar Papers, Institute of Commonwealth Studies*, 18, 1975: 105–20; see for a critical appraisal the introduction to Beinart and Dubow, *Segregation and Apartheid*.

97   The Population Registration Act was published in the Extraordinary Union Gazette on 7 July 1950, pp. 3–19, the Natives (Abolition of Passes and Co-ordination of Documents) Act in the Government Gazette on 7 November 1952, pp. 1013–29.

98 The example shown here (figure 18) is filed under KAB 1/UTA 6/1/79. The book was issued to Xalisile John Tiwani, a man classified as Xhosa, on 25 February 1958. This reference book doesn't contain any information on Tiwani's personal history of residence and work, nor on his tax payments. As all pages are left blank, the book was not collected and never used by its intended owner.

99 Keith Breckenridge, Verwoerd's Bureau of Proof: Total Information in the Making of Apartheid. *History Workshop Journal*, 59, 2005: 83–108, here p. 85.

100 On these paper regimes see Rizzo, Visual Aperture.

101 The following summary of the main features of the registration scheme is based on Breckenridge, Verwoerd's Bureau, which remains the main reference on the topic. The essay is included in Keith Breckenridge, *The Biometric State*, as chapter 5.

102 The most prominent instance of collective resistance to the reference books was the nationwide campaign organised by the Pan-African Congress in 1960. See Kwandiwe Kondlo, *In the Twilight of the Revolution. The Pan-Africanist Congress of Azania* (South Africa) 1959–94. Basel, 2009, p. 65.

103 Athol Fugard, *Township Plays*. Oxford, 2000. See also Lily Saint, Reading Subjects: Passbooks, Literature and Apartheid. *Social Dynamics*, 38, 1, 2012: 117–33.

104 Deborah Posel, *Influx Control and the Construction of Apartheid*. Oxford, 1987; Julia C. Wells, *We Now Demand: The History of Women's Resistance to Pass Laws in South Africa*. Johannesburg, 1994; Gary Minkley, How, in Heaven's Name, Are These people to Provide Photographs for Themselves? The Intimate Photographic Event, the Provision of Politics, and the Encounter of an "Empire of Love" in South Africa, unpublished conference paper, n.d.

105 Wells, *We Now Demand*; Pamela E. Brooks, *Boycotts, Buses, and Passes. Black Women's Resistance in the US South and South Africa*. Amherst, 2008, chapter 8.

106 KAB CMT 3/1435 30/F – Population Registration and Abolition of Passes. Issue of reference Book to Bantu. Itinerant Photographer, 1962–1963.

107 For a more comprehensive national perspective on the population registration scheme see again Breckenridge, *Biometric State*.

108 See Ann L. Stoler, *Along the Archival Grain. Epistemic Anxieties and Colonial Common Sense*. Princeton, 2009.

109 The chronologies of the scheme as it developed in the former Transkei help nuance the temporalities suggested by Breckenridge with regard to an overall national framework based on the analysis of records produced by the central state authorities in Pretoria. See: Breckenridge, Verwoerd's Bureau. There were earlier applications to the magistrates for reference books in the region, yet they appear to have remained occasional. See e.g.: KAB, 1/MTA 8 N1/23/2, Population Registration Mount Ayliff, 1953–1961, Magistrate Mount Ayliff to the Central Reference Bureau Pretoria, 14 January 1955.

110 See e.g. KAB, 1/UTA 6/1/79 N1/23/2, Population Registration of Natives, 1955–58, volume 3, Circular of the Chief Magistrate of the Transkeian Territories, 7 February 1958. The registration scheme in fact enabled the state and the Native Affairs Department in particular, to control and monopolise the practices of labour registration by recruitment agencies that had been in place before. For a discussion of migrant labour in South Africa that keeps an eye on chronological and geographical shifts see e.g.: David Yudelman and Alan Jeeves, New Labour Frontiers for Old: Black Migrants to the South African Gold Mines, 1920–85. *Journal of Southern African Studies*, 13, 1, 1986: 101–124.

111 See e.g. KAB, 1/TSM 7/1/46 N1/23/2, Magistrate Tsomo, n.d.

112 KAB, CMT 3/1434 30/B, volume 1, Chief Magistrate Transkeian Territories to the Magistrate Umtata, 29 April 1955.

113 KAB, CMT 3/1434 30/B, Population Registration and Abolition of Passes. Native Registration. Main File, volume 1, The Central Reference Bureau Pretoria to the Chief Magistrate Umtata, 10 June 1955.

114 KAB, CMT 3/1434 30/B, Population Registration and Abolition of Passes. Native Registration. Main File, volume 1, Chief Magistrate Transkeian Territories to the Secretary for Native Affairs Pretoria, 7 January 1958.

115 KAB, 1/UTA 6/1/79 N1/23/2, Population Registration of Natives 1955–58, volume 1, The Central Reference Bureau Pretoria to the Magistrate Umtata, 8 April 1957.

116 KAB, 1/XAA 172 N1/23/2, volume 1, Identical Minute No. SB 1/16: Issue of Reference Books to Natives by District Offices, sent by the Magistrate in Umtata, 22 April 1956.

117 Filed under KAB, 1/ECO 6/1/32 N1/23/2.

118 This is the case at least throughout the early stages of the scheme, i.e. before the *dompas* became compulsory for men in 1958, and for women in 1960. See: Mark Sher, From Dompas to Disc: The Legal Control of Migrant Labour, in Dennis Davis and Mana Slabbert (eds.), *Crime and Power in South Africa: Critical Studies in Criminology*. Cape Town, 1985, 72–89. Green reference books were issued to those who were exempted from the pass laws, namely teachers, students and church or mission employees.

119 The notion of invisible backdrop is taken from Arjun Appadurai, The Colonial Backdrop. *Afterimage*, March/April 1997: 4–7.

120 Goodrich, The Theatre of Emblems.

121 Marcus Banks and Richard Vokes, Introduction: Anthropology, Photography and the Archive, *History and Anthropology*, 21, 4, 2010; 337–49, here p. 339.

122 Miriam Bratu-Hansen, Benjamin's Aura. *Critical Inquiry*, 34, 2008: 336–75, here p. 340.

123 Bratu-Hansen, Benjamin's Aura, 340.

124 The original image is ca. 4 × 3 cm in size. Pinkerton Booi submitted two images that were not identical.

125 Appadurai, *The Colonial Backdrop*, p. 4.

126 Ibid., p. 5.

127 Mika Elo, Walter Benjamin on Photography: Towards Elemental Politics. *Transformations*, 15, 2007: n.p.

128 The official photographers whose names come up in the files are: N.L.J. van Wyk, E.V. Kent, and J. Conn.

129 KAB, 1/UTA 6/1/79 – N1/23/2, volume 3, Circular by the Chief Magistrate of the Transkeian Territories, Umtata, 7 February 1958; KAB, CMT 3/1434 30/B, volume 1, District Superintendent, Native Recruiting Corporation Ltd., to Chief Magistrate of Transkeian Territories, Umtata, 28 January 1958; KAB, CMT 3/1434 30/B, volume 1, C.R. Bannister, Secretary of Illovo Sugar Estates Ltd., to the Chief Native Commissioner Umtata, 30 January 1958.

130 F.L. Simpson owned Transkei Studio in Umtata, and Raymond Lee Studios was in Queenstown. Amateur photographers were e.g. G.C. Costello in Umtata, R.T.A. Stobart in Bizana, J.J. Kruger in Indwe, V.G. Hart in Tsomo, or N.S. Harrison in Kentani. It seems as if some missionaries, such as Father Kieran McCrann of the Catholic Diocese of Kokstad stationed in Lusikisiki, also owned cameras and took photographs for the registration scheme.

131 Some of the photographers, such as Edward B. Ntsane, sent sample images to convince the magistrate of their professionalism. See KAB, CMT 3/1434 30B, volume 1, Letter by Edward B. Ntsane to the Chief Magistrate in Umtata, 1 May 1958. These photographs have not survived in the archive. The archives suggest that most of the men did eventually produce photographs for the population registration scheme. I have to date not been able to trace their personal archives.

132 Figure 21 was enclosed as a model image in KAB, 1/TSM 7/1/46 N1/23/2, The Director of the Registration Office Pretoria to the Magistrate Tsomo, 28 April 1960.

133 See e.g. KAB, 1/XAA 172 N1/23/2, volume 1, Department of Native Affairs Pretoria, Identical Minute No. SB 1/16: Issue of Reference Books to Natives by District Offices, 22 April 1956.

134 Box cameras of various types seem to have been quite popular among local photographers. See e.g. KAB, CMT 3/1434 30B, volume 1, Magistrate Qumbu to Chief Magistrate Umtata, 11 March 1958. On the prescribed Polaroid cameras see KAB, CMT 3/1435 30B, Secretary for Bantu Administration, Circular No. B.B. 15/6, re: Sale of cameras. W.B. Diko, a photographer in Mount Frere, for example managed to buy himself a Polaroid camera in mid-1963. See KAB, CMT 3/1435 30/F, Letter by W.B. Diko to the Magistrate Mount Frere, 9 August 1963.

135 See e.g. KAB, 2/KMN 22, volume 2, NC Kuruman to Chief Native Commissioner Potchefstroom, 27 January 1958. The Polaroid cameras produced two identical photographs that developed within a couple of seconds.

136 Those photographers who had no studio of their own asked clients into their homes or worked as itinerant photographers who would take images at locations selected by those who commissioned portraits. See e.g. KAB, CMT 3/1434 30 B, volume 1, Magistrate Elliotdale to Chief Magistrate Umtata, 14 March 1960.

137 Polaroid likewise changed the material form of the photographs produced and the process of reproduction. No negative image is available here, only positive ones. Accordingly, the instant cameras changed the materiality of photographic archives.

138 On Lemmer, see: Breckenridge, Verwoerd's Bureau, p. 88.

139 KAB, CMT 3/1434 30 B, volume 1, Chief Magistrate Transkeian Territories to the Secretary for Native Affairs Pretoria, Umtata, 29 June 1953. The magistrate enclosed notes he had taken of Lemmer's speech.

140 KAB, 1/UTA 6/1/79 – N1/23/2, volume 2, Letter by Mputi women to the magistrate D.O.G. Sparg, 12 June 1957.

141 KAB, 1/ECO 6/1/32 – N1/23/2, volume 2, Letter of complaint by Malingonke Jijingubo to the Magistrate Engcobo, 26 January 1961.

142 Union of South Africa, Department of Bantu Administration and Development, Pretoria, General Circular no. 20 of 1959 (File No. SB 9/1), Reference Book System: Finger-prints, 1 September 1959. The circular stated on page 3: "The finger-print system offers a complete solution of the problem which always existed of positively identifying a Bantu." See also: Breckenridge, Verwoerd's Bureau.

143 Christopher Pinney, *The Coming of Photography in India*. London, 2008, p. 61.

144 What comes up recurrently in the archive are cases in which local headmen or residents are asked to identify persons on photographs, a request that usually produces confusion and ambivalence about individuals' identities. See e.g. KAB, 1/XAA 172 N1/23/2, volume 2, Statement by Ngonyama Gecelo, headman, in front of magistrate, Cala (Xalanga), 6 June 1958; KAB, 1/ALC, Minister B.A.B. Gasa, Bantu Presbitarian Church of South Africa, Lovedale, to the Magistrate in Alice, 24 March 1958.

145 Walter Benjamin, The Work of Art in the Age of Its Technological Reproducibility, in Hannah Arendt (ed.), *Illuminations*, New York, 1969, pp. 1–26. The distinction between semblance and play is also discussed in Elo, Walter Benjamin on Photography, though the argument developed here takes a different direction.

146 Benjamin, Work of Art, p. 26.

147 Benjamin, Work of Art, p. 48, footnote 23.

148 Benjamin, Work of Art, p. 45, footnote 11.
149 Benjamin, Work of Art, p. 27.
150 Ibid., p. 27.
151 See Esposito's argument explained at the beginning of this chapter.
152 Breckenridge, *Biometric State*; Posel, *Influx Control*: Wells, *We Now Demand*.
153 There is, typically perhaps, no reference whatsoever in this archive to the settlement of "coloureds" on the frontier around the Kei River in the first half of nineteenth century by the Cape colonial government. See: Martin Legassick, *The Struggle for the Eastern Cape 1800–1854. Subjugation and the Roots of South African Democracy.* Johannesburg, 2010. On the category of "coloured" within racial classification in twentieth century South Africa see Sean Jacobs, Coloured Categories. Review of Mohamed Adhikari, Not White Enough, Not Black Enough: Racial Identity in the South African Coloured Community, H-South Africa, H-Net Review, May 2007.
154 KAB, CMT 3/1443, The Secretary for Bantu Administration and Development to the Chief Native Commissioner Umtata, Pretoria, 26 June 1960. "Coloureds" were issued the so-called "persoonskarte" and were not required to carry reference books.
155 KAB, CMT 3/1443, Native Commissioner Kentani to the Chief Native Commissioner Umtata, 25 July 1960.
156 KAB, 1/KTN 127 N1/23/2, volume 1, Bantu Affairs Commissioner Kentani to Chief Bantu Affairs Commissioner Umtata, 13 March 1963.
157 The source materials that relate to the Northern Cape, which was an entirely different area in terms of administration, different area, might seem misplaced at first sight. But I would argue that it is precisely the problem of semblance that explains their integration into the Eastern Cape magistrate's archives.
158 The photograph was part of a set of two identical images kept in a brown envelope and filed under KAB, 2/KMN 22, N 1/23/2, volume 1. The envelope was stitched to the N.V.R. 7 form of Martha Swarts van Wyk, certified on 17 March 1956.
159 In early 1958 the native commissioner in Kuruman had confirmed that there was a commercial photographer in the town, who took studio photographs of people, yet didn't use Polaroid cameras (KAB, 2/KMN 22, N 1/23/2, volume 1). The Native Commissioner Kuruman to the Chief Native Commissioner Potchefstroom, 27 January 1958. Martha Swarts van Wyk and others, who registered before Polaroid cameras were introduced by the registration teams to the region, probably had to find the closest photographer themselves. It's not clear where Swarts van Wyk's photograph was taken. Obviously the numbers in the image reference conventions of prison and police photography. See chapter I, and Minkley, How, in Heaven's Name, p. 9.
160 The text was part of standard form B.V.R. 30/3.
161 Interestingly, Pretoria advised magistrates and commissioners to remain conservative with regard to reproduction of new photographs in case images proved inappropriate. The registrar asked his regional addressees to keep in mind costs and other expenditures that would incur.
162 Some of the applications were indeed rejected due to alleged lack of image quality or, generally, because the photographs did not correspond with the requirements set out for registration.
163 The reclassification was simply noted by the magistrate on the N.V.R. 7 form. See KAB, 2/KMN 22, N 1/23/2, volume 1, Martha Swarts van Wyk, 17 March 1956.
164 Impersonation is a common theme in historical studies, though it has been covered less in twentieth-century colonial histories. See for a discussion Cynthia Wu, Review of Tina Chen, Double Agency: Acts of Impersonation in Asian and American Literature and Culture. *Journal of Asian American Studies*, 9 February 2006: 209–12.

165 All cases concern men, and I have not encountered a single instance in which a woman was charged with or suspected of impersonation in these archives.

166 KAB, 1/KNT 127 N1/23/2, volume II, Bantu Affairs Commissioner, Cape Peninsula, Langa, to the Bantu Affairs Commissioner Kentani, 17 August 1960.

167 See Andrew Macdonald, The Identity Thieves of the Indian Ocean: Forgery, Fraud and the Origins of South African Immigration Control, 1890s–1920s, in Keith Breckenridge and Simon Szreter (eds.), *Recognition and Registration: Documenting the Person in World History*. Oxford, 2012, pp. 390–428.

168 See: Cynthia Wu, Review of Tina Chen, Double Agency: Acts of Impersonation in Asian and American Literature and Culture. *Journal of Asian American Studies*, 9, 2, 2006: 209–12, here p. 210.

169 Roberta McGarth, Geographies of the Body and the Histories of Photography. *Camera Austria*, 51–2, 1995: 99–106, here p. 99.

170 Esposito, The *Dispositif* of the Person, p. 25. He refers here to the etymological origin of the word person in the actor's mask. See also Goodrich, The Theatre of Emblems.

171 Esposito, The *Dispositif* of the Person, p. 30. His formulation is derived from a reading of Simone Weil, Human Personality, in Simone Weil, *An Anthology*, edited by Siân Miles. London, 1986, pp. 49–78.

3   Augenblick
The moment in Namibian photography, 1930s–1950s

Introduction

The most transitory of things, a shadow,
proverbial the emblem of all that is fleeting and momentary,
may be fettered by the spells of our natural magic,
and may be fixed forever in the position
which it seemed only destined for a single instant to occupy.

Henry Fox Talbot, 1839[1]

Let me begin this chapter with a photographic image, one chosen to provide an entrance into the problem of the photograph's interplay with time, and by implication, with history – into what scholars of photography call "the burden of the moment".[2] Here we have a black-and-white portrait of a child, a boy slightly leaning his head towards a horizontal wooden beam on his left, on which he has gently placed the tips of his fingers on his left hand. The child's look is directed towards the photographer, and he smiles, sweetly and almost impishly. He wears a white shirt, dark braces, and trousers; the shirt looks a bit dirty, and is tattered on the right arm he's raised to protect his face from the sunlight, and perhaps from the eye of the camera. Two kids crowd around him, partially entering the frame from the right bottom corner and from the left-hand side. In the background, two figures are vaguely perceptible, the shadow and partial silhouette of two grown-ups, one of them most likely a woman. The photograph is aesthetically appealing, its careful composition inviting us to contemplate the beauty of the smiling child. What appears to be captured here, at first, is but a moment, though one with different levels. It is at an unspecified time during the day – the children are dressed for school, for a family event, for church, or perhaps just for leisure and play; photographically, it is just after the boys have gathered in front of the camera, where they briefly keep still, to be photographed, once, possibly several times, before they fidget and run off anew; and finally biographically, it is in childhood, at the beginning of the boys' lives, before they grow up and pursue their future paths.

We do not know the boy portrayed or his sketchy photographic cohort by name, nor do we know precisely where and when the photograph was taken. There is an archival context though, which provides first clues: This image is part of the personal archives of Ernst Rudolf and Anneliese Scherz, who took numerous photographs in Namibia during a period spanning several decades. Within this collection, the photograph is among a group of images produced in the late 1930s and 1940s, presumably in central Namibia. On one hand, given the absence of further textual information relating to the photograph, the image remains suspended, arresting a fleeting, haphazard moment, which cannot be described as exceptional, if only because there is a second photograph depicting the same group of children in the collection. On the other hand, both the careful composition and aesthetic quality of this particular photograph and the material and visual context of the photographic archive – the fact that it features numerous portraits of African children – invite us to move away from the fleetingness of the moment and commonness of the everyday towards representation and signification, i.e. towards a meta-reading. Indeed, as much as the portrait of the boy remains linked to a singular event and therefore to a particular moment and site, it likewise appears as "a constellation of several histories"[3] that might speak, e.g. of children as subjects of colonial rule, of the fragility of bonds between infants and their parents and custodians, of the instability of their social worlds marked by residential and racial segregation, and of emotional registers authorising children's forced insertion into regimes of colonial state and missionary welfare.[4]

In what follows, we shall remain in the period addressed in the preceding chapter, the 1930s, 1940s and 1950s, but we will focus more specifically on Namibia, at the time the colonial hinterland of the South African segregationist and, after 1948, apartheid state. Chapter 2 discussed photographs produced and circulated in the context of individual and collective classification, and the control of mobility across and beyond the South African territory as part of a larger project of racial mapping. While our concern there was primarily with the photographic image and medium's use in the administrative or official realm, here we will shift attention towards private photographic collections, and hence pursue different avenues of image production and reception. However, as we shall see, the photographs to be discussed remain part of the same visual landscape deeply marked by the politics of racial segregation in mid-twentieth-century South Africa and Namibia. This is undoubtedly the case for the E.R. and A. Scherz collection, which we will consider more carefully in a moment. But first, we will have to explicate how the problem of the photographic moment, touched upon in the above reflection on Figure 3.1, helps frame the questions guiding the subsequent discussion.

The point of departure is a simple one and takes us back to the "burden of the moment". What is this "burden" in relation to a photograph? Does the photograph, as the scholarship likes to suggest, reiterate *but* a moment,

Figure 3.1 Untitled photograph, n.d.[5]

a fragment of time, an elusive, ephemeral, even trivial instant, what Benjamin calls the "tiny spark of contingency" and the "here and now",[6] the coincidence of what happens to be in front of the camera at the moment between the shutter's opening and closing?[7] Or is the moment in and of photography, instead, the freezing of time, since the photograph extracts a *particular* moment from the undifferentiated temporal flow, turning it into something significant, decisive, momentous,[8] and, by virtue of its material and visual persistence, extends beyond itself and becomes a monument – or as Barthes would have it, the past re-enacted as memory?[9] How does the photograph transform the moment it captures, and what is the temporality of the transfiguration? How is the transformation acted out, and what are its historical effects? How are photographic moments historically situated and lodged in notions of time and temporality? How are they, if we echo Reinhard Koselleck's intricate notion of historical time, placed in specific spaces of experience and on particular horizons of expectation?[10] Finally, and in view of the historical context addressed here, what does an inquiry into "the moment" in Namibian photographs from the 1930s and 1940s tell us about photography, time, and history? How, in other words, do *specific* photographs work through the problem of the moment and momentousness in relation to historical representation?

The heading of this chapter – *Augenblick* – points to the way in which we might begin to attend to these questions, while keeping in mind some of the affiliated concepts that cluster around the division and ordering of time, before we inquire what these concepts offer for a reading of historical photographs from Namibia. While moment, instant, and Augenblick are often used interchangeably to simply denote a short unit of time, Balibar et al. take us through some of the more intricate linguistic, semantic, and philosophical differentiations that concern the specific meanings and connotations these terms carry once they are brought in relation to each other.[11] The authors retrace how classical rhetoric establishes a distinction between a *tempus generalis* or *khronos*, which concerns the regular flow of historical time and allows for measurement and dating, and a *tempus speciale* or *kairos*, which describes indeterminable time and can refer to periodical recurrence, unpredictable occurrence, a propitious moment, or a moment of decision and good action in terms of *occasio* or *tempus opportunitatem*.[12] The distinction serves as conceptual ground on which modern philosophical thought develops an existential concept of Augenblick underpinned by *kairos*, asserting that while in the everyday experience of the world, in the ordinary course of life, a moment is just another instant in the flow of time, Augenblick comes to describe an experience which is elevated from ordinary, everyday temporality and takes on particular significance.[13] Literally the "blink of an eye", Augenblick metaphorically serves to express knowing and understanding through the language of the embodied act of seeing, the swift opening and closing of the blink – sight becomes insight, the moment of vision one of revealing.[14] But this kind of knowing and understanding is, more specifically, premised on a moment of crisis and collusion, and one of the recurring aspects of Augenblick that arises in existential philosophy is a concern precisely with the crisis of human existence, a concern that results in a marked disposition towards eschatological or apocalyptic thinking.[15] It is against this backdrop that Augenblick holds the possibility of exposing the limitations of contemporary modes of being, of the basic historical condition of human existence, and thereby opens the temporal being to a field of new possibilities by the suspension of the existing order of things.[16]

Significantly, this kind of opening and inhabiting of Augenblick as a moment of vision and revelation seems available, at least implicitly as Suvi Alt has noted, to but a few, and indeed requires the presence of an exceptional, visionary individual.[17] Remarkably enough, it is the idea of the visionary subject as "the right man in the right time"[18] that has found clearest correspondence in the modernist fetishisation of the photographer's eye and the notion of the "decisive image", most prominently associated with the photographs and writings of Henri Cartier-Bresson.[19] Originally published as *Images à la Sauvette* (1952, literally "images on the run"), Cartier-Bresson's notion of the decisive moment concerned both what was in the image and the moment of photographic capture. Augenblick here describes the heightened awareness of the photographer, his or her "authentic" encounter with an event, and the production of an image that would reveal "a moment come to presence", an actualisation, a now that is not simply a matter of time, but something underlying the ordinary surface of everyday appearances. Yet, as Roberts has rightfully argued, the desire to "get the decisive moment right" tends to foreground an unproblematic relationship between the photograph and the event as a moment of historical disclosure, failing to explain what constitutes the event in the first place – that is, both historically and photographically, how the event is historicised and brought to visibility, and how photography positions itself in relation to the temporality of an event.[20]

The following discussion of historical photographs from Namibia builds on these critical inquiries into photography's relationship to the representation of the event as a form of historical knowledge and explores the kind of analytical work "moment" and "Augenblick" might do here. While acknowledging that Augenblick can denote an existential moment that concerns the very condition of being, it is nevertheless not disconnected from the historical situation. Hence, adopting a less subjectivised, more relational, and historical perspective will enable us to pay attention to Augenblick as a moment and site of photographic transformation, and interrogate the photograph's implication not only in the arresting, freezing, or interrupting of the flow of time, but also in its function as a passage or threshold, i.e. in terms of a transfiguration of the moment into a spatio-temporal arrangement.[21] As in the earlier chapters, here we will again have to attend to the ways in which we encounter particular historical photographs in the archive, how the archive shapes the notion of historical event and establishes hierarchies in the photographic mediation of what comes to constitute a moment and Augenblick in and of history.[22] As we shall see, there will be no unity or consistency, and the diversity of photographic practices will inevitably and productively evidence diverse sensibilities towards the problem of time and the temporality of the photographic moment.

The moment in and of photography – images from the A & E.R. Scherz collection

Let us move back then to the abovementioned Scherz collection, which is part of a personal archive that assembles photographs, correspondence, and manuscripts authored by Ernst Rudolf Scherz and his wife Anneliese, and covers a period of several decades beginning in the 1930s and reaching into the 1970s.[23] The Scherz photographs are situated in the domain of German cultural work in Namibia that began in the interwar period, and more specifically the field of semi-professional visual production and writing, in which sections of the wider settler community, individuals of diverse ethnic descent, social standing, and political *couleur*, showed a growing preoccupation with establishing niches of intellectual engagement and knowledge production that drew on South African as well as metropolitan culture.[24] As we shall see, once we consider settler photography from this period more generally, the Scherz photographs are quite in line with the broader image economy, in terms of both genres and subjects chosen for photographic documentation.[25]

But since we will look at a very particular part of their collection and a specific moment in time, namely the late 1930s, when Anneliese moved to Namibia to join her husband there, the photographs discussed here need to be situated against the backdrop of a more specific historical situation and understood as one expression of particular aesthetic sensibilities among German-speaking immigrants to the colony.

The late 1930s were a period of crisis and collusion, in colonial Southern Africa as much as in the European metropoles; in particular, the growing war threat as well as the spread of National Socialism was deeply felt across the sub-continent.[26] In Namibia, a South African mandate and de facto colony since 1915, international turmoil ripped across a complicated political and ideological landscape in which South African settler society, divided by antagonist imperial, national, and ethnic affinities, was in the process of renegotiating the nature and texture of a crumbling category of whiteness. The brittleness of white cohesion was not new, though, as it had haunted the South African nation state since its constitution with Union in 1910 and the subsequent attempt to establish itself as a "white man's land".[27] While intra-white conflict had been predominantly understood as a symptom of British-Boer antagonism, an unresolved tension between British imperial interest and Afrikaner nationalism, political anxiety and sensibility shifted by the late 1920s as the South African administration took into account the antagonism it faced from a significant section of South West African settler society – i.e. those of German descent.

What caused particular concern here was the possibility of settler alignment with fascism, since the interwar period had seen a process of considerable German ethno-national revival, partly caused by a growing sense of sociopolitical erosion and cultural marginalisation, and intensifying competition between Afrikaner and German settlers over land.[28] Also, after 1933, fascist propaganda in Namibia adopted more aggressive tones, and South African concerns over the "smooth functioning of the mandate" increased accordingly.[29] Settlers of German descent had indeed long wavered between assimilation into the South African racial fabric of whiteness and a retreat into a politics of reified ethnicity based on *Deutschtum*.[30] These tensions intensified once growing Afrikaner nationalism and talk of South West Africa's inclusion into South Africa as a fifth province threatened to bury German colonial revisionist desires and hopes for the colony's return to its "true motherland".[31] While critical voices could be heard among those who called into question the alignment with European imperial interests of any colour and orientation, and instead insisted on the colony's self-determination,[32] far-right ideas very compatible with the emerging National Socialist notion of a master race and "blood and soil ideology" were cherished by many members of white Southern African society at the time. In fact, the South African United Party government under J.B.M Hertzog showed persistent difficulties in adopting a clear position in view of the fascist threat, and at the outbreak of the Second World War, Afrikaner nationalist demands for neutrality almost foreclosed South African alignment with Britain in the war effort against the Third Reich.[33]

African perspectives, of course, were different. We know of a range of political organisations on the left, such as the All-African Convention founded in South Africa in 1935, and of numerous African intellectuals in the diaspora who sought to mobilise against fascism and linked African support for the Allied cause to the demand for decolonisation and liberation. But everyday responses to imperial competition, ethnic nationalism, and intra-white conflict, let alone the threat of fascism in Namibia, remain largely unstudied.[34] Also, there were challenges faced on the ground. African societies had undergone a profound transformation in the first two decades of South African occupation. In contrast to the period of German colonial administration, the entire Namibian territory had been brought under military and administrative control by the early 1920s.[35] The South African authority's main interest had been in securing further land for settlers and in establishing a system of indirect rule in northern Namibia that would guarantee the continuation of migrant labour recruitment in support of the commercial farming and mining economies.[36] A systematic policy of segregation provided for small, marginal reserves set aside for the African population within the Police Zone (i.e. in central and southern Namibia), while the northern territories, where most people lived, were divided into consolidated native reserves.[37] Urban areas were likewise segregated along racial and ethnic lines, and Africans accordingly relegated to locations on the periphery of cities and towns.[38] Additionally, a barrage of legislation delineated the conditions of black mobility between reserves, farms, and urban areas, and forced removals of entire populations throughout the 1920s and 1930s became an integral part of colonial containment strategies.[39] While administration remained weak, and limited policing provided loopholes, by the 1930s, the South African authorities began to impose more systematic and rigorous control on its Namibian colony.[40] The tightened administrative grip on people and lands, and the drive towards economic isolation and retribalisation in the reserves brought far-reaching social changes, particularly once the structural decline in the wake of the depression, and a series of severe droughts in the early 1930s largely eroded African prospects for sustainable economic and social reproduction.[41] Access to wage labour, for example, which had become an important strategy in accumulating livestock and social capital and in countering famine, declined dramatically, and numbers of recruited migrant workers dropped from more than 6000 in 1928 to only a few hundred in 1932.[42] Only towards the end of the decade would there be signs of recovery, and mainly in the colonial economy, with mining gradually recuperating and white settlement steadily resuming in the Police Zone in 1937.[43]

This is, in short, the context in which the Scherz couple began their photographic work in Namibia. As we shall see, the landscape they traversed remained marked by the difficult political climate and the aftermath of the socioeconomic transformation sketched out above. More specifically, their photographic response to the Namibian environment would articulate itself in an idiosyncratic photographic mediation of two contemporary issues: the fragility of the category of whiteness and the presence of the "black" in the colony, i.e. what came to be known as "the native question".[44] The pre-occupation with *whiteness* and *the native* seemed to reveal something about the very condition of being and its complicated historical grounding.

A group of Scherz photographs from the late 1930s circles around the space and subject matter of farm life. The fact that Anneliese Scherz was in the process of relocating from Germany to South West Africa, and once in the colony, joined her husband on their honeymoon during 1938, explains why this part of the Scherz collection seems to encourage a reading of these pho-tographs within the domain of the personal and familial and is bound up with an intrinsic politics of sentiment.[45] This is all the more so since most of these early images were never published nor were they ever intended for public viewing or broader circulation.[46] However, as I will try to show in a moment, the photographs nevertheless prove suggestive of the intricacies involved in drawing an aesthetic line between the private and the public, the individual and the social – and ultimately the specific and the typical – particularly if read against the backdrop of an uncertain and heated political climate.

Figure 3.2 is an example from a series of portraits, photographs of farm inte-riors, and everyday objects taken during the 1938 honeymoon, many of which reveal an aesthetic sensibility treating the family as an emotional space enshrined in transgenerational solidarity, personal affection, and intimate sociality.

Figure 3.2 Untitled photograph, 1938.[47]

This image illustrates how the Scherz portraits work through the problem of *the moment* and *Augenblick* discussed at the beginning of this chapter. At one level, there is a particular moment captured in this photograph, which is one of ease and serenity, of a man in work wear, interrupting his farming duties, and retreating to the cooling shade of the porch, smoking his pipe, gently holding a child in his lap, and visibly feeling comfortable. Softly lit, the photograph enhances the beauty of the situation – of *a* father lovingly attending to *his* child – while concurrently evoking generic sentimental registers associated with the photographic trope of parental love.[48] While the man, like many of the photographic subjects in this group of images, remains unidentified, the Scherz photographs introduce us to individuals, particular men and women, who inhabit the privacy and intimacy of their families and farm worlds, and who appear relaxed, smiling, enjoying the rare moments of rest, the pleasure of a shared meal – while also introducing us to the poetics of photographic contemplation. When we keep in mind that the Scherz couple had recently arrived in Namibia, and Anneliese had before moved among cosmopolitan photographers and artists in a Europe that was by then about to enter a disastrous period of war and fascist terror, the 1938 farm portraits and scenes appear as a photographic homage to the *pastoral*, to the simplicity and beauty of the rural. They display a visual valorisation of a primordial spatiality and temporality embedded in farm work and domestic life that required the camera to approach the photographic subjects and the sites of physical and emotional recovery with appreciation and respect. While the focus on the familial and transgenerational cohabitation possibly emanated in part from a romantic anticipation of what the future might have held for the newlyweds, the honeymoon photographs clearly inserted themselves into longer and wider trajectories of aestheticising farm life and its configuration as a sentimentally charged imaginary.[49]

Yet, there is another, different moment foreshadowed in this photograph, one that concerned the before-mentioned positionality of the German-speaking settler community in relation to the political perturbations that undermined white cohesion in the colony at the time, particularly because of the persistence of fascist sentiment among Southern African whites in the late 1930s.[50] Keeping in mind the contemporary photographic economy, the question of the ideological alignment of German settlers in Namibia had by then passed through a series of visual mediations, most importantly in the domain of German colonial revisionism and national-socialist propaganda.[51] Within these ideological imaginaries, photographs of German settler life, especially those taken on farms, were used to signify the actuality of *Deutschtum*, the values of communal and family life often embodied by German women, the maintenance of racial purity, and – in an audacious gesture towards revisionist amnesia – the peacefulness of the relations with a sympathetic colonised subject population.[52] Placed against this visual backdrop, the Scherz portraits clearly chose a different, more careful tone and gaze, one that deliberately shunned the limelight of abrasive ideology. It seems plausible then to assume that the privacy and intimacy in the framings of farm and family life, the beauty of the portraits that individualised their subjects, *and* the archival seclusion of this particular group of images in the Scherz collection aesthetically and materially eluded an overt absorption into the political hegemony of late-1930s propaganda. It was indeed the moment as *Augenblick* rather than as monument, which asserted itself in the portraits,[53] whose aesthetic language described the German-speaking farmer community neither as an abstract category composed of individual types, nor as an essentialised register for the articulation of political, i.e. fascist subjectivity, but as an historically situated and visually receding social milieu, in which to quietly fathom the intimacy and privacy of individual positionality. In this sense, the photographic Augenblick here emerged as what we might call a *visuality of retreat*; as a visual articulation of the interiority and subjectivity of space and time that served as a counter-narrative to the exteriority and objectification of much more vociferous ethnic-nationalist and national-socialist visualities.

Still, one does come across images that reveal the photographic collection's more venturous openings towards the public, political, and ideological. One of these openings is provided by a series labelled "Boers on the move", in which the camera left the farmhouse and its immediate surroundings and moved into the open *veld*.[54] The labelling of the photographs included in this group was quite suggestive of situating the subjects and scenes depicted in the images within a particular sociocultural and important political and ideological frame – Afrikaner nationalism. As shown in Figure 3.3a–c, the photographs of Afrikaans-speaking rural dwellers, or *bywoners*, brought into focus the subjects and objects of a nomadic lifestyle shadowed out by household utensils clumsily placed in the open and embodied by women performing domestic work under unfavourable environmental conditions.[55] Selected material markers of the *trek,* among them ox-wagons, horses, and female garb, further specified the vernacular iconography of Afrikaner historical mythology and folklore.[56] And it is precisely thanks to that particular historical imagination that these photographs, once placed on the historical horizon of Afrikaner rootedness in the land, harboured monumentalising effects.

An important context for discussion here was the contemporary debate on "poor whites", which had become a key theme in the political and ideological fabrication of a consolidated white identity in South Africa.[57] While the trope of "poor white-ism" did operate in the Namibian colony as well, it largely crumbled along the fault lines of a frail white solidarity – one marked, throughout the 1930s, by the pointed rivalry over land between settlers of German descent and Afrikaner immigrants, exacerbated by significant Boer influx to the colony since the mid-1920s.[58] It remains unclear if and to what extent the Scherzes were familiar with the trope of "poor white-ism", or the wider photographic discourse that the poverty and vulnerability among white settlers and farming communities had produced in Southern Africa and – perhaps more prominently – the United States (US). In any case, the "Boers on the move" series unquestionably shares

(a)

(b)

Figure 3.3 (a, b & c) Boers on the move, 1938.[59]   (*Continued*)

(c)

Figure 3.3 (Continued)

representational and aesthetic characteristics with photographs commissioned by both the South African Carnegie Commission of 1932 and the Farm Security Administration in the 1930s and 1940s in the US.[60] While these photographic precedents and analogues might shape the ways in which the Scherz photographs from this series can be contextualised historically,[61] we should nevertheless attend to the specificity of their distinct photographic approach to the question of the Afrikaner lifeworld in Namibia at that time. Their images elude an unambiguous alignment with any ideological position available in the complicated political situation described above, and – aside from the archival labelling of the series – there is no textual evidence pointing towards a clear political agenda that the Scherzes would have pursued at the time. While the relationship between photography and ideology is generally a complicated one – neither uncontested nor self-evident – it seems unjustifiable to read the Scherz photographs in terms of an explicit programmatic orientation towards a politics of ethnic difference that fostered anti-Afrikaner sentiment and/or partisan articulations of Germanness.[62] This is not to say that these photographs did not resonate with the political – they did, albeit in complicated ways.

In order to substantiate this argument, we should pay attention to what the camera captured, to the apparent photographic focus on the material – namely the objects, fabrics, and sites of the nomadic – and inquire what precisely this materiality would have referenced and what kind of historical imagination it would have evoked. In fact, the question of lifestyles and living standards, based on permanent settlement and meticulously defined requirements for housing, had become normative for a generic notion of "being white" in Namibia and South Africa in the 1930s.[63] It was this particular materiality of whiteness that endowed the "Boers on the move" series with the quality of what could be called a *visual philanthropy*; one that proved sensitive to the everyday, conceived of as a temporal framework in which any moment in the ordinary course of Afrikaner life would reveal something about the essence of what it meant to be white, particularly under adverse conditions, and would hence invite the viewer's empathy. Here lay the key transformative labour of the "Boers on the move" photographs, in that they situated the moments captured not in the signifying idiom of an evident politics of ethnic essentialism, but in an aesthetic register that testified to white solidarity while it concurrently eclipsed its parasitic dependence on the colonial racial order.[64] Ultimately, that is what the "Boers on the move" series unintentionally reminds us of, the photographic subject inhabiting this Augenblick as an interruption, a suspension, an opening: certainly the Afrikaner woman, but much more so the marginalised figure of the black worker, her and especially his ghostly appearance recurring throughout the series (see, e.g., Figure 3.3a).

Let us then move on to this second issue, the presence of the native, and inquire how the Scherz photographs speak to the colonial racial order as both a space of experience and a framework of photographic expression, while keeping in mind that the sedimentation of race at the level of the visual and, if at all, the single image remains problematic.[65] As argued earlier on, the political turmoil lurking on the colony's horizon – the tension between ethnic sectarianism and white cohesion – seems to have given cause for caution in analysing the Scherzes' photographic reflection of "whiteness". But what was its bearing – if any – on the camera's framing of "blackness"?

The figure of the "black labourer" in the collection emerged first while the camera wandered around farms and, keeping a notable distance, captured unidentified, solitary women washing linen or fetching water, and men cleaning shoes or stowing away tools and appliances.[66] The workers' presence in the photographs is a silent and unobtrusive one, inserting itself almost naturally into the physical environment of farm life. But the impression is deceiving, since farm labour in the 1920s and 1930s was anything but a simple or stable matter, but determined by tightening colonial native policy and legislation and the volatility of economic developments recurrently affecting the agricultural sector.[67] Once South Africa had secured a permanent mandate for the Namibian colony in 1921, the state's main interest lay in providing cheap labour for the public sector, the mining industry, and settler farming, and controlling the distribution of the workforce between these.

The establishment of native reserves, taxation, master and servant and vagrancy laws, pass regulations, and even the penal system were all geared towards binding the African population to more or less compulsory labour service.[68] While in the Police Zone, workers would often negotiate labour agreements with farmers in ways that allowed families to stay together, keep their livestock, and secure access to grazing – claims they could successfully assert in periods of acute labour shortage and in view of the financial weakness of many farm owners in the late 1920s and early 1930s[69] – migrant workers from the northern reserves situated beyond the Police Zone boundary were subjected to contracts that targeted single men, fixed wages and the period of employment, and imposed the obligation to return to the reserve once the contract expired.[70] The period of sustained economic growth in the late 1930s and early 1940s, which rested heavily on agriculture and on the karakul sheep boom in particular, significantly shifted the parameters of farm labour and dramatically transformed the composition of the workforce on farms.[71] Regulations regarding the numbers of male workers to be employed on farms were imposed more strictly,[72] and the farming economy became the main recipient of migrant labour, ousting the mining sector as most competitive recruiter by 1935.[73] Labour conditions deteriorated accordingly, and primitive accommodation (if any), long hours, minimal sustenance, and almost complete isolation that exposed farm workers to physical exploitation and mistreatment was common throughout.[74]

It is against this backdrop that we have to consider the Scherz photographs of farm workers, among them Figure 3.4. In this image, taken on farm Haribes in southern Namibia in 1938, we look at a group of women, children, and one man who had lined up in front of the Scherzes' camera. There is an oppressing quality to the way in which this photograph exposes the vulnerability of the black subject's positioning, and the little girl's marvel at the scene proves to be the image's arresting detail, its intriguing *punctum*.[75] Keeping in mind the rationale of farm labour recruitment and, given the composition of the group in the image, its differentiating and corroborating effects in relation to age and gender, this photograph moved onto sensitive terrain, as if deliberately seeking a problematic ambiguity in signification. As mentioned before, the labour regimes in Namibia in the late 1930s treated men as primary workers and, accordingly, relegated women and children to a secondary role with uncertain legal status, no or limited eligibility for payment in cash and, hence, greater dependence on black men and white employers.[76] Yet, the photograph might have evoked a different register as well, one that assumed promiscuity, polygamy, and an abundance of children to be a generic feature of African kinship and social life.[77] These potential evocations become more evident once we consider the archival proximity of Figure 3.4 to the portraits of German farmer families and, more importantly, the "Boers on the move series", where it ultimately simply denotes the poverty and precariousness of colonial servitude and raises the question of if and how these *"other" poor* figured in the visual philanthropy described above. In light of the historical

Figure 3.4 Farmworkers at Haribes, 1938.[78]

continuum of African servitude in colonial Namibia, we have to ask if and how the Scherz collection addressed "black poverty" captured in a photographic moment in a way that allowed for *blackness as vulnerability* to emerge as a shared status with whiteness and, accordingly, invited the viewer's empathic response.[79] While this possibility is lodged in the photograph itself, it seems foreclosed by the ideological and photographic placing, i.e. under a colonial regime that assumed that Africans existed chiefly to serve as labour *and* on the farm as a constitutive site of a colonial economy, in which empathy ran against the fact that – for the "black subject" – labour was the only way out of the poverty it had produced in the first place. The photographic site burdened the image even further, since the photograph helped fix its subjects, the women, children, and one man, *on the farm* and, more specifically, in the space and time of an agricultural labour regime, thereby working against the importance of African agency: men and women's reluctance to perform farm labour in the first place, given that it was often taken only as a last resort, and the prevalence of desertions, breaches of contract, escapes, or forms of life and subsistence that remained beyond the colonial farming economy.[80]

We might nevertheless have to give the Scherzes the benefit of the doubt and consider the possibility of a moment of catharsis, an Augenblick of photography that might have alleviated the ethical malaise in seeing the "black subject" through the social rank of whiteness; one that was held available in the imag(in)ing of the "native".[81]

Before taking a closer look at Figure 3.5, we should consider the Scherzes' late 1930s photography of "native people" against the range of contemporary images produced of Africans in Namibia at the time, particularly those authored by members of the settler community. Here, the field of ethnographic photography had begun to gain traction since the mid-1920s, even if it remained weak and widely dependent on either work of amateurs and missionaries, pseudo-scientific production of colonial officials and bureaucrats, or the unsteady yields of tourist photography that remained in its very early stages.[82] In very general terms, ethnographic conventions and their photographic expression tended to be charged with settler anxiety about African detribalisation caused by cultural and racial mixing, high mobility, socio-economic transformation, and growing urbanisation.[83] These preoccupations were countered with a pointed visual inclination towards the "tribal", or "native picturesque", and the discursive relegation of Africans beyond the domain of history to the one of culture.[84] A significant publication from the interwar period was *The Native Tribes of South West Africa* (1928), a co-edited volume, which gathered the writings and photographs of Rhenish missionary Heinrich Vedder, the native commissioner of Ovamboland C.H.L. Hahn, and the medical officer to the administration Louis Fourie.[85] Vedder's and Hahn's work in particular had huge implications for the objectification

Figure 3.5 Landscape, 1930s.[86]

of black subjects and the shaping of ethnic constructions in Namibia in the first half of the twentieth century,[87] as much as it nurtured both white settler mythologies and a deeply ingrained confidence in knowledge of "the native" among whites.[88] But, as scholars of Namibian visual history have rightly noted, "one of the most enduring tenets of colonial photography seems to be that when colonial officials, settlers, and outsiders took photographs of the colonised, this constituted ethnography", and "when white men (or women) took pictures of themselves, this was something different. It was personal, biographical [...]".[89] The Scherz collection clearly challenges these assumptions, and it complicates a neat distinction between ethnographies of the black and biographies of whites. Indeed, assuming that ethnographic photography's fiction was the direct encounter between the camera and the photographic subject, and concurrently the desire to conceal photographic mediation in order to enable a direct encounter between the viewer and those depicted in an image,[90] Figure 3.5 does hardly qualify as ethnographic. Instead, the genre and aesthetic convention through which this photograph mediated the presence of "the native" was rather another one – namely landscape.

Our reflection on this photograph shall proceed from three questions: How exactly does this landscape photograph mediate the presence of the native? What kind of moment does the camera capture? And what is the relationship of the photographic moment to landscape? But let us look at the image first: we are taken to the Atlantic coast and probably into the vicinity of the coastal town of Swakopmund. We see two backlit women, one with a baby on her back, and a man walking along the coast towards the town, carrying wood, and their basic belongings. The figures are surrounded by an expansive desert, which is delicately circumscribed by the receding ocean on the left and the hazy contours of Swakopmund emerging on the horizon. This is a highly atmospheric picture, by virtue of the photographer's sophisticated *mise-en-scène*, with its evocation of ambience – the texture of the sandy shore, the intense light and fleeting shadows, and the elegance of the moving figures, whose depiction in the image seems ambiguous, strangely reminiscent of animal portraiture.[91] The real protagonist of this framing and staging, though, is the desert, expanses of sand that bind every place, object, and body in the image within a single horizon of a present moment, thereby establishing a sense of cohesiveness and coevalness.[92] Seen from this angle and recalling the political tensions within the settler community at the time, Figure 3.5 was, again, quite in line with photographic representations and imaginaries in the 1930s, a significant part of which precisely strove to ground an inclusive, non-partisan notion of whiteness in a particular perception of and disposition towards the Namibian landscape, one that liked to represent Africans as bearers of culture *and* as part of the natural environment.[93] But we should look more carefully and take time to contemplate this image and the specificities of it being a landscape photograph. Though it is not clear what kind of camera equipment the Scherzes used at this point,[94] the image was taken while the photographer kept a certain distance, one that prevented him or her from casting a close eye on the photographic subjects and instead enabled a panoramic view of the scene. But, since viewers are concurrently kept at a distance, what kind of photographic moment are we confronted with? In other words, what kind of event of photography was this, since there seems to have been no (perceivable) interaction between the camera and those photographed, as if the photographer refused to move into the space of "the landscape's lived parameters",[95] and the photographic subjects ostensibly ignored the operation behind their backs? Finally, why would this non-encounter and non-event nevertheless result in the production of a photograph?[96]

The observations just offered rest upon a notion of landscape as a cultural construction, a cognitive or symbolic order, one that is deeply imbedded in histories of imperialism and colonialism. In line with this, W.T.J. Mitchell proposed an understanding of landscape as "social hieroglyph", as emblem of the social relations it conceals,[97] a formulation that will help us historicise the distance kept by the Scherzes' camera. Does landscape prescribe distance, and if so, how does this affect our reading of landscape photographs as historical documents? As much as "keeping a distance" might have been a matter of aesthetic concern and sensibility, one that required the photographer to place him/herself in the position of an external observer with a single, sovereign point of view, we need to keep in mind that distance was as much determined by the colonial situation and racial segregation, both of which defined the contingencies and character of and, especially, the restrictions to social interaction between white settlers, photographers included, and colonised subjects, in and beyond the photographic event.[98] Placed alongside the images of farmworkers produced by the Scherz couple, where interracial interaction was moulded by the rationale of an exploitive farming economy, the terms of the social encounter between them and the wayfarers on the shoreline seemed less evident. The camera was, indeed, moving towards a potential threshold, without ever crossing it; this landscape, charged with the tensions in the encounter between black and white, was much more ambiguous than its eventual photographic representation would suggest.

But there is something else, a further visibility in this photograph, which is most likely to catch the viewer's attention and takes us back to the texture of the desert depicted in the image, or specifically to the uncountable footprints and tracks highlighted by the camera. These traces of previous human and animal passage and the tracks indicating the circulation of carts or, possibly, motor vehicles along the coast evidence longer trajectories of movement and mobility across the Namibian environment.[99] The tracks and prints, hence, constitute visual clues to a different understanding of landscape – not as a picture of imagination, not as a representation or ordering of nature, but constituted *temporally*, as an enduring record of the lives and works of those who have and continue to dwell in it.[100] If we pursue this line of thought, what exactly is this landscape, and what is its temporality in this particular photographic reproduction?

The traces and tracks tell us something about this, and they offer a compelling visual entry point to some of the histories lodged in Figure 3.5. Thinking about landscape and temporality, and their mutually constitutive relation, Tim Ingold has pointed to the ways in which "paths and tracks impose a habitual pattern on the movement of people, and yet they also arise out of that movement, for every path or track shows up as the accumulated imprint of countless journeys that people have made – with or without their vehicles or domestic animals – as they have gone about their everyday business. Thus the same movement is embodied, on the side of the people, in their 'muscular consciousness', and on the side of the landscape, in its network of paths and tracks".[101] Translating these considerations to the particular moment depicted in the Scherz photograph and to the political geographies of late 1930s Namibia, we are reminded of the limitations and constraints imposed on African mobility, entrenched as it was in residential segregation, and the time regime regulating African presence and employment in and around urban centres.[102] Still, the presence of the man and the two women in the image, as temporary and restricted as it might have been, constituted a performative act – one among many, the tracks tell us, that constituted the form and shape of the landscape and, being part of a history of moving bodies, qualified its temporality as an essentially social one.[103]

Understanding the Namibian shoreline in this way, i.e. as an environment constituted by the agencies of those who inhabited and traversed it, might require us to revisit the moment of this photograph and its earlier qualification as a non-event, given that the three figures in the image and the photographer's presence behind the camera would always point to a space of social interaction, if only a ruptured one. This is why Figure 3.5 invites us to consider how the photographic subjects, kept at a distance, first and foremost attended *to one another*: as viewers of this photograph we can only see them, they were themselves engaged in acts of looking, while orienting themselves, gazing towards the ocean, watching the tide, or looking out towards the town of Swakopmund in order to observe if someone would come towards them, if there was activity in and around the town, or if there was trouble or danger looming on the horizon.[104] It is their movement through this sensitive landscape, inevitably a space of colonial policing and surveillance, their eyes scanning the terrain, and perhaps even sensing the presence of the photographers behind their backs, which were constitutive of and essential to the world they were living in. It is, in other words and as way of closing our reflections on the Scherz collection, the moment of the African subjects' presence leaving its visual trace and therefore providing an opening to the photograph's *Augenblick*.

In what follows, we will continue to investigate the question of landscape and time further, as we need to be more precise about its manifestation across diverse photographic practices in Namibia in the period before and after the Second World War, particularly those that are considered ostensibly different from each other. While the Scherz photographs discussed so far focused on

Namibia's rural and coastal areas, the collections, which will be of interest to us now, take us into a different landscape, namely the urban milieu, and *the location* more specifically.[105] This will enable us to explore more carefully, how – echoing Ingold's argument – Africans shaped the environment they lived in and how moments of photographic encounters *among* Africans became constitutive of possibly different understandings of landscape and the visual mediation of its intricate temporality.

Entr'acte – sighting the African location

There is need for a parenthesis here, one that will help us more carefully make the transition from the Scherz photographs to African photographic encounters and to the location as a particular space of photography in 1930s and 1940s Namibia. To this end, our interim visual companion is an image taken by Ottilie Nitzsche-Reiter, a Windhoek-based photographer of German descent.[106]

Nitzsche-Reiter's photographic work has received some attention in the Namibian public and scholarship, especially the series of photographs she took in locations in Windhoek and, less frequently, other African urban residential areas between the 1940s and 1960s.[107] Considered to aspire towards social engagement photography, even if only unassertively,[108] Nitzsche-Reiter's images have increasingly been valued as exceptional historical evidence for African urbanisation in that period, and for their strenuous efforts to sustain social and cultural life among black Namibian communities affected by residential segregation and apartheid urban planning.[109] While she became one of the most commercially successful photographers in Namibia, her international and artistic reputation was and remains much less established.[110] But notwithstanding her undeniable provincialism, Nitzsche-Reiter's location photographs could have earned her a plausible place alongside contemporary white documentary photographers covering township life in South Africa, such as Ellen Hellmann, Bryan Heseltine, and Constance Stuart Larrabee.[111]

Figure 3.6 is an example that illustrates Nietzsche-Reiter's photographic coverage of African urban residential areas as both built and social environments. Her location photographs cover a diverse range of subjects and genres, but they tend to focus on street views, houses, public buildings, and churches,[112] and cluster around a few social events such as weddings, dances, and fashion shows,[113] on the occasion of which Nitzsche-Reiter succeeded in producing a series of quite remarkable portraits, some of which stand out thanks to their particular aesthetic quality.[114] The image reproduced here was taken in the African location in Usakos, a small town on the margin of the Namib desert in central Namibia, located between the capital of Windhoek and the coastal town of Swakopmund. The photograph shows a group of women and one child, most of them seated, in front of a typical location house built of flattened oil drums and other makeshift construction materials. A solitary goat has joined the group and baffles viewers with its curiosity

Figure 3.6 Usakos location, n.d.[115]

for the camera. Originally captioned as "Natives: Damaras, Usakos location", the image was part of a series depicting African women, usually in
Windhoek and sometimes in other central Namibian towns.[116] Here, as was
the case with many of Nitzsche-Reiter's location photographs, the encounter
between the photographer and the photographic subjects had been mediated
by members of the Rhenish Mission Society, an instance that reminds us –
as was the case for the Scherz photographs – that social interaction between
black and white was at the time subject to restrictions and a sensitive matter, especially once it took place in segregated African residential areas.[117]
Obviously, Nitzsche-Reiter and the women photographed did not inhabit
the same material, social, and cultural worlds, nor would they ever share the
same photographic frame; their encounter remained exceptional and limited
to a fleeting moment, their roles prescribed by the photographic event, their
relationship marked by distance and inequality. Given these limitations, and
bringing to mind that the women were unnamed and the precise location
and time of the photographic encounter unspecified – in short, that there
was a deliberate concealment of context – we seem required to qualify this
photograph and the location images more generally, as extrinsic, pertaining
less to the location world than to settler imaginaries of African urban life and
the desire for its visual containment.[118]

Within these, the focus on women was significant. While missionary
mediation and the gendered pattern of labour migration might have served
as an everyday explanation for the frequent absence of men, particularly
young ones, from the photographic field, the predominant female presence

in the location photographs resonated with a growing concern with women in South African urban policies starting in the mid-1930s.[119] Against this backdrop, the relationship between image and world proved complicated, even on the surface, once, e.g. the camera shadowed the everyday objects of women's economic productivity. Obviously, the assortment of tins and kitchen utensils used for cooking, soap making, or beer brewing would have simply helped to visually emphasise domestic time and space and, hence, to fix women in specific understandings of traditional gender roles. But it also spoke to their social vulnerability under segregation and apartheid urban planning, since beer brewing in particular had increasingly been under sanction by the authorities and was used as a means to expel female residents from urban areas.[120]

However, Nitzsche-Reiter's location images referenced the undesirability of female urbanisation more explicitly, once she notoriously classified her photographs as native studies, regardless of image content or social occasion – a procedure that seems particularly disturbing in relation to the popular ball events and fashion shows.[121] Ethnic and racial captioning bespoke the classification inherent in the wider collection, i.e. one that fed into the unabated interest in ethnography and strove for a survey of "the tribes and people of South West Africa", even if it would never mature.[122] Quite in line with the post–Second World War commodification of "native culture",[123] Nitzsche-Reiter's location photographs ultimately belied social engagement photography, given that they remained fundamentally marked by an ambiguity constitutive of settler imaginaries at the time: as the photographs of women in the Windhoek and Usakos locations suggest, the visualisation of African urban life was whittled down to fragmented snapshots, photographic moments conceived of as programmatic thresholds that marked Africans' problematic transition away from (rural) culture to (urban) modernity, invoking the spectre of moral decay.[124] Women were seen to embody these idiosyncratic settler understandings of "native degeneration" in particular ways.[125] Yet, at the same time, the location was precisely the paradigmatic photographic site – the urban pendant to the farm – where white audiences could envision the inevitable progression of a colonial spatio-temporal regime: the enforcement and solidification of spatial segregation, and the entrenchment of African urban presence as an essentially transitory condition. Even if life in the locations across central Namibia between the 1930s and 1960s was in fact marked by fluidity and high mobility, of both men and women,[126] the fleetingness and shallowness of settler photography fostered a problematic aestheticisation, which eclipsed the reality of political disenfranchisement, economic precariousness, residential instability, and the constant threat of eviction. As we shall see, and as a way of closing our transition via Figure 3.6, the period of Nitzsche-Reiter's photographs coincided – though this is, to be sure, no coincidence – with the progressive destruction of the location in Usakos, as well as the one in Windhoek, and the forced removal of African residents to new townships further distanced from the white residential areas.[127] The "burden" of her photographs was indeed a heavy one – it was nothing less than the beginning of dreadful apartheid urban planning in Namibia.

The group of women photographed in front of a house in the Usakos location remains inaccessible to us, and we hardly recognise them as historical subjects who shaped the landscapes they lived in *or* as participants in a photographic event. In what follows, we will linger on in the streets of Usakos' former African neighbourhood, in order to understand how segregation and apartheid affected African photographic practices in an urban milieu. Were they different from the photography of the Scherz couple and Ottilie Nitzsche-Reiter? And if so – in what sense? In trying to reflect on these questions, we will return to the problem of moment and Augenblick in and of photography and explore how the moment builds up once the location's residents and black photographers appropriated the camera.

The space-time of Augenblick – the Usakos old location photographs

Thus far, this chapter has looked at private photographic collections from Namibia in the period between the 1930s and 1950s. Both the Scherz and Nitzsche-Reiter collections have at some point entered institutional archives, and their photographs have partly been digitised – instances which have facilitated their gradual consideration in academic research and their circulation and exhibition in public history initiatives.[128] These collections and their trajectories seem exemplary for the broader colonial photographic archive of Namibia, in which photographs produced by members of the settler community, colonial officials, and missionaries continue to make up the larger part of the archive's holdings and accordingly receive closer attention. While the archival fade-out of African photography was perhaps particularly severe in Southern African apartheid societies, it has nevertheless been identified as a lacuna in visual histories of the continent more generally.[129] Research and curatorial practices have increasingly explored ways of decentring the colonial archive, through critical revisions of its institutional, conceptual, and disciplinary grounding, and by expanding the latitude of visual images, photographic practices, subjects, and locations to be considered under the rubric of an extended and dynamic notion of an African photographic archive.[130] Private collections, particularly those that have remained beyond the public or institutional domain, have proved crucial here, for both enhancing our knowledge of African photographic practices and complicating received understandings of photography as a theoretically coherent and historically uniform object.[131]

We thus enter the realm of a reframed visual archive by turning to a body of historical photographs from Usakos, all of which belong to the private collections of four women residents of this central Namibian town.[132] Let me briefly describe the corpus at hand: Kept within larger personal archives, among a diverse assemblage of objects, written materials and a variety of images, a group of about 250 black-and-white photographs relates to what has come to be known as the *Usakos old location*. The photographs vary in size and style, and they are printed on different papers and in various formats. Most often stored in cardboard boxes and tin cans, and sometimes in plastic bags or leather handbags, they have occasionally been placed in file folders or in more elegant leather albums. Many of the images feature traces of frequent use – residues of adhesive tapes, scratches, tattered margins, pinholes – and signs of decay are visible all over.[133] As is often the case with private collections, their materiality points to intricate patterns of handling and circulation, moments of image exchange and display, as photographs were enclosed in letters sent to family and friends, placed in frames or displayed in cabinets and on walls, and eventually stored away, temporarily or possibly for good, inserted individually in envelopes or simply piled and assembled in groups of loose images. To date, they remain part of an ongoing practice of collecting, preserving, and curating by the women and their families.[134]

The Usakos old location photographs cover the period between the late 1920s and the early 1960s, and hence date back to the beginnings of the establishment of a segregated African neighbourhood there. The town's history is closely linked to the development of the railway system in central Namibia, with first steps made during the German colonial period and greater infrastructural extension after South African occupation in 1915.[135] Started as a railway station with maintenance and repair facilities in 1906, the place gradually developed into a vibrant, if small, urban centre, which attracted white and black railway workers and residents from across Namibia and abroad. By the early 1910s, the population had reached 2500, and the townscape was characterised by its prominent railway infrastructure, surrounded by dozens of residential houses, administrative buildings, shops, hotels, schools, churches, a police station, two hospitals, and a large number of informal dwellings. Racial segregation shaped the social and physical environment; though residential patterns remained interwoven up until the early years of South African administration, housing for white workers and their families tended to cluster around the railway station in what began to emerge as the centre of town, while Africans were relegated to different locations scattered on the edges.[136]

The situation changed in the late 1920s, when urban planning was aligned more consistently with central state policy requirements, and the closing down of racial grey-zones, i.e. the creation of proper white neighbourhoods, neatly separated from black residential areas, became a generalised priority.[137] State-financed building programs were launched in response to what emerged as an alleged "European housing crisis" – a variation of the broader debate on white poverty referred to earlier – and helped secure the economic, social, and moral "uplifting" of the local settler community throughout the 1930s.[138] Things looked very different for the black population: In 1927, the Usakos municipality designated a space for a consolidated "native location", in which all non-white residents were henceforth required to live; but otherwise, municipal activity remained low and was limited to tax collection, the provision of basic sanitary services, and minimal policing and control. A system of internal ethnic division, with Damara, Herero, and Ovambo sections, respectively, set apart, along with a railway compound for migrant workers, provided a merely superficial sense of order and administration in a situation that was otherwise marked by an official *laissez-faire* approach.[139] The structural measures of residential consolidation and socio-economic marginalisation were notably imposed in the context of economic depression and a period of severe droughts in the early 1930s.[140] While archival sources remain scant,[141] it is safe to assume that living conditions in the location were harsh. Male residents were mostly employed with the railways, or pursued work at local businesses, while women predominantly performed domestic labour in private white households, in hotels, or administrative offices; in all cases, wages were shockingly low.[142] To be sure, the cramped location space (single plots were strictly limited to 50 × 50 feet) and hardly any access to water and land set tight limits on subsistence, which was possibly reduced to rudimentary small-stock husbandry and gardening in and around the location.[143] Services provided by the Catholic and Rhenish missions, both of which attended to their African congregations in the location starting in the early 1910s, would have made no essential difference, though they granted access to basic schooling and health care.[144] The situation seems to have eased after the mid-1930s – or so the building of a water reservoir in 1935 and the opening of a community hall in 1936 suggest – and relative stability, at least with respect to the colonial economy, seems to have persisted into the early 1950s.[145]

Placed against the backdrop of a nascent social history of location life in central Namibia in the first half of the twentieth century,[146] the Usakos old location photographs promise to provide additional insight. But any inflated hopes of catching a direct, unmediated glimpse at reality might be thwarted[147] and in any event should of course always be avoided. We remain on safer ground if we approach these photographic collections less as historical evidence, i.e. less on the forensic plane, than as objects of aesthetic practice and as a form of historical performance, which invite us to ask how location residents used photography to sense and make sense of the worlds they lived in and to enact awareness of their past, present, and future (Figure 3.7).[148]

This photograph is part of the collection of Wilhelmine Katjimune – one of the women collectors mentioned before – and it exemplifies the conceptual shift made here, away from the photographer as author and pivotal agent towards a broader notion of *photographic practice*, including collecting, preserving, and curating photographs.[149] Katjimune herself is depicted in the photograph, alongside family members – her aunts with husbands – and childhood friends. She has identified the photographic subjects, the occasion represented in the image – her first communion – and the precise site and moment of photographic recording, i.e. one of the family houses in the Usakos old location in the 1930s. The photograph and Katjimune's

Figure 3.7 Usakos old location; Wilhelmine Katjimune (in a white dress) at her first communion, with Sibilla (girl on the right, surname unknown), Petrus Chabagae and Maria Schiefer (on the left), Gertrud Schiefer and Alex Hagendorn (on the right), names of children unknown, late 1930s.[150]

knowledge about it remind us of the necessity of understanding photography in the social institutions in which it is embedded and activated, including – as is the case here – in orality and the familial (we will come back to these later on).[151] For the time being, though, we shall pay attention to what the women collectors and curators tell us about photography in the Usakos old location in the 1930s, 1940s, and 1950s, first insofar as they explain the character and quality of the photographic encounter among Africans.[152] Unlike in the Namibian capital Windhoek and the coastal towns of Swakopmund and Walvis Bay, there was no professional photographer or photo studio in the old location of Usakos at the time. But there were cameras, and by the 1930s, social gatherings, festivities, or family events offered welcome opportunities for public and private picture taking; indeed, some of the old location photographs were produced by family members, friends, or neighbours.[153] But the significant part of these collections are images taken by African itinerant photographers, men from as far as Cape Town or Johannesburg, who travelled along the railway lines, stopped in towns and villages, and offered their services to the local clientele.[154]

As one of the main nodal points of the Namibian railway system and therefore a place that attracted immigrants from all over the country, the Cape, and the wider African continent throughout the first half of the twentieth century, Usakos was undoubtedly among the more attractive destinations for ambulant photographers operating in central Namibia at the time.[155] We have no information on photographic equipment and cameras used, but we know that these itinerant professionals, who usually sojourned in the location for a certain time period, enjoyed room and board there, moved around the African neighbourhood comfortably, and were naturally considered as members of the local community and respected craftsmen who offered affordable service.[156] While it would be misguided to understand the social embeddedness of black photographers as providing the basis for a privileged gaze – and with it a greater, realist authority of the image[157] – the character and quality of their integration was important for negotiating the terms of the photographic occasion, for choosing photographic sites, selecting attire, accessories and requisites, deciding on who would be in the image, alone or in company, and – crucially – how clients would receive copies of their photographs.[158] In sum, there was a difference here, a contrast to the ways in which location residents experienced the presence and practice of external, unfamiliar photographers – administrative officers, missionaries, and members of the settler community alike.[159]

That being said, we still need to explore if and how the photographs themselves indicate the particularity of interaction between African photographers and their clients in the Usakos old location. Is the moment in and of photography here a different one? Let us briefly survey the photographic *sujets* and genres that constitute these collections, before we explore possible ways of answering the question.

Many of the images kept in all three collections are portraits, either of individuals or of groups. Figure 3.8 is one of these, a photographic portrait of Cecilie//Geises taken in the old location, probably in the early 1950s.[160] It is clearly a posed image, which was carefully enacted by the photographic subject herself and the photographer, who remains unidentified. Taken in an outside location – as was the case for most old location portraits – Cecilie//Geises was pictured here sitting on a chair, which had been placed close to an exterior wall built of flattened metal sheets. Her dress and impeccably neat apron – markers of her status as domestic worker – stood out against the dark backdrop, while her characteristic woollen cap, a personal accessory she wore in many photographs, broke up the homogeneity of the uniform and provided the young woman sitter with individuality, elegance, and dignity.[161] If we remember the portraits of farmers taken by the Scherz couple, there are obvious similarities, proof of how photography can capture the distinctiveness of the moment, highlighting how the situational works against the generic: We encounter an individual, a self-confident young woman, at ease with herself, her gaze directed towards the camera, concerned with obtaining a beautiful portrait of herself, one she in fact commissioned. For this, she was willing to take her time, possibly before going to work, spend parts of her hard-earned income, and finally, preserve

Figure 3.8   Cecilie//Geises, Usakos old location, n.d.

the received photograph in her personal archive, for decades to come. As the collections evidence, the matter of ensuring that she and other residents of the old location would acquire copies of their images also concerned photographic occasions that were less staged and intimate and included snapshots taken during the popular sports events, dances, concerts and cultural festivities.[162] Once we recall the broader visual landscape in Namibia at the time, and how the political economy of photographic production and circulation remained dominated by the colonial authorities, missions, and settler community, African ownership of photographs appears as no self-evident matter.[163]

Placed alongside photographs of family events such as weddings, communions, baptisms, and funerals – i.e. the more conventional tropes of family photography – the images taken at social and cultural gatherings convey a sense of visual self-determination and of multifaceted community life and vibrant sociality considered worth of photographic recording, by its participants and the photographers who habitually visited the African neighbourhood.[164]

Securing photographic prints was likewise desired in relation to the rare photographs taken inside people's homes, at their workplace, at church, or in schools, i.e. in private realms as much as in public ones. Unlike the photographs of location life in Windhoek authored by Nitzsche-Reiter and her employees, the photographic practices that cluster around the collections kept by the four women were hence firmly rooted in the location itself and part of the worlds its residents inhabited. The predominance of outdoor photographic sites is, in fact, important, and it has complicated bearings on these personal archives' effects. While the images offer detailed views of the built environment, streets, and squares (we will come back to these in a moment), the photographic corpus is inevitably bound to visually reproduce the location as a discrete space, one that had, *nota bene*, come into being as a space of confinement and segregation in the first place. Viewed in this light, the old location photographs seem "compounded", their time and space circumscribed by the physical and representational confines of a category of colonial urban planning, the "native location".[165] But then again, there are lines of flight, images that break up the perceived visual solidification and inhibit an overly homogenising view (Figure 3.9).[166]

Figure 3.9 Petrus Chabagae (left) and Mr. Reiter; photographer: C.F. Fenton, Walvis Bay.[167]

Such openings are first provided by portraits taken in the towns on the coast, Swakopmund and Walvis Bay, as well as in Windhoek or Rehoboth in central Namibia, and they include photographs produced in professional studios as early as the 1900s.[168] Against the backdrop of a tightening regime of residential segregation and the constriction of African mobility – preferably determined by the labour economy, as far as the colonial administration was concerned – these images point to intricate cultures of movement and travel, while they concurrently evidence how old location residents, men and women alike, drew from distinct iconographic conventions and imaginaries of class mobility marked by the studio space, impeccable attire, and visual conceptions of respectability, as a way of expressing their social and cultural aspirations.[169]

While these expanded trajectories and ambitious practices of cosmopolitan photography remained exceptional,[170] there were further efforts to water down the hegemony of the location as a homogenising administrative category that blocked the view onto social and cultural diversity, the variety of everyday experience, and the limitlessness of individual appearance. These visual contestations from within, if you like, become clear once we reconsider the question of the moment and Augenblick in the old location photographs, by especially turning our attention to the concept's spatial connotation.

We have explained earlier that while Augenblick describes an experience, one which is elevated from ordinary, everyday temporality and takes on particular significance, the term denotes both the moment *and* the site of photographic transformation.[171] It is the more specific question of the space-time of Augenblick that is at stake here, and Figure 3.10 can help us explain why and how. The image is part of the collection owned by Gisela Pieters and Olga//Garoës, who identified the subjects of the photograph and named the precise place where it was taken.[172] While the photographer remained unknown, and the date of the picture was given only approximately, Pieters' and //Garoës' specifications provide important clues to the social and physical environment in which such images were produced. Naming people and sites, and sometimes adding relevant handwritten notes on the back of single photographs, changed the "native location" from an undifferentiated, administrative space of containment into a particularised place of social interaction, habitation, and dwelling.[173] Once considered together, these photographic collections come to constitute an intricate form of visual mapping, in which the urban environment, i.e. the streets, squares, and buildings familiar to the location's residents; the characteristic mountain range delineating the horizon; and the nearby Onguati River and its peculiar scrub and thorn-bush vegetation, its particular trees, pastures, or fields were conducive to photographic composition, as much as they bespoke nuanced topographical knowledge. As in Figure 3.10, the built and natural spatial markers added to the visual recurrence of particular accoutrements and accessories – carefully selected chairs, tables, rugs, and household effects – in short, personal showpieces that

Figure 3.10 Herodia Goreses (left) and Gisela Pieters (right), next to Olga//Garoës' house, Usakos old location, ca. 1950s.[174]

smoothed the distinction between the exterior and interior, and introduced viewers to the materiality and texture of location life. Unlike in the "Boers on the move" series produced by the Scherz couple,[175] where scattered household utensils had marked the harshness of nomadic lifestyle and economic vulnerability of Afrikaner rural dwellers, here the domestic objects and pieces of furniture did the precise opposite. Working against official perceptions of African residential areas as slums or hotbeds of filth, crime, vice, and disease,[176] these personal items were involved in a performative act that visually marked the location as an inhabited and featured space – in short, as home.

It should be clear by now how the Usakos old location photographic collections configure what we have called the space-time of the Augenblick. Against the backdrop of racist colonial policies, which legitimised the confinement of Africans to segregated urban residential areas with the necessity to patronise backward colonised subjects for the reputed benefit of their economic, social, and moral improvement – audaciously framed in terms of colonialism's and apartheid's modernising commitment[177] – it is reasonable to understand the photographic practices cultivated by location residents and itinerant photographers as a form of visual dissent, one which bound itself to a different temporality and positionality. Embedding the photographs in the space-time of the location – i.e. in a place shaped by the agency of those who live there, in a landscape formed by the everyday experiences of those who dwell in it – helped situate each and every moment captured in a photographic image within the framework of the biographical, familial, and social; concurrently, the character and quality of the encounter between residents and photographers provided the appropriate visual language. It is this intricate photographic mediation, one that went far beyond the photographic occasion and the photographic image itself,[178] which helped constitute the location *per se* as the Augenblick in and of photography.

The moment of memory

There is, though, a later moment that weighs on these collections, one that feeds on an important historical caesura – the destruction of the Usakos old location in the early 1960s and the forced removal of its residents to racially segregated townships on the periphery, beyond the Onguati river.

This radical transformation of Usakos' urban landscape was by no means a matter of chance, but part of a larger scheme concocted by politicians and technocrats in the South African Native Affairs Department in Pretoria.[179] Based on the prescriptions formulated in the Group Areas Act of 1950, cities and towns across South Africa and southern and central Namibia were reorganised according to a general blueprint that aimed at securing the constitution and radical separation of white and black residential areas according to racial and ethnic classification of urban dwellers.[180] In Usakos, the hour of tragedy struck on a day in July 1955, when a Native Affairs Department inspection resulted in a request to remove the African location, since it was said to be situated in disturbing proximity to the town's white residential areas. From this moment forth, the municipal authorities began to look for a site that would conform to the requirements and norms set out for the establishment of segregated townships and the construction of standardised low-cost houses.[181] They soon hit pay dirt: an area located north of the town, several kilometres away, henceforth called Hakhaseb. Architects and town planning consultants, who had been awarded the contract, proposed a township to be built from scratch, providing space for more than 1500 permanent residents and a variety of administrative and community service buildings. Classified as a public housing scheme, the construction of the township began in 1960, but it took years to be completed, and in mid-1964, only 150 houses were ready for occupation.

The delay did not cause grounds for policy revision, and the forced removals of location residents commenced in 1961. Three years later, one-third of the 770 dwellings in the old location had been emptied. People's response to the removals was complex: Political leaders and mission societies operating in the location had promoted the scheme, arguing that the new neighbourhoods offered better housing and improved living conditions.[182] More importantly, though, there had been a violent precedent that curbed residents' willingness to resist the removals: the shootings at the old location in Windhoek in 1959, in the course of which 11 people were killed and more than 40 wounded, while thousands fled the violent police incursion.[183] Still, by 1964, those who had been moved to Hakhaseb revolted, since they had been defrauded and fooled: they had received neither compensation for their former houses nor new ones that met their expectations – there were no floors, no electricity, and no running water.[184] Given that the municipality had enforced the removals in a situation of an acute economic crisis, caused by the decline of the railway and the transfer of workshops from Usakos to Windhoek that left many Africans jobless, the repercussions were severe.[185] Up to the mid-1960s, more than half of the remaining households in the old location were run by women, and the municipality's threat to relocate whoever refused to move or pay rent for the allotted township house in the reserve hit them particularly.[186] While we do not know how many people were eventually deported, to the reserves or to their countries of origin, the last group of residents left the old location in 1968. Almost 800 privately owned houses had been destroyed. A few years later still, in the mid-1970s, the town established a second township, Erongosig, this time for those classified as "coloured", and again their houses in and around the old location were razed to the ground.

What remains of the old location today – what "people are left with" – are ruins (see Figure 3.11). This phrasing refers to Ann Laura Stoler's reflections on ruins as imperial debris, and her propositions are conducive of an understanding of photographs that document seismic destruction under colonialism and apartheid beyond a dystopic notion of ruination.[187] Ruins, Stoler argues, provide an image of what has vanished from the past and long decayed, and they have readily served as objects of colonial melancholy and imperial nostalgia.[188] On the other hand – and in the Southern African context especially – ruins often result from destruction, and hence point to violent

Figure 3.11 Paul Grendon, old location showers, Usakos, 2013.[189]

processes and experiences of trauma and fear.[190] It comes as no surprise, perhaps, that both nostalgia and trauma constitute the entangled registers within which the Usakos old location photographs take effect. The collections considered here are embedded in contemporary memory work, cultivated in a Namibian urban community engaged in coming to terms with the experience of forced removal, racial segregation and apartheid, and a dramatic socioeconomic decline since the early 1960s.[191] These traumatic events are deeply ingrained in people's historical consciousness, and they are considered important for explaining why the town of Usakos remains marked by widespread poverty, demographic and infrastructural decline, and the lack of socioeconomic, educational, and cultural prospects.[192] Since the current dispensation feels difficult and problematic to many, there is a widespread sense of loss and nostalgia for a place and moment irrevocably gone and, more precisely, for life in the old location before the advent of apartheid.[193]

The practice of collecting, preserving, and curating old location photographs, as done by //Geises, Katjimune, Pieters & //Garoës, is undoubtedly situated in this framework of loss and nostalgia, and their photographs have become important *aides-mémoire*, which – once shared with family, friends, neighbours, and other viewers and interlocutors – help recall and narrate the past in particular ways. Here and now, the photographic collections constitute the material manifestation and symbolic expression of their understanding of and sustained connection to precisely that past.[194] But, memory and nostalgia do not explain these photographic practices comprehensively; they are just one modality of how the women activated their collections, since the images have moved and continue to move between different forms of assemblage, narration, and performance – between the personal, intimate, and reflective on the one hand, and the social and public on the other hand, taking on various meanings whenever they are looked at, spoken about, displayed, and reproduced.[195] Because many of the photographs are portraits of individuals who are no more, they have become cherished objects and important tokens of affection that outline the contours of an intricate landscape of personal articulation, remembrance, and memorialisation.[196]

Yet, other images – such as those depicting the built environment or sites of social gathering – open up different avenues and invite commentaries, critical reflections, and sometimes even moral judgements about community life, economic well-being, social justice and solidarity, or generational conflict – in short, an evaluation of the past, present, and future. These collections are and do multiple things; they are – as Martha Langford put it – sagas, chronicles, life stories, autobiographies, legends, photo-romances, and private and public histories, all at once.[197] If we want to understand the Usakos old location photographs as an example of aesthetic and cultural forms and practices that worked against the disruption of the physical and social environment of Africans placed under colonial and apartheid rule, and value them today as a creative way of sustaining the continuity of personal and collective memories, we need to pay attention to the shifting ways in which photographs figure in the crafting and composing of historical narratives.[198] The space-time of the old location constitutes a decisive frame of reference for its former residents, one in which every moment of photography, every photographic event and encounter among Africans, was an instantiation of visual self-articulation in a context otherwise marked by almost complete heteronomy. Thanks to their continued material existence, the Augenblick of these collections, finally, rests on their maintenance in an ongoing practice of collecting and curating, on the potentiality that arises from their persisting and insisting gesture towards a preoccupation with and desire for revising, and sometimes even disrupting, a colonial aesthetic order, or, as one might well say, a hegemonic distribution of the sensible.[199]

Conclusion

At the opening of this chapter, we looked at a photograph taken by either Ernst Rudolf or Anneliese Scherz in central Namibia in the late 1930s in order to raise questions about the moment in photography and its relation to time and history. Photographs are often said to capture but a moment, a fragment of time; what they present us with is elusive, ephemeral, and simply a reproduction of whatever happened to be in front of the camera at the moment between the shutter's opening and closing. On the other hand, photographic images are likewise said to freeze time, and by extracting a particular moment from its undifferentiated flow, they precisely turn that moment into an event, something significant, decisive, and hence momentous. Much of the literature continues to vacillate between these phenomenological propositions, understood less as antagonist poles than as mutually constitutive yardsticks, in an attempt to come to terms with photography's role in historical signification. While remaining indebted to these debates,[200] this chapter has been preoccupied with addressing the question of the moment in photography from a slightly different angle: it made recourse to *Augenblick*, a concept defined as a moment of vision and revelation that enables the production of an image, which manifests a moment come to present, a "now that is not simply a matter of time, but something underlying the ordinary surface of everyday appearances"[201] and is hence, importantly, considered a moment of historical disclosure. Augenblick provided a productive analytical tool for exploring how photography, understood as an image form and medium around which a wide range of social and cultural practices coalesce, transforms the temporality and spatiality of the moment it captures. Departing from a stringent existential philosophical understanding by arguing that Augenblick and its visual manifestation remain historically grounded, the concept has been put to work here in relation to a series of archives and collections from mid-twentieth century Namibia in order to unravel how particular historical subjects engaged with photography as an aesthetic expression of historical consciousness, and as a form of mediating their being-in-the-moment.[202]

What exactly did we gain from making use of moment and Augenblick in a discussion of the Scherz, Nitzsche-Reiter, and Usakos old location photographs? On one hand, and obviously perhaps, we moved to the specific and contingent; to the subjectivity and interiority of space and time, which is, ultimately, what all these private photographic collections, the ones compiled by the Scherz couple *and* those collected by Katjimune, //Geises, Pieters & //Garoës, do above all. The portraits of farmers of German descent, photographed as individualised subjects who inhabit the privacy of their social worlds, belong here, as do intimate snapshots of family and friends feasting in the location backyard. Yet still, because the photographs became part of collections held in private and public archives, and because of the ways in which they continue to be activated – in public history initiatives, in scholarship, and in memory work – these images resonate beyond themselves, into further semantic spaces, both within and beyond the archival frame. They do so, as we have seen, for example, in view of the question of whiteness and blackness in settler photography, or while thinking about the conditions of dwelling in and moving across the segregated urban landscape of colonial Namibia. Moment and Augenblick help describe this intricate tapestry and complicated polyphony of the medium, i.e. those qualities which emerge precisely once we interrogate photographic images and their assemblage as both historical form and practice.

There is another moment configured throughout this chapter, one that points to the historical conditions of being in the Namibian colony and to how we might use historical photographs for understanding them. This is why placing the photography of settlers such as the Scherz couple and the Nitzsche-Reiter studio *alongside* the work of African itinerant photographers and African photographic practices that included collecting, curating, and displaying photographic images was important. The visual line-up proceeded from the desire to understand these collections as part of *one* visual economy – as coeval and concurrent visual manifestations, which are often treated separately or antagonistically. While we obviously need to take into account that racial segregation and apartheid had bearings on cultural production and aesthetic practice, as much as on social and political life, we should be careful not to naturalise and perpetuate the logics of difference intrinsic to the distinction made between white and black photography in Southern Africa. Instead, thinking about Namibian photographic production in the period between the 1930s and 1950s along the lines of Augenblick presented us with a problem of another kind: the need to reconsider what we mean by the moment in and of photography in the first place; to direct our gaze beyond the fleetingness of the moment and constriction of the site of image making, towards what Ariella Azoulay has called the event of photography[203] – which includes, as we have argued, social interaction and negotiation, photographic afterlives, the archive, and memory. These are the grounds on which we need to explain not so much an assumed difference between settler and African photography, but rather why the former had no eye for the latter, and the latter was constantly overshadowed by the former. A return to the archive is an appropriate reminder: in 1942, Ernst Rudolf Scherz embarked on a journey that took him and his wife Anneliese from Windhoek to Swakopmund, but after a terrible car accident, the couple was stranded in Usakos. E.R. Scherz recalled the moment as follows:

> In Usakos, a boring nest of lice, we had obviously missed the connecting Union train to Swakopmund. 24 hours of waiting. Boring, but everything passes. This hell has but one object of interest, a graveyard surrounded by a fence – three meters high and certainly hyena-proof.[204]

Scherz was describing, *nota bene*, what had emerged as the white part of the town. While he and his wife produced a substantial amount of photographs during their numerous trips across Namibia – and we have discussed some of them – it did not occur to them that their judgement about Usakos' appeal might have shifted had they considered the African location and its vibrant photographic culture. Going along with their blindness, even if understood as simply a symptom of how things were kept apart, today seems at least problematic; certainly, it should not continue to serve as the grounds on which we look at historical photographs from the Namibia at the time.

Notes

1   Quoted in Peter Burleigh, The Burden of the Moment: Photography's Inherent Monumentalising Effect, in Ladina Bezzola Lambert and Andrea Ochsner (eds.), *Moment to Monument. The Making and Unmaking of Cultural Significance*. Bielefeld, 2009, pp. 185–95.
2   See Burleigh, The Burden of the Moment; also Lynn Hunt and Vanessa R. Schwartz, Editorial. Capturing the Moment: Images and Eyewitnessing in History. *Journal of Visual Culture*, 9, 3, 2010: 259–71.
3   Eduardo Cadava, Of Veils and Mourning: Fazal Sheikh's Widowed Images, in Fundacion MAPFRE, *Fazal Sheikh*. Madrid, 2009 [exhibition catalogue].
4   See Silvester et al., "Trees Never Meet", p. 41; Keith Gottschalk, The Political Economy of Healthcare: Colonial Namibia 1915–61. *Social Science and Medicine*, 25, 6, 1988: 577–82. For South Africa see e.g. Azeem Badroodien, Race, Crime, Welfare and State Social Institutions in South Africa from the 1940s. *Social Dynamics*, 25, 2, 1999: 49–74, and more generally Grace Davie, *Poverty and Knowledge in South Africa. A Social History of Human Science, 1855–2005*. Cambridge, 2015. For liberal preoccupations with the volatility of African family life and respective photographic documentation see Marijke du Toit, The General View and Beyond: From Slum-yard to Township in Ellen Hellmann's Photographs of Women and the African Familial in the 1930s. *Gender & History*, 17, 3, 2005: 593–626, here pp. 612–13.
5   Basler Afrika Bibliographien (BAB), E.R. and A. Scherz Collection, S08_0097, untitled photograph.
6   Shepherd Steiner, Reading in Benjamin's "Little History of Photography". *InTensions*, 1, 2008: 1–20, here p. 3.
7   Edwards, *Raw Histories*, p. 5.

8 Hunt and Schwartz, Editorial, p. 259.

9 Barthes, *Camera Lucida*, p. 77.

10 Anders Schinkel, Imagination as a Category of History: An Essay Concerning Koselleck's Concepts of Erfahrungsraum and Erwartungshorizont. *History and Theory*, 44, 2005: 42–54.

11 Françoise Balibar, Philippe Büttgen, Barbara Cassin, Jean-Pierre Clero, and Jacques Collette, Der/das Moment, der Augenblick, die günstige Gelegenheit. *Trivium*, 15, 2013: 1–12.

12 Balibar et al., Der/das Moment, p. 4.

13 See Koral Ward, *Augenblick. The Concept of the "Decisive Moment" in 19th and 20th Century Western Philosophy*. Hampshire, 2009. The "philosophers of the moment" discussed by Ward are Kierkegaard, Nietzsche, Jaspers and Heidegger.

14 Ward, *Augenblick*, p. xi. Also Gary Shapiro, Nietzsche's Story of the Eye: Hyphenating the Augen-blick. *Journal of Nietzsche Studies*, 22, 2001: 17–35.

15 Outi Pasanen, Notes on the Augenblick in and around Jacques Derrida's Reading of Paul Celan "The Meridian". *Research in Phenomenology*, 36, 2006: 214–37, here p. 222.

16 See Shapiro, Nietzsche's Story, p. 20.; and Hans-Georg Gadamer, The Continuity of History and the Existential Moment. *Philosophy Today*, 16, 3/4, 1972: 230–40, here 232.

17 Suvi Alt, Darkness in a Blink of an Eye. Action and the Onto-Poetics of a Beyond. *Angelaki*, 21, 2, 2016: 17–31, here p. 24.

18 This is Martin Heidegger's formulation, referred to in Ward, *Augenblick*, p. xii.

19 See the chapter on Henri Cartier-Bresson in Ward, *Augenblick;* also John Roberts, Photography After the Photograph: Event, Archive, and the Non-symbolic. *Oxford Art Journal*, 32, 2, 2009: 281–98.

20 Roberts, Photography; also Ariella Azoulay, What Is a Photograph? What Is Photography? *Philosophy of Photography*, 1, 1, 2010: 9–13.

21 Cadava, *op.cit.*, p. 304: Burleigh, The Burden of the Moment, p. 194. This is what the original meaning of "moment" implies, i.e. both a temporal and a spatial element, in terms of the moment as movement, opening and entrance. See Balibar et al., Der/das Moment, p. 2.

22 Roberts, Photography.

23 The couple spent 40 years in Namibia before relocating to Germany in the late 1970s. See Dag Henrichsen, Teilnachlass E.R. and A. Scherz im Personenarchiv der Basler Afrika Bibliographien. Internal library finding aid, Basel, 1990, p. 6.

24 Lorena Rizzo, Between the Book and the Lamp–Interiors of Bureaucracy and the Materiality of Colonial Power. *African Historical Review*, 45, 2, 2013: 31–51.

25 Hayes et al., Photography, History, and Memory, p. 3.

26 Brian Bunting, *The Rise of the South African Reich*. London, 1964; Howard Simson, *The Social Origins of Afrikaner Fascism and Its Apartheid Policy*. Stockholm, 1980; Albrecht Hagemann, Nationalsozialismus, Afrikaaner Nationalismus, und die Entstehung der Apartheid in Südafrika. *Vierteljahrshefte für Zeitgeschichte*, 39, 3, 1991: 413–36; Herman Giliomee, The Making of the Apartheid Plan, 1929–48. *Journal of Southern African Studies*, 29, 2, 2003: 373–92.

27 Saul Dubow, Afrikaner Nationalism, Apartheid and the Conceptualization of Race. *Journal of African History*, 33, 2, 1992: 209–37; Silvester et al., "Trees Never Meet", p. 38.

28 Heinrich Struebel, Die Entwicklung des Nationalsozialismus in Südwestafrika. *Vierteljahrsherfte für Zeitgeschichte*, 1, 2, 1953: 170–76; Robert J. Gordon, The Impact of the Second World War on Namibia. *Journal of Southern African Studies*, 19, 1, Special Issue: Namibia: Africa's Youngest Nation, 1993: 147–65,

here 149; Martin Eberhardt, *Zwischen Nationalsozialismus und Apartheid. Die deutsche Bevölkerungsgruppe Südwestafrikas 1915–1965*. Berlin, 2005, p. 106; Reinhart Kössler, *Namibia and Germany: Negotiating the Past*. Windhoek, 2015, p. 106.

29   Silvester et al., "Trees Never Meet", p. 37.

30   Struebel, Die Entwicklung, p. 172; Richard Dale, Reconfiguring White Ethnic Power in Colonial Africa: The German Community in Namibia, 1923–50. *Nationalism and Ethnic Politics*, 7, 2, 2001: 75–94, here p. 82.

31   Brigitta Schmidt-Lauber, *Die abhängigen Herren. Deutsche Identität in Namibia. Interethnische Beziehungen und Kulturwandel*. Münster, 1993, p. 77; Hagemann, Nationalsozialismus, p. 422.

32   Silvester et al., "Trees Never Meet", p. 38; Struebel, Die Entwicklung, p. 176; Schmidt-Lauber, *Die abhängigen Herren*, p. 77.

33   South Africa did join Britain as an ally after a thin parliamentary vote enabled them to do so. The vote in parliament forced Hertzog to resign and it was his successor, Jan Smuts who led South African troops into World War II. For the divisions within white South African society caused by the participation in World War II see Albert Grundlingh, The King's Afrikaners? Enlistment and Ethnic Identity in the Union of South Africa's Defense Force during the Second World War, 1939–45. *Journal of African History*, 40, 1999: 351–65.

34   Tony Emmett, *Popular Resistance and the Roots of Nationalism in Namibia, 1915–66*. Basel, 1999; Les Switzer, *South Africa's Alternative Press. Voices of Protest and Resistance, 1880–1960*. Cambridge, 1997, p. 335; Marc Matera, *Black London: The Imperial Metropolis and Decolonisation in the Twentieth Century*. Oakland, 2015, p. 96. There is one exception in the Namibian historical literature, which is W. Werner, "Playing Soldiers": The Truppenspieler Movement among the Herero of Namibia, 1915 to ca. 1945. *Journal of Southern African Studies*, 16, 3, 1990: 476–502. Werner briefly refers to the spread of "Nazi millenarianism" among mission educated black men in the 1930s (see Werner, "Playing Soldiers", p. 494); see also Wallace, *A History*, p. 241.

35   Silvester et al., "Trees Never Meet", pp. 16–17.

36   Richard Moorsom, The Formation of the Contract Labour System in Namibia, 1900–1926, in Abebe Zegeye and Shubi Ishemo, *Forced Labour and Migration: Patterns of Movement Within Africa*. London, 1989, pp. 55–108.

37   Giorgio Miescher, Facing Barbarians: A Narrative of Spatial Segregation in Colonial Namibia. *Journal of Southern African Studies*, 38, 4, 2012: 769–86, here p. 778.

38   Thomas Rodney Hope Davenport, *The Beginnings of Urban Segregation in South Africa. The Natives (Urban Areas) act of 1923 and Its Background*. Grahamstown, 1971; and for Namibia, Marion Wallace, *Health, Power and Politics Windhoek, Namibia, 1915–45*. Basel, 2002.

39   Silvester et al., "Trees Never Meet", p. 19.

40   Wallace, *A History*, p. 222.

41   While this describes a general trend, economic and social repercussions varied regionally. See Wolfgang Werner, *"No One Will Become Rich". Economy and Society in the Herero Reserves in Namibia, 1915–46*. Basel, 1998; Lorena Rizzo, *Gender and Colonialism. A History of Kaoko in North-Western Namibia, 1870s–1950s*. Basel, 2012; Emanuel Kreike, De-Globalisation and Deforestation in Colonial Africa: Closed Markets, the Cattle Complex and Environmental Change in North-Central Namibia, 1890–1990. *Journal of Southern African Studies*, 35, 1, 2009: 81–98; Silvester et al., "Trees Never Meet", p. 22.

42   Giorgio Miescher, *Namibia's Red Line. The History of a Veterinary and Settlement Border*. New York, 2012, p. 128.

43 Miescher, *Red Line*, p. 128; Wolfgang Werner, A Brief History of Land Dispossession in Namibia. *Journal of Southern African Studies*, 19, 1, 1993: 135–46, here p. 143; Silvester et al., "Trees Never Meet", p. 28.

44 See e.g. Ifor Leslie Evans, *Native Policy in Southern Africa: An Outline*. Cambridge, 1934; Saul Dubow, Holding "A Just Balance Between White and Black". The Native Affairs Department in South Africa, ca. 1920–33. *Journal of Southern African Studies*, 12, 2, 1986; Ivan Evans, *Bureaucracy and Race: Native Administration in South Africa*. Los Angeles and London, 1997, p. 3.

45 There are two digital albums, or folders rather [S003 and S004] in the Scherz photographs collection that are labelled with "Honeymoon" and dated 1938. My phrasing is loosely referring to Gillian Rose's *Doing Family Photography. The Domestic, the Public and the Politics of Sentiment*. Ashgate, 2010, though I do not engage her argument closely.

46 As Roberts has noted in a different context is that what lies waiting for all photographic images, and particularly those that achieve no sustained circulation is the archive. See Roberts, Photography, p. 294.

47 S004_123, BAB Scherz collection; no caption; from album Hochzeitsreise 1938.

48 Wendy Kozol, Madonnas of the Fields: Photography, Gender, and 1930s Farm Relief. *Genders*, 2, 1988: 1–23.

49 Marijke Du Toit, Blank Verbeeld, or the Incredible Whiteness of Being: Amateur Photography and Afrikaner Nationalist Historical Narrative. *Kronos*, 27, 2001: 77–113.

50 Patrick J. Furlong, The National Party of South Africa: A Transnational Perspective, in Martin Durham and Margaret Power (eds.), *New Perspectives on the Transnational Right*. New York, 2010, pp. 67–84.

51 Cadava, Of Veils and Mourning, p. 303; Henrick Stahr, *Fotojournalismus zwischen Exotismus und Rassissmus. Darstellungen von Schwarzen und Idianern in Foto-Text-Artikeln deutscher Wochenillustrierter 1919–1939*. Hamburg, 2004.

52 Willeke Sandler, Deutsche Heimat in Afrika: Colonial Revisionism and the Construction of Germanness through Photography. *Journal of Women's History*, 25, 1, 2013: 37–61; Daniel Joseph Walther, *Creating Germans Abroad. Cultural Policies and Settler identities in Namibia*. Athens, 2002, p. 55.

53 Burleigh, The Burden of the Moment.

54 *Veld* is the Afrikaans term for field or bush.

55 Bywoners were tenants on farms owned by other Afrikaner or German farmers. Throughout the 1920s and 1930s, the South African administration encouraged Boer immigrants to Namibia to settle on farms in order to make them used to farming. See e.g. Renee Sylvain, Bushmen, Boers and Baasskap: Patriarchy and Paternalism on Afrikaner Farms in the Omaheke Region, Namibia. *Journal of Southern African Studies*, 27, 4, 2001: 717–37, here p. 727.

56 Du Toit, Blank Verbeeld.

57 Robert Morrell, *White but Poor: Essays on the History of Poor Whites in Southern Africa*. Pretoria, 1992.

58 Christo Botha, The Politics of Land Settlement in Namibia, 1890–1960. *South African Historical Journal*, 42, 1: 232–76, here pp. 242–44.

59 S004_152, 148, 153, BAB Scherz collection, Hochzeitsreise 1938, 'Boers on the move' series.

60 See e.g. Darren Newbury, The Visibility of Poverty: A Rural Vision of Depression in the Photographs of the Farm Security Administration. *Visual Anthropology*, 8, 1996: 1–31; Marijke du Toit, 'Binnelandse Reise' (Journey to the Interior): Photographs from the Carnegie Commission of Investigation into the Poor White Problem, 1929/32. *Kronos* 32, 2006: 49–76.

61 Roberts, Photography, p. 285.

62   See Silvester et al., "Trees Never Meet", pp. 37–8.

63   Giorgio Miescher, Usakos' Urban Past. Traces in the Archive, in: Paul Grendon, Giorgio Miescher, Lorena Rizzo, Tina Smith (eds.), *Usakos. Photographs beyond Ruins. The Old Location Albums, 1920s–1960s*. Basel, 2015, pp. 28–63.

64   Tiffany Willoughby-Herard, *Waste of a White Skin: The Carnegie Corporation and the Racial Logic of White Vulnerability*. Berkeley, 2015, p. 2.

65   Eleanor M. Hight and Gary D. Sampson, Photography, "Race", and Postcolonial Theory, in: Eleanor M. Hight and Gary D. Sampson (eds.), *Colonialist Photography. Imag(in)ing Race and Place*. New York, 2002, pp. 1–19.

66   See e.g. images S001_106, S003_141, S004_156, S004_157, S004_179, S004_181, S004_183 in the Scherz photographic collection in the archives of the Basler Afrika Bibliographien.

67   See Wolfe W. Schmokel, The Myth of the White Farmer: Commercial Agriculture in Namibia, 1900–1983. *The International Journal of African Historical Studies*, 18, 1, 1985: 93–108.

68   Robert J. Gordon, Vagrancy, Law & 'Shadow Knowledge', in Hayes et al., *op. cit.*, pp. 51–76, here pp. 55–56.

69   Jeremy Silvester, Beasts, Boundaries & Buildings. The Survival and Creation of Pastoral Economies in Southern Namibia, 1915–1935, in Hayes et al., *Namibia under South African Rule*, pp. 95–116, here p. 111.

70   Richard Moorsom, Underdevelopment, Contract Labour and Worker Consciousness in Namibia, 1915–72. *Journal of Southern African Studies*, 4, 1, 1977: 52–87.

71   Silvester, Beasts, p. 115; Wallace, A *History*, p. 235. Significantly, E.R. Scherz worked as a purchasing agent for the Karakul breeding association, of which he became the manager in 1947. See Henrichsen, Teilnachlass, p. 5.

72   Since 1927 no farm owner could allow unemployed black men over the age of 18 to reside there. Not more than 10 African men could be employed on the farm on which the owner resided, and not more than 5 on any other. See Gordon, Vagrancy, p. 57.

73   Wallace, *A History*, p. 235.

74   Moorsom, Underdevelopment, p. 73; Kletus Likuwa, Contract Labour System and Farm Labourers' Experiences in Pre-Independent Namibia: Historical Reflections, Perspectives and Lessons, *BAB Working Paper*, 2, 2014.

75   Barthes, *Camera Lucida*, p. 27.

76   Sylvain, Bushmen, p. 719; Moorsom, Underdevelopment, p. 76 footnote 50; Meredith McKittrick, The 'Burden' of Young Men: Property and Generational Conflict in Namibia, 1880–1945. *African Economic History*, 24, 1996: 115–29, here p. 116.

77   See on white discourse on the African family in the interwar period the discussion in Chapter 2.

78   S004_160; "Eingeborene in Haribes", BAB Scherz collection, Hochzeitsreise 1938.

79   Willoughby-Herard, *Waste of a White Skin*, 9.

80   Moorsom, *op.cit.*, p. 76.

81   Hight and Sampson, Photography, "Race", and Postcolonial Theory.

82   Giorgio Miescher and Lorena Rizzo, Popular Pictorial Constructions of Kaoko in the 20th Century, in: Giorgio Miescher and Dag Henrichsen (eds.), *New Notes on Kaoko. The northern Kunene Region (Namibia) in Texts and Photographs*. Basel, 2000, pp. 10–47, here p. 12.

83   Silvester et al., "This ideal conquest", p. 17.

84   Du Toit, The General View, p. 599.

85   See Wallace, *A History*, p. 237.

86 S001_0026, BAB Scherz collection, 1933–1938. A positive print of this photograph is included in an album, S037, which includes a list of captions. Figure 27 is the first print in the album and captioned as "Natives on the beach north of Swakopmund" (Eingeborene am Strand nördlich von Swakopmund). The list specifies that this image was taken by E.R. Scherz before 1938.

87 Silvester et al., "Trees Never Meet", pp. 44–5

88 Gordon, Vagrancy, p. 69; Lorena Rizzo, A Glance into the Camera. Gendered Visions of Historical Photographs in Kaoko (North-Western Namibia). *Gender & History*, 17, 3, 2005: 682–713, here pp. 688–92.

89 Silvester et al., "This ideal conquest", p. 16.

90 Cadava, Of veils and mourning, p. 301.

91 See James Ryan, *Picturing Empire. Photography and the Visualisation of the British Empire.* London, 1997, pp. 99–110.

92 Du Toit, The General View, p. 608; Tim Ingold, The Temporality of the Landscape. *World Archaeology*, 25, 2, 1993: 152–174, here p. 168.

93 Lorena Rizzo, Faszination Landschaft – Landschaftsphotographie in Namibia. *BAB Working Paper*, 1, 2014; Jeremy Foster, "Land of Contrasts" or "Home we have always known"? The SAR&H and the Imaginary Geography of White South African Nationhood, 1920–1930. *Journal of Southern African Studies*, 29, 3, 2003: 657–80.

94 Possibly a Leica or a Rolex.

95 Du Toit, The General View, p. 608.

96 Azoulay, What is a photograph?, p. 12.

97 W.J. Thomas Mitchell, *Landscape and Power*, p. 15.

98 On legislation regulating and criminalising social relations between white and black in Namibia in the 1930s see Wallace, *A History*, p. 238; also Melissa Jeanne Betts, *Namibia's No Man's Land. Race, Space, and Identity in the History of Windhoek Coloureds under South African Rule 1915–1990.* Unpublished PhD, UCLA, 2009, pp. 108–14; for debates among settlers of German descent see Ulrike Lindner, Contested Concepts of "white"/"native" and Mixed Marriages in German South-West Africa and the Cape Colony 1900–1914: A Histoire Croisée. *Journal of Namibian Studies*, 6, 2009: 57–79.

99 On motorised transport in Namibia in the interwar period, see Jan-Bart Gewald, Missionaries, Hereros, and Motorcars: Mobility and the Impact of Motor Vehicles in Namibia before 1940. *The International Journal of African Historical Studies*, 35, 2/3, 2002: 257–285.

100 Ingold, The Temporality of the Landscape, p. 152.

101 Ingold, The Temporality of the Landscape, p. 156.

102 See Wallace, *A History*, p. 218.

103 Ingold, The Temporality of the Landscape, p. 162.

104 The risks and anxieties linked to African movement in and around towns and cities is described e.g. in Vinnia Ndadi, *Breaking Contract.* London, 1989, p. 50, who describes the situation in the 1940s in Windhoek; for South Africa in the 1950s and 1960s see Athol Fugard, *The Township Plays.* Oxford, 1993.

105 Location refers to the residential area set apart for Africans in towns and cities. As a consequence of the Group Areas Act of 1950 passed by the apartheid government, African locations across South Africa and Namibia were either destroyed or consolidated into townships. See Paul Maylam, Explaining the apartheid city: 20 years of South African urban historiography. *Journal of Southern African Studies*, 21, 1, 1995: 19–38. We will come back to this later on in the chapter.

106 Here Ottilie Nitzsche-Reiter refers to the photo studio, as it remains unclear if she took the photographs herself or if they were authored by one of her employees.

107 The Windhoek Old Location was the Namibian capital's main segregated area for black and so-called coloured residents. It existed since the early twentieth century until the late 1950s, when the South African administration removed its inhabitants to a new township, Katutura. See Dag Henrichsen, "A Glance at Our Africa". The History and Contents of South West News, in: ibid., *A Glance at Our Africa. Facsimile Reprint of South West News 1960.* Basel, 1997, pp. 13–44, here p. 23; Henning Melber, Revisiting the Windhoek Old Location. Unpublished paper presented at the 3rd Namibia Research Day organised by the Basler Afrika Bibliographien, Basel, 2016.

108 Hartmann et al., *Colonising Camera*, p. 19, footnote 16.

109 Martha Mukaiwa, Social Life in the 1950s. *The Villager*, 304, 2011; Wallace, *A History*, pp. 254–55. In 2001 the National Archives of Namibia bought Nitzsche-Reiter's photographic archive and began to digitise her negatives. The collection can be viewed at http://dna.nust.na/ (Digital Namibian Archives).

110 For some biographical information, see Patricia Hayes, Compound Nation: Migrant Worker Portraits in the Politics and Photography of 1980s Namibia, in: Costanza Caraffa and Tiziana Serena (eds.), *Photo Archives and the Idea of the Nation.* Berlin, Munich, Boston, 2015, pp. 279–300, here p. 291 footnote 25. Nitzsche-Reiter completed an apprenticeship with the photographer Franz Fiedler in Dresden in the early 1930s, from whom she inherited a predominant interest in portraiture. After returning to Namibia in 1934, she established a photo studio with her husband in Windhoek, and their business would take thousands of passport and advertisement photographs in the decades to come. Nitzsche-Reiter regularly took on work commissioned by local newspapers, businesses and the South West African administration, documenting many events on the official calendar, social and cultural festivities and gatherings of the white settler community in Windhoek throughout the 1940s, 1950s and 1960s.

111 See Du Toit, The General View; and Darren Newbury, Photographs of Windermere: The Brian Heseltine Collection. *Photography and Culture*, 3, 2, 2010: 225–237; Peter Palmquist, Women in Photography: Archives and Resources for Second World War Women Photographers. *History of Photography*, 18, 3, 1994: 247–255.

112 See e.g. Digital Namibian Archives, Ottilie Nitzsche-Reiter (ONR) Collection, images No. 03483-034402. These numbers do not correspond with the numbers of negatives in the original collection kept at the National Archives of Namibia in Windhoek.

113 There are two main events that took place in the Windhoek location photographed by Nitzsche-Reiter (or one of her employees): The Old Location Dance in 1959 and The Herero Function (fashion show) in 1963. See Digital Namibian Archives, ONR Collection, images No.: 001635-001695 and 034510-034550.

114 See e.g. Digital Namibian Archives, ONR Collection, images No.: 034384, 034421, 034405, 034406.

115 Digital Namibian Archives: National Archives, Ottilie Nitzsche-Reiter Collection, image number 034486, "Natives: Damaras. Usakos Location", n.d.

116 E.g. Digital Namibian Archives, ONR Collection, images No.: 034381, 034391, 034412, 037881.

117 Melber, Revisiting the Windhoek Old Location, p. 3. The captions to the photographs reference the Rhenish mission society respectively, though it remains unclear if their involvement was limited to mediation or if they were indeed commissioning Nitzsche-Reiter's photographic work. See also footnote 98 for further references.

118 Again, while all photographs in the collection are attributed to Nitzsche-Reiter, it may well be that some of the photographs taken in the location in Windhoek

in the 1950s and early 1960s were authored by her employees (all members of the settler community or German immigrants), among them e.g. Dieter Hinrichs. Some of his Photographs were Published, in: Dag Henrichsen, Naomi Jacobson and Karen Marshall (eds.), *Israel Goldblatt. Building Bridges. Namibian Nationalists Clemens Kapuuo, Hosea Kutako, Brendan Simbwaye, Samuel Witbooi.* Basel, 2010, pp. 47, 48 and 53.

119 See Wallace, *History of Namibia*, p. 236.

120 Jan-Bart Gewald, Diluting Drinks and Deepening Discontent. Colonial Liquor Control and Public Resistance in Windhoek, Namibia, in: Deborah Fahy Bryceson (ed.), *Alcohol in Africa: Mixing Business, Pleasure, and Politics.* Portsmouth 2002, pp. 117–138, here p. 120.

121 'Natives: Damara' for figure 28. All original captions, including those accompanying the glamorous dances and fashion shows that took place in the Windhoek location in the 1950s and 1960s, feature *Eingeborene* (natives) as generic label. For dancing and fashion shows see Henrichsen, *A Glance*, pp. 24–25.

122 Digital Namibian Archives, ONR Collection, e.g. images No. 034352, 034484, 034483, 03357, 03356, 034488.

123 See Lorena Rizzo, A Glance, p. 686.

124 See the earlier discussion on pp. 21–2 and footnote 84.

125 See for this argument Marion Wallace, Looking at the locations: the ambiguities of urban photography, in Hartmann et al., *Colonising Camera*, pp. 132–37.

126 Wallace, Looking, p. 135.

127 See for the Windhoek location e.g. Brigitte Lau (ed.), *An Investigation of the Shooting at the Old Location on 10 December 1959.* Windhoek, 1995; Melber, Revisiting the Windhoek Old Location.

128 The Basler Afrika Bibliographien (BAB) acquired the Scherz collection in the 1980s, and have digitised parts of the photographs (see http://baslerafrikabibliographien-archiv.faust-web.de/); the National Archives of Namibia (NAN) received the Ottilie Nitzsche-Reiter collection (ONR) in 2001 and parts of the photographs have been included in the Digital Namibian Archives (see footnote 109). The NAN used images from the ONR collection for the exhibition '50th Anniversary of the Old Location Massacre' in Windhoek in 2009; and the BAB exhibited some of the Scherz photographs in the exhibition 'White Lady – Black Lady. On photography and everyday life in during African rock art research' in Basel in 2016.

129 Christopher Morton and Darren Newbury (eds.), *The African Photographic Archive. Research and Curatorial Strategies.* London, New Delhi, New York, Sidney, 2015.

130 See for an early contribution Paul Landau and Deborah Kaspin (eds.), *Images and Empires. Visuality in Colonial and Postcolonial Africa.* Berkeley, Los Angeles, London, 2002; Erin Haney, *Photography and Africa.* London, 2010; Richard Vokes (ed.), *Photography in Africa. Ethnographic Perspectives.* Woodbridge, Rochester, 2012; and the various contributions to Morton and Newbury, *The African Photographic Archive.*

131 See Christopher Morton and Darren Newbury, Introduction. Relocating the African Photographic Archive, in ibid., *The African Photographic Archive*, pp. 1–16.

132 The women collectors are Cecilie//Geises, Wilhelmine Katjimune, Gisela Pieters and Olga//Garoës. We were introduced to these collections in the course of research done in central Namibia in 2012. The photographic collections have been part of a collaborative exhibition project. See Paul Grendon, Giorgio Miescher, Lorena Rizzo, Tina Smith, Usakos. *Photographs Beyond Ruins. The Old Location Albums, 1920s–1960s.* Basel, 2015.

133 Edwards and Hart, Introduction, in ibid., *Photographs Objects Histories*, pp. 1–15.

134 On women as collectors see Martha Langford, *Suspended Conversations. The Afterlife of Memory in Photographic Albums*. Montreal, Kingston, London, Ithaca, 2008.

135 Giorgio Miescher, The NE51 Series Frontier: The Grand Narrative of Apartheid Planning and the Small Town. *Journal of Southern African Studies*, 41, 3, 2015: 561–80, here p. 570.

136 Giorgio Miescher, Usakos' Urban Past – Traces in the Archives, in Grendon et al., *Usakos*, pp. 26–61, here p. 39. According to the magistrate in Karibib, the neighbouring town, there were 1205 African residents – 529 men, 405 women, and 271 children – who lived in the various locations in Usakos in 1926. In comparison: there were 600 white residents in the town at the time.

137 The Natives Urban Areas Act of 1923 was the crucial legislative incentive here. See Davenport, *op. cit.*; and Bill Freund, Cities in Revolt: The Long-Term Crisis of South African Urbanism, in: ibid., *The African City. A History*. Cambridge, 2007, pp. 107–43, here p. 113

138 See the discussion on page 15.

139 Miescher, The NE51 Series Frontier, p. 571.

140 See the discussion on p. 10.

141 Miescher, Usakos' Urban Past, p. 26.

142 Information is more solid for the period after the Second World War, but interviews conducted in Usakos in 2012 and 2013 allow to describe work and labour relations in the 1930s and 1940s accordingly. There's no doubt that the railway was the main employer of African men at the time and much less important for women, who often found work in private households. Interview with Cecilie//Geises, Usakos, 20. November 2012.

143 Residents paid fees for grazing and watering stock. See Miescher, Usakos' Urban Past, p. 47.

144 Ibid., p. 40.

145 Miescher, The NE51 Series Frontier, p. 580.

146 Melber, Revisiting the Windhoek Old Location, p. 1. But see Wallace, *Health, Power, and Politics*.

147 Elizabeth Edwards, Introduction: Observations from the Coal Face, in ibid., *Raw Histories*, p. 5.

148 Edwards, Photography and the Material Performance of the Past, here p. 131.

149 See e.g. the introduction to Christopher Morton and Elizabeth Edwards (eds.), *Photography, Anthropology and History: Expanding the Frame*. London, New York, 2009, pp. 1–26.

150 Wilhelmine Katjimune Collection, image No. 29, Usakos Old Location; Wilhelmine Katjimune (in a white dress) at her first communion, with Sibilla (girl on the right, surname unknown), Petrus Chabagae and Maria Schiefer (on the left), Gertrud Schiefer and Alex Hagendorn (on the right), names of children unknown, late 1930s [11.5×8.5cm].

151 Morton and Newbury, *The African Photographic Archive*, p. 7.

152 Interviews with Cecilie//Geises and Wilhelmine Katjimune in Usakos, and with Gisela Pieters and Olga//Garoës in Okombahe, between 2012 and 2014.

153 There is still little to no research on everyday African photography in 1930s and 1940s Namibia, see Jeremy Silvester, Your space or mine? The photography of the Police Zone, in Hartmann et al., *Colonising Camera*, pp. 138–44, here p. 138.

154 Again, there is almost no knowledge about itinerant or ambulant photographers in Namibia. See for a recent contribution to itinerant photography in South Africa Sophie Feyder, Lounge Photography and the Politics of Township Interiors: The Representation of the Black South African Home in the Ngilima Photographic Collection, East Rand, 1950s. *Kronos*, Special Issue on Documentary Photography in South Africa, 38, 2012: 131–53. More generally

on ambulant photographers in Africa see Vera Viditz-Ward, Photography in Sierra Leone, 1850–1918. *Africa. Journal of the International African Institute*, 57, 4, 1987: 510–518; and the introduction to Heike Behrend, *Contesting Visibility. Photographic Practices on the East African Coast.* Bielefeld, 2013.

155 Lorena Rizzo, Paul Grendon, Giorgio Miescher, Tina Smith, Photographs Beyond Ruins. The Usakos old location albums, 1920s to 1960s, in Grendon et al., *Usakos*, pp. 7–25, here p. 11. See for the conjuncture of railways and settler photography in South Africa Jeremy Foster, 'Land of Contrasts'.

156 Interviews with Cecilie//Geises, Usakos, 19 November 2012, and Gisela Pieters and Olga//Garoës, Okombahe, 8. August 2014, who remembered the price for photographs, 15 cents per image, and the names of some of the photographers. There is a photograph of one of the ambulant photographers in the Gisela Pieters and Olga//Garoës collection, the portrait of Jan Christian with his camera, taken in the 1950s. See Grendon et al., *Usakos*, p. 10.

157 See Simon Njami quoted in Kylie Thomas and Louise Green, Stereoscopic Visions: Reading Colonial and Contemporary African Photography. *Social Dynamics*, 40, 1, 2014: 1–11, here p. 1.

158 Clients paid on the spot and would either receive their images by mail or would wait for the photographers return, since most of the photographs had to be developed in professional studios in Windhoek, Swakopmund or Walvis Bay. Interview with Gisela Pieters and Olga//Garoës, Okombahe, 8. August 2014.

159 Interview with Gisela Pieters and Olga//Garoës, Okombahe, 8. August 2014.

160 The Cecilie//Geises Collection is included in Grendon et al., *Usakos*, pp. 62–75.

161 Interview with Cecilie//Geises, Usakos, 19. November 2012.

162 See images reproduced in Grendon et al., *Usakos*. Football for men and netball for women were among the most popular and photographically best documented sports in the Usakos old location. Dances, concerts and other festivities took place most commonly at the community hall opened in 1936.

163 It remains unclear if Ottilie Nitzsche-Reiter's photographs taken in the old location in Windhoek were commissioned by location residents, or if people could buy copies of photographs at her studio and shop. For South Africa see Santu Mofokeng, *Black Photo Album/Look At Me, 1890–1950.* Göttingen, 2013.

164 Heike Behrend, *Contesting Visibility*, pp. 121–46.

165 The notion of compounded photographs is developed in Patricia Hayes, Okombone: Compound Portraits and Photographic Archives in Namibia, in Morton and Newbury, *The African Photographic Archive*, pp. 177–96.

166 'Lines of flight' is a concept developed by Giles Deleuze and Felix Guattari. See Chapter 1 for explanation and references.

167 Wilhelmine Katjimune Collection; Petrus Chabagae (left) and Mr. Reiter; photographer: C.F. Fenton, Walvis Bay (8.5 × 13.5 cm).

168 The oldest images in the Usakos old location collections are a portrait of Cecilie//Geises' grandmother Johanna with an unknown female friend, taken in Rehoboth in the 1900s, and the portrait of Wilhelmine Katjimune's grandmother Elisabeth Schiefer taken in ca. 1910 in an unspecified photo studio, see Grendon et al., *Usakos*, p. 68 and p. 92.

169 See Lorena Rizzo, Gender and Visuality: Identification Photographs, Respectability and Personhood in Colonial Southern Africa in the 1920s and 1930s. *Gender & History*, 26, 3, 2014: 688–708, here p. 696; Richard Vokes, Introduction, in ibid. (ed.), *Photography in Africa*, pp. 1–29, here p. 9; Amar Wahab, Race, Gender, and Visuality, p. 7. For a broader discussion of respectability in South Africa in the interwar period see Lynn Thomas, The Modern Girl and Racial Respectability in 1930s South Africa. *Journal of African History*, 47, 2006: 461–90.

170 While the Katjimune Collection contains many studio photographs taken in various Namibian locations, there are less such images in the //Geises and the Pieters & //Garoës Collections.

171 The spatialised notion of time is derived from Archimedean thought on the mechanical grounding of time and its measurement. The German distinction between *der* Moment (temporal) and *das* Moment (spatial) has kept the double connotation of the term. In the Nitezschean elaboration on Augenblick in *Also Sprach Zarathustra* (*Thus Spoke Zarathustra*) the site of the transformative experience of the Augenblick is likewise preserved. See Balibar et al., Der/das Moment, p. 2, and Shapiro, Nietzsche's Story, pp. 27–8.

172 Interview with Gisela Pieters and Olga//Garoës, Okombahe, 8 August 2014.

173 See for a more general discussion of naming people and places in South African photography Ruth Simbao, Review of Figures & Fictions: Contemporary South African Photography by Tamar Garb. *Kronos* 38, 2012: 272–75.

174 Gisela Pieters and Olga//Garoës Collection, Herodia Goreses (on the left) and Gisela Pieters, next to Olga//Garoës' house, Usakos old location, ca. 1950s (11 × 6.5 cm)

175 See this chapter pp. 15–7.

176 The debate on native locations as slums gained momentum in the 1930s and 1940s and was a popular argument among architects and town planners, which helped legitimise residential segregation and apartheid urban planning. See Miescher, The N51 Series Frontier, p. 565.

177 See e.g. Union of South Africa, *South West Africa and the Union of South Africa. The History of a Mandate.* (n.p.), 1947; and for the period before and after WW II, Wallace, *A History*, pp. 244–45.

178 Azoulay, What is a photograph?, p. 13.

179 Miescher, The NE51 Series Frontier, p. 576. The following paragraphs draw significantly from Miescher's work on the history of urban planning in Usakos.

180 The Group Areas Act was never officially applied to Namibia, but it undoubtedly served as informal guideline. See also footnote 105.

181 The regulations also prescribed buffer zones between towns and townships, and the allocation of plots and houses according to race. The standardised NE 51 house was one version of non-European housing. See again Miescher, The NE51 Series Frontier.

182 Interviews with Cecilie//Geises, 11 August 2014.

183 Milly Jafta, Nicky Kautja, Magda Oliphant, *An Investigation of the Shooting at the Old Location on 10 December 1959.* Windhoek, 1991.

184 Interview with Wilhelmine Katjimune, Usakos, 12 August 2014.

185 Miescher, Usakos' Urban Past, p. 58.

186 Interview with Cecilie//Geises, 11. August 2014.

187 Ann Laura Stoler, Imperial Debris: Reflections on Ruins and Ruination. *Cultural Anthropology*, 23, 2, 2008: 191–219, here p. 194.

188 For Namibia see George Steinmetz, Colonial Melancholy and Fordist Nostalgia. The Ruinscapes of Namibia and Detroit, in: Julia Hell and Andreas Schönle (eds.), *Ruins of Modernity*. Durham and London, 2010, pp. 294–320.

189 Paul Grendon, Old location showers, Usakos, 2013. The image is reproduced in colour in Grendon et al., *Usakos*, p. 116.

190 See e.g. Daniel Herwitz, Monument, Ruin, and Redress in South African Heritage. *The Germanic Review: Literature, Culture, Theory*, 86, 4, 2011: 232–48.

191 In collaboration with the town of Usakos, the Museums Association of Namibia, the University of Namibia and the University of Basel, and the four women collectors we opened an exhibition at the local museum in Usakos in 2015. See Grendon et al., *Usakos*.

192 See for a more general discussion Ciraj Rassool and Sandra Prosalendis (eds.), *Recalling Community in Cape Town: Creating and Curating the District Six Museum.* Cape Town, 2001.

193 Obviously, this resonates with Jacob Dlamini's *Native Nostalgia.* Johannesburg, 2009, though it is important to note that historical narratives in Usakos work with an intricate chronology that makes a decisive difference between the period before and after the implementation of apartheid urban planning and the forced removals in the early 1960s.

194 Rizzo et al., Photographs beyond Ruins, p. 12.

195 Langford, *Suspended Conversations.* While we have mentioned the exhibition at the local museum in Usakos, there have been mobile versions of the exhibition travelling Europe and the USA since 2016.

196 Andrea Kunars, Traditions of Collecting and Remembering. Gender, Class and the 19th Century Sentiment Album and Photographic Album. *Early Popular Visual Culture*, 4, 3, 2006: 227–43.

197 Langford, *Suspended Conversations*, p. 20.

198 See for a synthesis of current scholarship on public history, memory and historical narration in South Africa, Witz et al., *Unsettled History.*

199 Jacques Rancière, *Dissensus. On Politics and Aesthetics.* London, New Delhi, New York, Sydney, 2010, p. 36.

200 See the references on p. 4.

201 See page 6.

202 The formulation echoes the notion of Heidegger's being-in-the world. For a discussion of this concept in relation to photography, see Chaudhary. *Afterimage of Empire.* Minneapolis, 2012, pp. 24–5.

203 See page 24.

204 BAB Scherz collection, I.A:3.2., E.R. Scherz, Fahrt nach Swakopmund. März 1942, p. 10. [German original, my translation.]

4 Heterotopia

Aerial photography and mapping in the Eastern Cape, 1930s–1960s

Prelude – a view from above

The opening of this chapter is, again, provided by an image – more specifically, an aerial photograph. It is a view from above, a vertiginous picture of an expanding landscape fleshed out in shades of black and white and qualified by scattered geographical forms: lines, squares, and dots. It is a barren landscape with no distinctive features such as prominent mountain peaks, great waters, ravines, or extended forests that would help guide the eye. Here and there, however, we discern gravel roads, perhaps small rivers where the lines darken, individual fields, and – it would seem – clusters of dwellings with bordered gardens. There is evidence of the photograph's provenance on the image's right hand margin: it was taken on the 7th of November 1938, at 01h25, at a height of 12,000 feet (3560 metres), on behalf of the Aircraft Operating Company of Africa in Johannesburg, and as part of the topographical survey of the South East Coast. The photograph is filed in the image collection of the National Geo-Spatial Information in the Department of Rural Development and Land Reform in Cape Town among a series of images taken within the vicinity of Umtata in the Eastern Cape and assembled under flight job 132. We also learn about the camera and lenses used, the scale of the photographs taken (1:25,000), the size of single prints (7′ × 7″), the extent of the area covered in job 132 (1600 square miles, or 4000 square kilometres), and the section depicted in the image – the border area between Libode, Tsolo, and Qumbu districts, including sections of the Zandukwane and Wolo-wolo rivers.

Before returning to this information retrieved from the geospatial archive and the photographic print itself, it is worth paying attention to some of the more general characteristics of aerial photography as a distinctive image form. To non-specialists, aerial photographs appear to be rather obscure, highly encoded, and hard to "read", understand, or make sense of.[1] They are ambiguous, simultaneously evocative and banal, aesthetically appealing, but strangely blank in their metrical layout.[2] Their legibility is all but obvious; their larger perspective is comprehensive yet – depending on image scale, quality, and resolution – limited in detail.[3] While aerial photography is often associated with the emergence of a modern industrial image economy and

Figure 4.1 Aerial photograph of Umtata, 1938.[4]

the desire for an all-encompassing, panoptic gaze – underpinned by milita-ristic surveillance[5] – the high level of abstraction and the intrinsic verticality confuse habitual, lateral, and even more embedded ways of seeing the world, the uncertain vantage point causing discomfort if not major disorientation.[6] Thus, the slightly unskilled description of Figure 4.1 proposed above seems, perhaps, typical for an untrained viewer.

Aerial photographs scan and survey the earth and present it as a flat-tened, geometricised surface, on which the landscape's natural features appear transformed and restored as collated data in an abstract and uniform pattern.[7] Thanks to extreme scaling, the image underscores a radically detached and removed view, thereby reducing traces of human presence and intervention, if visible at all, to mere superficial phenomena, or eclips-ing them entirely.[8] In the case of Figure 4.1, the location and date of the photograph provide some grounding, but this itemised information remains strangely at odds with a persistent sense of the non-situated and ahistorical, nurtured by the visual production of an unspecified, unre-solved spatiality and temporality.[9] There is, then, reason for caution, since the model of formal abstraction and, as Paula Amad has noted, the generic notion of visual panopticism are susceptible to swallowing up more spe-cific and oblique histories of image production and visual practice, even in what we like to conceive of as the closely regulated domain of aerial photography.[10] Indeed, the archive itself gives cause for nuancing – more specifically, a remark made in a report on aerial photography and topographical surveying prepared by the Director of the Trigonometrical Survey in Cape Town, W. Whittingdale, for the Secretary for Lands in Pretoria, on the 21st of September 1936:

> Aerial survey may mean anything from taking photographs in the air to plotting detailed and contoured maps from them using complicated and expensive machines.[11]

The director's report went on to paint an intricate picture composed of the diverse image forms and formats, scales and materialities that included verticals and obliques, contact prints, mosaics, or enlargements; topographical map sheets; flight plans, line drawings and sketches. He also conveyed a sense of the various practices clustering around aerial photography, among them taking photographs, adding notations on photographic surfaces, recording field notes, translating photographs into maps, and operating the sophisticated technological equipment required for all these interventions: aeroplanes, cameras, theodolites, and stereoscopes. With an eye to explaining the growing interest in aerial photography, he listed those involved in image production, be they the South African Air Force, private companies, or adventurous individuals armed with the required visionary enthusiasm, pecuniary means, and technical skills. And finally, he enumerated diverse fields of application, such as agriculture and geology, irrigation and forestry, railways and roads, native affairs and mining, all of which provided an account of public and private image use and consumption.

We will concern ourselves with the image forms, visual practices, agents, and vectors of image distribution referred to in the report throughout the chapter. Here, we shall simply observe that what makes the director's account remarkable is the way in which it sheds light, if cursorily and in patches, on the complicated material, institutional, and technological networks within which aerial photographs were produced, circulated, and deployed.[12] There is, as we shall see, a specific history to the configuration of aerial photography in South Africa in the late 1930s, one that we will retrace in detail since it provides the backdrop against which the images' shifting deployments in a particular location need to be understood. Yet before we do so, we should explain why we relinquish here the close-up views adopted in the earlier chapters in favour of moving towards the more distanced view from above. The way there leads us back, first, to a more elaborate, general discussion of aerial photography in order to mark off the historical and theoretical frameworks within which we will later tease out iterations of this peculiar image form across the Eastern Cape.

Aerial photography as heterotopia

As suggested above, aerial photographs appear as "enigmatic puzzles".[13] They are characterised by a tension between their richly aesthetic appeal and an ostensible flatness induced by their geometrical and mechanical texture – a tension that the Swiss architect and urban planner Le Corbusier described as one between "imagination and cold reason".[14] Aerial photographs, we noticed, provide a vertiginous view of space that produces a sense of radical miniaturisation and visual totality, and since, importantly, the image does away with the horizon, we are deprived of one of the key orientation guides. The described ambiguity in assessing aerial photography as an image form runs like a thread through its history and goes back to its very beginnings. Cosgrove and Fox have retraced how the desire to view and represent the world from above and to contain it in a single image have stimulated and intertwined histories of landscape art, surveying, and mapping.[15] Decisively transformed by the co-evolution of photography and flight beginning in the mid-nineteenth century, first by balloon and later powered aircraft, the pre-occupations with what is alternately referred to as the bird's-eye or God's-eye perspective encouraged a gradual shift away from panoramic vistas grounded in eighteenth-century landscape painting towards more elevated notions of an all-encompassing aerial vision, be it in its oblique or vertical mode.[16]

The French photographer Nadar's adventurous experiments at and eventually his success in producing a high-altitude photographic image of a village outside of Paris in 1858 is generally identified as the beginning of the photographic expression of the long-evolving aspiration to overcome the physical restriction to – and visual limitations of – ground-level perspectives.[17] Spectacular illustrations of cities, produced in large-scale cartographic or pictorial form, had become fashionable by the late eighteenth century; but it was only during the late eighteenth century that aerial photographic views of places such as Paris, London, Melbourne, and New York began to be hugely popularised.[18] Stereoscopic photographs reduced the earth's vastness to a material and visual scale readily consumable by growing numbers of armchair-travellers.[19] With the advent of aviation at the turn of the last century, the striving for a detached and transcendent photographic view from above received its decisive boost, and the utopian desire for the unimpeded, omnivoyant gaze – what had hitherto been an exclusive, divine privilege but was now considered an emblem of modern advancement – became a reality brought about by technological innovation.[20]

Aerial photography's momentous development and perfection as a technology used in recording, mapping and, crucially, reconnaissance, ensued during the period of the First World War, when an increasingly industrialised process underpinned the unprecedented demand for, and production of, accurate maps (at various scales) of monitored territory to facilitate the study and anticipation of enemy positions and movements.[21] Seeing was considered decisive for prevailing in battle. As Peter Collier has noted, intelligence and map revision first involved the acquisition of photography from low-flying aircrafts using largely improvised camera equipment, but the threat of being shot down required planes to fly higher and hence encouraged the development of cameras with longer focal lengths.[22] In addition, the photographic medium was widely used to aestheticise the war and promote the heroic image of the soldier – dead or alive. The outrageous scale and horror of human loss, destruction, and devastation necessarily revealed the medium's problematic and deeply dystopian facets, especially in its aerial manifestation.[23] An increasingly technologised and rationalised form of warfare mediated through images that de-realised the military engagement, rendering it through an abstract, anonymous view from above, seemed to deliver a detached and dehumanising perspective. Once human presence was removed from the field of vision, killing was ultimately made easier and more efficient.[24] In the dystopian understanding of aerial photography, it was made clear that war had, at some level, stopped being about enemy activity and fighting, and had become about what Robert Dixon describes as a "matter of applied science", for which the photograph would deliver the information required about abstract patterns, systems of intelligence, and flows of material processes.[25]

The tension between enthusiastic and utterly negative, if not rejectionist, responses to aerial photography continued to go along with the growing proliferation of the medium across a broad range of bureaucratic, civil, and commercial realms in the interwar period. Expectations were high in the domain of mapping and surveying, which in the early twentieth century became a principal tool for planning infrastructural projects, agricultural production, and urban development, and aerial photography would indeed feature prominently here.[26] The military control of air surveys was inherited from the war, and after 1916, it gradually gave way to the involvement of commercial companies and the emergence of a specialised field of photo-interpretation.[27] Photogrammetric techniques for the development of mapping from aerial photographs had been developed in France as early as 1851,[28] yet they were significantly improved in the 1930s, making photogrammetry much more widely accepted.[29]

Notwithstanding the prevalent belief in aerial photography's ability to bring about new, more efficient, and less expensive methods of surveying and mapping, the medium's value and contribution remained contested and vividly debated in specialist journals and the popular press.[30] Conventional ground survey remained a crucial reference once aerial photographs were used for cartographic purposes.[31] Still, aerial photography ushered in important shifts in the perception and management of the earth's surface, which was henceforth more tightly linked to remote aerial representation.[32] The peculiar appeal, as Cosgrove and Fox argue, arose from what aerial photographs managed to do: they established a visible context for individual features on the ground, placed them in relation to one another and to a broader topography, and, crucially, revealed patterns to the eye – in short, they "created geographies".[33]

It is common knowledge that surveying and mapping have also been instrumental tools of imperial expansion and colonial conquest,[34] and indeed, it was in this context, and more specifically in Gaza, Palestine, where the first successful attempts at mapping from aerial photographs were made.[35] Private air survey companies first became involved in mapping the Anglo-Belgian boundary in the Copper-Belt in 1927, in what is today Zambia and the Democratic Republic of Congo.[36] These commercial endeavours soon spread across the continent into Uganda, Tanzania, Zimbabwe, and, as the information given to the opening figure to this chapter evidenced, South Africa. We will come back to the commercial advance into aerial surveying later on, but for now, the "creation of geographies" quoted above shall take us into a second domain in which aerial photography's reception was mixed, and its strengths and weaknesses, promises and deceptions, were discussed in ways that are relevant for our purposes here – the disciplines of geography, history, and the science of space.

An important effort in reflecting on aerial photography's value for understanding the relationship between the human and natural environment was made by historians grouped around the French *Annales School*, most prominently by Fernand Braudel and Marc Bloch.[37] Believing that history was less about individuals and events alone, but rather about understanding the entanglement of physical and social landscapes, Bloch and others promoted an interpretive model that would bring together history and geography and would look at human existence across multiple perspectives – a view that would, surprisingly perhaps, resonate with the South African state's approach to "native administration".[38] To the French scholars, aerial photography appeared propitious, since it seemed to offer a fresh macro-perspective that overlooked the complexities of the earth's surface and could be brought into dialectical conversation with the micro-perspectives of social life.[39] Underpinning these deliberations was the emergence of what Paula Amad identified as a new paradigm in human geography during the interwar period, which began to conceive of the earth as face and, concurrently, to read and interpret it in physiognomic terms. In Amad's own words: "The world appeared as an expressive, skin-like surface with an objective correlate".[40] Placed alongside each other, natural features such as rivers, mountains, and vegetation, *and* the material traces of human intervention would now constitute elements of a highly encoded text. Aerial photography's appeal lay in its ability to precisely record this text, understood as being made up of documents from the "planet's living archive".[41] Comparing aerial photography to an archive ingeniously introduced temporal depth to the view from above, a conception that clearly differed from the immediacy and presentism of military reconnaissance, bringing it closer to an archaeological understanding of space and landscape.[42] Landscape thus understood appeared as a palimpsest of material layers, in which the sedimentation of history became *visible* as soon as it was recorded in the aerial photograph.[43] Though the aerial view compressed space – onto the image, within its frame, through miniaturisation – it preserved time, since it precisely allowed a temporal excavation of that space.

While evidently attracted to the view from above, Bloch and his peers acknowledged the need to ground it by linking geography with social, political, and economic structures.[44] In their ambitious preoccupation with understanding the history of humankind in relation to the environment, aerial photography was an attractive tool of observation and research, and – because the photographic medium was generally understood in terms of mechanical objectivity – it would remain so in the social sciences. As Jeanne Haffner has argued, the view from above became crucial in reflecting on the nature and morphology of social space.[45] In its benevolent reception, the distanced perspective afforded by aerial photography was seen as the privileged representational modality through which the "disorders and pathologies on the ground" – especially, though not exclusively, associated with urban contexts – assumed a distinct, abstract form.[46] And yet it was the formal abstraction of a particular landscape surveyed that would ultimately shed most light on the character and mentality of people who inhabited it.[47]

There were, though, more critical voices among those concerned with aerial photography's role in producing, mediating, and experiencing the physical and social landscape. Henri Lefebvre's careful reflections on the production of space could not fail to note how much attention aerial photography was attracting from contemporary social scientists and theorists of space. His own response was much more suspicious, based on both the aerial image's intrinsic affinity for abstraction and the medium's significant appropriation by the state.[48] Considered against the backdrop of an anthropocentric theory of space that emphasised the intersection of spatial experience, perception, and imagination,[49] a technology of representation such as aerial photography appeared to flatten and reduce the richness and meaning of social life and the complexity of how humans experienced and inhabited their environments.[50] The view from above was considered, in this critical reading, a top-down perspective, and of particular use and value to those in power, especially state bureaucracies. State officials and planners, Lefebvre argued, considered visual methods to be objective and quantifiable means of recording and documenting,[51] with a privileged status in a hegemonic regime of control and surveillance that increasingly imposed an epistemology of science on examinations of space.[52] This is why aerial photography epitomised to its critics the ways that "the world was reduced to an image, to an icy coldness", in which "space had no social existence".[53] Lefebvre's reasoning seems dystopic, indeed, when we read that "the space of state control can also be defined as being optical and visual. The human body has disappeared into a space that is equivalent to a series of images".[54] In this view, there was little to gain, ultimately, from a visual technology that produced nothing more than inventories of what was *in* space but would never give rise to meaningful knowledge *of* space.[55]

Notwithstanding his desire to rip aerial photography to pieces, Lefebvre was well aware of how the medium brought about a new aesthetic of space, how it interfered with spatial perception by establishing new signs, signals, and codes that importantly reshaped the sensual interaction between actors and physical space.[56] Roland Barthes has most consistently reflected on the ways in which the view from above underscored a series of shifts in the perception and conceptualisation of the physical world, and on the extent to which the aerial perspective captured the world's unique spatial and temporal qualities.[57] For Barthes, aerial photography changed the possibilities lodged in the very act of seeing, since the photograph appeared as the portent of a daring "Promethean seer" endowed with the creativity to perceive the world anew and with an eye granting an "incomparable power of intellection".[58] In Adnan Morshed's reading of Barthes, aerial photographs hence produced an aesthetic of lightness, an anti-gravity, which radically reconceived the relationship between material forms and ground and in an act of "marvellous mitigation of altitude" suspended the sense of spatio-temporal dependence.[59] Barthes, then, understood the aesthetic value of the bird's-eye view in terms of a specific sensibility of vision:

> The bird's-eye view [...] gives us the world to read and not only to perceive; this is why it corresponds to a new sensibility of vision; in the past, to travel [...] was to be thrust into the midst of sensation, to perceive only a kind of tidal wave of things; the bird's-eye view, on the contrary, [...] permits us to transcend sensation and see things in their structure.[60]

Aerial seeing and perceiving, the new visual sensibility, appears here as an imaginary process; one that enables the eye to subsume fragments of space and multiple, dispersed objects into a visual continuum and a signifying whole. However, this is not, as Barthes continues to argue, simply a matter of geography; it is just as much an attempt to recompose the layers of time and imagine history in a way that makes, as he boldly concluded, "duration itself become panoramic".[61]

Clearly, Barthes was tracing aerial photography's *transformative* effects on the perception and imagination of space and landscape, and his thinking is highly suggestive for probing the medium's ability to reconfigure something we might call the "other" space, or the utopian no-place.[62] This brings us to a final deliberation that has relevance for our discussion of aerial photography: Michel Foucault's concept of heterotopia, and his attempt to outline the characteristics of spaces he considered to be somewhat different, i.e. contradictory, incompatible, transformative, and which he understood to be singular in how they formulate a complex relationship between the spatial and the temporal.[63] He wrote: "Heterotopias are counter-sites, a kind of effectively enacted utopia in which the real sites that can be found within the culture are simultaneously represented, contested, and inverted. Places of this kind are outside of all places, even though it may be possible to indicate their location in reality".[64] Continuing along these lines, we are told that heterotopias, or "emplacements" as Foucault generally seems to prefer,[65] can either function as spaces of illusion, when they expose every real space, all the sites inside of which human life is partitioned, as still more illusionary, or as spaces of compensation by "creating a space that is other, another real space, as perfect, and meticulous as [the real space is] messy, ill constructed, and jumbled".[66] Importantly, these explications assume that heterotopias do not designate an entirely detached realm but instead remain connected with all other spaces or emplacements, though in a way that suspends, neutralises, or inverts the relations designated, reflected, or represented by them.[67] Refining the texture of the concept further, Foucault notes that whatever function heterotopias might have – be it as illusion or compensation – their effect on all other spaces will always depend on the restructuring, redistribution, and carving out (*découper*) of flows of time. He accordingly declares that this is important since it pursues "the idea of constituting a place of all times that is itself outside of time and inaccessible to its ravages" in order to organise "in this way a sort of perpetual and indefinite accumulation of time in an immobile place".[68] Hence, while heterotopia describes the interpenetration of spaces, it also implies, crucially, the "crossing" and accumulation of "temporal streams" that make the question of temporality, and by implication, history, "extremely messy".[69]

Foucault's notion of heterotopia seems suggestive for thinking about aerial photography as an image form with particular spatio-temporal effects that impinge on the production of space. Recalling the ambiguities of the medium referred to above, aerial photographs appear, on one hand, as abstracted, detached and transcendent images that seem, therefore, to be somewhat unreal. On the other hand, the photographic medium itself and the notion of mechanical objectivity suggest that they are anchored in reality, merely mirroring, as it were, what is there on the ground.[70] In addition, the central importance of scaling – miniaturising as much as enlarging – is essential for aerial photography, which strongly resonates with Foucault's ocular language and his idea that heterotopias produce "spatial intensities" precisely because they replicate, exaggerate, or reduce another world.[71] And it is indeed here, embedded in Foucault's visual undertone, that a remarkable congruence between aerial photography and heterotopia shows and helps us identify them both as "concrete technologies" *and* "rhetorical machines".[72]

If we review the various reflections on aerial photography discussed above, what seems common to all is a tension between two understandings. One sees the medium in terms of mimetic representation and objective rendering and considers these photographs as documents in an archive of space that enables us to see the relationality and complexity of features that make up a particular landscape. The other one views aerial photography as an image form and technology through which landscapes are fundamentally transformed and reconstituted, thereby acquiring an entirely new aesthetics that reshapes the spatio-temporality of the space they claim to represent. It is, in other words, perhaps the unresolved matter at the heart of photography and more generally technology, which looms here: its function to either *record* – or "enframe" in Heideggerian parlance – or to *reveal*.[73] These ambiguities and tensions, which seem to cluster around aerial photographs in an intense manner, will continue to be of concern to us once we look at the medium's deployment in the South African context. We will also pay particular attention to the question of aerial photography acquiring heterotopian characteristics and functions, with a specific spatio-temporality that essentially depended on an aestheticised view from above.

"Seeing our land from above"

First experiments with aerial views in South Africa were made between the late nineteenth and early twentieth century. Gas balloons had been introduced by the British on a large scale during the Anglo-Boer War, "for the purpose of observing enemy movements and directing artillery fire", as well as for airmail and passenger flights in the early 1900s.[74] The advent of powered aircraft wouldn't change this, and sightseeing balloons kept ascending into the skies over Durban and Johannesburg, providing – in one instance – the opportunity for pioneering aerial image making by the Swiss balloonist Eduard Spelterini in 1911 (Figure 4.2).[75] However, the first known aerials produced for military purposes seem to have been taken, tellingly, during the South African invasion of Namibia in 1915, though – ironically perhaps – from a German plane monitoring the bombing of an enemy military camp at Tsaukhaib in the southern Namib Desert.[76] Indeed, the military would remain a critical actor in the production of aerial photography in South Africa in the twentieth century, including in one of the main fields in which the medium was deployed – namely, surveying and mapping.[77]

Figure 4.2 Johannesburg, 1911.[78]

The connection between emerging colonial bureaucracies and mapping as an essential feature of early colonial rule and one of the basic forms of state formation has been noted, as mentioned above, by many historians of Africa.[79] As mechanisms of spatial reorganisation, surveying served to produce general maps of newly acquired territories as well as subjugate colonised peoples, enable labour extraction, and, importantly, extend private land ownership. On a representational level, mapping helped render claimed lands legible and navigable to those willing to exploit them. Lindsay Frederick Braun has meticulously retraced the process of surveying and mapping rural South African landscapes between the 1850s and the early 1910s – a process which in its early decades remained widely inaccurate and incoherent, given a fair amount of "geographical confusion", the lack of precise methods of triangulation, and the uneven implementation of surveying across the colonial territory.[80] In the Cape Colony, for example, and with regard to "native lands", military surveillance and administrative concerns with controlling, managing, and classifying land and population intensified between the 1860s and 1880s. However, it was the Native Locations Act of 1879 and the Glen Grey Act of 1894 (providing for the imposition of a village system and the precept of "one man one plot") that constituted important thresholds for the transformation of land occupation and use. This legislation energised the extension of a system of freehold and quitrent tenures into African space that concurrently required more consistent surveying across the Northern and Eastern Cape.[81]

Mapping and surveying were placed on new footing after Union in 1910, when efforts were oriented towards a comprehensive national framework, and the intention declared, by 1919, to base all surveys across the country on modern triangulation. Under the auspices of a centralised organisation, this ensured future economic development.[82] Aerial photography would not enter the scene yet, however, since at this moment the priority was still institutionalisation and systematisation, which did in fact come to fruition. In 1920, the Trigonometrical Survey Office opened in Cape Town, and a commission was appointed to inquire into matters concerning the survey of lands, which recommended an overall topographical survey of the country and the passing of a National Survey Act, effectuated in 1927.[83] The medium of aerial photography itself emerged in 1922, literally coming like a bombshell, when the South African Air Force took the first vertical aerial photographs during the Rand Rebellion and concomitant bombings of parts of Johannesburg and the Witwatersrand in 1922.[84] While technological improvements throughout the 1920s – especially the acquisition of state-of-the-art theodolites for geodetic triangulation – stirred up hopes, it was only in the mid-1930s that the central government decided to map the entire South African territory at a scale of 1:50,000. The use of aerial photography in this ambitious, large-scale programme would become, as we shall see, an intensely discussed matter (Figure 4.3).

Figure 4.3 Aerial photograph of Fordsburg, 1922.[85]

Aerial photography remained firmly in military hands throughout the 1920s, and even though after the First World War there were a few commercial enterprises that continued to offer short flights around the main South African cities to moneyed customers, or to those who wanted to take oblique photographs of the Cape Peninsula or privately owned farming estates that could be sold as postcards and collectors' items.[86] Commanding both exceptional powered and photographic technology, the Air Force preserved its monopoly on aerial surveying, offering their services to a number of government agencies. However, these activities remained limited to certain areas in the country and included, for instance, aerial photography for the Kalahari and Vaal-Harts irrigation schemes, surveying the route for the Belfast-Waterval railway line and stretches of the coast for hydrographic purposes, and, as we shall see in more detail later in this chapter, an aerial survey of the Transkei.[87] First experiments with terrestrial photogrammetry in 1928 hinted at the potentials for mapping, but the systematic use of aerial photography for capturing topographical data remained a long way off. A correspondence among officers in various government departments and agencies – relating to a set of aerial photographs taken of Groot Constantia in Cape Town and submitted by a member of the local flying club in 1930 – confirms some of the areas in which the new technology began to be applied, yet it likewise depicts a sense of reserve, if not reservation, that prevailed among bureaucrats and state technicians:

> While it [aerial photography] is destined to figure largely in future development, it is not considered, however, that the department [of agriculture] is yet in a position to advocate to farmers its use […] The Chief of the Division of Chemistry states that aerial photography would prove useful in soil survey work while the Division of Plant Industry also recognises its value in field husbandry, but is unable just yet to use it in that direction. The Chief Conservator of Forests has noted your remarks with interest as has also the Director of Irrigation who points out that similar work is being carried out for his Department by the Air Service of the Department of Defence […] This type of work is still in its infancy and as it develops is sure to receive the closer attention of the Departments of State which it can assist.[88]

Farming was, indeed, a problem child. Here aerial surveying was seen, by some, as valuable in countering a phenomenon that served as a subtext to the above quote. Since the 1920s, soil erosion had become of general concern. William Beinart has provided the most comprehensive historical analysis of environmental degradation and the emergence of conservationist concerns in South Africa.[89] According to this study, evidence of severe soil erosion was accumulating in the early twentieth century, and the official position, as it was formulated in two major reports submitted by the Drought Commission in 1923 and the Native Economic Commission in 1932, tended to see methods and practices of both white and black farmers as the main reason for environmental degradation.[90] Statistical data evidences the intensification of livestock farming in this period, and sheep and cattle numbers grew significantly, reaching a peak in 1930. While the distribution of livestock was uneven throughout the country, soil erosion was "painfully evident" almost everywhere.[91] Hence, by the early 1930s, the state was determined to act, and soil conservation became one of the major justifications for intervening in land use, animal husbandry, and agricultural production.[92] Beinart shows how this would have different repercussions in districts dominated by white-owned farms and in African communal areas, and we will come back to this later on. Here, our interest is in how, at this stage, soil conservation briefly emerged as a subject matter in the archive of aerial photography.

The occasion to see the emergency of this subject was provided by the principal of the Grootfontein Agricultural School in Middelburg in the Karroo, which would become the major agricultural research station in the Eastern Cape, in December 1932. In a letter entitled "Soil erosion: propaganda", this is what the correspondent had to say:

> After having flown over parts of Grootfontein and surroundings, I am of the opinion that a series of photographs, taken of soil erosion from the air, would make excellent propaganda in bringing home to the public

(particularly the non-farmers who have little idea of what soil erosion means) the extent of the damage which the country is suffering.

Photographs of such places as the Kundulu Valley, Lady Grey District, and the bottom valleys in the Transkei, showing ramifications of main side sloots [sic], come to mind as being suitable subjects.

I need not emphasise the value of propaganda work in arousing public opinion to call for combative measures.[93]

A few months later, he specified what he thought to be the specific value of photographic documentation, how sites affected by erosion could best be turned into "suitable scenes and subjects", and what scales and image sizes were most appropriate for "propaganda work" – enlargements for use in agricultural research and fieldwork and small scales in education and publicity.[94] By that point, the Secretary for Agriculture seemed convinced, and notwithstanding roundabout negotiations with the Air Service in the Department of Defence that mainly concerned expenditure, an unspecified number of aerial photographs across four South African provinces was taken in 1933 and 1934, usually of privately and government-owned farms.[95] Still, Grootfontein's verve and sophisticated argument in favour of the bird's-eye view was not rewarded, ultimately, beyond occasional provisions of photographs taken by the Air Force, at a price acceptable to the Department of Agriculture. Indeed, while soil erosion had clearly become a genuine preoccupation among state officials, and would remain so, importantly, at this stage, it seemed not a sufficient argument *per se* to justify large pecuniary investments in systematic aerial photography. A more successful incentive would come, as noted earlier on, from mapping, and – perhaps as a scrap of comfort to Grootfontein – it already loomed on the horizon.

Critical at this juncture was less a conservationist agenda and the concern for the soil's well-being than a larger vision of survey and spatial measurement. That is, "seeing our land from above" expressed less the particular interest in a subject matter than the desire for a foundation to future state action *in space*. At this stage, it remained unclear what material and visual form the rationale would assume, and it is precisely this question, which set the tone of written deliberations over aerial photography and mapping, that intensified in 1936. Because of this, it is thus worth returning to the director of the Trigonometrical Survey, W. Whittingdale, and follow some of his lines more attentively:

Many exaggerated claims have been made by interested parties and amateur enthusiasts on behalf of aerial photography as a direct means for rapid and cheap mapping. Air photographs themselves are a big help in the field and a technique is being developed to enable the topographer to make full use of them when they are available. But the possibility of the profitable employment of aerial survey methods in this country are [sic] still being investigated. Colonel Hoare, Director of Technical Services at Roberts Heights, is trying out a new 7-lens camera which has great possibilities for certain classes of work. Dr. Fourcade, a world authority upon the difficult subject of precise measurement and plotting from photographs is at present engaged in building a comparatively simple automatic plotting machine which from theoretical considerations is a great advance upon the performance of the complicated and expensive machines now in use on the Continent; machines which are not suited to South African scales of mapping. Apart from the possible success of these investigations, the aeroplane and the camera will play a very definite part in the work. The question of ways and means is still under consideration, and further information is required before concrete proposals can be put forward in regard to air survey work.[96]

If we would venture a guess, it was probably the Department of Defence's generous offer in the form of ample material resources and technical services – including flights, photography, and film processing – that made Whittingdale submit more than favourable recommendations for aerial photography and mapping to the central government a few days later. They were part of the report referred to at the beginning of this chapter, in which the senior surveyor itemised image forms and formats, practices and actors, scales of mapping, technological equipment, and fields of application that constituted the intricate terrain of aerial photography. These recommendations would, as we noted, establish the basis for the decision made in 1936 to map the entire country at a scale of 1:50,000 by making extensive use of aerial photographs. Now, no time was wasted, and soon after Whittingdale's submission a newly appointed inter-departmental Air Survey Committee met in Pretoria in late December 1936. The composition of its members was revealing, and it included, as would seem natural, the Director of Trigonometrical Survey and a technical officer from the Defence Department, but also representatives of the geological survey, forestry, the National Road Board, South African Railways, and officers from the divisions of plant industry, soil erosion, and irrigation.[97] The minutes of the meeting evidence the persistent ambivalence towards aerial photography and its methodological and economic viability for topographical mapping. Enthusiasts as much as sceptics voiced their respective arguments, and there was a fair amount of bureaucratic pettiness occasionally compromising a favourable outcome. Eventually, the committee passed its resolutions, which defined the strategic guidelines for the scheme.[98]

We will get a more detailed sense of the future *modus operandi* conditioned by these decisions once we look at the Eastern Cape material. Here, it may suffice to comment on just two issues raised in the report, both of which will remain important for our discussion. Critical to the lengthy debates among the committee members on technical matters relating to air survey and mapping was a remarkable confidence in the accuracy and reliability of the photographic medium. As one of the clerks in the office of the Trigonometrical Survey phrased it: "Mapping from air photographs could be reduced to a scientific method, whereas the plane-table method was *an art* to which no adequate checks were applicable".[99] This appraisal depended on high image quality, state-of-the-art camera equipment, and the skills of pilots and photographers, and it was also due to these demanding premises that the committee decided to water down the Air Force's monopoly in aerial surveying and commission some of the required photographs through a private tenderer, namely the Aircraft Operating Company (AOC). AOC had opened an office in Johannesburg in 1931 and had since been involved in a number of localised aerial surveys on behalf of various government departments.[100] We first encountered this company as producer of the aerial photograph taken near Umtata in 1938 (Figure 4.1), and we will come across them repeatedly once we move to the Eastern Cape. But first let us follow the work of the Aerial Survey Committee for a bit longer, and finally take a brief look at how aerial photography would loom up after the Second World War. Paying careful attention to these defining discussions among state technicians and specialists will shed light on the historical genesis of a specific South African notion of aerial photography. On a more theoretical level, it will help us anticipate some of the questions this particular form of photography raises in relation to time, space, and history addressed in the final part of this chapter.

The Committee held its second meeting in late June 1939, and since the aerial surveying scheme had been underway for more than two years, reviewing the process produced remarkable conversations on some of the most interesting aspects of the technology's application in South Africa at the time. In addition, the committee now felt much more confident in reformulating aerial photography's forms and formats, practices and guidelines, aims and ambitions. They would, indeed, set the course for the medium's prospects in important ways. But we shall begin, as we did for the committee's first meeting, with its members: the "usual suspects" had remained present, including Whittingdale as chairperson and officers from forestry, geological survey, soil erosion, agriculture, roads, railways, irrigation, and lands; but there were newcomers who joined the distinguished circle, among them representatives of provincial government, public health, and "native affairs".[101] Whittingdale's review of the scheme's first two years, which opened the June meeting, renewed the Trigonometrical Survey's commitment to a "modern form of mapping" and the critical role filled by aerial photography. He also iterated important investments made, among them the acquisition of an aircraft and the employment of an additional pilot. Methodological and technological improvements had been induced as well, and there was even space for invention, since South Africa could pride itself in having blessed the world with a new plotting machine: the stereoprojector.[102]

It came as no surprise, then, that the scheme had exceeded all expectations and generated an unprecedented and overwhelming demand for aerial photographs, as well as – since there had been delays in providing images to departments – a thorough reassessment, by the committee, of the areas that needed to be photographed most urgently, while others would have to wait.

Whittingdale's narrative of success was followed by two reports, and they are both full of surprises and revelations. The first one by the Director of War Supply, General Hoare, spoke directly to the problem of urgency and delay, and – apart from its disconcerting martial tone – conveyed an intricate picture of aerial photography's idiosyncratic temporality and materiality. In first explaining how the overall scheme could be improved and made more efficient, he lobbied for investments in the latest craze in aviation – the British-produced Bristol Blenheim aircraft – and state-of-the-art camera equipment; but ultimately, things simply came down to "better pilots do a better job".[103] However, Hoare's report struck a more poetic note once he spoke about a critical factor in aerial photography: the weather – which made the view from above materially and temporally vulnerable and capricious; weather conditions had, in Hoare's own words, serious consequences, and there were lessons to be learned. He tells us:

> With modern high speed film and large aperture lenses, photography could commence at 8.00–8.30 and be continued to 4.00 or 4.30 according to the time of the year. On perfect days [...] it should be possible to cover 1000 square miles. [...] For photography in coastal areas and for urgent work elsewhere which might have to be undertaken in the rainy season, it was essential to use an all-metal aircraft. The Envoy [the aircraft in use at that point] was largely constructed of three ply wood and alternate wet and hot days had a most deleterious effect on this material. After the East London survey both aircraft required very extensive repairs which would have put an end to the work for some months if another aircraft had not been loaned by the Air Force.[104]

The second report by the mapping officer in the Trigonometrical Survey Office, N.G. Huntly, continued to reflect upon the question of time in aerial photography, by first insisting on "urgency" of the requested survey work and "suitable photographic season" for the areas in question as key to the guidelines for the order in which aerial photography would be carried out. However, in contrast to his fellow executive, the lack of appreciation for the weather as a critical factor among non-specialists, who were crowding government departments and lamenting delays, had apparently broken his nerves. Therefore, displaying a certain degree of arrogance, Huntly too saw the need for elucidation:

> In connection with the weather it must be realised that in order to be satisfactory for air photography weather had to reach a much higher standard than the average picnic conception of a fine day [...] It was essential that there be virtually no clouds, as these caused shadows as well as obscuring detail, and the wind must not be very high, or very changeable, otherwise the drift of the aircraft would be upset.[105]

After giving vent to his annoyance, the mapping officer shared more pleasing news regarding the normal scale of photography (set at 1:20,000 for contact prints and 1:10,000 for enlargements), the areas that had been surveyed between 1937 and 1939 either by the AOC or the Air Force, and the number of images ordered by the various government departments.[106] Most importantly, though, he spoke about a crucial innovation, which concerned the creation of an archive and library of aerial photography and the hope to set up an efficient system of image circulation between the Trigonometrical Survey Office and the departmental divisions requiring photographs for their work. The plan was as follows:

> The Trigsurvey [sic] Office ordered two contact prints of every photograph taken. One set of these prints was for use by the field parties and would be filed as part of the survey records at the topographical survey. The other set was filed in special volumes as a photo library (An example of these volumes was shown to the Committee). Thus there was in Pretoria a complete photo library of one contact print of every photograph taken and these were available for examination for departments interested. It was possible that this would be extended so that departments interested might use this as a lending library and take out photographs provided they were not marked in any way.[107]

What emerges here, notably, is an exceptional readiness to establish a connection between the world-encompassing view provided by aerial photography and the archive's desire for a totalising taxonomy.[108] It will be important to consider more the relationship between aerial photographs, the archive, and the landscape they intend to represent as it took shape in the South African context, and we will do so at a later stage. However, in the late 1930s, the grand plan sketched out above remained an idle wish, since the outbreak of WWII slowed down the aerial surveying scheme significantly – not least because of the South African Air Force's involvement on East African battlefields.[109] Yet once the war was over, fresh attempts were made, and now state preoccupations with the farming sector and the precept of soil conservation seeped in once again. The renewed initiatives were grounded on new legislation passed in the early and mid-1940s, among them the Soil Conservation Act in 1946. This act provided for the systematic appointment of district-based soil conservation committees, who would monitor and enforce environmental regulations and supervise – discipline, in fact – white farmers in managing their farms along conservationist lines.[110] Here, aerial photography, and more specifically aerial mosaics, became an important basis for farm planning, since they provided a visual template for border fencing, internal camp erection, dispersion of water resources, and implementation of rotational systems of grazing.[111] The Act's impact was very uneven across the white-owned farming areas, but up to the 1950s, more than 10,000 farms were planned.[112] As we shall see, intensifying state intervention in agricultural management after WWII, and the transformation of land use it triggered, would remain important for aerial photography's role in the Eastern Cape context as well. However, here things would look fundamentally different.

The technological remaking of the Eastern Cape

Experiments with aerial photography in the Transkei began in 1926, when the South African Air Force received a request from the Surveyor General in Cape Town, who at that stage wished to ascertain "what accuracy could be obtained by means of photographic survey under certain conditions as regards preliminary ground survey".[113] The site chosen for the test was Ndabakazi, a village on the railway line approximately 15 kilometres west of Butterworth, and the more specific rationale indicated by the Native Affairs Department was its objective to survey "Native allotments in the Transkei".[114] Since this was the first time aerial photography was carried out in an African communal area, the way to go seemed sensitive, and as a result, the Secretary for Native Affairs urged authorities on the ground, i.e. the magistrate and police, to inform residents about the operation and provide them with details of dates and areas to be photographed. Otherwise, he feared, "Natives may be upset unless matter is fully explained (Figure 4.4)".[115]

We do not know if the requested efforts to explain were made, nor if the presence of planes circling above villages caused concern or possibly fear among residents of Ndabakazi and surroundings. However, we do know that the results from the experiment were not considered to be of good quality; the representative of the Defence Department explained that the mountainous nature of the country, as well as prevailing winds and air currents, had made accurate flying difficult. In any case, the photographs taken were disappointing,[116] and the Surveyor General gave a distinctly negative judgement:

> I have to inform you with regret that the experiment carried out by the Air Force in conjunction with a qualified land surveyor has not proved to be as satisfactory as was anticipated.
>
> The plan of the allotments constructed by Mr. Surveyor Eagle of Kokstad from the photographs supplied by the Air Force does not represent the actual position of the allotment boundaries with a correctness which is required to determine the areas of the individual holdings within a reasonable limit of error.
>
> A careful consideration of all circumstances forces me to the conclusion that, at the present state of aerial development in this country, survey work of the sort required for cadastral purposes cannot successfully be undertaken from the air.[117]

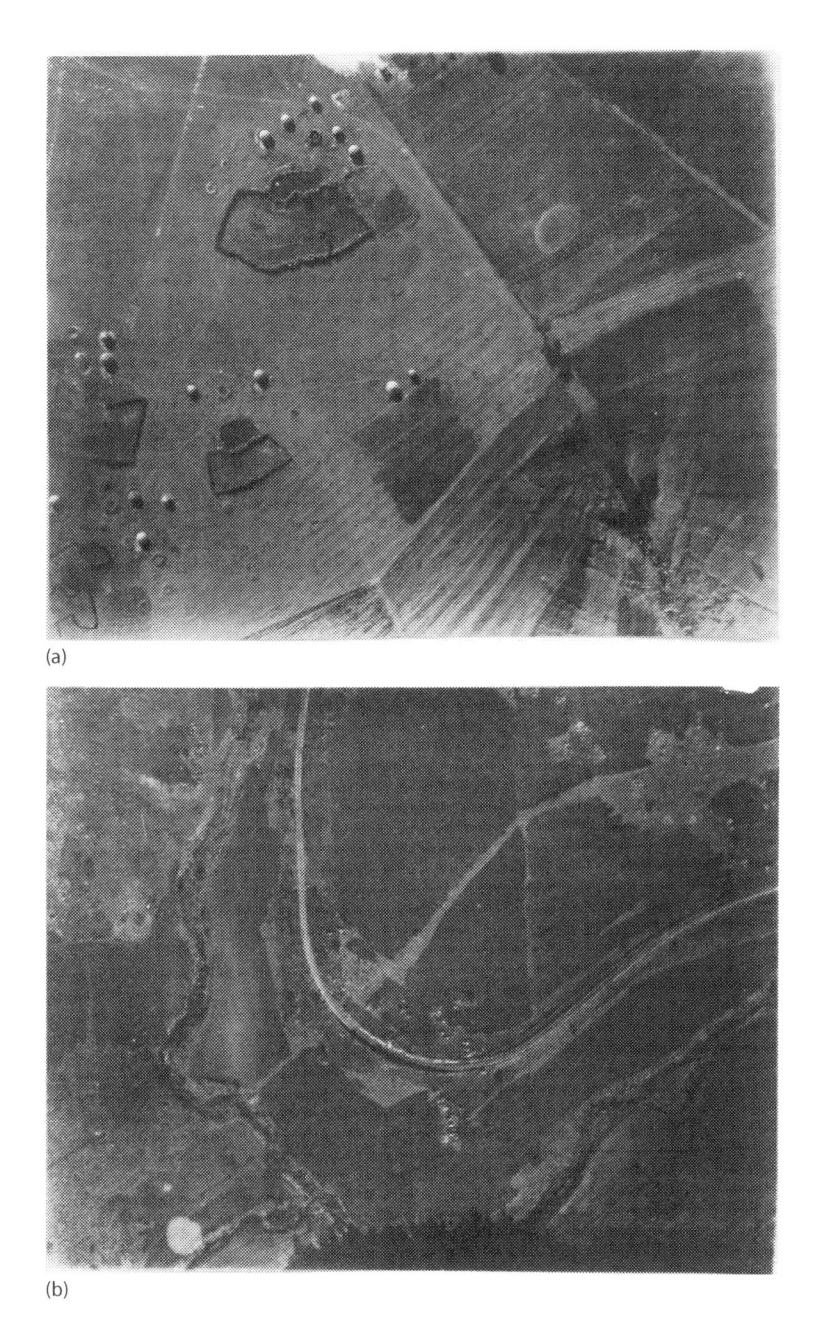

(a)

(b)

Figure 4.4 (a & b[118]) Aerial photograph, Ndabakazi, Eastern Cape.

There was obviously some disappointment on the Surveyor's side, and the Secretary for Native Affairs must have felt similarly. Surveying African freehold settlements and private land titles held by Africans in the reserves became an important concern of an invigorated Native Affairs Department in the 1920s.[119] While nineteenth-century legacies of African title had survived into the early decades of the twentieth century, after the Land Act of 1913 and the creation of reserves they tended to be abandoned in favour of a vision of communal land tenure under truncated customary law.[120] Enforcing the corresponding policy and regulating African access to and use of land was henceforth conceptualised within the framework of "native administration", as it would be drawn up in the respective Act passed in 1927 and restricted to what was called African locations within the reserves.[121] Aerial photography, as both high-ranking officials seem to have hoped, would have simplified assessing property and mapping conditions on the ground. However, in 1926, it was not to be. A slight chance for redress emerged, albeit with remarkable delay, through an offer submitted to Native Affairs in May 1928.[122] The author of the respective letter was the manager of the AOC, who at that point were trying to enter the South African market via their African outpost in Bulawayo, in what was at the time Southern Rhodesia. Their initiative to contact the Secretary for Native Affairs had been preceded by correspondence between AOC and E.S. Eagle, the Kokstad surveyor mentioned in the above quote, and this had apparently given reason for proposing what the letter presented as a solution to the problem of surveying and cadastral mapping of African estates in the reserves across the country: the "modern scientific method of surveying based on aerial photography". AOC prided itself on having at their disposal the required capital, technological equipment, photographic knowhow, *and* archival system in place that would enable them to produce and manage high-quality photographic images. Clearly, the Secretary was tempted and the offer was laid before the Surveyor General.[123] But, for no apparent reason, the auspicious conversation fizzled out and silence descended – if temporarily – on aerial photography's accruing inception in the Eastern Cape.

There was fresh momentum in the mid-1930s, when new legislation and policy inaugurated a period of important state interventions in African communal areas at large, and the Eastern Cape more specifically. The following two-and-a-half decades saw a critical transformation of how land use and landscape here would be conceived of, and aerial photography thrived in a context marked by increasing technologising and the rule of experts.[124] Before explaining these developments, though, we should recall some of the questions raised at the beginning of this chapter, since they will continue to guide our discussion of the Eastern Cape material. Moving, again, along the lines of the report on aerial photography and topographical surveying prepared by the Director of the Trigonometrical Survey, W. Whittingdale, in 1936,[125] our interest will be on the image forms, materialities and technologies, and practices and actors that shaped aerial photography's iteration in an African rural area. These questions shall enable us, in a second step, to investigate if and how aerial photography contributed to the production of a specific notion of the Eastern Cape landscape, or – echoing our earlier discussion of Foucault's heterotopia – a somewhat different and transformed space, by drawing on a particular spatio-temporal reconfiguration that vitally depended, as we have suggested, on the technological mediation of the view from above.

Aerial photography's gradual comeback in the Eastern Cape began in the immediate aftermath of the Native Trust and Land Act passed in 1936. This act and later legislation provided the legal framework within which the South African government acquired land in order to extend and consolidate reserves, administer and allocate land to Africans through the newly formed Native Trust, and initiate a radical transformation of peasant agriculture under the rubric of "betterment".[126] The new phase of state intervention had been preceded by a growing concern with crumbling ecological, agricultural, and economic conditions in rural areas. The report produced by the Native Economic Commission in 1932 described the situation in the "native reserves" as disastrous and, as we saw earlier on, blamed African farmers and their agricultural practices for the impending ecological collapse. Indeed, the 1920s and 1930s saw mounting pressure on land, growing livestock numbers, and more intensive use of fields and pastures, whereby across the Eastern Cape region access to and distribution of land and livestock resources became very uneven, with clear signs of economic decay and widespread poverty.[127] Occasional and localised attempts were therefore initiated by the newly formed agricultural division in the Department of Native Affairs in both the Transkei and Ciskei, where they opened agricultural schools and demonstration farms, through which demonstrators in the field attempted to encourage the use of farming practices considered less strenuous on the soil and vegetation.[128]

But nothing was systematic at this stage, even if the 1932 commission had provided for more compulsory regulation and intervention and underscored the necessity for comprehensive surveys of soil erosion, ravines, and gullies.[129] Four years later, the worry and request for action advanced by the commission met with a response from the Secretary for Native Affairs, D.L. Smit, and a nationwide conservation survey of African locations with the aim of re-planning settlement "to save them from absolute ruin" began.[130] This was just the thing for those who were concurrently concerned with entrenching aerial photography in survey and mapping, and offers submitted to Native Affairs did, indeed, not fail to appear.[131] However, at this stage, Smit's imagination had not been ignited yet, and his response was dismissive:

> The question of surveys to be carried out by the South African Native Land Trust has not yet been considered but it is unlikely that the work will be of such nature and magnitude as would warrant the utilisation of aerial methods of survey.
>
> Your suggestions will, however, be borne in mind for consideration in due course.[132]

Surveying in the Eastern Cape did not take off in any significant way in the mid-1930s, and it remained very limited for at least the next decade.[133] Even if we keep in mind that the mills of the state grind slowly, Smit's judgement of aerial photography's future role could not have been more inaccurate, since he did not foresee how important technicians and technologies would become, especially within his own department.[134] Both would, in fact, reap the full benefits of a significant shift from bureaucratic to instrumental state rationality gaining ground between the 1920s and 1950s.[135] The Control and Improvement of Livestock in the Native Reserves Proclamation – commonly known in the literature as Betterment Proclamation – passed in 1939, was indicative of this programmatic *revirement*, and it created the framework within which state officers would henceforth perceive and act upon the physical and social landscapes of the Eastern Cape. As stipulated by the Native Trust and Land Act, betterment was designed for a radical transformation of reserve agriculture.[136] The scheme provided for changes in the organisation of grazing by introducing a system of camps and paddocks; it prescribed significant limitations of livestock numbers and accordingly required culling of surplus animals; and it promoted contour farming and the spread of water resources as measures directed at the prevention of further soil erosion. Most importantly, betterment introduced systematic fencing – of camps, fields, and forest areas – and thereby imposed the newly designed radical separation of pastures, arable, and residential land. Finally, in order to allow for a more rational utilisation of land, homesteads were grouped into consolidated villages, either lined up along roads or organised in township grids.[137] Obviously, enforcing all these measures required a large amount of work on the ground, and the presence of administrative and technical officers – among them surveyors, agricultural extension workers, soil conservationists, foresters, engineers, road constructors, native commissioners, and police, joined by local chiefs and headmen urged to support the various departments in their work – became much more extensive and frequent.[138]

As one might expect, betterment elicited strong responses from African farmers and residents in the reserves. African critiques of government mapping and alienation of land and natural resources in the Eastern Cape had been expressed from as early as the 1900s,[139] but betterment clearly increased the levels of resistance among rural communities, gradually in the 1930s and significantly, as we shall see, after World War II.[140] Discontent was generally directed against the scheme *per se* – euphemistically termed "rehabilitation" in official parlance – but especially against stock-culling provisions, restrictions on the use of grazing, and reductions on the availability of arable land.[141] Still, the range of African responses to betterment policy in the Eastern Cape varied geographically, as Hendricks has noted, and it often hinged on local conditions. Thus, while implementation was possible in some areas, it was inconceivable in others. The path of betterment was not uniform, nor linear, and it meandered its way into the reserves following the line of least contestation.[142]

How, then, did the beginning of betterment in the late 1930s affect aerial photography? In what way does betterment surface in aerial photography's archive, and to what extent, in turn, did government "rehabilitation" schemes change the configuration of this photographic archive in the making? As we shall see, the implementation of betterment in the reserves would gradually invigorate the production and circulation of aerial photographs – and other image forms – though the effect was more complicated than one might assume. While up to 1939, various government departments had selectively commissioned the AOC to do project-based aerial surveying, the second meeting of the Aerial Survey Committee initiated, as we explained earlier on, stronger regulation and systematisation of procedures.[143] Nationwide topographical surveying and mapping remained a priority, and particular interests that belonged to individual departments and administrative units had to be weighed against budgetary concerns. Consequently, requests for aerial photographs needed to be justified, the selection of geographical areas explained, and the urgency of matters argued for. Once betterment was declared a justification for state intervention in African rural areas, the Native Affairs Department went from being a minor commissioner of aerial photographs in the late 1930s to a much more important recipient of photographic images a decade later.[144]

At first, betterment and aerial photography did not go together well, and the procedural guidelines and constraints imposed by the Trigonometrical Survey were felt negatively. Still, Native Affairs' wants and needs grew rapidly; aerial photographs of "native settlements and holdings" as well as enlargements to various scales had been requested for the Transvaal in 1937 and for areas around Mafeking and Vryburg in the northern part of the Cape Province in 1938.[145] One year later, correspondence between W. Whittingdale, various officers in Native Affairs, and the Native Commissioners in King William's Town and Pietermaritzburg swelled, since reclamation committees were keen to begin betterment in various districts of Natal and the Ciskei.[146] However, even if 1939 did mark a turning point in aerial photography's advancement in "native administration", the archival evidence is quite puzzling.

One certainly wonders who, at this stage, was in fact setting the agenda, since the availability of aerial photographs in the archives of the Trigonometrical Survey and the AOC seemed to determine the choice of betterment locations as much as anxieties among Native Affairs officers about imminent agricultural collapse in the reserves. Besides, intractable issues appeared wherever one looked, especially in the premises of regional and local authorities: decisions to be made on the scale of photographs most appropriate for reclamation work; the choice and acquisition of photographic paper and technological equipment; the qualified operation of the necessary devices, most importantly stereoscopes; or the required methodology for using aerial photographs for survey work on the ground. These were complex matters officials grappled with, and they did so even before taking into consideration the most critical problem they would face: securing the consent of local farmers and residents, who were meant to be subjected to betterment in the first place.[147] An exchange between D.L. Smit, the Secretary for Native Affairs, and the Chief Native Commissioner in King William's Town on planning soil conservation measures in a number of districts of the Ciskei reveals some of the conditional dynamics at play and the ad hoc nature of betterment planning:

> In order to place soil conservation work on a better basis it has been decided that, wherever possible, the planning of measures to be undertaken shall be done by a committee consisting of the Reclamation Committee and a soils man. [...] In order to provide topographical maps on which field notes regarding the physical properties of the soil can be made it is proposed to supply air maps of the respective areas. [...] The soil man will require the photographs for recording the results of his observations in the field before the full committee commences work.
>
> With regard to the selection of the actual localities to receive attention by the committee [...] the decision should be made by you in consultation with the Engineer and the Assistant Director of Agriculture.
>
> It is considered that work should not be done in arable lands in a surveyed location at this stage and also that it would be advisable to select areas that are not unduly difficult to commence with, leaving the problem areas until such time as the committee has had more experience of this type of work.[148]

Building upon experiences on the ground might possibly have helped improve the work and practice of betterment's rank and file, but as mentioned earlier, World War II significantly slowed down survey work across the country, and while it did not bring "rehabilitation" in the reserves to a general halt, it temporarily put off most plans.[149] Still, inactivity on the "home front" was of short duration, and 1945 inaugurated a new era of reclamation, which was now extended more resolutely into the Transkei.[150] The first location to be chosen for betterment in the region was Butterworth on the Gcuwa River. The site for one of the earliest Wesleyan Mission stations in the Eastern Cape, founded in 1827, Butterworth had been the target of survey work in the early 1900s, when the Cape colonial government began to measure and map individual allotments and household plots across the district.[151] Lindsay F. Braun has shown how these early surveys depended on complicated negotiations between local headmen and colonial technicians, making the entire process much more costly and time consuming than anticipated.[152] While the Butterworth model was gradually applied to neighbouring districts – since against all odds it had gone fairly well – the idea of mapping the area based on precise surveys and translating the new order into realities on the ground had proved to be mere illusion. Survey work in the Transkei was abandoned, if temporarily, in 1923.[153] Yet, the Butterworth exercise had nevertheless produced, Braun argues, a significant geographical archive – an instance that seems to have informed the decision to begin betterment work here two decades later.[154] We can only speculate if Butterworth was considered an "unproblematic area", where "rehabilitation" would not have encountered "unduly difficult conditions". In any case, while it had been chosen for betterment as early as 1939, for reasons that remain somewhat unclear, actual survey work only began in the early 1940s.[155] Thenceforth, Butterworth would, again, acquire a remarkable place in the archive, this time silhouetted against a visual assemblage of maps, sketches and – obviously – aerial photographs.

Betterment essentially hinged upon surveying and mapping; it was grounded in specialised expertise, and it therefore became a domain in which technicians tended to have greater leverage vis-à-vis their untrained fellow bureaucrats, including at times their superiors. What betterment would in fact require, first, was knowledge of the photographic archive and proficiency in a highly encoded visual language. Butterworth precisely exemplifies these dynamics, and the case reveals the level of technicality and the variety of visual practices involved in drafting what would become the general template for "rehabilitation" in the Eastern Cape in the post-World War II period. Engineers in the Native Affairs Department and officers of the Trigonometrical Survey Office would distinguish themselves as key actors in selecting and setting up betterment locations in the reserves, whereby they relied, as we shall see in a moment, on on-site personnel to provide some of the necessary data. The overall aim was to record conditions on the ground as accurately as possible, thereby providing both a scientific working basis *and* the technical prerequisites for any future action. However, there were preliminary steps to be taken, among them clarifying which sections of the Transkei had previously been surveyed by means of aerial photography, and establishing if there were up-to-date topographical maps available. While after the war there was undoubtedly growing pressure and enough enthusiasm among officials to begin betterment work in the reserves, assessing the archive of aerial photographs caused a fair amount of confusion. The Secretary for Native Affairs, G. Mears, seemed to take the view that more than 60% of the Transkei had not been surveyed, and the available photographs did not cover the districts selected, including Butterworth.[156]

Others knew better, among them Native Affairs' senior engineer: Not only did he enlighten his superior about the state-of-the-art of aerial surveying, he also understood the unforeseen lack of clarity as an inducement to suggest a new spatial classification, which would facilitate the production and provision of aerial photographs for betterment work. The proposition was critical, and once accepted, plan No. 1651/45 laid the grounds for what was to come: the division of the Transkei into six air surveyed areas, each qualified by priority (Figure 4.5).[157]

Echoing the engineer's initiative, the Trigonometrical Survey Office saw a need for clarification as well, issuing their own instructions to be complied

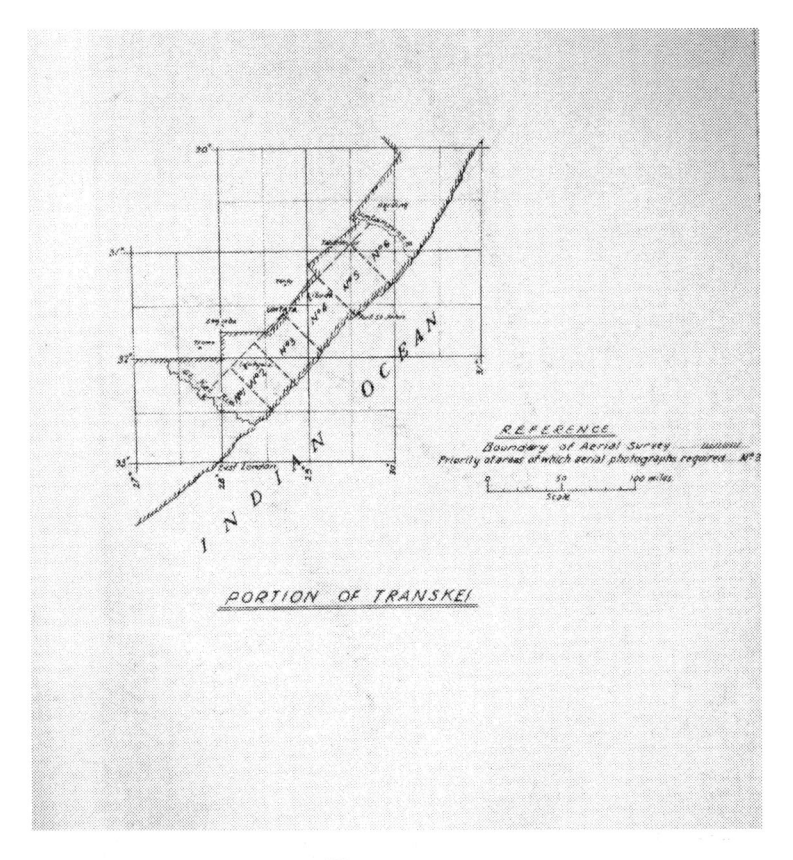

Figure 4.5 Plan No. 1651/45, 1945.[158]

with in an extended memorandum on surveying and mapping requirements prepared for the departmental divisions involved.[159] Calling to mind the main aims of "rehabilitation" and land use planning in the reserves, the officer in charge summarised the pilot scheme as it had been drafted for the Butterworth district. It was here where the first location planning committee in the Transkei had been established, and it was meant to work in close collaboration with two commissioned surveyors on the ground. However, any planning work required the committee to be furnished with a basic, large scale topographical map at a scale of 1:9,000, upon which information gathered in the field – such as population density, environmental characteristics, and crops grown as well as new demarcations of residential, arable, grazing, and afforestation land – would have to be recorded. As far as aerial photography was concerned, the officer in charge finally explained that Butterworth had indeed been surveyed from the air in 1942, but since he felt that those images were both out of date and at a scale too small to be of use to the planning committee, he strongly advised the progressive production of new aerial photographs.[160]

The mapping requirements and the aerial survey zoning did not bring clarity, and the bureaucratic process remained cumbersome. The Chief Magistrate in Umtata had asked for enlargements of aerial photographs for Butterworth – overall 400 images – as soon as plan No. 1651/45 was in circulation, but his request was put off temporarily, given that the Air Force was only resuming its domestic surveying work gradually.[161] In addition, the provision of topographical maps that covered the entire district proved overly ambitious, wherefore magistrates in the region were eventually asked to specify five priority locations in which the planning committee would commence its work. All of these had to lie in surveyed districts.[162] Requesting local information put flesh on the bone and revealed more particulars of the landscape, and by late May 1945, G. Mears received a complete list and detailed sketch maps indicating huts, fields, roads, and vegetation of 26 surveyed locations in the Butterworth and adjoining Nqamakwe districts (Figure 4.6).[163]

It is at this point that the senior local magistrate made mention of how residents of Butterworth responded to the implementation of betterment

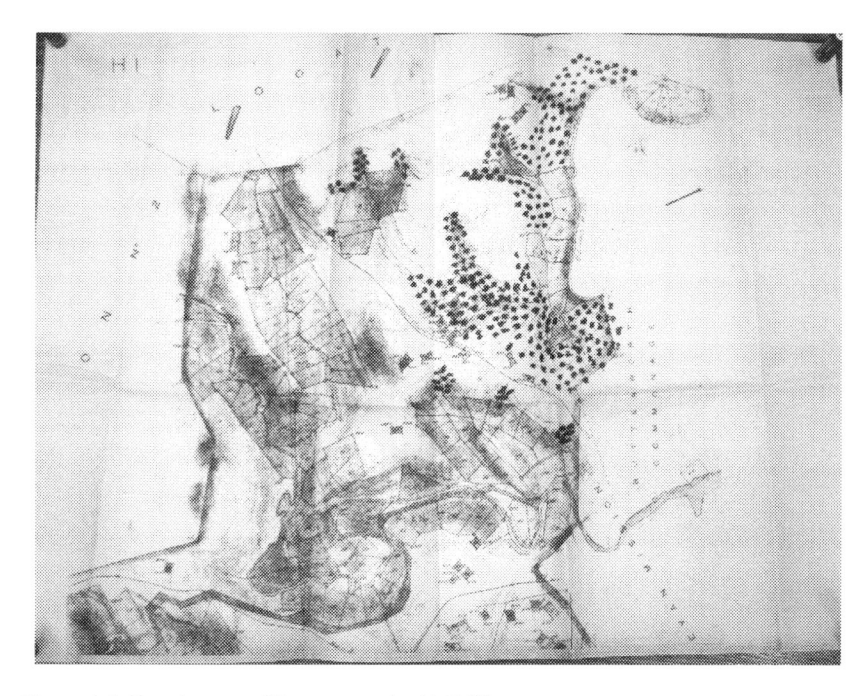

Figure 4.6 Sketch map of Butterworth, 1945.[164]

measures in their area – though the information remained brief and was most likely euphemistic:

> In the former [Butterworth] district ten locations have already accepted or have asked for the application of the betterment area system with a view to rehabilitation. In the Nqamakwe district some 35 locations have made application to be declared betterment areas.
>
> As you are aware rehabilitation measures have already been carried out in three locations and when this has been done in the case of some of the further locations which have accepted the betterment area system I anticipate that the remaining locations will not be slow in following suit. So far as the Nqamakwe district is concerned it will be observed that practically the whole district has asked to come under the system.
>
> For this reason I would ask that if possible, aerial survey maps be furnished of all locations in the two districts of Butterworth and Nqamakwe.[165]

Strong resistance in fact marked betterment in Butterworth, but contestation from local farmers and residents was not reflected in the visual archive formed around the scheme.[166] What shows instead is how, by late 1945, the procedure established here and the idiosyncratic sequence between surveying, mapping, sketching, and photographing the landscape were first extended to other districts across the Transkei and Ciskei, and then to reserve areas in Natal and the Transvaal.[167] While the lack of material and human resources and complex determinations of priority areas continued to delay both the production of aerial photographs and enlargements and, concurrently, the implementation of betterment, from the late 1940s onwards the quantity of images ordered by the Native Affairs Department and their technical staff operating in the Eastern Cape and beyond increased steadily and significantly.[168]

This growing circulation of aerial photographs within Native Affairs mirrored further attempts at rationalisation and pointed to looming adjustments within the overriding betterment scheme and policy shifts after the National Party's seizure of power in 1948. From September 1949 onwards, all aspects concerning the production and use of aerial photography by government departments had to be approved by the newly appointed National Advisory Survey Council, and the Trigonometrical Survey Office further increased its control over archiving and circulating aerial photographs, and issuing and prescribing the scale of photographic enlargements and topographical map sheets.[169] Rationalising survey methods and image distribution was readily explained with soaring costs, lack of human resources, and poor efficiency in coordinating image requests across the state bureaucracy.[170] But clearly, there was a critical concern with centralisation and political control, and the fact that by the beginning of 1950 the South African Defence Department had reacquired its monopoly on the production of aerial photographs, driving private tenderers such as the Aircraft Operating Company out of the market, is indicative.[171] Still, delays remained a huge issue – if not actually increasing – and surveying remained slow: in 1956 for example, only 86 locations out of a total of 887 had been planned in the Transkei, and betterment work in all but 37 locations was completed.[172] This was in spite of the fact that Native Affairs had just announced yet another era of betterment, entailing a paradigmatic reformulation of the scheme and the role attributed to the "native reserves" within the broader South African political economy.[173]

By this time, the central government had already begun to link its land policy much more explicitly to labour, thereby responding to an altered economic and demographic situation. Curbing African presence in towns and cities, together with the displacement of labour tenants on farms and inhabitants of "native settlements" outside the reserves, resulted in a massive enlargement of the population in the reserves. As a result, their function changed fundamentally from serving as a generator and source of cheap migrant labour, to acting predominantly as a source of social control over the growing rural population.[174] Consequently, resettlement began to take precedence over conservation and "rehabilitation" concerns, which had been part, at least rhetorically, of betterment policy in its early years. The new rationale of the apartheid state's social engineering plans for the reserves provided for an essential distinction between a farmer class on the one hand and migrant labourers on the other hand, and even their separate relocation in different villages was envisioned.[175] Indeed, the orchestrated social stratification and residential segregation came to some fruition, and while a small agricultural elite benefitted from the realignment of betterment in this period, the imposed measures generally led to widespread landlessness and structural impoverishment.[176]

As a result, resistance against the scheme grew massively, and the Eastern Cape entered a period of recurring violent confrontations between African rural communities and an increasingly ruthless state.[177] Still, by the mid-1960s, 44% of the Transkei had been subjected to betterment.[178] But by then, Native Affairs, and the rank and file of bustling technicians and surveyors who had populated the region for almost two decades, had abandoned the tedious but thorough system of detailed location-by-location planning. There are in fact strong archival indications that, accordingly, the commitment to aerial photography, as a basis for what technicians and bureaucrats alike had praised as a modern and sophisticated methodology for "native administration" in the rural areas, swiftly deteriorated.[179]

Eastern Cape heterotopia

It is by now time to ask what the above retracement of aerial photography's deployment across a diverse range of administrative contexts in South Africa tells us about the technological remaking of the Eastern Cape landscape.[180] Does the archive of aerial photography provide us with a different lens through which to look at the transformation of landscape here, as it was brought about, for example, by betterment policy between the late 1930s and the mid-1950s? One might wonder if a focus on practices that clustered around photography somewhat misses the point, given that this archive would release little information on rural communities' responses to state-imposed agricultural transformation – including widespread resistance to betterment schemes – or African farmers' and reserve residents' understandings of how the landscapes they inhabited changed as a result of state-imposed agricultural schemes.[181] The scholarship referred to in this chapter clearly privileges a sociohistorical approach that is preoccupied with retrieving people's agencies in view of exploitative land and labour policies pursued by both the United Party and apartheid governments. However, even within this framework, a number of authors have noted that agricultural policy and even a scheme as significant as betterment had limited environmental, let alone conservational effects, and it did not alter the distribution of natural resources in rural areas in a significant or sustained way. What state intervention did, essentially, is that it engendered an important spatial transformation and imposed new categories on the perception and understanding of the physical landscape (Figure 4.7).[182]

It is precisely the question of spatial transformation that takes us back to the discussion proposed at the beginning of this chapter. We should reconsider

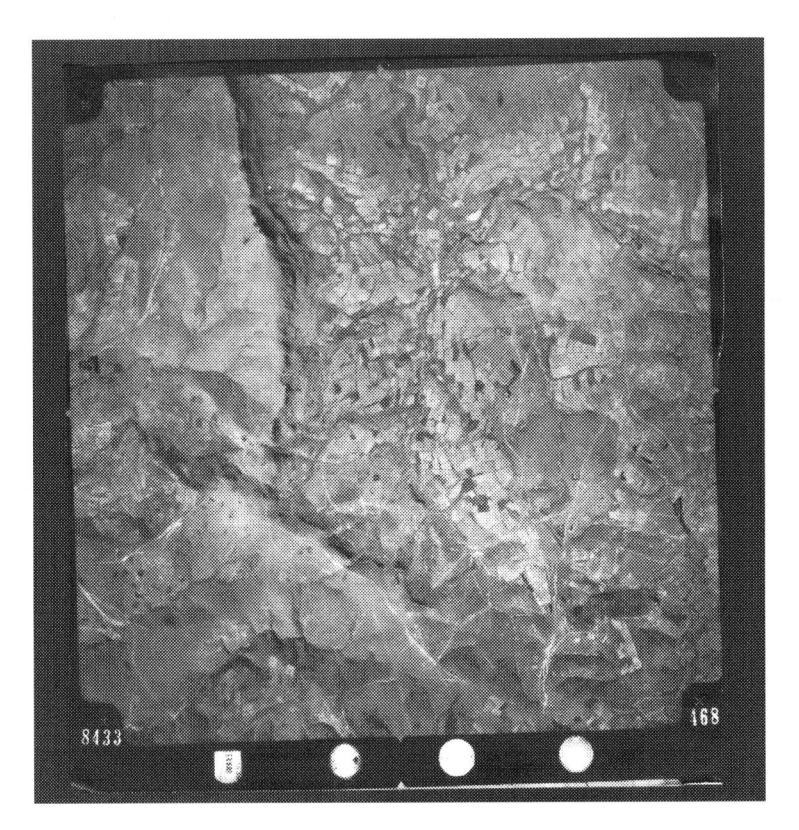

Figure 4.7 Aerial photograph of Butterworth, 1961.[183]

more carefully the ways in which the Eastern Cape material speaks to the literature on aerial photography generally and the proposition to think about aerial photographs in terms of heterotopia more specifically. As we saw earlier on, both the theoretical and practical reflections on aerial photography were marked by a tension between utopian and dystopian understandings of the medium and image form. South African state officials clearly tended to subscribe to its advantages, believing in aerial photography's mechanical objectivity and its capacity to record the complexity and relationality of surface features of natural landscapes, thereby enabling the trained eye to better understand and act upon the environment. For them, aerial photography constituted a critical tool in implementing an efficient approach to the physical world and its specific requirements – be it the quality of soils, the management of natural resources, or the viability of agricultural production – increasingly understood as technical problems that, accordingly, required technological responses and solutions. What they seemed to acknowledge less was how aerial photography, far from simply delivering a mimetic representation of space, fundamentally transformed their perception of and interaction with the physical environment.

There were, though, rare moments of insight, reflections on how interventions in space authorised by the state would entail or possibly give rise to a new aesthetics of landscape, a transformed sensibility of vision. A first clue is provided in a text authored by F.R.B. Thompson, then the principal of Teko Agricultural School, Butterworth, and later the director of agriculture in the Transkei, sometime in the late 1920s. Elaborating his thinking on "agricultural economics and methods in the territories", he summarised his own sense of a technician's vision of the landscape:

> As the artist revels in the jagged peaks of the mountains silhouetted against the sky, so the delight of the Agriculturalist should be "straight lines"[184]

Once aerial photography had entered the South African stage, and its advocates as much as state officials praised and assessed its role in changing how one perceived the environment, some became more explicit about the medium's contribution to a fresh and essentially different view. Obviously, there were practical advantages that emerged from the conjunction of aviation and photographic recording, since remote areas across the country, which had beforehand only been accessible "on foot or horseback" could now be penetrated by a potentially all-pervasive technological eye. Seeing seemed almost unlimited.[185] Also, as has been noted repeatedly, the belief in modern scientificity, visual accuracy, and mechanical objectivity significantly contributed to aerial photography's general appeal among government's technical staff. Speaking to the growing interest in precise and cost-efficient mapping and surveying in the late 1920s and throughout the 1930s, AOC's promotional writings had subtly highlighted how once aerial photographs were used *correctly*, nature would replace the surveyor on the ground and plot her own field notes onto the image.[186]

But some of the medium's aura and the belief that it was indeed revolutionising vision likewise stemmed from its cryptic visual language. In fact, there was a literacy issue, given that many among the ranks and file of Native Affairs were unable to "read" aerial photographs, and the more these images circulated, the more there was need for educating and training the eye.[187]

However, bureaucrats and technicians alike were not willing to be daunted by the complexity and coding of the aerial photographic idiom, and there was unbroken enthusiasm for how seeing the world was renewed. Scaling was critical here. While there is little evidence for a widespread appreciation of the *aesthetic* appeal of small-scale aerial photographs in the archive, there was explicit aesthetic appreciation of enlargements – to scales of 1:10,000 or 1:8,000 – i.e. the material that surveyors and technicians on the ground actually worked with. Once reservations regarding the handling of stereoscopes were vanquished, engineers, geologists, soil conservationists, and surveyors employed by Native Affairs marvelled at the "plasticity" of a terrain that could now be studied, in detail, "in the 3rd dimension".[188] In the light of such refreshing appreciation of the enlargements, finally, officials and scientists began to pay attention to just about everything about them: the image's texture and materiality, the quality of resolution, or the most appropriate paper – glossy, ordinary, or smooth matte – to be chosen for the prints.[189]

Scaling is, hence, pivotal for understanding how the perception of the Eastern Cape landscape was modified thanks to aerial photography, and even if these shifts were not made explicit, the archive is suggestive of a changing disposition towards the environment and state representatives' growing propensity to use photography as a basis for acting in and upon this reconfigured space. As was just proposed, we might begin to understand these shifts once we probe the idea of aerial photography as heterotopia against the specifics of the South African case study, while also asking how the production of *an-other*, different space surfaced the possibility of rendering some features of the landscape visible while blinding out others – in other words, how aerial photographs swayed between visibility and concealment. Let us recall the Foucauldian idea of heterotopia, which understands it as counter-site that simultaneously represents, contests, and inverts "real spaces" by reformulating a complex relationship between the spatial and the temporal. In doing so, heterotopias can function as illusions – exposing the illusionary nature of reality itself – or as compensations – projecting a meticulous perfection that counters the messiness and misconstruction of the "real world".

Considering the specific domain in which aerial photography was used – mapping, surveying, and environmental expertise – understanding the ways in which the medium worked through the temporal proves complicated. Clearly, mapping and photography constitute technologies that accumulate time and fix it in an immobile space flattened so much that it collapses into the surface of the earth.[190] In the aerial photograph, the visibility of time was first a matter of its manifestation and sedimentation at the level of surface features, predicated on the slowness of geographical and geological change, both in turn contingent on scaling.[191] It was, indeed, nature chronicling herself that provided the language technicians in the field were keen to decode. Accessing this idiosyncratic temporality, though, essentially depended on the technologically mediated view from above, since it enabled the abstracted eye to subsume the fragments and layers of time and recompose them, as Barthes rightfully noted, in a way that made duration itself, and (we need to add) the underlying structures and patterns of time, visible.[192] However, the South African archive of aerial photography in fact yields more "down-to-earth", concrete hints at the temporal transformations brought about by the medium, though they are less a matter of image content and style alone than of the practices that induced and engendered it.

Remember, for example, the Aerial Survey Committees' preoccupation with the weather and the ways in which wind, rain, and clouds conditioned the production of aerial photographs in 1939. While these considerations might seem minor to lay persons, weather conditions and seasons clearly introduced a specific temporality to aerial photography, which critically determined if and when landscapes would come into view in the first place, and how many photographs of one site could be taken within any given period of time. Weather and the seasons produced important interruptions in the temporal flow of aerial surveying, and it left numerous blind spots that undermine the continuity and consistency of the South African landscape's official photographic record.[193] Not that continuity and consistency could have otherwise been taken for granted. In fact, retracing the advent of aerial photography in the Eastern Cape reveals a specific temporality at work. This temporality was patterned by an intricate negotiation process of establishing priority and urgency in the production of aerial photographs, and a number of unpredictable factors – trivia such as lack of human and material resources as much as more important events such as the outbreak of WWII – often caused significant postponements and delays.

The motif of urgency and priority, which runs as an important thread through the archive of aerial photography, also transpired in the reconfiguration of space. We have mentioned the division of the Transkei into six (photographic) areas, which determined the progress of aerial surveying. Added to this were the prerequisites of flight and the production of a series of images according to flight plans and assembled into flight jobs, respectively. It was, ultimately, not so much the single image but the *seriality* of aerial photographs that, in a necessarily imaginary act, merged fragments of space and dispersed objects into a visual continuum and a signifying whole.[194] This reduction of space to images is precisely what Henri Lefebvre understood as the problematic effect of visual technologies controlled by the state. The result was, in Lefebvre's argument, an understanding of space that flattened and reduced the richness and meaning of social landscapes and instead favoured a detached view that produced mere inventories of what was to be recorded in that space. The key absence here was, obviously, human presence, and the ways in which those who inhabited the landscape experienced, perceived, and imagined it. On this reading, aerial photography in the Eastern Cape seemed indeed to fulfil the promise of heterotopia as compensation, configuring a space and archive that concealed the "pathologies on the ground" – socioeconomic decay, landlessness, demographic congestion, migrant labour, and political turmoil – and instead directed attention towards the physical environment and its own wants and needs.[195]

But there is no inevitability in emphasising the compensatory value of aerial photographs, and their relation to the world they represent might be less stable and unilateral. Reconsidering Foucault's distinction, we might have to ask if the Eastern Cape photographs likewise functioned as illusions, thereby undermining their own claim to refer to any representable reality, but also reintroducing the question of their very grounding. Here again, the archive has something to tell us, bringing to mind first how the materiality of aerial photographs – the paper chosen and the different scales and sizes of prints – was designed in view of recording *field notes* on the image itself, and then, more importantly, how aerial photographs had to be coordinated with ground surveying in order to be useful to topographical mapping in the first place. The technical term used to describe this process is, tellingly, *ground-truthing*, and there is indeed more to say about this.[196]

Native affair's photographic ground-truthing

Contrary, perhaps, to what one might expect, what we will turn to now is ground-truthing of a different kind, one that helps us establish a relationship between aerial photography and one of its "other" spaces along the lines of photography, rather than surveying and mapping. We will consider a space charted in a photographic album composed by the Department of Native Affairs, filed under the rubric "land affairs" and headlined "Projects".[197] While no dates are given, the photographs assembled here certainly cover the post-World War II period throughout the 1950s. Since Native Affairs authored it, the album focused on the reserves, mainly covering areas in the Ciskei, Transkei, Natal, and the Orange Free State. What will concern us here is the possibility of thinking about this album in terms of a grounded visuality – the view from below, so to speak, that mirrored aerial photography – that therefore helps us retrace how in the mid-twentieth century, South African state institutions looked at the "native world", notably, across multiple perspectives.[198]

The album follows a fairly systematic geographical and thematic pattern and it addresses some of the key interests of mid-twentieth century agricultural policies in African rural areas. Isabel Hofmeyr has proposed that we consider the South African state's desire to possess and mark the countryside in terms of "political inscription", which required a "rigid grammar" in order to be kept in place.[199] This proposition is fruitful regarding the album at hand, since the photographic assemblage precisely identified the visual and material signifiers of this process of inscription. Scattered oblique photographs of towns across the Eastern Cape reminded the viewer of the album's "shadow archive" of aerial photography.[200] But throughout the album, the abstracted

Figure 4.8 Fencing, Eastern Cape.[201]

language of the view from above was broken down into close-ups that made the transformation of the physical and social landscapes of the Eastern Cape much more tangible (Figure 4.8).

While only occasionally referenced as a thematic focus, we come across what appears as a visual inventory of betterment measures: the classification and demarcation of land into arable, grazing, and residential areas; breeding high-quality livestock (as opposed to the alleged "unreasonable native propensity" to merely accumulate animals); the sustainable use and dispersal of water resources; the improvement of farming practices under the guidance of agricultural instructors; contour farming and dryland cultivation; and – importantly – fencing.[202] As the various captions to the images make clear, the overall narrative framing of the photographic images was explicitly developmental, and the album seemed keen to provide evidence for the apartheid state's role as saviour, whose measures were intended to benefit the reserves' African population.[203] The album thus featured images of roads built throughout the Eastern Cape, the administrative buildings of territorial authorities in Umtata, hospitals, and mission and agricultural schools. Added to these were photographs of those men *and* women (there was an explicit focus on gender) who seemed to benefit from betterment and were trained as dairy farmers or planters or had been supported in starting local trade shops that specialised in selling agricultural produce. Evidently, Native Affairs was furnishing visual proof of their commitment to build up a class of "good farmers" in the "native reserves".[204] Finally, images of engineers, agricultural inspectors, cars, trucks, and ploughs registered the actors and objects of betterment as a modern and technical endeavour, while at the same time clarifying that the reserves' transformation hinged on the expertise and guidance of a paternalist state.

Indeed, the view from below held many possibilities that aerial photography was denied, since there was ample opportunity to bring into view human presence and to do so in strategic ways. The album accordingly moved beyond betterment's showpiece figure of the idealised farmer and pursued an ethnographic programme, which featured numerous photographs of "native life", such as everyday scenes taken in villages, "native huts" lining the soft ridges of the hilly landscape, lonely shepherds escorting their herds towards wooden enclosures, and men and women in traditional attire, carrying infants and modest belongings while heading towards unspecified destinations beyond the hazy horizon. While ethnography seems an obvious interest for a Native Affairs Department, what mattered especially in this particular album was the conjunction of two complementary aesthetic modalities: an instrumental visuality concerned with the photographic itemisation of betterment's key transformative effects on the landscape, *and* ethnographic photography that conjured the culturalised "native".[205] The conjunction was critical, since it essentially leaned on understanding the physical landscape as the prerequisite to the knowledge of those who inhabit it (Figure 4.9).[206]

Needless to say, the visualisation of Native Affairs' "Projects" made no reference whatsoever to "pathologies on the ground". Eastern Cape heterotopia remained in place as an illusion, given that – once brought into conversation – aerial photography and the album would entertain an intricate, dialectical relationship with one another, one reinforcing the other's imaginative and transformative force.

Figure 4.9 Rural village, Eastern Cape.[207]

Epilogue

The Native Affairs' "Projects" album was just one manifestation of what we have called visual ground-truthing, and we could have chosen others. In 1939, for example, just when betterment was launched as an agricultural scheme in the Eastern Cape, Alfred Duggan-Cronin published his photographs in a volume pertaining to a series entitled *The Bantu Tribes of South Africa*, with a section on "The Nguni" that covered the Ciskei and southern Transkei.[208] Premesh Lalu has offered an important critique of Duggan-Cronin's photographs within the context of Eastern Cape history and against the backdrop of South African articulations of ethnography as a disciplinary project.[209] Determining that while the scholarship has tended to discuss Duggan-Cronin's oeuvre as a record of vanishing culture, and his photographic studies of "native life" as an exclusive ethnographic exercise, Lalu invites us to understand how this kind of ethnography depended on a particular notion of history, and what the separation of the ethnographic from the historical in the domain of photography might tell us about the constitution of South African landscapes and the subjects expected to dwell in them. He thus proposes that we think about Duggan-Cronin's Eastern Cape photographs as "an attempt at photographing African history", by investigating how the photographs worked through multiple narratives of loss (Figure 4.10).

The portraits included in the volume clearly subscribed to a salvage ethnography committed to the recuperation of a "native subject" lost to the march of industrial modernity and progress, but it is the "massive reconstruction of an idealised landscape" that provides clues to a more submerged history of loss.[210] Using the photograph of Hohita Falls as an example, Lalu argues that while such an image nurtured an imaginary of a pre-industrial past that functioned antithetically to the realities of a rapidly changing society, it likewise constituted a re-enactment of "a scene reminiscent of a form of political power laid to rest by industrial modernity – or history for that matter".[211] This ambiguity of time, the tension between timelessness and history lodged in the photograph was, in fact, reinforced by the accompanying caption, which read:

> Plate XXII: The Hohita Falls in Thembuland. These falls are near to the spot where the paramount Xhosa Chief, Sarili [Sarhili], had his Great Place, until he was compelled to leave it after the cattle-killing in 1857.
>
> Herd-boys spend much of their time in amusing themselves beside the river, especially on warm summer days.[212]

Placing Alfred Duggan-Cronin's Eastern Cape photographs alongside the photographic album authored by the Native Affairs department a few years later helps us add a further layer to Premesh Lalu's analysis, one which

A. M. Duggan-Cronin

THE HOHITA FALLS IN THE MBULAND

Figure 4.10 Duggan-Cronin, *Bantu Tribes*, 1939: Plate 22, Hohita Falls, Eastern Cape.[213]

concerns the ways in which, by the late 1930s, for the South African state (and, there is reason to assume, for the discipline of ethnography as well) "seeing" became essentially a matter of scale. James Scott has argued that state bureaucracies generally tended to privilege the removed, distanced perspective, especially in the domain of surveying, agricultural planning, and the management of landscapes.[214] But the Eastern Cape photographic archive shows that matters might be more complicated, especially once, unlike Scott, we pay careful attention to the visual forms and technologies through which the question of scale can be made more explicit.[215] As we have argued in this chapter, South African state bureaucracies harnessed the possibility of choosing alternatively the bird's-eye or close-up view – and anything in-between – when looking at the "native world", each time reconstituting this world's spatio-temporal placing. Photographic scaling, or the strategic alternation of the parameters of vision, was particularly pertinent here, since it provided a means by which the world could be indefinitely replicated, exaggerated, or reduced. This spatial and temporal intensity was, as we have seen, critical to the imaginary production of both landscape and the "native subject". Scaling was thus among the defining strategies that helped constitute the Eastern Cape as a heterotopian site, and the region's archive of aerial photography is suggestive of why heterotopia – and, we will add, photography – have been deemed to be at once concrete technologies and rhetorical machines.[216]

Notes

1 Paula Amad, *Counter-Archive. Film, the Everyday, and Albert Kahn's Archives de la Planète.* New York, 2010, p. 272; Paula Amad, From God's-eye to Camera-eye. Aerial Photography's Post-humanist and Neo-humanist Visions of the World. *History of Photography*, 36, 1, 2012: 66–86, here pp. 81–2.

2 Charles Waldheim, Aerial Representation and the Recovery of Landscape, in: James Corner (ed.), *Recovering Landscape: Essays in Contemporary Landscape Architecture.* Princeton, 1999, pp. 121–39, here p. 131; Adnan Morshed, The Aesthetics of Ascension in Norman Bel Geddes's Futurama. *Journal of the Society of Architectural Historians*, 63, 1, 2004: 74–99.

3 The question of what can be seen in an aerial photograph is in some ways a matter of technology – especially for aerial photography produced in the 1920s and 1930s; but it is likewise a matter of abstraction and scaling, a point made e.g. by Henri Lefebvre. See the discussion in Jeanne Haffner, "Historicizing the View from Below: Aerial Photography and the Emergence of a Social Conception of Space". The Proceedings of Spaces of History/Histories of Space: Emerging Approaches to the Study of the Built Environment. A Conference at the University of California, Berkeley, 30 April and 1 May 2010 [published online on eScholarship, University of California, 15 September 2010], p. 15.

4 National Geo-Spatial Information (NGI), Umtata, Flight job 132, Strip 001, Image Number 18174, 1938.

5 See especially Allan Sekula, The Instrumental Image. Streichen at War. *Artforum*, 14 April 1975: 26–35; also Davide Deriu, The Ascent of the Modern Planeur: Aerial Images and Urban Imaginary in the 1920s, in: Christian Emden, Catherine Keen and David Midgley (eds.), *Imagining the City.* Oxford, 2006, pp. 189–211, here p. 189.

6 Jeanne Haffner, *The View from Above: The Science of Social Space.* Cambridge, MA, 2013, p. 21, Waldheim, Aerial Survey, p. 124.

7 Deriu, The Ascent, p. 198.

8 Amad, From God's-eye, p. 71; Robert Dixon, *Prosthetic Gods: Travel, Representation and Colonial Governance.* St Lucia QLD, 2001, p. 53.

9   Amad, From God's-eye, p. 86; Denis Cosgrove and William L. Fox, *Photography and Flight*. London, 2010, p. 8.

10   Amad, *Counter-Archive*, p. 264.

11   National Archives Repository (SAB), LDB_2099/R3730, Vol. 1, Department of Agriculture. Aerial Photography. General Correspondence, 24 July 1930–24 October 1947, Director of Trigonometrical Survey to Secretary for Lands, 21 September 1936.

12   Amad, From God's-eye, pp. 67 and 86; Deriu, The Ascent, p. 196.

13   Amad, From God's-eye, p. 81.

14   Quoted in Amad, From God's-eye, p. 86.

15   Cosgrove and Fox, *Photography and Flight*, p. 8.

16   According to Cosgrove and Fox (*Photography and Flight*, pp. 12–13), the vertical perspective taken at 90 degrees to the earth's surface flattens the third dimension in favour of a plan and pattern. The oblique view, i.e. looking down at an angle of more or less 45 degrees, producing high and low obliques respectively, allows for more topographic forms, vegetation, buildings and other three-dimensional elements to be observed. It is therefore more akin to the perspective of landscape painting, while the vertical view resembles more a map. See also Deriu, The Ascent, p. 190.

17   Amad, From God's-eye, p. 68; Cosgrove and Fox, *Photography and Flight*, p. 25.

18   Waldheim, Aerial Representation, p. 122.

19   Amad, From God's-eye, p. 68; Cosgrove and Fox, *Photography and Flight*, p. 22.

20   Amad, From God's-eye, p. 69; Morshed, The Aesthetics of Ascension, pp. 78–9; Deriu, The Ascent, p. 189.

21   Amad, From God's-eye, p. 71; Bernd Hüppauf, Experiences of Modern Warfare and the Crisis of Representation. *New German Critique*, 59, 1993, pp. 41–76, here p. 49.

22   Peter Collier, The Impact on Topographic Mapping of Developments in Land and Air Survey, 1900–1939. *Cartography and Geographic Information Science*, 29, 3, 2002: 155–74, here p. 160.

23   See for a more elaborate discussion Bernd Hüppauf, The Emergence of Modern War Imagery in Early Photography. *History & Memory*, 5, 1, 1993: 131–51.

24   Among the canonical texts that formulate this critique are Siegfried Kracauer's essay on photography (Siegfried Kracauer, *The Mass Ornament. Weimar Essays.* Edited by Thomas E. Levin. Cambridge (MA), London, 1995, pp. 47–64) and Walter Benjamin's The Work of Art in the Age of Its Mechanical Reproduction, in Hannah Arendt (ed.), *Illuminations*, New York, 1969, pp. 1–26. For a discussion see Amad, From God's-eye, pp. 69–70. Also, Sekula, The Instrumental Image.

25   Dixon, *Prosthetic Gods*, p. 53.

26   Cosgrove and Fox, *Photography and Flight*, p. 16; Deriu, The Ascent, p. 196.

27   Peter Collier, The Impact, p. 161; Cosgrove and Fox, *Photography and Flight*, p. 60.

28   Amad, From God's-eye, p. 68; Cosgrove and Fox, *Photography and Flight*, p. 24.

29   Collier, The Impact, p. 167.

30   Morshed, The Aesthetics of Ascension, p. 80; Collier, The Impact, p. 164.

31   Cosgrove and Fox, *Photography and Flight*, p. 24.

32   Waldheim, Aerial Representation, p. 121.

33   Cosgrove and Fox, *Photography and Flight*, p. 9; see also Deriu, The Ascent, p. 200.

34   The literature is extensive but see for an overview Morag Bell, Robin Butlin, and Michael Heffernan (eds.), *Geography and Imperialism, 1820–1940*. Manchester and New York, 1995; and for Africa Jeffrey C. Stone, Imperialism, Colonialism, and Cartography. *Trans. Inst. Geogr.*, 13, 1988: 57–64; and Peter Collier, The Colonial

Survey Committee and the Mapping of Africa. Unpublished Paper presented at the International Symposium "Old Worlds-New Worlds": The History of Colonial Cartography, 1750–1950, Utrecht University 21–3 August 2006.

35 Dov Gavish, *The Survey of Palestine under the British Mandate, 1920–1948.* London, 2005, pp. 167–68.

36 H.M. Stationary Office, *Colonial Reports – Annual. No. 1410 Northern Rhodesia. Report for 1927.* London, 1928, p. 31. The aerial survey of the Anglo-Belgian border was done by the Aircraft Operating Company, i.e. the same company, which produced figure 34 in the opening of this chapter. See also Collier, The Impact, p. 80.

37 Adam Smith, *The Political Landscape: Constellations of Authority in Early Complex Polities.* Berkeley, 2003, pp. 48–9.

38 Amad, *Counter-Archive*, p. 262; Morshed, The Aesthetics of Ascension, p. 94.

39 Amad, From God's-eye, p. 67; Haffner, Historicising, p. 7.

40 Amad, *Counter-Archive*, p. 271.

41 Ibid., p. 272.

42 Amad, From God's-eye, p. 86; Smith, *The Political Landscape*, p. 49.

43 Amad, From God's-eye, p. 86; Morshed, The Aesthetics of Ascension, p. 81.

44 Haffner, *The View from Above*, p. 20.

45 Haffner, Historicising, pp. 14–18.

46 Morshed, The Aesthetics of Ascension, p. 92; Deriu, The Ascent, p. 193

47 Haffner, *The View from Above*, pp. 21–2.

48 See Henri Lefebvre, Space. Social Product and Use Value, in: ibid., *State, Space, World: Selected Essays.* Minneapolis, 2009, p. 194.

49 Smith, *The Political Landscape*, p. 73.

50 Haffner, Historicising, p. 15.

51 Ibid.

52 Smith, *The Political Landscape*, p. 54.

53 Haffner, *The View from Above*, p. 3.

54 Haffner, Historicising, p. 21.

55 Smith, *The Political Landscape*, p. 54; Henri Lefebvre, *The Production of Space.* Oxford and Cambridge (MA), 1991, pp. 96–7.

56 Smith, *The Political Landscape*, p. 73.

57 Amad, From God's-eye, p. 86.

58 Morshed, The Aesthetics of Ascension, p. 81.

59 Ibid.

60 Deriu, The Ascent, p. 203. Note the correspondence with Marc Bloch's notion of the earth's surface as a readable text discussed earlier on.

61 Deriu, The Ascent, p. 203; Amad, From God's-eye, p. 86.

62 Amad, From God's-eye, p. 69.

63 Michel Foucault, Of Other Spaces: Utopias and Heterotopias. *Architecture/Mouvement/Continuité*, October, 1984: 1–9.

64 Foucault, Of Other Spaces, pp. 2–3.

65 Peter Johnson, The Geographies of Heterotopia. *Geography Compass*, 7, 11, 2013: 790–803, here p. 798.

66 Foucault, Of Other Spaces, p. 8

67 Johnson, Geographies, p. 794.

68 Foucault, Of Other Spaces, p. 7.

69 Rui Assubuji and Patricia Hayes, The Political Sublime. Reading Kok Nam, Mozambican photographer (1939–2012). *Kronos* 39, 1, 2013: 66–111, here p. 96.

70 Amad, *Counter-Archive*, p. 274.

71 Johnson, Geographies, p. 798.

72 Johnson based on J. Faubion, in Johnson, Geographies, p. 798.

73 Martin Heidegger, *The Question Concerning Technology and Other Essays*. Translated and with an Introduction by William Lovitt. New York, London, Toronto, Sidney, 1977, pp. 3–35. See also the introduction to Zahid R. Chaudhary, *Afterimage of Empire*. Minneapolis, 2012; Patricia Hayes, The Production of Red: Aesthetics, Work, and Time. *Kronos*, 42, 1, 2016: 103–20, here p. 107.

74 John Illsley, Seeing Our Land from Above: the first decades. *PositionIT*, 2012: 22–6, here p. 22.

75 Alex Capus, *Eduard Spelterini: Photographs of a Pioneer Balloonist*. Zürich, 2007.

76 The image is accessible online through the catalogue to the image collection of the German Colonial Archive, as image No. 037-0600-44, catalogue entry: 'Bombardement des südafrikanischen Truppenlagers am Bahnhof von Tschaukaib (DSWA) durch k. u. k. Leutnant Fiedler am 17 December 1914' [sic].

77 See for details A. Jacobs and A. Smit, Topographic Mapping Support in the South African Military during the 20th Century. *Scientia Militaria*, 32, 1, 2004: 32–50.

78 Swiss National Library, Eduard Spelterini Collection, EAD-WEHR-32111-B, Johannesburg 1911.

79 Denver A. Webb, Lords of All They Surveyed? The Royal Engineers, Surveying, Mapping and Development in South Africa's Eastern Cape. *African Historical Review*, 45, 1, 2013: 22–45, here p. 25.

80 Lindsay Frederick Braun, *Colonial Survey and Native Landscapes in Rural South Africa, 1850–1913: The Politics of Divided Space in the Cape and Transvaal*, Leiden and Boston, 2015.

81 Webb, Lords of All, p. 28; Roger J. Southall, *South Africa's Transkei. The Political Economy of an Independent Bantustan*. New York, 1983, p. 76; Les Switzer, *Power and Resistance in an African Society. The Ciskei Xhosa and the Making of South Africa*. Madison, 1993; Clifton Crais, *The Politics of Evil. Magic, State Power, and the Political Imagination in South Africa*. Cambridge, 2002, pp. 76–78.

82 Richard Wonnacott, 90 years of Surveying and Mapping. *PositionIT*, 2010: 26–32, here p. 26.

83 Wonnacott, 90 Years of Surveying, p. 28.

84 Illsley, Seeing Our Land, p. 23; Baruch Hirson, The General Strike of 1922. *Searchlight South Africa*, 3, 3, 1993: 63–93, here p. 73; Keith Breckenridge, Fighting for a White South Africa: White Working-Class Racism and the 1922 Rand Revolt. *South African Historical Journal*, 57, 2007: 228–43; Tilman Dedering, Air-power in South Africa, 1914–1939. *Journal of Southern African Studies*, 41, 3, 2015: 451–65, here p. 457.

85 Museum Africa, PH 2006_8907, Fordsburg 1922.

86 Illsley, Seeing Our Land, p. 23 refers to e.g. the Solomon brothers and their 'Aviation Ltd'.

87 Illsley, Seeing Our Land, p. 24, Wonnacott, 90 Years of Surveying, p. 29.

88 South African National Archives (SAB) LDB_2099/R3730, vol. 1, Department of Agriculture. Aerial Photography. General Correspondence, 24 July 1930–24 October 1947, Editor to Captain A.R. Cook, 9 August 1930.

89 William Beinart, *The Rise of Conservation in South Africa. Settlers, Livestock, and the Environment 1770–1950*. Oxford, 2003.

90 Beinart, *The Rise of Conservation*, p. 304.

91 Ibid., p. 376

92 Ibid., p. 374.

93 SAB_LDB_2099/R3730, vol. 1. Department of Agriculture. Aerial Photography. General Correspondence, 24 July 1930–24 October 1947, Director Grootfontein Agricultural School Middelburg to Division of Agricultural Education and Extension, Department of Agriculture, Pretoria, 21 December 1932.

94 SAB_LDB_2099/R3730, vol. 1. Department of Agriculture. Aerial Photography. General Correspondence, 24 July 1930–24 October 1947, Director Grootfontein School of Agriculture Middelburg to Division of Agricultural Education and Extension, 4 March 1933.
95 SAB_LDB_2099/R3730, vol. 1. Department of Agriculture. Aerial Photography. General Correspondence, 24 July 1930–24 October 1947, Secretary for Agriculture, Memorandum on Aerial Photographs – Glen, 10 November 1933, and SAB_LDB_2099/R3730, vol. 1, Department of Agriculture. Aerial Photography. General Correspondence, 24 July 1930–24 October 1947, Director of the Technical Division, Department of Agriculture, to the Secretary for Agriculture, 7 May 1934; and Illsley, Seeing Our Land, p. 24.
96 SAB_LDB_2099/R3730, vol. 1. Department of Agriculture. Aerial Photography. General Correspondence, 24 July 1930–24 October 1947, Director of Trigonometrical Survey, Whittingdale, to the Director of Technical Services Union Defence Forces, 17 September 1936.
97 SAB_LDB_2099/R3730, vol. 1. Department of Agriculture. Aerial Photography. General Correspondence, 24 July 1930–24 October 1947, Report on the Meeting of the Air Survey Committee held in the Union Buildings, Pretoria, on the 21st and 22nd December 1936, 30 January 1937.
98 SAB_LDB_2099/R3730, vol. 1. Department of Agriculture. Aerial Photography. General Correspondence, 24 July 1930–24 October 1947, Report on the Meeting of the Air Survey Committee held in the Union Buildings, Pretoria, on the 21st and 22nd December 1936, 30 January 1937, p. 11.
99 SAB_LDB_2099/R3730, vol. 1. Department of Agriculture. Aerial Photography. General Correspondence, 24 July 1930–24 October 1947, Report on the Meeting of the Air Survey Committee held in the Union Buildings, Pretoria, on the 21st and 22nd December 1936, 30 January 1937, p. 2. The plane-table method is a graphical method of survey, in which the field observations and plotting are done simultaneously. It is most suitable for small-scale maps.
100 Illsley, Seing Our Land, p. 24.
101 SAB_LDB_2099/R3730, vol. 1. Department of Agriculture. Aerial Photography. General Correspondence, 24 July 1930–24 October 1947, Director of Trigonometrical Survey, Whittingdale, to the Secretary for Agriculture and Forestry, Report and minutes of the Second meeting of the Air Survey Committee on 26 June 1939, 8 August 1939.
102 Developed by H.G. Fourcade, see G. Petrie, A Short History of British Stereoplotting Instrument Design. *Photogrammetric Record*, 9, 50, 1977: 213–38.
103 SAB_LDB_2099/R3730, vol. 1. Department of Agriculture. Aerial Photography. General Correspondence, 24 July 1930–24 October 1947, Director of Trigonometrical Survey, Whittingdale, to the Secretary for Agriculture and Forestry, Report and minutes of the Second meeting of the Air Survey Committee on 26 June 1939, 8 August 1939, p. 6.
104 SAB_LDB_2099/R3730, vol. 1. Department of Agriculture. Aerial Photography. General Correspondence, 24 July 1930–24 October 1947, Director of Trigonometrical Survey, Whittingdale, to the Secretary for Agriculture and Forestry, Report and minutes of the Second meeting of the Air Survey Committee on 26 June 1939, 8 August 1939, pp. 6–7.
105 SAB_LDB_2099/R3730, vol. 1. Department of Agriculture. Aerial Photography. General Correspondence, 24 July 1930–24 October 1947, Director of Trigonometrical Survey, Whittingdale, to the Secretary for Agriculture and Forestry, Report and minutes of the Second meeting of the Air Survey Committee on 26 June 1939, 8 August 1939, p. 13.

106 SAB_LDB_2099/R3730, vol. 1. Department of Agriculture. Aerial Photo-graphy. General Correspondence, 24 July 1930–24 October 1947, Director of Trigonometrical Survey, Whittingdale, to the Secretary for Agriculture and Forestry, Report and minutes of the Second meeting of the Air Survey Committee on 26 June 1939, 8 August 1939, p. 11. Between 1937 and 1939 numbers of photographs ordered by different departments and divisions were as follows – Geological Survey: 8600; Irrigation: 6200; National Roads: 5600; Agriculture and Forestry: 5400; Provincial Roads: 1000; Native Affairs: 200.

107 SAB_LDB_2099/R3730, vol. 1. Department of Agriculture. Aerial Photography. General Correspondence, 24 July 1930–24 October 1947, Director of Trigonometrical Survey, Whittingdale, to the Secretary for Agriculture and Forestry, Report and minutes of the Second meeting of the Air Survey Committee on 26 June 1939, 8 August 1939, p. 8.

108 Amad, *Counter-Archive*, p. 262.

109 Illsley, Seeing Our Land, p. 24.

110 Beinart, *The Rise of Conservation*, p. 381.

111 See the copious documentation filed under SAB_LTD_461/R3730, vol. 2. State controlled farm planning seems to have been a complicated process of negotiation between farmers and the technical staff in the Department of Agriculture. With regard to the production of aerial mosaics the main conten-tious issue was that farmers were required to pay £5 for mosaics of their farm – many of them refused or insisted on not being charged for service deliveries by the state.

112 Beinart, *The Rise of Conservation*, p. 381.

113 SAB_NTS_8356 20/355, vol. 1. Native Affairs Department, Survey of Native Allotments by Air photography. Aerial Survey, Lieutenant Colonel for Chief of General Staff Defence Department to Secretary for Native Affairs, 3 December 1926.

114 SAB_NTS_8356 20/355, vol. 1. Native Affairs Department, Survey of Native Allotments by Air photography. Aerial Survey, Secretary for Lands to Secretary for Native Affairs, 18 September 1926.

115 SAB_NTS_8356 20/355, vol. 1. Native Affairs Department, Survey of Native Allotments by Air photography. Aerial Survey, Secretary for Lands to Secretary for Native Affairs, 18 September 1926.

116 SAB_NTS_8356 20/355, vol. 1. Native Affairs Department, Survey of Native Allotments by Air photography. Aerial Survey, Lieutenant Colonel for Chief of General Staff Defence Department to Secretary for Native Affairs, 3 December 1926.

117 SAB_NTS_8356 20/355, vol. 1. Native Affairs Department, Survey of Native Allotments by Air photography. Aerial Survey, Surveyor General to the Secretary for Native Affairs, 24 December 1926.

118 SAB_NTS_8356 20/355, vol. 1. Native Affairs Department, Survey of Native Allotments by Air photography. Aerial Survey, Lieutenant Colonel for Chief of General Staff Defence Department to Secretary for Native Affairs, 3 December 1926.

119 Saul Dubow, "Holding a Just Balance Between White and Black": The Native Affairs Department in South Africa c. 1920–1933. *Journal of Southern African Studies*, 12, 2, 1986: 217–39.

120 Rosalie Kingwill, Papering over the Cracks: An Ethnography of Land Title in the Eastern Cape. *Kronos*, Special Issue on Paper Regimes, 40, 1, 2014: 241–68, here p. 245; Switzer, *Power and Resistance*, p. 194.

121 See the above discussion of the Native Locations Act of 1897 on page 15 and references given in footnote 82.

122 SAB_NTS_8356 20/355, vol. 1. Native Affairs Department, Survey of Native Allotments by Air photography. Aerial Survey, Manager Aircraft Operating Company, African Expedition, Bulawayo, to the Secretary for Native Affairs, Pretoria, 3 May 1928.

123 SAB_NTS_8356 20/355, vol. 1. Native Affairs Department, Survey of Native Allotments by Air photography. Aerial Survey, Secretary for Native Affairs to Manager Aircraft Operating Company, 10 May 1928.

124 Timothy Mitchell, *Rule of Experts. Egypt, Technopolitics, Modernity*. Berkeley, 2002. We will come back to this later on.

125 See discussion on page 3.

126 Colin Bundy, Land and Liberation: The South African National Liberation Movements and the Agrarian Question, 1920s–1960s. *Review of African Political Economy*, 29, 1984: 14–29; Fred T. Hendrick, Loose Planning and Rapid Resettlement: The Politics of Conservation and Control in Transkei, South Africa, 1950–1970. *Journal of Southern African Studies*, 15 February 1989: 306–25; Chris de Wet, Betterment Planning in South Africa: Some Thoughts on Its History, Feasibility, and Wider Policy Implications. *Journal of Contemporary African Studies*, 6, 1/2, 1987: 85–122.

127 Southall, *South Africa's Transkei*, p. 84; Switzer, *Power and Resistance*, p. 206. Switzer notes here that by the late 1930s 30% of the population in the Ciskei was landless.

128 Beinart, *The Rise of Conservation*, p. 334; Switzer, *Power and Resistance*, pp. 229/30.

129 Ibid., p. 206.

130 Quoted in Beinart, *The Rise of Conservation*, p. 358.

131 SAB_NTS_8356 20/355, vol. 1. Native Affairs Department, Survey of Native Allotments by Air photography. Aerial Survey, Managing Director Aircraft Operating Company to the Secretary for Native Affairs, 16 July 1936.

132 SAB_NTS_8356 20/355, vol. 1. Native Affairs Department, Survey of Native Allotments by Air photography. Aerial Survey, Secretary for Native Affairs to Managing Director Aircraft Operating Company, 27 July 1936.

133 Switzer, *Power and Resistance*, p. 206. Switzer notes that between 1913 and 1950, only seven African locations were surveyed in the Transkei, and similarly, in the Ciskei most locations remained un-surveyed.

134 William Beinart, Soil Erosion, Conservationism and Ideas about Development: a Southern African Exploration, 1900–1960. *Journal of Southern African Studies*, 11, 1, 1984: 52–83, here p. 75.

135 Crais, *The Politics of Evil*, p. 103.

136 Southall, *South Africa's Transkei*, p. 107.

137 Beinart, Soil Erosion, p. 69; Switzer, *Power and Resistance*, p. 230; P.A. McAllister, Resistance to "Betterment" in the Transkei: A Case Study from Willowvale District. *Journal of Southern African Studies*, 15, 2, Special Issue on The Politics of Conservation in Southern Africa, Jan. 1989: 346–68, here p. 346; P.A. McAllister, The Impact of Relocation on Social Relationships in a "Betterment" Area in the Transkei. *Development Southern Africa*, 3, 3, 1986: 467–78, here p. 468.

138 Beinart, Soil Erosion, p. 75; Southall, *South Africa's Transkei*, p. 107.

139 Jacob Tropp, The Contested Nature of Colonial Landscapes: Historical Perspectives on Livestock and Environments in the Transkei. *Kronos*, 30, 2004: 118–37, here p. 130.

140 Bundy, Land and Liberation, p. 15; William Beinart and Colin Bundy, State Intervention and Rural Resistance: The Transkei, 1900–1965. In: Martin A. Klein (ed.), *Peasants in Africa*. Beverly Hills, 1980, pp. 271–315.

141 Bundy, Land and Liberation, p. 21; McAllister, Resistance to "Betterment", p. 346.

142 Fred T. Hendricks, Loose Planning and Rapid Resettlement: The Politics of Conservation and Control in Transkei, South Africa, 1950–1970. *Journal of Southern African Studies*, 15, 2, 1989: 306–25, here p. 320; and for how gender affected dynamics and variations in responses to betterment Anne K. Mager, "The People Get Fenced": Gender, Rehabilitation and African Nationalism in the Ciskei and Border Region, 1945–1955. *Journal of Southern African Studies*, 18, 4, 1992: 761–82.

143 See footnote 107 for the departments involved. In the period between 1937 and 1939 the AOC surveyed a total of approximately 50,000 square miles (or 129,000 square kilometres), i.e. ca. 10.5% of South Africa's entire territory. In contrast, the South African Defence Force surveyed only 9950 square kilometres (or 25,770 square kilometres) during the same period of time. Aerial photographs were taken mainly in Transvaal, the Cape Province, along the Natal Coast and selectively in the Eastern Cape (East London area). For a detailed list of areas covered, see SAB_LDB_2099/R3730, vol. 1, Department of Agriculture. Aerial Photography. General Correspondence, 24 July 1930–24 October 1947, Director of Trigonometrical Survey, Whittingdale, to the Secretary for Agriculture and Forestry, Report and minutes of the Second meeting of the Air Survey Committee on 26 June 1939, 8 August 1939, p. 10.

144 See footnote 107.

145 SAB_NTS_8356 20/355, vol. 1. Native Affairs Department, Survey of Native Allotments by Air photography. Aerial Survey, Director Trigonometrical Survey to Secretary for Native Affairs, 4 August 1937, and Director Aircraft Operating Company to the Secretary for Native Affairs, 21 November 1938.

146 SAB_NTS_8356 20/355, vol. 1. Native Affairs Department, Survey of Native Allotments by Air photography. Aerial Survey, Assistant Director Native Agriculture to Chief Native Commissioner Pietermaritzburg, 13 April 1939; Secretary for Native Affairs to Chief Native Commissioner Pietermaritzburg, 27 April 1939; Secretary for Native Affairs to Director of Trigonometrical Survey, 23 May 1939; Director of Trigonometrical Survey to Secretary for Native Affairs, 15 June 939; Secretary for Native Affairs to Chief Native Commissioner King William's Town, 25 August 1939.

147 SAB_NTS_8356 20/355, vol. 1. Native Affairs Department, Survey of Native Allotments by Air photography. Aerial Survey, Director of Trigonometrical Survey to Secretary for Native Affairs, 30 July 1937; Director of Trigonometrical Survey to Secretary for Native Affairs, 4 August 1937; Manager AOC to Secretary for Native Affairs, 30 May 1939.

148 SAB_NTS_8356 20/355, vol. 1. Native Affairs Department, Survey of Native Allotments by Air photography. Aerial Survey, Secretary for Native Affairs to Chief Native Commissioner King William's Town, 25 May 1939.

149 Beinart, Soil Erosion, p. 73; De Wet, Betterment Planning, p. 88.

150 Hendricks, Loose Planning, p. 316; De Wet, Betterment Planning, p. 89.

151 Switzer, *Power and Resistance*, pp. 113–17; In the early nineteen century Gcuwa was where the Great Place of the Xhosa Paramount Chief Hintsa was situated; see Jeffrey B. Peires, *The House of Phalo: A History of the Xhosa People in the Days of Their Independence*. Berkeley, Los Angeles, London, 1982, p. 109, and Premesh Lalu, *The Deaths of Hintsa. Postapartheid South Africa and the Shape of Recurring Pasts*. Cape Town, 2002, p. 288, footnote 63.

152 Braun, *Colonial Survey*, pp. 180–89.

153 Braun, *Colonial Survey*, p. 187.

154 Braun, *Colonial Survey*, p. 189.

155 There is disagreement in the literature. Beinart and Bundy argue that while lack of staff and materials, and problems with survey work might have played a role, opposition from local farmers and residence was decisive for delays. See Beinart, Soil Erosion, p. 80, and Bundy, Land and Liberation, pp. 21–2. Hendricks notes that in 1945 in only three wards (village sections of districts) culling of livestock had been completed (see Hendricks, Loose Planning, p. 317), while Ngcaba states that betterment in the Butterworth district only began in 1945. See Siyanda Vincent Ngcaba, The Decline of Agriculture in Rural Transkei: The Case of Mission Location in Butterworth. Unpublished MA Thesis, Rhodes University, Grahamstown, 2002, p. 5.

156 SAB_NTS_8356 20/355, vol. 2. Native Affairs Department, Survey of Native Allotments by Air photography. Aerial Survey, Secretary for Native Affairs to the Acting Undersecretary, 20 February 1945.

157 SAB_NTS_8356 20/355, vol. 2. Native Affairs Department, Survey of Native Allotments by Air photography. Aerial Survey, Notes by Major Roberts, Senior Engineer Native Affairs, 3 March 1945 and Engineer Native Affairs to Chief Magistrate Umtata, 19 April 1945.

158 SAB_NTS_8356 20/355, vol. 2. Native Affairs Department, Survey of Native Allotments by Air photography. Aerial Survey, Plan No. 1651/45 – Portion of Transkei Covered by Aerial Photography and Division into Areas 1–6, no date, [1945].

159 SAB_NTS_8356 20/355, vol. 2. Native Affairs Department, Survey of Native Allotments by Air photography. Aerial Survey, Officer in Charge Topographical Survey, Memorandum, Surveying and Mapping Requirements of Native Trust, 12 June 1945.

160 The series of aerial photographs of the Butterworth district taken in 1942 is filed under National Geo-Spatial Information (NGI), Butterworth, Flight Plan Job 5, 1942. The job includes a total of 1919 photographs taken at a scale of 1: 30,000.

161 SAB_NTS_8356 20/355, vol. 2. Native Affairs Department, Survey of Native Allotments by Air photography. Aerial Survey, Secretary for Native Affairs to Chief Magistrate Umtata, 26 April 1945.

162 SAB_NTS_8356 20/355, vol. 2. Native Affairs Department, Survey of Native Allotments by Air photography. Aerial Survey, Secretary for Native Affairs to Chief Magistrate Umtata, 14 May 1945.

163 SAB_NTS_8356 20/355, vol. 2. Native Affairs Department, Survey of Native Allotments by Air photography. Aerial Survey, Chief Magistrate Umtata to department of Native Affairs, 14 May 1945 and Chief Magistrate Umtata to Secretary for Native Affairs, 21 May 1945.

164 SAB_NTS_8356 20/355, vol. 2. Native Affairs Department, Survey of Native Allotments by Air photography. Aerial Survey, Secretary for Native Affairs to Chief Magistrate Umtata, 4 June 1945. Figure 39 shows one sketch map sheet out of three.

165 SAB_NTS_8356 20/355, vol. 2. Native Affairs Department, Survey of Native Allotments by Air photography. Aerial Survey, Chief Magistrate Umtata to department of Native Affairs, 14 May 1945 and Chief Magistrate Umtata to Secretary for Native Affairs, 21 May 1945.

166 For a brief discussion of resistance to betterment in Butterworth see Ngcaba, op.cit., pp. 22–3. Ngcaba notes that the government's satisfaction with how betterment took off was because most local chiefs and headmen supported the scheme, while the broader population did not.

167 SAB_NTS_8356 20/355, vol. 2. Native Affairs Department, Survey of Native Allotments by Air photography. Aerial Survey, Secretary for Native Affairs to Trigonometrical Survey Office, 12 November 1945.

168 SAB_NTS_8356 20/355, vol. 2. Native Affairs Department, Survey of Native Allotments by Air photography. Aerial Survey, Survey Directorate Pretoria to Chief Magistrate Umtata, 12 August 1947.

169 SAB_NTS_8356 20/355, vol. 3. Native Affairs Department. Survey of Native Allotments by Air Photography, Trigonometrical Survey Office, Circular: Proposed National Advisory Survey Council, 25 August 1949, and Secretary for Native Affairs to Chief Magistrate Umtata, Chief Native Commissioner Pietersburg, Chief Native Commissioner Potchefstroom, Chief Native Commissioner Kingwilliamstown, Chief Native Commissioner Pietermaritzburg, 21 September 1949.

170 SAB_NTS_8356 20/355, vol. 3. Native Affairs Department. Survey of Native Allotments by Air Photography, Trigonometrical Survey Office, Circular: Proposed National Advisory Survey Council, 25 August 1949.

171 SAB_NTS_8356 20/355, vol. 3. Native Affairs Department. Survey of Native Allotments by Air Photography, Director of Trigonometrical Survey to Secretary for Native Affairs, 3 March 1950.

172 De Wet, Betterment Planning, p. 88.

173 Beinart, *The Rise of Conservation*, p. 359.

174 De Wet, Betterment Planning, pp. 88-9.

175 Hendricks, Loose Planning, p. 311.

176 Southall, *South Africa's Transkei*, p. 231.

177 Bundy, Land and Liberation, p. 24.

178 De Wet, Betterment Planning, p. 100.

179 The files on aerial photography kept by the Native Affairs Department end in 1961. It seems plausible to assume that the general state interest in aerial photography might have been redirected towards it "origins", i.e. the use of the medium for military purposes, e.g. in the context of the Pondoland Revolt in 1960 or the war in northern Namibia from 1966 onwards. See for Pondoland see Bundy, Land and Liberation, p. 26, and for Namibia Richard Dale, *The Namibian War of Independence, 1966–1989: Diplomatic, Economic, and Military Campaigns.* Jefferson (NC), 2014, p. 78.

180 Brian Larkin, Infrastructure, the Colonial Sublime and Indirect Rule, in ibid., *Signal and Noise. Media, Infrastructure and Urban Culture in Nigeria.* Durham and London, 2008, pp. 16–47, here p. 36.

181 See e.g. Farieda Kahn, Rewriting South Africa's Conservation History – The Role of the Native Farmers Association. *Journal of Southern African Studies,* 20, 4, 1994: 499–516; Paul Hebinck and Wim van Averbeke, Rural Transformation in the Eastern Cape, in Paulus Gerardus, Maria Hebinck, and Peter C. Lent (eds.), *Livelihoods and Landscapes: The People of Guquka and Koloni and Their Resources.* Leiden, 2014, pp. 33–66.

182 See e.g. McAllister, Impact, p. 468; Tropp, Contested nature, p. 118; De Wet, Betterment Planning, p. 101.

183 National Geo-Spatial Information (NGI), Butterworth, Job 468, Strip 1, Image Number 8433, 1961. Total of photographs: 638, scale 1:36,000.

184 Quoted in Beinart, *The Rise of Conservation*, p. 343.

185 SAB_NTS_8356 20/355, vol. 1. Native Affairs Department, Survey of Native Allotments by Air photography. Aerial Survey, Engineer Native Affairs Department to Chief Native Commissioner Natal, 15 June 1939.

186 SAB_NTS_8356 20/355, vol. 1. Native Affairs Department, Survey of Native Allotments by Air photography. Aerial Survey, Manager Aircraft Operating Company to the Secretary for Native Affairs, 3 May 1928.

187 SAB_NTS_8356 20/355, vol. 1. Native Affairs Department, Survey of Native Allotments by Air photography. Aerial Survey, Secretary for Native Affairs to Chief Native Commissioner Natal, 21 September 1939.

188 SAB_NTS_8356 20/355, vol. 1. Native Affairs Department, Survey of Native Allotments by Air photography. Aerial Survey, AOC to Secretary for Native Affairs, 18 June 1937 and Director of Trigonometrical Survey to Secretary for Native Affairs, 4 August 1937.

189 SAB_NTS_8356 20/355, vol. 1. Native Affairs Department, Survey of Native Allotments by Air photography. Aerial Survey, Director of Trigonometrical Survey to Secretary for Native Affairs, 30 July 1937 and Manager AOC to Secretary for Native Affairs, 30 May 1939. Smooth matt was considered the best for adding handwritten notes.

190 For a more detailed discussion of the time-space compression in mapping, see Barny Warf, *Time Space Compression. Historical Geographies.* Abingdon, 2008, especially the chapter on 'Late modern time-space compression', pp. 78–166.

191 See this chapter p. 9, and also Courtney J. Campbell, Space, Place, and Scale: Human Geography and Spatial History in Past and Present. *Past and Present, gtw006*, 2016.

192 See this chapter p. 11.

193 Weather remains one of the main factors conditioning aerial photography. See Ron Graham and Alexander Koh, *Digital Aerial Survey: Theory and Practice.* Caithness and Boca Raton, 2000, p. 180.

194 See footnote 62.

195 Morshed, Aesthetics of Ascension, p. 92.

196 Cosgrove and Fox, *Photography and Flight*, p. 24.

197 Ditsong National Museum of Cultural History (DNM), SA_dnmch_grondsake 133, Union of South Africa, Department of Native Affairs, Projects [n.d.]

198 See especially Haffner, Historicising.

199 Isabel Hofmeyr, The Spoken Word and the Barbed Wire. Oral Chiefdoms versus Literate Bureaucracies. In ibid., *"We Spend Our Years as a Tale That Is Told": Oral Historical Narrative in a South African Chiefdom.* Portsmouth, Johannesburg, London, 1993, p. 59–77, here pp. 67/68.

200 Allan Sekula, The Body and the Archive, p. 10.

201 DNM, SA_dnmch_grondsake 133, Union of South Africa, Department of Native Affairs, Projects [n.d.], Image No. 2244b, 'Fencing has been erected in the rural districts of the Eastern Cape. Development was undertaken by the South African Bantu Trust', p. 29.

202 Hofmeyr elaborates on the idea of the fence as the key political inscription in the landscape. See Hofmeyr, The Spoken Word, p. 61.

203 See Beinart, Soil Erosion, p. 69.

204 See e.g. Hendricks, Loose Planning, p. 309; Patricia Hayes, Jeremy Silvester and Wolfram Hartmann, Photography, History, and Memory, in wolfram Hartmann, Jeremy Silvester and Patricia Haayes (eds.), *The Colonising Camera. Photographs in the making of Namibian history.* Cape Town, Windhoek, Athens, 1998, pp. 2–9, here p. 5.

205 On ethnography as aesthetics see e.g. Silvy Chakkalakal, Margaret Meads Anthropologie der Sinne: Ethnographie als ästhetische und aisthetische Praxis. *Berliner Blätter,* 67, 2015: 14–28.

206 See for the emergence of this argument in the social sciences from the 1930s onwards Haffner, *The View from Above*, pp. 21–3.

207 DNM, SA_dnmch_grondsake 133, Union of South Africa, Department of Native Affairs, Projects [n.d.], Image No. 2241h, 'Social life in the rural districts of the Eastern Cape', p. 24.

208 Alfred M. Duggan-Cronin, *The Bantu Tribes of South Africa. Reproductions of Photographic Studies.* Vol III, Section I: The Nguni. Cambridge and Kimberley, 1939.

209 Premesh Lalu, *The Deaths of Hintsa. Postaparteid South Africa and the Shape of Recurring Pasts.* Cape Town, 2009.
210 Lalu, *The Deaths*, p. 181.
211 Lalu, *The Deaths*, p. 180.
212 Duggan-Cronin, *The Bantu Tribes*, caption to plate 22.
213 Duggan-Cronin, *The Bantu Tribes*, no page, plate 22.
214 James C. Scott, *Seeing Like A State. How Certain Schemes to Improve the Human Condition Have Failed.* New Haven, 1998. See especially Part 1, Chapter 1, Nature and Space, pp. 11–52.
215 Scott does refer to cadastral maps, though without reflection on them as a particular image form and technology of representation. See Scott, *Seeing Like A State*, p. 46.
216 Johnson, Geographies, p. 798.

5 Presence

The Breakwater prison albums, Cape Town, 1890s–1900s

The historian is, in every sense of the word, only the fictor, which is to say the modeller, the artisan, the author, the inventor of whatever past he offers us. And when it is in the element of art that he thus develops his search for lost time, the historian no longer even finds himself facing a circumscribed object, but rather something like a liquid or gas expansion – a cloud that changes shape constantly as it passes overhead. What can we know about a cloud, save by guessing, and without ever grasping it completely?[1]

Introduction

We begin the last chapter in this book with a return to its opening pages, where we explored a photographic image and object of policing in German South West Africa, the *Fotografiealbum 1b Farbige*. We recall Governor von Lindequist's letter to the consulate in Cape Town composed in 1906, in which the colonial dignitary complained of rampant criminal activity across the Namibian colony.[2] Drafting an ambitious blueprint for transnational cooperation in criminal prosecution, von Lindequist's hopes had been, as we saw, tempered by political pragmatism, and the German Consul-General in Cape Town had made a case for more modest demands.[3] Recalling an earlier, unsuccessful attempt by the German colonial administration to "get hold of the storied rogues gallery in the possession of the Cape Town prison authorities", the sagacious diplomat had possibly spared the governor's blushes.[4] Hence, von Lindequist's enthusiasm was stranded and his technocratic flirtation with the southern neighbour was in vain. But the German administration had good reason for nosiness, since there really was a "storied rogues gallery", one that by the early 1900s seemed almost shrouded in legend – and ought to arouse our own curiosity about the Cape Town doings.

Visual histories of colonial South Africa have loosely dealt with prison photography as a genre associated with specific contexts and locations and with particular moments in the making of the country's past. Robben Island, the site of the notorious prison, undoubtedly occupies a privileged position within the photographic narration of confinement and incarceration under colonialism in the nineteenth and early twentieth centuries and segregation and

Figure 5.1 Portrait of Magoma, Robben Island.[5]

apartheid in the period after South African Union in 1910.[6] It is a history that encompasses photographs as diverse as images of some of the most important Xhosa leaders captured during the frontier wars and after the Cattle Killings in the Eastern Cape in the early and mid-1850s and imprisoned on Robben Island (Figure 5.1), as well as iconic photographs of political prisoners from the rank and file of the anti-apartheid and liberation movements, most notably the Pan Africanist Congress (PAC) and African National Congress (ANC) leadership, held on Robben Island since the 1960s.[7] While Robben Island remains a landmark in the iconography of imprisonment in South Africa, there have been a number of inquiries into the history of photographic production in other penal institutions, as it emerged in the course of diverse deployments of the camera at the nexus of colonial surveillance and confinement since the mid-nineteenth century, that merit discussion (Figure 5.2).

A body of images taken of /Xam Bushmen in the Breakwater Convict Station in 1871 has received repeated attention.[8] Produced in the context of anthropological surveys throughout the British Empire, the Bushmen photographs have accordingly been understood within histories of scientific knowledge production, and interpreted as part of mid-nineteenth century articulations of race and the desire to produce visual evidence for "the

Figure 5.2 Group of prisoners, Robben Island, 1871.[9]

physical diversity of the human races" – as it was coined by contemporaries.[10] The Breakwater Convict Station is conspicuous in the formation of the practice of photographic surveillance in the Cape Colony, yet by considering a set of photographs beyond the burgeoning field of imperial acquisition of knowledge, this chapter hopes to draw nearer to the micro-politics of colonial institutions.

Moving to the Cape Colony in the late nineteenth century and to prison photography, will inevitably echo our earlier discussion of photography and policing in German South West Africa, both empirically and analytically. It is reasonable to expect that the deployment of the photographic medium in South African and Namibian police and prison institutions in the period between the late nineteenth and early twentieth centuries would have rested on comparable assumptions about and desires linked to the new image form and technology, e.g. in view of the promises it held for identification and classification purposes. Also, commonality with regard to forensic methodology, image genre, and materiality seems likely. As a result, and more specifically, one might proceed from the assumption that in both cases Bertillonage would have served as the overarching methodological framework, producing characteristic forms of documentation, recording, and archiving such as personal descriptions, fingerprints, registers of detainees, and signature images like the mug-shot. As we shall see, this rationale will be substantiated to some extent, once we take a look at the Cape Town rogues gallery. Still, history likes *Eigensinn*, and the past often reveals the wayward and capricious, all the more so if we approach it through the visual.[11] There is indeed evidence for such capriciousness in something that arouses curiosity: the Cape authorities' refusal to cooperate with and their explicit rejection of Windhoek's request to exchange photographs. We might assume Cape Town's hesitation to be an expression of British imperial mistrust and competition towards its unloved German rival, and perhaps it was.[12] But there might be more to it, and our inquisitiveness opens up the possibility of further considerations that may have induced the Cape colonial government to remain secretive about its pictorial possessions – considerations linked to photography's uneven and idiosyncratic trajectories across diverse moments in time, geographical locations, and institutional sites.

The following discussion of the Cape Town rogues gallery, which consisted, as we shall see, of a series of photographic albums, will help us shed light on some of the historical and analytical problems we have encountered in earlier chapters. An analysis of this particular collection of prison photographs will serve a reconsideration and refinement of our understanding of Bertillonage's resonances across the colonial world and lend credence to the scholarly argument that (since the method yielded more or less coherent and stable image genres) institutional practices and material objects preserved and recorded in the archive take us down a blind alley.[13] Throughout this chapter, the focus on Bertillonage is hence not so much an argument for empirical clustering as a rhetorical device to draw attention to the mutual contingency of the photographic image and the archive.[14] Yet, while the archive remains an important institutional site for the production of photographic meaning, we should not proceed as if the mutuality speaks for itself, but instead continue to explain if and how *specific* archives condition visual semantics, and how *particular* photographic collections shape the ways we encounter and make sense of Southern African pasts.[15]

There are, in other words, striking material and visual differences between the Cape Town albums produced in the late nineteenth century and the mid-1910s assemblage of South West African police photography that we considered in Chapter 1. In what follows, we will delineate these differences more carefully, first and foremost as they notably find expression in a distinct preoccupation with aesthetics and technological mediation within Cape colonial penal institutions. This is an instance that will, not surprisingly, take us back to the writings of Walter Benjamin and help us develop a notion of policing as both a function of social institutions and an aesthetic order.[16] We thereby hope to first show that it is important to attend to the historical contingency of the meaning and use of particular photographs in a specific colonial penal institution, and second, to complicate instrumental readings of historical photography that draw on a causal link between colonial disciplinary power and visuality.

Readers may wonder about this last chapter's title – "Presence" – so let us briefly explain before we move into the depths of the Cape Town archive and its remarkable photographic collection. As we shall see in a moment, archival research can lead us along unexpected paths. Historians like to believe in the archive's vital role in defining history; it contains the textual and material sources, the nitty-gritty from the past that informs our work. As much as we might read the archive critically, both *along* and *against* the grain, and acknowledge that it conceals as much as it reveals, the archive remains constitutive of historical thinking and writing.[17] This is not to say that we shall argue for a return to empiricism or positivism here, though historical photographs would be particularly tempting if we were to make such an argument. But it is a way of conceding that, while doing archival research, we may be taken by surprise and marvel at the ways in which it is precisely the archive that makes us believe we are being brought into privileged and meaningful contact with the past – through its texts, images, and objects. Presence will serve as an analytical tool to come to terms with these seductive but ultimately treacherous effects.

Ancestral fantasy

In the course of 2012–2013, I found myself conducting research in the Western Cape Archives and Records Services in Cape Town, South Africa. After I had looked at a substantial number of files and parts of the photographic collections, staff working at the archives gradually got an idea of what I was looking for and the head archivist told me about a series of albums with photographs of convicts imprisoned at the Breakwater Convict Station in Cape Town in the late nineteenth century. To my utter astonishment, and admittedly to my delight, it seemed as if no one – no *historian* of Cape Town or Cape colonial photography I knew of – had looked at these albums, let alone written about them. At the same time, while I spent several weeks trying to make sense of the presence of the albums in the archives and find additional sources that would help contextualise the photographs, I was repeatedly approached by other users of the archive who were very excited to see the albums again, and who recalled consulting them in the hope of finding portraits of their ancestors. I didn't pay much attention to this and continued to focus on my own historical interest in these albums that was, I believed at the time, of *an entirely different kind*.

However, when I came across the photographs of two men who had my surname – Rizzo (a southern Italian name) – my attitude changed. The younger of the two men was called Salvador,[18] the older John (Figure 5.3). Without thinking too much about it, I declared John to be my Cape Town "ancestor", as it seemed much harder to use the young man, Salvador, since it felt as if ancestors – particularly chosen ones – need to be of a certain age. Who was this John Rizzo? Was he an Italian in the first place, and if so, how could he have been related to me? Would there be any plausible, historically convincing narrative about him in relation to me? Was recourse to histories of southern Italian emigration in the second half of the nineteenth century, caused by large scale impoverishment of peasant populations and their desire to rebuild their lives abroad, in the Americas or in Africa, a plausible narrative line?[19] John Rizzo could have been among these emigrants seeking economic opportunity in the prospering Cape Colony then fuelled by the

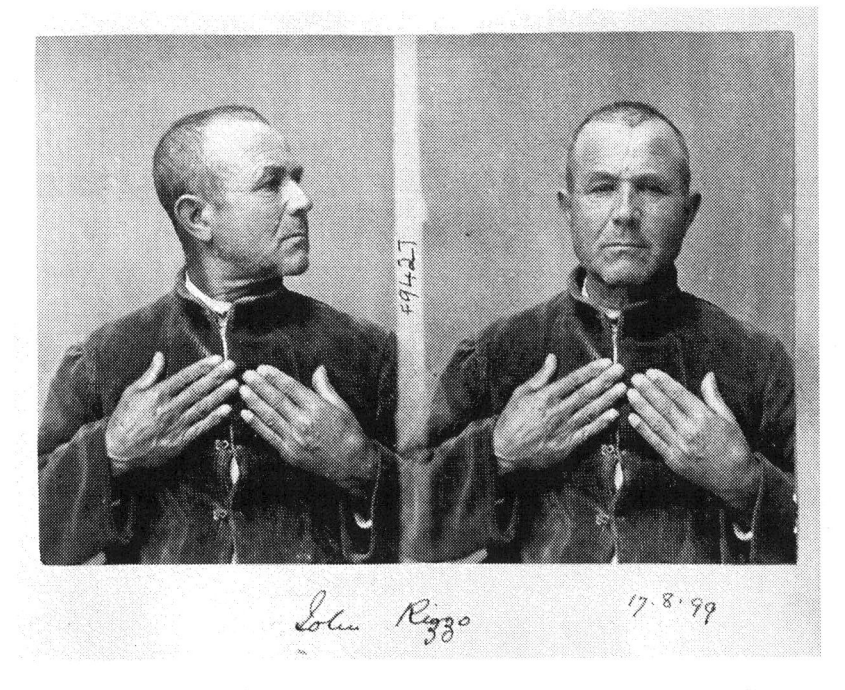

Figure 5.3 Photographs of John Rizzo, convict number F9427, 17.8.[18]99.[20]

discovery of diamonds in the Kimberley area in the 1870s and of gold in the Witwatersrand basin in the mid-1880s.[21] It was clear as daylight – I needed a copy of my "ancestral portrait".

The Breakwater prison albums are exceptional archival objects, not only because of the delicate collection of images they contain, but also – as the negatives have been lost – "original", all of which fuels a strong sense of *aura*. As noted in Chapter 1, there are various practical and conservational reasons why archives tend to privilege or even fetishise albums, and at times limit their accessibility; this is especially acute in the case of photographic albums, a point I will later return to.[22] Here, I mention it simply to explain why – in addition to my wish to secure an image of John – I immediately got permission to have high-quality reproductions of the photographs made. The reproduction process was laborious. Assisted by Cape Town-based photographer Paul Grendon, we took the albums to a small room set aside for reproduction work and began photographing every single page, details of pages, and single photographs. The process proved tiring, both physically and mentally; it was time-consuming, and the poor lighting complicated the task. I did my best in assisting Paul, holding album pages, shifting the albums into proper position, shifting pages up and down, depending on Paul's instructions as he stood on a chair with his camera fixed on the archival material. The space was so narrow

that we could barely move around, and after several days in which we managed to photograph five out of nine albums, both of us agreed that we needed
to stop. The men's faces we had been looking at for uncountable hours began
to haunt us and caused us nightmares. But there was an eventual moment of
catharsis when I reencountered John Rizzo's photographs while working on
Vol. 5. Paul generously took note of my ancestral fantasy and made a series of
perfect reproductions of these particular photographs, but it was the fact that
Paul and John – the photographer and the ancestor – were the spitting image
of each other that made the entire process end in laughter, and somehow
reconciled us with an otherwise gruelling overexposure to images of colonial
captivity and imprisonment.

My retelling of these moments of *archive fever* is more than the shaping of a
mere anecdote; more than a rhetorical move to seduce readers.[23] One could
do away with the significance of John Rizzo, of his images in the Western
Cape Archives, by declaring this trove of photographs a happy coincidence, a
curiosity, an example of how the past, as it reveals itself visually in an archive,
can surprise us. Yet, while working with these albums was indeed in many
ways an intense and exciting experience, I was still puzzled by something
these particular photographs did to me – which is that they *touched* me.

What might seem profoundly banal to some and unreasonable or pathetic
to others, is – admittedly – something that might embarrass our sense of scholarly composure and professionalism as historians; something that seems to
undermine the concern with a hermeneutic understanding of historical photographs and, hence, an analysis that has nothing to do with the frivolity and
irrationality of any of one's *personal* responses. We might find redemption in
a Barthesian reading of this longing, which, when looking at certain photographs, wants us to precisely avoid affective closure by becoming "[a person]
without knowledge", and – in speaking or writing about these photographs –
to privilege expressive, even affective rather than critical language.[24]

Probing presence

Revisiting Roland Barthes's *Camera Lucida* will in part inform the attempt to
come to terms with this one pair of historical photographs and my response
to them. Yet, what will help much more than the return to Barthes in understanding this moment of unexpected archival intensity is thinking along the
lines of Eelco Runia's *Moved by the Past*, especially the debate on what Runia
and other thinkers have proposed in terms of "presence".[25] Let us briefly
sketch out some of the key elements in Runia's argument, as outlined by
Runia himself that will bear upon our reflections on the prison photographs.

Runia's entry point is Hayden White's *Metahistory* published in 1973, a
text he considers key in the advancement of representationalism as the dominant mode of accounting for the past. While he concedes representationalism a temporary critical vigour, Runia nevertheless criticises the paradigm's
inability to explain recent phenomena such as memory, *lieux de mémoire*,

remembrance, and trauma. He establishes that the conceptual inadequacy and shortcomings of representationalism lie in the fact that it is solely interested in the transfer of meaning. It is at this point that Runia proposes "presence" as an epistemological alternative:

> What may be called "presence" ("the unrepresented way the past is present in the present") is at least as important as "meaning". "Presence" can be dealt with by employing a "topical" view of history [...] in which the whole of history is stored in "places" [...] that can be "visited" on the plane of the present. Presence can be said to be stored in metonymy. Whereas metaphor is instrumental in "the transfer of meaning", metonymy brings about a "transfer of presence". A metonymy is a presence in absence not just in the sense that it presents something that isn't there, but also in the sense that in the absence (or at least the radical inconspicuousness) that is there, the thing that isn't there is still present. The presence of the past thus does not reside in the intended story or the manifest metaphorical content of the text, but in what story and text contain in spite of the intentions of the historian [...]. Presence – being in touch with reality – is, I believe, just as basic as meaning.[26]

As Ethan Kleinberg has rightfully noted, "presence", in terms of a movement away from a constructed past towards a past that actually existed, is not simply a "return to positivism or realism before the linguistic turn", nor is it an expression of the modernist struggle between mimesis and representation. While "presence" does position itself in some ways as a counter to meaning, it is also an invitation to shift away from language towards experience, and reclaim meaning from the "clutches of [...] representationalism". Runia, Kleinberg tells us, ultimately seems to argue for a "return to a relationship with the past, predicated on our unmediated access to actual things that we can feel and touch and that bring us into contact with the past".[27]

Historians of photography will inevitably have strong responses to Runia's claims and propositions – positive as much as critical ones – most obviously so if we add to "the things we can feel and touch" those that we can *see*. There is, as many have noted, a tension between photography's seeming capacity to provide a privileged access to the past, to what happened, and ultimately to reality on the one hand, and an understanding of photographs as representations and signs on the other hand.[28] Photographs seem to embody what eludes language and (literally) bring to the surface "the revelation that speaks without words".[29] Unlike textual historical sources, perhaps, photographs appeal to the senses and the sensible, they "flirt with us",[30] and it is the evidence of *seeing* – an object, a place, a person – that tempts us to believe in an immediate if hallucinatory experience of the past as "presence".[31] But sight *does* like to play tricks, and photographs confuse historical consciousness not only because they blur the distinction between the past and the present,[32] but because of their denoting messiness and their seemingly undifferentiated recording of whatever happened to be in front of the camera, without assigning relevance. As much as we acknowledge – and we have argued accordingly throughout these chapters – that photographic images are *not* unmediated reflections of reality, or the past, but the product of framings and selection; spatial and temporal fragments; visual compositions in that they include and exclude; and hence a first act of *interpretation*, photographs have an uncanny ability to "undermine their own historicity; they lend themselves to instantaneous recognitions that we make in the present, from their presence, leading viewers into a misguided perception of having access to another time instead of merely access to an object, a photograph, that is old".[33]

The presence/absence of historical prison photographs in the archive

Let me go back, then, to the objects themselves – the Breakwater convict albums. As mentioned before, they are *auratic* because they're considered originals, privileged archival items.[34] But if we continue to spin the preceding narrative yarn, the albums' aura also emanates from their material and visual persistence over time that "categorically defines 'the presence of the past'".[35] Consider for a moment the archival image-object I was introduced to at the Western Cape Archives: The Breakwater convict albums are filed under a large archival conglomerate of Colonial Office records, i.e. the office that in the late nineteenth and early twentieth century supervised all convict stations and prisons.[36] There are nine large-sized (ca. 40 × 60 cm) bound albums, all of which are kept in a brown hard cover and, respectively, include fifty pages, each of which provides framed spaces for eight groups of double photographs. The albums are archived according to their numerical and chronological order, which begins with volume 1 produced in 1893 and ends with volume 9 in 1901/1902 (Figure 5.4).

The general pattern followed in all albums includes 16 black and white mounted portrait photographs, of which two at a time refer to one convict. Every pair of photographs is associated with a name and a date, and every convict supplied with a reference code composed of a letter and a number – a possible reference, we know by now, to Bertillonage. There is a strong uniformity with regard to image content and style: The men were photographed in front of neutral backdrops, they all wear prison uniforms, and all have their hands placed visibly on their chest. While some of the men face the camera, others appear in front and profile views. The serial and repetitive modality of visualisation is kept more or less consistent throughout the nine albums, but there are certain material and visual shifts concerning the printing technique and quality, the backdrops, the front and/or profile views, the colour, pattern and material of the uniforms, the position of the body, as well as the men's appearances. While in the first volume, every individual was photographed before and after his head and face had been shaved, the visual signs for similar transformations of appearance are less consistent in the later albums.

Figure 5.4 Convict Album, Vol. 1, p. 3.[37]

Recent scholarship has shifted the focus from an understanding of the archive as an institutional repository of information and data towards a notion of the archive as discursive formation, in which texts, objects, and images are rendered legible and valuable as historical sources.[38] Echoing this literature, once again, we might begin to explore some of the characteristics and config-urations of the archive of photography and policing in the Cape Colony. It is an archive, indeed, that raises the question of "presence" in particular ways.

To begin with, there is a problem of accessibility regarding police pho-tographs in South Africa (as is the case elsewhere), an instance that seems suggestive of what we might call the culture and cult of secrecy that often pervades colonial and postcolonial prison and police institutions and condi-tions the trajectories and locations of photographs in archives.[39] Much more significant, though, is a phenomenon that is less linked to the institutional ori-gins of photographs of policing but contingent on conservational and archival practices, resulting in a material and discursive dissociation of photographs from the heterogeneous assemblages in which they are usually embedded when they enter the archive. Photographs are often amalgamated into pho-tographic collections, a procedure that does follow the logics and require-ments of preservation, but is likewise grounded in certain notions of formal equivalence that tend to narrow the range of possible sights.[40] Beyond these archival constraints and inadequacies, there are historical explanations for why it proves complicated to trace photographs of policing and confinement in South African archives. In fact, both were remarkably non-photographic institutional practices far into the twentieth century, as photography's place and status in surveillance, imprisonment, and police work was often unsta-ble and highly contested.[41] This gives an additional explanation for why the Breakwater prison albums are considered privileged archival objects. As we mentioned in our discussion of the photographic collection from German South West Africa, by the late nineteenth century, police albums had become a favoured genre throughout the colonial world and the metropoles, and archival practices within police institutions themselves tended to choose this format.[42] It is this complex historical and contemporary production and evocation of exceptionality, as far as we can retrace it, that underscores the album's material presence in the archive today.

But what does the Breakwater convict albums' archival environment look like? Tracing additional sources that would help contextualise the photo-graphs proved difficult. Systematic consultation of Colonial Office records, police and prison records, and documents produced by associated depart-ments within the Cape colonial administration – most importantly the law department and attorney general's office – yielded little information on the production of photographs itself, and evidenced, again, how laborious and, at times, unrewarding it can be to reconnect images and texts preserved in archives.[43] It seems, indeed, as if written sources that referred to the convict albums *directly* would be scattered across the archive according to an impen-etrable pattern that ran against the desire to contextualise the photographs.[44] Such was the case, for example, in an undated list with the names of 18 convicts, their numbers, the crimes for which they'd been charged, the sen-tences passed, and the date and place of the court's ruling have been noted.[45] If compared with the albums though, neither the numbers nor the dates coincide, nor are there any comments made on the photographs themselves. This inconsistency or lack of congruence affects most of the men identified in the list, and while some of them were portrayed in the albums, most of the 18 men mentioned had not been, seemingly, photographed and/or included in the visual compendium. The list is one example of what seems constitutive of this archive: the fragmented geography and temporality of penal prosecution and visual documentation.[46]

There are further instances of archival disintegration, again in documents that stem from the period between 1902 and 1910, i.e. after the production of albums seems to have stopped.[47] This material consists of correspondences between various departments of the central government, among them the Colonial Office and the law department and different police and prison institutions throughout the Cape Colony. They address financial and technical issues related to convict photography, the pros and cons of the system, and ways in which the circulation of photographic images between the Breakwater prison and the various police and legal institutions would have been best organised and secured. While we find some information that is indeed important for the albums – including the name of one of the photographers – glossing over the temporal disjuncture and the fact that said discussions emerged only once the production of the albums seemingly ceased might be problematic, if not misleading.[48] We shall return to these records later on.

Let me dwell on the situation just described, since it is important beyond the question of methodology. As mentioned before, the albums as such, and the naming, dating, and numbering of the photographs, are suggestive in terms of the introduction of Bertillonage at the Breakwater prison, and the convict registers and descriptions make this assumption plausible indeed.[49] Yet, as I will try to show, the remaining messiness of the relationship between the photographs and related written materials – the classificatory, spatial, and temporal disjuncture – might become meaningful in slightly different ways. For now, we can simply note that they curb the inclination to classify the Breakwater albums in terms of format and genre and as part of a full-fledged method of criminalistics in the Cape colonial penal system in the 1890s. The doubts we had about the German colonial efforts seem as reasonable and appropriate here. Additionally, there are, once again, numerous empirical lacunae: There are no archival sources that tell us who the photographers were, where the photographs were taken, what technical equipment was used, or if there were more photographs.[50] Indeed, these nine albums remain a strikingly singular visual occurrence within the archive – an instance, we might remember, that has been described as quite common for European police and prison archives as well.[51]

The questions that inform the analysis proposed here, then, take us beyond an exercise of empirical aggregation. How do we make sense of the Breakwater albums? Why would a convict station in Cape Town in the late nineteenth century invest substantial resources and time in the production of more than 7000 photographs over a period of roughly ten years, if it wasn't meant to be part of a full-fledged system of Bertillonage? What were these albums and the photographs meant to do?[52] Finding answers to these queries will first take us to the moment and place of their production, i.e. the Breakwater Convict Station in Cape Town in the 1890s and early 1900s. Doing so does not conceal an argument about the primacy of historical context. Indeed context – in relation to photographs – is not a given, but an act of interpretation, as the history and theory of photography have rightfully argued.[53] Going back to the moment of production is simply informed by my specific historical interest in the place of photography within colonial regimes of surveillance. Beyond this, though, it will clear a space for more theoretical reflections on the problem of the (photographic) "presence of the past".

The political economy of imprisonment in the Cape Colony

The Breakwater Convict station was built in the context of the beginning of construction of the breakwater in Cape Town in 1859, a public works project that would occupy thousands of convicts for nearly half a century.[54] It was the colony's largest convict station for most of the nineteenth century, and it also secured labour for all further dock constructions along the coast and major road building throughout the colony. It had been part of a larger scheme initiated by Governor John Montagu in 1843, and by the 1880s, it was significant for the standardisation of penal practices and had the reputation of being the best convict station in terms of discipline and efficiency in the colony.[55] As a penal institution, the Breakwater prison was attuned to the demands of the colonial economy and part of a complex system of labour supply, in which prisons and compounds became crucial mechanisms for securing labour.[56] The Cape colonial economy throughout the nineteenth century was marked by a continuous labour shortage, first for the capitalisation of settler agriculture, and after the mineral revolution, triggered by the discovery of diamonds in the Cape in 1867 and of gold on the Witwatersrand in 1886, for the exploitation of mineral wealth.[57]

The transition from merchant to industrial capitalism is generally understood to have been crucial for the development of the prison system, and the chronic labour shortage and increasing demand for land by European settlers in the Cape Colony by the mid-nineteenth century seen as constitutive of the form and meaning of "criminality".[58] This is the backdrop against which the colonial authorities passed a conglomerate of legislation that criminalised colonial subjects by regulating master-servant relations (with an array of laws enforcing various forms of indentured and forced labour), securing privileged access to property (land) for settlers, and underscoring the proletarianisation of an increasingly disempowered subject population, particularly so in the course and aftermath of the wars of dispossession on the colony's northern and eastern frontiers.[59]

How, then, did the Breakwater convict station operate as an institution in view of the creation and control of an economically viable and disciplined working class? Within the colonial penal system, the Breakwater convict station was considered an important site for the establishment of "correct" penal practice *and* for the encroachment of colonial difference with regard to punishment. Montagu's prison reform in the mid-1840s had provided for the creation of classes of prisoners according to conduct (penal and probation classes), and the desire to implement an orderly regime at the Breakwater motivated attempts at classification, documentation, surveillance, and education. The distinctions between sexes, tried and untried prisoners, and recidivists and first-time offenders were seen as desirable since the early nineteenth century, but they took a long time to be implemented. In their actual formulation, all these concerns prompted the gradual emergence of two dominant discourses of control at the Breakwater prison: an argument for a strict European disciplinary regime that involved the exhaustive surveillance, classification, and separation of prisoners, on the one hand; and on the other hand, an evocation of the difference of the "Native" prisoner, considered in need of being punished by hard manual labour and hard to reform by conventional prison discipline. Labour was an integral part of the prison regime, though it took a hybrid form – with imprisonment and physical separation of convicts from society *and* work parties at the docks outside of the prison in collaboration with free labour. Up to the 1880s, though, the prison was poorly organised and ill-equipped; regulations and classifications remained vague, and there are only shadowy traces of disciplinary techniques applied at the convict station. The buildings used consisted of shacks sprawled over the docks and were by no means close to any form of disciplinary architecture. Consequently, convicts could neither be kept in cells nor segregated physically according to conduct or in line with racial classification.

This situation changed by the late 1880s, with the codification of prison practice in Ordinance 23 of 1888, the organisational amalgamation of all prisons and convict stations, the appointment of an inspector of prisons, and the increased availability of resources generated in the aftermath of the mineral revolution.[60] With the economic upturn, disciplined labour now became more affordable and more urgently needed, both on farms and in the mines.[61] The Breakwater convict station was situated at the forefront of a new disciplinary implementation: new cells were built in 1889, inmates began to be separated at work and during the night, and the system of penal and probation classes applied more consistently. The segregation of prisoners would be articulated, gradually, as a race-class divide: while British rule at the Cape demanded nominal equality in the treatment of "black" and "white" prisoners, and only allowed the differentiation of prisoners according to individual behaviour, transformation, and reform, in the 1890s, the distinction of prisoners at the Breakwater along racial lines began to be drawn more sharply and to involve differential treatment (e.g. with regard to diet) and different forms of punishment.[62] With regard to the labour regime, the convict station now secured suitable outdoor labour for "Native" and industrial indoor employment for European convicts; racial segregation increasingly demanded a spatial dimension within the penal system. This was ensured for good in 1901 with the construction of an industrial Breakwater built for "white" convicts only. "Black" prisoners remained in the old barracks and continued to work at the docks until they were eventually transferred to the De Beers convict station in Kimberly in 1905.

Prison aesthetics

Based on the political economy of imprisonment in the Cape Colony and the desire to implement a disciplinary regime at the Breakwater convict station in the last two decades of the nineteenth century, we can now reflect on the ways in which the convict albums might have been embedded in these particular institutional practices, informed, as we saw, by specific discourses of imprisonment and, by the late 1880s, strong concerns with racial difference and racial segregation. It is important to keep in mind the theoretical question about the relationship between the broader narratives of policing, incarceration, and governance – and photography as a visual form and medium. While the profound socioeconomic transformation, the recurrent labour shortage, and the growing racialisation of Cape society undoubtedly framed the conception of criminality and the functional orientation of the penal system, an instrumentalist reading of the photographs kept in the albums might prove problematic.[63]

In their visual vocabulary and aesthetics, the photographs in the Breakwater convict albums show a certain formal fluidity characteristic of pre-Bertillonage attempts at visualising the criminal.[64] We might hence consider these albums – in a generalising gesture and echoing the South West African context – as another example of the colony's imperfect flirtation with a metropolitan occurrence. The photographs seem, indeed, to occupy an ambiguous position between a number of separate and yet entrenched "traditions" of visualisation: photographic portraiture, modern police photography, and anthropological imagery, all of which drew from physiognomic readings of the body and served the desire to visualise social, cultural, and racial difference.[65] It is perhaps this formal ambiguity that obstructs the clear classification of the albums as either a technology of policing – i.e. of identification, surveillance, and prosecution – or as an instrument of knowledge production aimed at the construction and classification of racial alterity.

So what were these photographs meant to do at the Breakwater prison? What would a photographic project have offered, which was not available elsewhere? Let us move away, for a moment, from image content and style, and linger instead on the album pages, such as shown in Figure 5.5, and recall their archival character, composition, and design. As argued in Chapter 1, the page layout, the serial arrangement of the photographs, and the succession of pages is very suggestive – not so much for a particular discursive formation but for a specific spatial configuration: the prison and the isolation of every single prisoner in a cell.[66] Obviously, the visual construction of a disciplinary

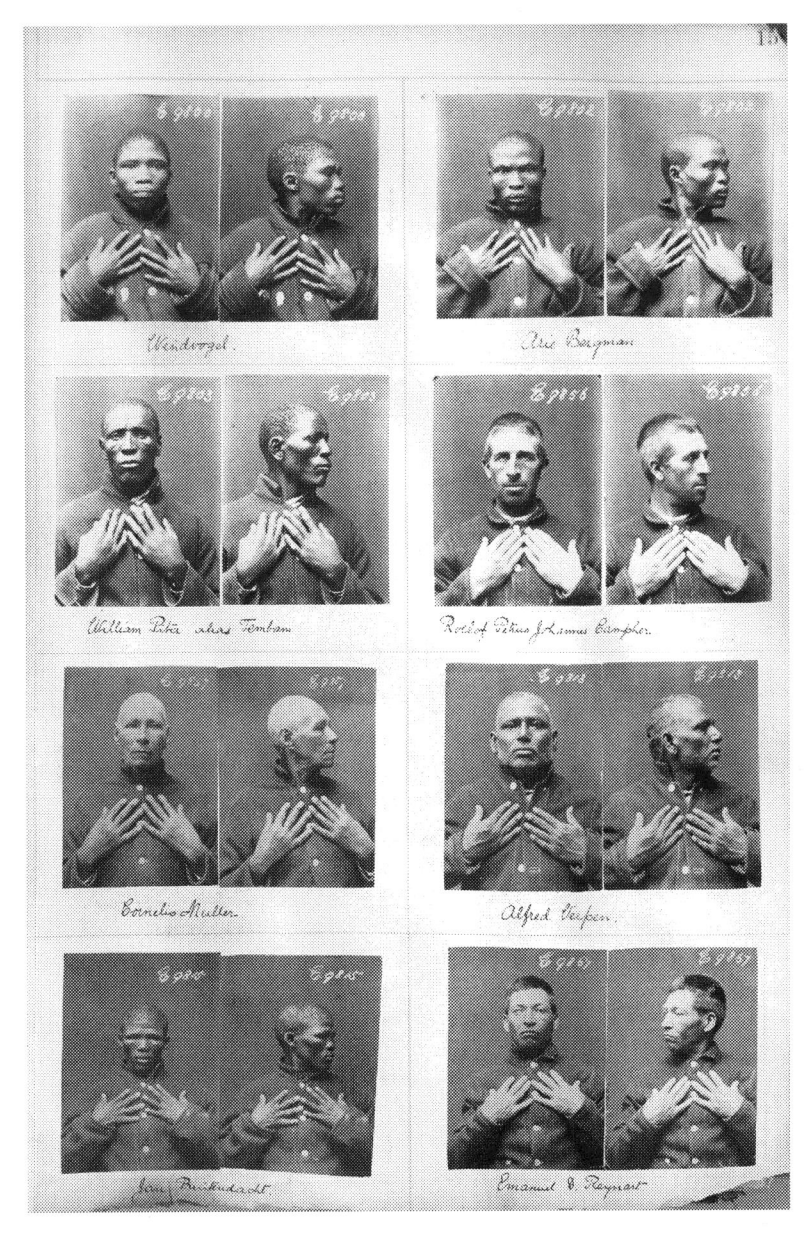

Figure 5.5 Convict Album, Vol. 3, p. 15.[67]

architectural form – a panoptic configuration – might have been, again, a way of obscuring or distorting realities on the ground that were marked, as we saw, by structural limitations, such as scattered prison buildings and the pragmatic association of prisoners at work and for accommodation purposes.

But the album page features additional effects that point towards a particular *modality of seeing* and root visuality in a specific sort of material existence, i.e. the spaces in which it is exercised and the techniques through which it is produced and circulated.[68] This is a glance taken through the lens of colonial power and governance, in as much as the close up view and minute distinctions enabled by the photographic camera become encoded into forms of rule. Unlike in the case of the German colonial album, Foucault's model of cellular power seems indeed almost indisputable here, since the ways in which the album pages and the single photographs expose the individual subjected to modern forms of discipline seem, or look rather, quite sophisticated.[69]

In terms of image content, on the other hand, the photographs' focus on the face and the body of the convict mirrored both prescribed framings within police imagery and the growing importance of late nineteenth century corporeal technologies.[70] In this way, the Breakwater albums acted as an object and form through which the peculiar modernity of colonial governance meshed with the constitution of social boundaries by visually inscribing difference on the body of an emergent "other".[71]

But what kind of "other" was the camera looking at? The narrative within the albums was, as noted before, organised chronologically, and several photographs were summarily allotted to particular dates. This might have been linked to the conditions of production, in which – as suggested earlier on – groups of convicts were either taken to a photographic studio or to separate venues within the Breakwater prison designated for the photographic session (the changing backdrops of the photographs make it difficult to decide on this matter).[72] In any case, the composition of the album kept the chronological order, and there are no indications of any further logic or pattern of classification. Neither were the albums segregated along racial lines – since "white", "black", "Chinese", or "Malay" convicts share the same visual field – nor would they inscribe any kind of classification of inmates according to crime, conduct, or sentence (Figure 5.6).

The chronological order added a further, significant narrative layer, thereby conceiving of the photographs not only as a form of spatialisation but likewise as a means of temporal configuration. This is particularly striking in Volume 1, where each couple of photographs references a *before* and an *after.* This is where the specific aesthetics of convict albums becomes most visible, in that it delineates a transformation of the individual on several levels.[73] First, the photographs evidence the physical transformation of the body – marked by the shaving of heads and faces. Likewise the visibility of the hands, while it followed prison image conventions, also echoed the core economic function of the Breakwater, which was to provide *manual* labour for public works.[74] And finally, every prisoner being neatly dressed in a white shirt and a dark uniform jacket materialised the condition of a clean and uncluttered being. Taken together, this form of visualisation helped constitute a particular kind of subject of rule, *the convict*, an individual emerging from a disciplinary transformation of criminals (from the visual "before") into physically, socially, and morally purified productive members of a modern coloniality (the visual "after").

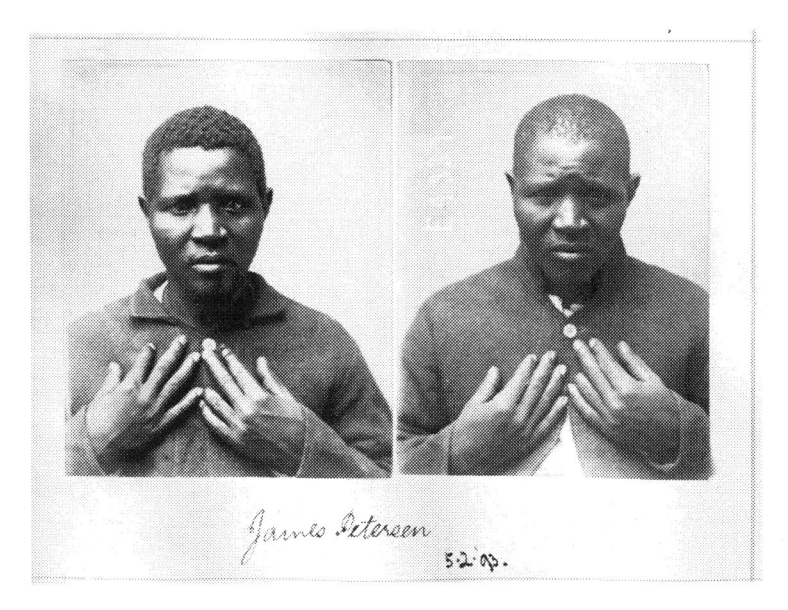

Figure 5.6 Convict Album, Vol. 1, detail from p. 2.[75]

The aesthetic articulation of a disciplinary, economic, and moral trans-formation of imprisoned individuals was an important effort made by the Breakwater convict station in view of the particular landscape of confine-ment at the Cape in the late nineteenth and early twentieth century. By this I mean that photography offered a modern means of ascertaining, envisioning, and conveying an image of a prison that, in the 1890s, was in the process of remaking itself. Produced for the Colonial Office, the albums potentially became objects of central government propaganda aligned with discourses of prison reform, which legitimised the material and symbolic investments in a modern penal institution and, simultaneously, distinguished the *public* convict station from its institutional counterpart – the labour compound on the mines. In contrast to the industrial and agricultural labour regimes in the colony at the time, the Breakwater convict station seems to have used this extensive photographic project as a means of substantiating its own progres-sive claims – the provision of cheap labour (on the economic benefit side) and the breeding of a modern category of individual (on the social benefit side).

An-aesthetics of the prison

There are, though, ruptures and fissures in the strategic fabrication of this modernising narrative, visual interruptions that we shall try to think about in terms of the *an-aesthetics* of the prison, the reason for which I explain in a moment. Visually, the sense of rupture emerges from a minor but recurrent

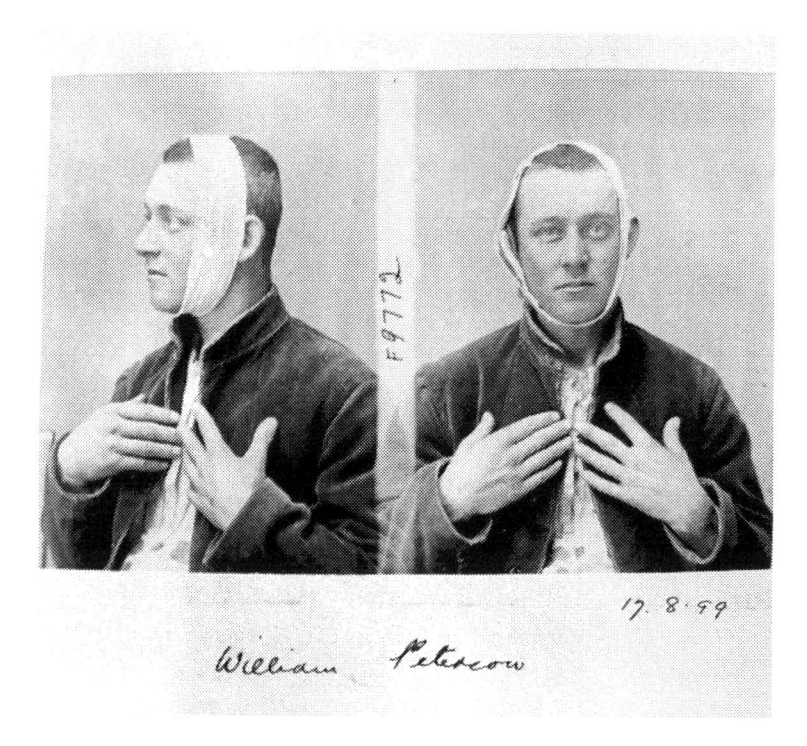

Figure 5.7 Convict Album, Vol. 5, detail from p. 25.[76]

detail throughout the photographs kept in the Breakwater convict albums. As this example from Vol. 5. shows (Figure 5.7), there are many photographs in which injuries and bandages on hands, fingers, and heads are made visible. While their presence evidences the risks, hazards, and casualties that were part of both the experiences within late nineteenth century colonial penal institutions and the regimes of forced and convict labour in the Cape Colony, their recurrence on the level of the photographic might point to some-thing else.[77] Historically, the visual traces of medical treatment mirror what Premesh Lalu has described as the biologisation of the British colonial state in South Africa in the 1890s, meaning a medico-political effort in the course of which doctors were increasingly consulted on matters related to social contagions caused by lunatics, inebriates, prostitutes, or criminals.[78] While the literature has considered the development of the medical profession at the Cape in the nineteenth century, the specificities of the constitution of an allegedly Western medical discourse in the colony, and the diversification of the professional field within and beyond the state administration, there are but a few scholarly references to the involvement and everyday work of medical practitioners within the Cape colonial institutions of confinement.[79] The annual prison reports published by the colonial government starting in the mid-1890s included summary information provided by the medical officers from various prisons and convict stations, and they reflected the main preoccupations with issues related to health and hygiene, and the prevalence of certain diseases within prison walls (such as scurvy and tuberculosis).[80]

Theoretically, then, it seems to be the conjuncture of a number of new technologies that regulate time, space, and the body, namely the prison, photography, and medical surgery, that enable these albums to unfold a particularly compelling narrative of modern colonial governance. Let me take this proposition further by exploring how the linkage between the visual and the medical might be translated into the semantic interface between aesthetics and an-aesthetics.[81] This argument draws from Susan Buck-Morss' reflection on Walter Benjamin's writings on aesthetics.

Benjamin, according to Buck-Morss, was less interested in aesthetics as a category of art (and a preoccupation with cultural forms) than with aesthetics in terms of sensible experience. For Benjamin, the essence of modern experience lay, eventually, in the experience of shock – in war, in industrial production, in urban overcrowding. And in order to protect the body against the trauma of shock caused by war or accidents, the sensory system inevitably needed to be marshalled, and modern aesthetics changed – from a cognitive mode of being "in touch" with reality to a way of blocking out reality. This is where Buck-Morss' reading of Benjamin guides her into a reflection on an-aesthetics, a medical technique which by the late nineteenth century had established itself, among an arsenal of drugs and therapeutic practices, as an intentional manipulation of the sensory system; first in order to counter what was perceived at the time as the disintegration of the capacity for experience and diagnosed as shattered nerves, nervous breakdown, or the fragmentation of the psyche; and then, most importantly, in desensitising shattered bodies and physical catastrophe. The semantic linkage, between aesthetics and an-aesthetics, lies in the double function of modern technology – it enhances the human senses and acuity of perception (with all the risks that this opening of the senses towards the world inevitably involves), and it doubles back on the senses as defensive, desensitising insulation.[82]

There are many ways in which Buck-Morss' theoretical reflections resonate with nineteenth-century Cape colonial history, marked as it was by experiences of war, institutionalised forms of violence, and the shattering of bodies placed under exploitive labour regimes. It is against this backdrop that the Breakwater prison albums appear to configure – on the level of the visual – analogies between the photographic camera's heightened perception – aesthetics – and the imprisoned body's dazed or numbed cognition – an-aesthetics. These effects become most visible if we think about the albums – again along the lines of Buck-Morss' reading of Benjamin – in terms of *fragmentation*: of vision and perception through photography, of power and control through the cellular, of the social through surveillance and confinement, and of the body through the regime of forced and manual labour. It is at this point that the albums appear as a unique set of images that provide space for interruption and dissonance and invite us to think about the convict photographs beyond surveillance and panopticism alone. The dissonance lies precisely in the photographic sensibility towards this multiple fragmentation of the body increasingly exposed to a technologised environment; a sensitivity that was not the photographer's or a matter of intentionality or agency, but intrinsic to the photographic medium. The Breakwater convict albums are, indeed, a privileged archival object and image, not simply because they constituted an exceptional occurrence within institutional archival practices, but because they are located at the interface of institutional histories of the convict body – as a productive, socially worthy, physically and morally disciplined entity, on the one hand – and histories of colonial subjectivity that account for the human body as the locus of pain, injury, and suffering, on the other hand.[83]

After the albums – building an archive of policing

Let us move back to the corpus of documents that refer to the period after the production of albums, as far as it is materially preserved in the archive, ceased. In the early 1900s, in the context of attempts at reconstruction and modernisation after the South African War of 1899–1902 and amplified definitions of criminality, the archival narrative on photography and policing in the Cape Colony changed, and we can trace the gradual emergence of an intensifying negotiation around questions of recidivism and identification.[84] Cape Town received its first Criminal Investigation Department (CID) in 1901, and the police became the driving force behind the reconfiguration of the role of photography within forensics.[85] The main debate, the archive suggests, developed over the question of the criminal's appearance in the image and the efficient recording and circulation of photographs between the various state departments involved. A communication among officers of the CID in 1902 is quite telling on this point:

> I beg to report that copies of photographs of criminals at the Breakwater Station are still being supplied to this Department and placed in our albums. We have found these photographs to be of service to us, but I wish to point out that they would be of greater use for police purposes if the convicts photographs were taken in their own clothes before they are clean shaven and their hair cut, instead of being taken in convict clothing, we do not want to know the man as a convict, we want his photograph as he would appear in ordinary life.
>
> If he escapes from prison he is not going to wear the convict uniform.[86]

Unfortunately, we have no further evidence for how photographs could have been "of service" to the police, nor do further image compendia such as the albums mentioned by the inspector of the CID survive in the archives. But we know that the question of the convict's appearance in the photograph remained an unresolved issue for years to come, precisely because the prison authorities and the police would not agree on the function of the images within their respective institutions. As argued before, the Breakwater prison used the photographic project in a process of institutional consolidation and in view of constituting the object of its practice, namely *the convict*. The police, on the other hand, were concerned with identification of criminalised individuals and with visual literacy within society. In an almost despairing tone, the inspector in charge of the CID would eventually note in 1910:

> Photographs of convicts sentenced to long terms of imprisonment are invariably taken in convict clothing, after their hair has been closely cropped and the face clean-shaven. This alters the appearance of the men so much that even their friends wouldn't recognise them. [...] Photographs have been very useful on many occasions when an individual who has previously been convicted and whose name is unknown is wanted for any offence, as in such cases the photograph of the person wanted has been picked out in the police album. I am referring to photographs of prisoners taken by police in their ordinary clothing and appearance, for in every instance where a witness has been shown the convicts' photographs they invariably would not swear to the photograph on account of the altered appearance. I have from time to time reported on this, but up to the present the only change allowed was that we were permitted to take photographs of short service prisoners for police purposes. The inspector wants this problem to be brought to the notice of the convict branch.[87]

Initiatives to implement a modern system of forensics remained tentative, and the first decade of the twentieth century is marked by unsystematic thoughts on filing systems, registers, and anthropometric description.[88] What becomes visible here, nevertheless, is a larger problem with regard to the use of photography in contexts of policing: namely, the ambiguity of the visual vocabulary and, accordingly, the containment of photographic meaning – we might say, indeed, the need for *policing the image* rather than the person alone.[89] And the only way of doing this would be, seemingly, the creation of an appropriate archive. Alphonse Bertillon, we remember, had reckoned this a long time before.[90]

The presence of the past

Let me return to the images of John Rizzo and the verve of genealogical recovery – the desire to re-trace (real and imagined) ancestors and beloved ones who are not anymore. This seemed to open up further possible sights and understandings of the Breakwater photographs that indeed forwent the problems of a particular configuration of presence (and absence) in archives of policing. We might argue, as Runia does, that, unlike work done by historians, ancestral discourse and practice speak much more powerfully to what "society is vehemently pursuing", i.e. "presence".[91] If we consider the larger knowledge fields that frame the genealogical initiatives in the Western Cape archives described at the outset of this chapter, the past two decades have indeed seen the emergence of a remarkably diverse range of social and cultural practices through which South African society negotiates forms and idioms of historical consciousness, among them in the domain of public history, memory, and memorialisation.[92] Here again, photographs, and the visual more generally, have figured prominently, validating the potentials of *photographic presence* and the promise it holds of being in touch with persons who ceased to exist, particularly if we keep in mind the level of individual and collective disruption, diasporic living conditions, disappearances, and deaths in the eras of segregation and apartheid.[93] Concurrently, the legacy of substantial collections of colonial photographs, many of which embody what has been called the "repressive mode of photography",[94] has fostered the desire to relocate photographs from disciplinary, classificatory spaces of viewing and knowledge production to more personalised, intimate framings within family histories, ancestry, remembrance, and memory work.[95] Through these relocations and recontextualisations, photographs can become – echoing Barthes and, more recently, Pierre Nora – *lieux de mémoire privés*, as they move from the domain of mere perception to the imaginary and affective.[96] In fact, biographical retracing that clusters around the Breakwater prison albums is a powerful indication of how contemporary practices of photographic redemption complicate the theoretical category of colonial photography in the first place – once they reactivate colonial prison photographs in shifting contexts of viewing and reopen new chapters in the images' afterlives.[97]

One case of such refiguring has been fleshed out in the framework of Northern Cape history and memory, and concerned Kgosi Galeshewe, a late nineteenth-century Bathlaping political leader and key figure in what came to be known as the Langeberg uprising of 1896–1897.[98] Galeshewe was sentenced to ten years of hard labour at the Breakwater Convict Station, but effectively remained imprisoned only between 1898 and 1903. In 2011, the Sol Plaatje Educational Trust commissioned research and the publication of a booklet, which assembled archival sources, oral histories, and historical photographs that referenced the personal life and political trajectory of Galeshewe and firmly anchored him in nineteenth-century southern Tswana dynastic politics (Figure 5.8).[99]

The narrative drafted in the booklet exposes the repeated imprisonment and criminalisation of Galeshewe as the illegitimate curtailing of political opposition to massive land expropriation, industrial capitalism, and British imperial expansion into the Northern Cape in the 1880s and 1890s. He becomes a hero, validated through a post-colonial framing of resistance histories. While the genealogical order and the figure of the hero both resonate into *and* decentralise national historical frameworks,[100] they provide one way to script contemporary negotiations of regional collective identification,

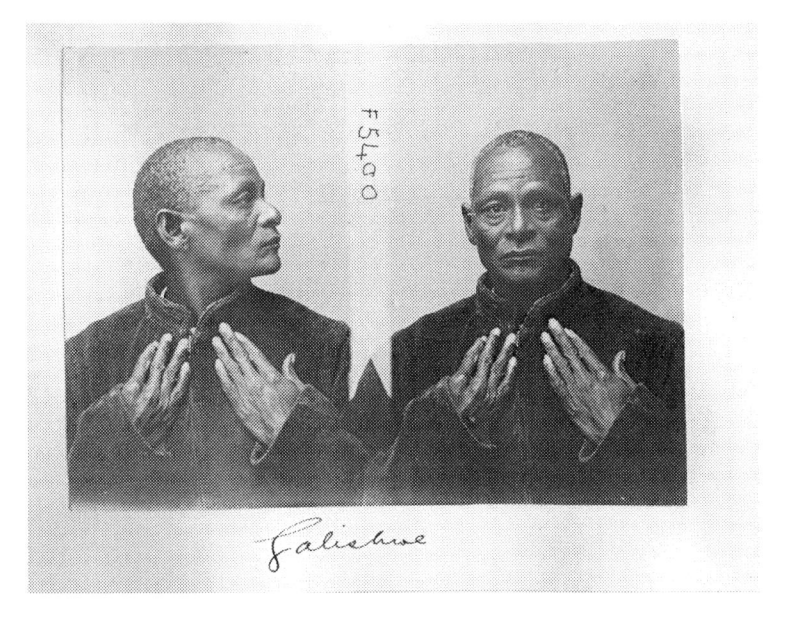

Figure 5.8 Photograph of Kgosi Galeshewe, Breakwater Prison, Cape Town, [1898–1903].

political mobilisation, and community building.[101] Furthermore, by unhinging the convict photographs from the carceral and moving them to the context of memory work, the booklet aimed to clear a representational space in which to remake these images as portraits, now embedded in orality and local historical imagination, and connected to particular sites of collective commemoration such as graves.[102] It is indeed within the genres and discourse of memory that Galeshewe's presence in the photographs is viewed as a metaphorical lens through which the narrative of resistance and national history can be appropriated, even if blending them into biography and the nation comes along with prescribed forms of vision.[103]

And indeed, the nationalist framework has ultimately failed to subvert the aesthetics of the Breakwater prison albums. Unaltered reproductions of the Galeshewe prison photographs continue to circulate in scholarly publications and online and remain haunted by the spectre of subjection, humiliation, objectification and death.[104] In the South African context, Galeshewe's and the many more images assembled in the Breakwater albums, as well as historical prison photographs in general, are likely to get embroiled in the "metaphysics of disorder"[105] that pervade the strong social preoccupation, if not obsession, with crime and proliferate across diverse visual landscapes and voyeuristic imaginaries of the uncanny.[106] Yet, there have also been more careful visual negotiations of the complicated history of criminalisation and imprisonment in South Africa and its resonances into the post-apartheid present, among them in the works by South African photographers David Goldblatt and Michael Subotsky.[107] These projects have indeed complicated the idea of "the presence of the past" – less in terms of an "intense and unmediated experience" than essentially as a problem of persisting aesthetic order and "distribution of the sensible".[108] For sure, art is ahead of the competition here, since academic histories of police and prison photography are only beginning to develop and nurture the analytical instruments required.

Coda – the presence and past of the Breakwater convict photographs

This chapter has concerned itself with the past and present of a particular photographic collection, the Breakwater prison albums, produced in Cape Town in the late nineteenth century. What served as a point of entry into the discussion and, thereafter, informed the conceptual approach to the photographic material, has been an archival coincidence, the moment at which encountering a pair of photographs opened up the admittedly speculative possibility of engaging the material through the lens of the ancestral. The photographs of John Rizzo, a convict at the Breakwater in 1899, required, it seems, thinking about the albums in view of how the past makes its way into the present, and what informs the various ways in which the past might speak to us. Eelco Runia's idea of presence – as a way of accounting for the unmediated, unprocessed, unintentional leaking of the past into the present; as a movement away from a constructed past to one that actually existed – has helped my coming to terms with the photographs of John Rizzo, in particular, and with the longing for a past lost – the inevitable absence that accompanies presence – more generally. But the reflections proposed here were not conclusive, and the desire to use photography in order to recover places, objects, or people who are not anymore (even if it assumes the form of ancestral fantasy) takes us onto uncertain and more risky grounds; into a domain that seems to elude language and, as Runia tells us, transcends the "mere" question of representation and meaning.

But as much as this line of argument appeals to us, as it makes space for thinking about the material presence of historical photographs as a particular instantiation of the past, it might still be worthwhile exploring the question of photographic meaning. Are photographs, to avail ourselves of one of Runia's borrowings, like W.G. Sebald's "kernels of reality", surrounded by "expanses of nothingness" – that is with no meaning, too much meaning, or no discernible meaning?[109] Or do we end up, ultimately, like Jean-Paul Sartre, bemoaning that while we look at photographs, there is nothing we can see?[110] This chapter has, hopefully, adopted a less melancholic tone, by thinking about these photographs across historical time and thereby resist the temptation of *presentism* that lurks in "presence".[111] Photographs, not only historical ones, are always embedded in multiple temporalities, of which "the presence of the past" is just one modality. Therefore, if we pay attention to the moment of their production, a retracing of how the photographs might have interwoven the past, presence, and future might be less easy to achieve, as time and temporality possibly interlace in unexpected ways. This is why when working with photographs as historical sources we might be well-advised to concede the possibility of different temporalities and to bear in mind "the pastness of the past".[112]

This chapter, then, has investigated what the Breakwater prison albums tell us about an engagement with the photographic medium at a particular moment in time, and interrogated how the specificity of the institutional and discursive contexts shaped the kinds of practices that clustered around this particular photographic project. The scholarship has generally been inclined to understand prison and police photography either within the framework of Bertillonage, and hence in terms of the emergence of a particular documentary practice, or as part of homogenising narratives of colonial othering and social pathology, e.g. in the fields of anthropology, racial science, and criminology.[113] While all of these epistemological projects had a bearing on institutionalised photographic production in the Cape Colony at the time, the Breakwater convict albums exemplified how historically contingent the use of photographs was, and how expectations about the medium could easily shift. The conflictual debate between the Cape Town prison branch and the police in the early 1900s helped substantiate the need to account for the dynamics involved in negotiating photographic meaning.

In a more theoretical gesture, making sense of these albums at the moment of their production served to revisit the relationship between colonial power and visuality, and we have insisted – very much in line with visual theory – that there is no causally determined link between the exercise of power and the photographic image.[114] While we may interpret convict photographs as visual representations of power, we still need to explain when, how, and why power resorts to the visual and what kinds of power effects photographic images might have.[115] South African prison and police officials in the late nineteenth and early twentieth centuries were quite aware of the difficulties faced once they tried to extract unambiguous information from photographs. Within photographic projects such as the production of the Breakwater convict albums, much of their energy was, as we saw, spent on attempts to contain – I've used the term *police* here – the image as such, hoping that this would reward their hopes to harness the medium for their respective agendas. The prison authorities at the Breakwater had a particular vision, and the albums tell us how photography enabled the convict station to configure a particular kind of subject of rule – *the convict*, as he emerged from the disciplinary transformation of the body placed under a modern penal regime. But, once again, we have argued that in this set of albums, the relationship between the body and the photographic medium proved an intricate matter, a capricious assemblage, which preserved its own aesthetic contingency.

Taking note of the recurrence of visual minutia, bandaged injuries that referenced the exposure of the convict body to the risks and hazards of labour and imprisonment and – in a Benjaminian sense – to the numbing effects of a technologised environment, helped us understand the specific histories lodged in photographs, histories that tell us something about the body as the locus of pain and vulnerability.

Returning, finally, to the problem of presence, and situating the discussion of the pair of photographs of John Rizzo in the context of diverse genealogical initiatives at the Western Cape Archives, has introduced us to a particular attempt to unhinge convict photographs from the carceral – and its affiliated discourses of racialisation and criminalisation – and reframe them in contexts of local historical narration and memory work. The case of the late nineteenth-century Batlhaping political leader Kgosi Galeshewe served as a lens through which we briefly looked at the possibilities and limitations that might come along with such reframing, since in this case, we have argued that neither anti-colonial liberation nor nationalist histories succeeded in disrupting the aesthetic order of prison photography in sustainable ways. One reason for this seems linked to the notion of "presence" and its desire for an immediate and visceral access to the past, which falls short of attending to precisely the question of mediation and medium, i.e. the problem of *how* the past makes its entrance into the presence. Photography's appeal to thinkers like Runia – although his explicit reference to the visual consist only of one single mentioning of Barthes punctum[116] – obviously derives from the photograph's analogical rather than rhetorical orientation.[117] But this draws, essentially, on image content and/or subject, rather than on what makes the photographic image different from any other historical *form*.[118] Attending to this problem will inevitably disclose the problem of photographic meaning, i.e. how photographs constantly drift between the shores of metonymy and metaphor, without – as Sartre remarked long ago – ever approaching either.[119]

Notes

1 Georges Didi-Huberman, *Confronting Images. Questioning the Ends of a Certain History of Art.* Pennsylvania, 2005, Pennsylvania State University Press.
2 NAN ZBU 751 II a 4, Verbrecheralbum, Fingerabdrücke, Bd 1. Kaiserliches Bezirksgericht Swakopmund, von Lindequist an das Konsulat in Kapstadt, 10 February, 1906.
3 NAN ZBU 751 II a 4, Verbrecheralbum, Fingerabdrücke, Bd 1. General-Konsul Kapstadt an den Kaiserlichen Gouverneur von Lindequist, 5 Juni, 1906.
4 Ibid. Original in German, translation is mine.
5 Ethnographic Museum Berlin, EM-SMB/32/915 (357), Magoma as Prisoner, Robben Island, Table Bay, Photographer: Gustav Fritsch. See also K. Dietrich and A. Bank (eds.), *An Eloquent Picture Gallery. The South African portrait photographs of Gustav Theodor Fritsch, 1863–1865.* Johannesburg, 2008.
6 See Hayes, Power, Secrecy, Proximity.
7 See D. Newbury, *Defiant Images. Photography and Apartheid South Africa.* Pretoria, 2009, Chapter 5; E. Haney, *Photography in Africa.* London, 2010, p. 103ff.

8 E. Edwards, Professor Huxley's "Well-considered Plan", in ibid., *Raw Histories*, pp. 131–55.

9 Unlike the anthropometric photographs of /Xam Bushmen taken at the Breakwater Convict Station, which have received repeated academic attention, the photograph depicted here, taken by the same photographer – David Selkirk – in 1871 and depicting some of the "research subjects", is part of a series that remains widely unknown. The image is part of the photographic collection housed at the Pitt Rivers Museum, PRM Photograph Nr. 1998.211.13.10: David Selkirk, 1871, Group of prisoners.

10 M. Godby, Images of //Kabbo, in P. Skotnes (ed.), *Miscast. Negotiating the Presence of the Bushmen*. Cape Town, 1996, pp. 115–27; A. Bank, Anthropology, Race and Evolution: Rethinking the Legacy of Wilhelm Bleek. *History and African Studies Seminar paper*, 1993.

11 Alf Lüdtke, *The History of Everyday Life. Reconstructing Historical Experiences and Ways of Life*. Princeton, 1995, pp. 313–14. Lüdtke developed his argument in view of understanding the social; he was less interested in questions of visuality.

12 See Roger B. Beck, *The History of South Africa*. Santa Barbara, Denver, Oxford, 2014 (2nd ed.), p. 98.

13 S. Edwards, The Machine's Dialogue. *The Oxford Art Journal*, 13, 1, 1990: 63–76, here p. 67; G. Baylis, A Few Too Many Photographs? Indexing Digital Histories. *History of Photography*, 38, 1, 2014: 3–20, here p. 13.

14 Sekula, The Body and the Archive.

15 Alan Sekula, The Body and the Archive; and for a southern Africa more specifically Carolyn Hamilton, Verne Harris, Jane Taylor, Michele Pickover, Graeme Reid and Razia Saleh (eds.), *Refiguring the Archive*. Cape Town, Dordrecht, 2002.

16 See Jacques Rancière, *Dissensus*.

17 Stoler, *Along the Archival Grain*. For a more ironic reflection on the archive and its limits and possibilities for the writing of history see Carolyn Steedman, *Dust: The Archive and Cultural History*. New Brunswick, 2002.

18 See Western Cape Archives (KAB) CO 6982, Vol. 5, page 21, photographs of Salvador Rizzo, convict number F9325, 6.7.[18]99.

19 See e.g. Donna R. Gabaccia, *Italy's Many Diasporas*. Seattle, 2000.

20 See Western Cape Archives (KAB) CO 6982, Vol. 5, page 23, photographs of John Rizzo, convict number F9427, 17 August [18]99.

21 Robert Buranello, Between Fact and Fiction: Italian Immigration to South Africa. *Altreitalie*, (January-December) 2009: 23–44. According to Buranello (p. 28) statistics listed 210 Italian citizens in the Cape colony in 1891, as compared to 60 in the Transvaal and 10 in the Orange Free State.

22 See for a discussion on archival salvage discourses and practices in curating African photographic collections Morton and Newbury, Introduction: Relocating the African Photographic Archive, in Morton and Newbury, *The African Photographic Archive*, pp. 1–16.

23 This is a very vague reference to Jacques Derrida, *Archive Fever. A Freudian Impression*. Chicago, 1996.

24 Roland Barthes, *Camera Lucida*, p. 8. Barthes's original phrasing is "to be a primitive, without knowledge".

25 Eelco Runia, *Moved by the Past. Discontinuity and Historical Mutation*. New York, 2014; and for the arguments made in this paper see particularly Chapter 3, Presence, pp. 49–83. See for the debate on "presence" Ranjan Ghosh and Ethan Kleinberg (eds.), *Presence. Philosophy, History, and Cultural Theory for the Twenty-First Century*. Ithaca and London, 2013.

26 Eelco Runia, "Presence", *History and Theory*, 45, (February) 2006: 1–29, here pp. 1 and 5. I'm using this version of Runia's essay, which had minor revisions made for its inclusion as a chapter in *Moved by the Past*.

27 Ethan Kleinberg, Presence in Absentia, in R. Ghosh and E. Kleinberg (eds.), *Presence*, p. 11.
28 See for a detailed discussion the introduction to Edwards, *Raw Histories*.
29 Susan A. Crane, of Photographs, Puns, and Presence, in R. Ghosh and E. Kleinberg (eds.), *Presence*, pp. 62–78, here p. 65.
30 Julia Adeney Thomas, The Evidence of Sight, *History and Theory*, Theme Issue 48, (December) 2009: 151– 68, here p. 151. Thomas' phrasing is also quoted in Crane, *op.cit.*.
31 See the discussion of the photograph of Andile Pinkerton Booi in Chapter 2.
32 Crane, Of Photographs, Puns, and Presence, p. 69.
33 Ibid. The claim that viewers would be "misguided" is, of course, problematic, not least because of how (photographic) "presence" actually works, e.g. in memory and remembrance. I'll come back to this point later.
34 The term *aura* in studies of photography is usually associated with the work of Walter Benjamin and in particular his essay *The Work of Art in the Age of Mechanical Reproduction*. For a critical revision of the dimensions of the concept in Benjamin's work see Miriam Bratu Hansen, Benjamin's Aura. *Critical Inquiry*, 34, 2008: 335–75.
35 Crane, Of Photographs, Puns, and Presence, p. 69; Bratu Hansen, Benjamin's Aura.
36 Western Cape Archives (KAB), CO 6978-6986 (Vol. 1–9).
37 Western Cape Archives (KAB), CO 6978, Vol. 1, p. 3.
38 See Stoler, Colonial Archives and the Arts of Governance. For the southern African context in particular see again Hamilton et al., *Refiguring the Archive*. Also Chapter 2.
39 See e.g. Richard J. Cox, Secrecy, Archives, And the Archivist: A Review Essay (Sort Of). *The American Archivist*, 72, 2009: 214–31.
40 See Edwards, Photography and the Material Performance of the Past, p. 142; and Sekula, The Body and the Archive.
41 This assessment is in some sense preliminary and needs qualification in as much as up to 2013 it was not possible to access the photographic collections of the former Criminal Identification Department (CID) kept in Pretoria. The CID branch in Cape Town was first opened in 1901 and most probably produced numerous photographs. See on Cape Town's CID Charles van Onselen, Jewish Police Informers in the Atlantic World, 1880–1891. *The Historical Journal*, 50, 1, 2007: 119–44, here p. 126.
42 See Susanne Regener, *Fotografische Erfassung*, p. 31; also Edwards, Ordering Others.
43 See C. Morton and D. Newbury, Introduction, Relocating the African photographic archive, in Morton and Newbury, *The African Photographic Archive*, pp. 1–16.
44 The Colonial Office records kept at the National Archives of the UK at Kew remain silent on the photographic project at the Breakwater Convict Station. For a broader discussion of these holdings see Edwards, Photographic Uncertainties.
45 KAB CO 2090 484, Rules re Convict photographs. Return of Convicts sentenced at Port Elizabeth and confined at the Breakwater convict station Cape Town, n.p., d.d.
46 Compare with the discussion in Chapter 1. As similar argument is made by Tina Campt in Haptic Temporalities: The Quiet Frequency of Touch, in ibid., *Listening to Images*, pp. 69–100, here pp. 84–91. In her work on the Breakwater albums Campt unravels different temporalities by meticulously comparing the serial numbers that accompany the convict photographs with entries in the Nominal Rolls of Convicts of 1869–1902, (KAB CO Vol. 8981–8997) and the Descriptive Returns

of 1866-1910 (KAB CO 8784–8930). Since she discerns correspondences at the level of numbers and dates, her interpretation differs from the one developed here.

47 These are the files kept in KAB AG (Attorney General) 1391 1461; KAB JUS (Department of Law) 108 23029; KAB CO (Colonial Office) 2090 484; KAB AG (Attorney General) 1738 8057; KAB AG (Attorney General) 1557 287; AG 1491 8605.

48 KAB AG 1391 1461, Under Colonial Secretary to Superintendent Breakwater Prison, 13 August 1903, specified that a photographer named Ambrose Jarman was taking photographs at the Breakwater Convict Station.

49 See again Campt, *Listening to Images*. While Campt's archival work would substantiate this line of argument, she doesn't read the archive in terms of Bertillonage either.

50 The albums disclose a pattern of dating, which tells us something about the recurrence of particular occasions on which groups of convicts were photographed. See also Campt, *Listening to Images*.

51 Regener, *Fotografische Erfassung*.

52 W.J.T. Mitchell, *What do Pictures Want? The Lives and Loves of Images*. Chicago, 2004.

53 See Morton and Newbury, *The African Photographic Archive*, p. 6. See also Chapter 1.

54 The main reference for the following paragraph is, if not mentioned otherwise, H. Deacon, *A History of the Breakwater Prison from 1859 to 1905*. Unpublished Honours Thesis, University of Cape Town, 1989; and to a lesser extent also H. Deacon, Racial Segregation & Medical Discourse in 19th century Cape Town. *Journal of Southern African Studies*, 22, 2, 1996): 287–308.

55 See N. Penn, "Close and merciful watchfulness": John Montagu's convict system in the mid-nineteenth-century Cape Colony. *Cultural and Social History*, 5, 4, 2008.

56 See e.g. S. Marks and R. Rathbone (eds.), *Industrialization and Social Change in South Africa, 1870–1930*. London and New York, 1982.

57 Ibid.

58 Charles van Onselen, Crime and total institutions in the making of modern South Africa. *History Workshop Journal*, 1985. For a broader perspective on the political economies of African penal systems see M. Gibson, Review Essay. Global Perspectives on the Birth of the Prison. *The American Historical Review*, 116, 4, 2011: 1040–1063.

59 A.J. Christopher, Land Policy in Southern Africa in the 19th century. *Zambezia*, 2, ii, 1971; Ch. Walker, The limits to land reform: reviewing "the land question". Unpublished paper presented at the African Studies/History seminar University of Natal, Durban 19 November 2003; see also C. Bundy, Lessons on the frontier: aspects of Eastern Cape history. *Kronos*, 30, 2004: 9–21.

60 See J.P. van Niekerk, An Introduction to South African Law Reports and Reporters 1828 to 1910. *Fundamina: A Journal of Legal History*, 19, 1, 2013: 106–145.

61 For the transformation of labour regimes on the Kimberley mines in the late 1870s and early 1880s see P. Harries, *Work, Culture and Identity. Migrant Laborers in Mozambique and South Africa, c. 1860s–1910*. Portsmouth, Johannesburg, London, 1994, pp. 50–55.

62 These developments within the penal system mirrored the more generalised growing concern with racial segregation in late 19th century Cape society. See V. Bickford-Smith, *Ethnic Pride and Racial Prejudice in Victorian Cape Town. Group Identity and Social Practice, 1875–1902*. Cambridge, 1995, p. 25.

63 Mitchell, *Landscape and Power*, p. 3.

64 Regener, *Fotografische Erfassung*, p. 61.

65 See Regener, *Fotografische Erfassung*; E. Maxwell, *Picture Imperfect. Photography and Eugenics 1870–1940*. East Sussex, 2008. See also Chapter 2.
66 See Tagg, *The Burden of Representation*. Chapter 3. On photography and the configuration of space-time see e.g. Edwards, Photography and the Material Performance of the Past. We have noted the analogy between the photograph and the prison cell in Chapter 1.
67 Western Cape Archives (KAB) CO 6980, Vol. 3, p. 15.
68 J. Rajchman, Foucault's Art of Seeing. *October*, 44, 1988: 88–117.
69 Jäger, Photography: A Means of Surveillance?
70 See S. Pierce and A. Rao, Discipline and the Other Body. Humanitarianism, Violence, and the Colonial Exception, in ibid. (eds.), *Discipline and the Other Body. Correction, Corporeality, Colonialism*. Durham, London, 2006, pp. 1–21; A. L. Stoler, Colonial Studies and the History of Sexuality, in ibid., *Race and the Education of Desire: Foucault's History of Sexuality and the Colonial Order of Things*. Durham, 1995, pp. 1–18.
71 Pierce and Rao, Discipline and the Other Body, 5.
72 Both practices were common in metropolitan and colonial prisons. See Regener, *Fotografische Erfassung*; Maxwell, *Picture Imperfect*.
73 See Baylis, A Few Too Many Photographs?, p. 9.
74 Tagg, *The Burden of Representation*, pp. 87–8.
75 Western Cape Archives (KAB) CO 6978, Vol. 1, detail from p. 2.
76 Western Cape Archives (KAB) CO 6982, Vol. 5, detail from p. 25.
77 H. Deacon, Racial Segregation; and more generally Gibson, Review Essay.
78 P. Lalu, Medical Anthropology, Subaltern Traces, and the Making and Meaning of Western Medicine in South Africa, 1895–1899. *History in Africa*, 25, 1998: 133–59.
79 H. Deacon, H. Phillips, E. van Heyningen (eds.), *The Cape Doctor in the Nineteenth Century*. Amsterdam, New York, 2004; E. van Heyninge, Agents of Empire: The Medical Profession in the Cape Colony, 1880–1910. *Medical History*, 33, 1989: 450–71; H. Deacon, Racial Segregation. There are but a few references to service to medical institutions as an early career step for a number of medical doctors in South Africa in E. Burrows, *A History of Medicine in South Africa up to the End of the Nineteenth Century*. Cape Town, 1958. For a critical reassessment of Burrows and social histories of medicine in South Africa see Lalu, Medical Anthropology.
80 See e.g. Cape of Good Hope, *Report on the Management and Discipline of Convict Stations and Prisons for the Year 1895*. Cape Town, 1896.
81 S. Buck-Morss, Aesthetics and Anaesthetics: Walter Benjamin's Artwork Essay Reconsidered, *October*, 62, 1992, 3–41.
82 Buck-Morss, Aesthetics and Anaesthetics, p. 22, and there in particular footnote 80.
83 Pierce and Rao, Discipline and the Other Body, p. 6.
84 See K. Shear, *Constituting a State in South Africa: the Dialectics of Policing, 1900–1939*. Unpublished Ph.D., Evanston, Illinois, Northwestern University, 1998, p. 26
85 Ch. van Onselen, Jewish Police Informers in the Atlantic World, 1880–1891. *The Historical Journal* 50, 1, 2007: 119–144, here p. 126. As mentioned earlier on, the photographic collection of the CID is not accessible, nor has it been integrated into the South African Police Service Museum and Archives in Pretoria. Some of the CID photographs were published, though, in the South African Police Gazettes from the 1920s onwards, which are stored at the SAP Archives.
86 KAB AG 1391 1461, Inspector of Criminal Investigation Department Cape Town to the Officer in Charge Criminal Investigation Department Cape Town, 23 May 1902.

87 KAB JUS 108 23029, Inspector in Charge of CID Cape Town to the Commissioner of Police Cape Town, 11 March 1910.

88 See e.g. KAB AG 1391 1461, Secretary to the Law Department Cape Town to Commissioner of Police Kimberley, x.10.1903, and Superintendent of Breakwater Convict Station to the Secretary to the Law Department, Cape Town, 12 November 1903; KAB AG 1738 8057, Acting Commander of Police to Secretary to the Law Department, Cape Town, 5 December 1906; and KAB AG 1419, Acting Secretary for the Law Department, Circular Bo. 2 of 1905: Adoption of Fingerprint system, Cape Town, 13 January 1905.

89 Rancière, *Dissensus*, pp. 36–7.

90 See Sekula, The Body and the Archive.

91 Runia, Presence, p. 5.

92 See e.g. Ciraj Rassool, Power, knowledge and the politics of public pasts. *African Studies*, 69, 2010, and his Human Remains, the Disciplines of the Dead, & the South African Memorial Complex, in Derek Peterson, K. Gavua and C. Rassool (eds.), *The Politics of Heritage in Africa: Economies, Histories, and Infrastructures.* Cambridge, 2015; Annie E. Coombes, *History after Apartheid: Visual Culture and Public Memory in a Democratic South Africa.* Durham, 2003.

93 See Coombes, *History After Apartheid*.

94 Sekula, The Body and the Archive.

95 Morton and Newbury, *The African Photographic Archive*, p. 8. See also Chapter 2.

96 See on this point Nao Sawada, Sartre et la photographie: autour de la théorie de l'imaginaire. *Etudes Françaises*, 49, 2, 2013: 103–121, here p. 109.

97 See John Peffer, Vernacular recollections and popular photography in South Africa, in Morton and Newbury, *The African Photographic Archive*, pp. 115–133. For a critical discussion of photography and redemption see David Zeytlin, Redeeming some Cameroonian photographs: Reflections on photographs and representations, in Morton and Newbury, *The African Photographic Archive*, pp. 61–76, here p. 63.

98 See H. Saker and J. Aldridge, The Origins of the Langeberg Rebellion. *Journal of African History*, 2, 1, 1971: 299–217.

99 S. Swanepoel and S. Mngqolo, *Galeshewe, Champion of the People.* Kimberley, 2011. Figure 5.8 is reproduced on p. 30. Note that the authors worked with a copy of the photograph kept at the Kimberley Africana Library and not with the originals in the Breakwater albums preserved at the Western Cape Archives.

100 John Aldridge, Luka Jantjie: A Publisher's View of a Highly Illustrated Historical Biography. *Botswana Notes and Records*, 45, 2015: 141–79.

101 See Christopher Morton, The Ancestral Image in the Present Tense. *Photographies*, 8, 3, 2015: 253–270. Swanepoel and Mngqolo, *Galeshewe, Champion of the People*, p. 38.

102 Ibid., p. 35; Aldridge, Luka Jantjie, p. 178. I propose a different reading of the prison photographs of Galeshewe (and his imprisoned allies) against the backdrop of the Langeberg/Phokwane rebellion of 1897 and contemporary Bathlaping preoccupations with history, the ancestral, and land in Lorena Rizzo, Presence and Absence – Photography and the aesthetics of historical return and disappearance (forthcoming).

103 See Costanza Caraffa and Tiziana Serena, Photographs, Archives and the Discourse of Nation, in Caraffa and Serena (eds.), *Photo Archives and the Idea of Nation.* Berlin, Munich, Boston, 2015, pp. 3–16.

104 See Sontag, *Regarding the Pain of Others*; and, in contrast, Didi-Huberman, *Images in Spite of All*.

105 Jean Comaroff and John Comaroff, Criminal Obsessions, after Foucault: Postcoloniality, Policing, and the Metaphysics of Disorder. *Critical Inquiry*, 30, 4, 2004: 800–24.

106 This resonates with discussions of the uncanny produced in film and cinema as e.g. in Anjeana K. Hans, *Gender and the Uncanny in Films of the Weimar Republic*. Detroit, 2014, p. 3.

107 See Hayes, Power, Secrecy, Proximity. Subotsky's project in Pollsmoore prison in Cape Town was completed in 2006, while Goldblatt's series on *Ex-Offenders* toured South Africa in 2012. For a critical discussion see *Chimurenga*, November Issue, 2013, p. 37.

108 See Jacques Rancière, The Distribution of the Sensible: Politics and Aesthetics, in J. Rancière, *The Politics of Aesthetics*. London, 2004, pp. 12–19.

109 Runia, Presence, p. 16.

110 See Barthes, *Camera Lucida*, p. 107; and Nao Sawada, Sartre et la photographie: autour de la théorie de l'imaginaire.

111 Runia is actually quite explicit about the "presentism" in his proposition. See Runia, Presence, p. 8.

112 See Ed Benson, Martin Guerre, the Historian and the Filmmakers: An Interview with Natalie Zemon Davis. *Film & History: An Interdisciplinary Journal of Film and Television Studies*, 13, 3, 1983: 49–65, here p. 62.

113 Ibid.; Regener, *Fotografische Erfassung*, or Maxwell, *Picture Imperfect*. More nuanced readings are proposed in Ch. Pinney, *The Coming of Photography in India*. London, 2008, pp. 61–8; C. Anderson, Voir/Savoir: Photographing, Measuring and Fingerprinting the Indian Criminal, in ibid: *Legible Bodies. Race, Criminality and Colonialism in South Asia*. Oxford, New York, 2004, pp. 141–80.

114 See for this theoretical argument e.g. Edwards, Photography and the Material Performance of the Past.

115 Such as e.g. in Jäger, Photography: A Means of Surveillance? The argument on power effects of images echoes W.T.J. Mitchell, *Seeing Through Race. The W.E.B. Du Bois Lectures*. Cambridge (MA), 2012, part I.

116 Runia, Presence, p. 16.

117 W.J.T. Mitchell, *Picture Theory*, p. 283.

118 Ewa Domanska, The Material Presence of the Past. *History and Theory*, 45, 2006: 337–348, here p. 337.

119 See Barthes, *Camera Lucida*, p. 20.

Epilogue

Monads and the spacing of history

The initial idea of *Photography and History in Colonial Southern Africa* was to place a series of archival encounters with Southern African historical photographs at the centre stage of a historical study. This approach has taken us on an explorative journey that covered extensive geographical distances and bridged long periods of time. Yet, as argued throughout the chapters, the trajectory did not necessarily follow linear vectors along predefined chronologies, even if now and again Southern African historiography provided a safe haven for an essentially eclectic and risqué project. More than proposing a continuous account of Southern African photographic history, one that would sit well on received parameters of the region's past, the narrative cultivated here was deliberately built from circuits, overlaps, repetitions, and returns.[1] The book opened with a photographic archive produced in central Namibia under German colonial rule; it continued to investigate different collections of photographs from across South Africa and Namibia during the interwar and apartheid periods; it moved on to the Eastern Cape in the 1950s and 1960s; and it returned to the Cape Colony in the late nineteenth and early twentieth centuries. Over the course of this extensive probing, we came across a wide range of what we might still call, for the sake of convenience, photographic genres – police and prison photographs, portraiture, landscape, and aerial photography. We likewise covered a diverse field of photographic practices, which included taking images, being photographed, collecting, curating and displaying pictures; ordering, selecting, discarding, describing, interpreting and classifying them; and finally, activating photographs in various situations, for multiple reasons, and with different aims in mind. In short, we delineated some of the contours of Southern African historical photography as an aesthetic and social domain, which encompassed a wide range of images, objects, and texts, acts, and agents, photographic conventions and sensibilities, hopes and desires, classificatory registers and epistemological preoccupations, and institutional achievements and failures, which eventually materialised in intricate archival formations.

In view of this diversity and complexity, some readers might wish to know if and how, in the region considered and the period covered, there are ways to sum up, in terms of an historical synthesis, the comings and goings of the photographic image, object, and medium.[2] As noted in the introduction, I have not necessarily been concerned with retracing the history of photography in Namibia and South Africa since the late nineteenth century, much less within the framework of a progressive development and unfolding throughout the twentieth century. Still, we have come across instances of photographic consolidation and pervasiveness, which – if desired – could be organised along axes of spatial and temporal continuity and discontinuity, though both would have to be accounted for.[3] Photography's implication in projects of imperial expansion and colonisation (as discussed explicitly regarding aerial photographs); their deployment in epistemological projects pursued by colonial science and the state, such as in the context of identifying and classifying colonised subjects along the lines of race, gender, citizenship, and nationality; as well as viewing photography as a cultural practice, which by the 1940s was increasingly shaped by Africans themselves (evidenced for example in the case of private photographic collections from central Namibia), has yielded insights into the dynamics of emerging visual economies in the region. On the other hand, there have been clues to an important degree of non-visuality, a wide range of responses to photography that included, but were not tantamount to, forms of renunciation or contestation, expressions of deep suspicion, articulations of criticism, and, sometimes, a remarkable awareness of the flaws and limitations of the photograph as an unmediated, truthful representation of reality.[4] These doubts and dismissals were common among Africans – especially when photography was rightfully associated with state surveillance – but they also existed among members of colonial state administrations, including, as we saw, in the police and penal system.

What do we intend by the above-mentioned circuits, overlaps, repetitions, and returns? How are these to be understood, if we do not conceive of them at the level of the narrative alone but in view of the historical nature of vision? *Photography and History in Colonial Southern Africa* attended to these issues by means of a recurring reflection on the photographic archive and a critical assessment of photographs as historical form. This discussion was neither conclusive, nor was its intention to provide final answers. There are, nevertheless, three points worth recalling, since I consider them critical for understanding what a series of archival encounters tells us about the relationship between photography and history in colonial Southern Africa. It is obvious, perhaps, that the region's history revolves around questions of difference, and scholarship remains preoccupied with how coloniality parasitically grew on an ongoing production and rigour of racialised bodies and spaces.[5] As argued throughout the book, "colonial(ist) photography" has often been made to stand in for ideas and ideologies of race and racism and the social and physical architecture of racial segregation. While we need to continue to refine our understanding of the relationship between the image and power, between the visual and ideation, and retrace its historical iterations, we should not limit ourselves to tying photographic images to colonial epistemologies of difference alone.

Several of the chapters in this book have therefore reframed the problematic and explored ways in which to understand the photographs' role less at the level of image content, but instead in view of the effects of the technological medium in the broader sense and in relation to the changing terms of vision. This has helped specify the ways in which photography took part in a range of material and social practices that helped constitute and differentiate bodies and things, the physical and the human, nature, and culture. Our consideration of these practices attempted to describe different conditions under which particular modalities of seeing were generalised and normalised, while others receded and disintegrated.[6] Scopic regimes enforced by colonial states could become very powerful, and as we saw repeatedly, especially in the case of population registration in South Africa in the 1950s and 1960s, they had real effects on peoples' lives. Yet, while the visualities so produced were totalising in their attitude and outlook, they were never comprehensive or uniform; instead, they had important limitations, showed intrinsic loopholes, and sometimes ended up in meaningful failures.

Let us dwell on population registration a bit longer and explain how, on a more theoretical note, it poses a different question that concerned most of the photographic collections considered here: the problem of scale. Firstly, scale is inevitably considered in terms of multitude, fed from photographic seriality, repetition, and reproduction, and perceptible, in some instances, as the return and omnipresence of the ever-same kinds of images. Standardised identity photographs from the 1960s are a case in point, but likewise we could recall images of "the native" in settler photography since the interwar period. Secondly, we need to view scale in terms of magnitude: recall the change in perspective that took us from the microscopic photographic registration of individuals, discussed in Chapter 2, to the macroscopic purview of aerial photography in Chapter 4. This shift highlighted the importance of the strategic alternation of the parameters of vision, which, for example, provided the colonial state with the means to indefinitely replicate, exaggerate, or reduce the world it wished to appropriate and control. *Photography and History in Colonial Southern Africa* has argued for the analytical possibilities lodged in exploring these dynamics of visual formatting and zooming, within and beyond the state, and to qualify the "cold and affective imaginaries" – to play on Le Corbusier's phrasing (Chapter 4) – attached to them.

However, retracing processes of scaling in a given historical context differs from scaling as a method of historical inquiry. In other words, while there are long histories of "zooming in and out", the ocular metaphor might be less appropriate for describing levels of reality.[7] The distinction is important, especially once we consider photographs as a form of historical representation, and ask how we proceed in inserting photographic images into historical narration. Photographic and visual studies have readily fostered Kracauer's idea of photographs (or cinematic stills) as close-up views, micro-narratives that allow us to grasp what eludes broader views and thereby to modify the comprehensive, large narrative of history.[8] That may well be, and *Photography and History in Colonial Southern Africa* certainly relates to this kind of historical understanding of photography. However, some of the analytical lines developed in the book – for example, in relation to Southern African landscapes – were more preoccupied with showing how specific spatio-temporal constellations mediated by the photographic image and medium involved the making and unmaking of the object and subject they represented. Photography's transformative effects, therefore, encouraged the possibility of conceiving of photographic collections less in terms of a logics of verticality that distinguishes shifting levels of perception – micro or macro, small or large scale – than along the lines of a flat ontology.[9] Within this framework, photographic archives were conceived of as emerging and unstable material and visual entities, which could be interrogated in view of the dynamic properties of images and objects and the changing connections and constellations between them. Tracing processes of material and visual clustering and connectivity, then, offered a critical methodological strategy for assessing how photographs become historically meaningful. Thus, the decision to situate each chapter within a particular theoretical discussion can be reaffirmed. It is essential, however, to state that *Assemblage*, *Bodies and things*, *Augenblick*, *Heterotopia*, and *Presence* does not constitute an eclectic selection of theoretical tools that mark different analytical approaches, but instead announce something regarding the nature of the photographic material itself. That is, these "tags" identify multiple points of view, what Benjamin calls "monads", meant to reflect the perspectival and fragmentary character of photographic collections, the archival encounter, and photography's galvanising resonances in the past, present, and future.[10]

Notes

1 Repetition and return in relation to photography point to a different experience and representation of time, and introduce a temporal plurality to historical narration. See Paul Ricoeur, Narrative Time. *Critical Inquiry*, 7 January 1980: 169–90, here pp. 179–80; also Hutcheon, *Poetics of Postmodernism*, p. 97.
2 See again Hayes, Power, Secrecy, Proximity.
3 Runia, Presence, p. 6.
4 Vokes, Introduction, in ibid. (ed.), *Photography in Africa*, p. 11.
5 See more generally Walter Mignolo, Introduction. *Cultural Studies*, 21, 2–3, 2007: 155–67.
6 See Sumathi Ramaswamy, Introduction: The Work of Vision in the Age of European Empires, in Martin Jay and Sumathi Ramaswamy (eds.), *Empires of Vision. A Reader*. Durham and London, 2014, pp. 1–22, here p. 3.
7 Bruno Latour, Anti-zoom, in Michael T. Clarke and David Wittenberg (eds.), *Scale in Literature and Culture*. Cham, 2017, pp. 93–6.
8 Edwards, *Raw Histories*, pp. 2–3.
9 See Sallie A. Marston, John Paul Jones III and Keith Woodward, Human geography without scale. *Trans Inst Br Geogr*, 30, 2005: 416–32, here pp. 7–8.
10 Cadava, *Words of Light*, pp. 60–1; also, Peter Osborne (ed.), *Walter Benjamin. Critical Evaluations in Cultural Theory*. Vol. I Philosophy. London and New York, 2005, pp. 146–7.

Bibliography

Adjaye, Joseph K., Review of *Bringing the Empire Home: Race, Class, and Gender in Britain and Colonial South Africa* by Zine Magubane. *Comparative Studies of South Asia, Africa, and the Middle East*, 26, 2006: 523–4.

Aldridge, John, Luka Jantjie: A Publisher's View of a Highly Illustrated Historical Biography. *Botswana Notes and Records*, 45, 2015: 141–79.

Alt, Suvi, Darkness in a Blink of an Eye. Action and the Onto-Poetics of a Beyond. *Angelaki*, 21, 2, 2016: 17–31.

Amad, Paula, *Counter-Archive: Film, the Everyday, and Albert Kahn's Archives de la Planète*. Columbia University Press, New York, 2010.

Amad, Paula, From God's-eye to Camera-eye: Aerial Photography's Post-humanist and Neo-humanist Visions of the World. *History of Photography*, 36, 1, 2012: 66–86.

Anderson, C., Voir/Savoir: Photographing, Measuring and Fingerprinting the Indian Criminal, in ibid., *Legible Bodies: Race, Criminality and Colonialism in South Asia*. Oxford, New York, 2004, pp. 141–80.

Appadurai, Arjun, The Colonial Backdrop. *Afterimage*, March/April, 1997: 4–7.

Assubuji, Rui and Patricia Hayes, The Political Sublime: Reading Kok Nam, Mozambican Photographer (1939–2012). *Kronos*, 39, 1, 2013: 66–111.

Azoulay, Ariella, What Is a Photograph? What Is Photography? *Philosophy of Photography*, 1, 1, 2010: 9–13.

Badroodien, Azeem, Race, Crime, Welfare and State Social Institutions in South Africa from the 1940s. *Social Dynamics*, 25, 2, 1999: 49–74.

Baker, George, Photography between Narrativity and Stasis: August Sander, Degeneration, and the Decay of the Portrait. *October*, 76, 1996: 72–113.

Balandier, Georges, La situation coloniale: approche théorique. *Cahiers Internationaux de Sociologie*, 11, 1951: 44–79.

Balandier, Georges, The Colonial Situation: A Theoretical Approach, in Immanuel Wallerstein (ed.), *Social Change and Colonial Situation*. New York, 1966, pp. 34–61.

Balibar, Françoise, Philippe Büttgen, Barbara Cassin, Jean-Pierre Clero and Jacques Collette, Der/das Moment, der Augenblick, die günstige Gelegenheit. *Trivium*, 15, 2013: 1–12.

Bank, A., Anthropology, Race and Evolution: Rethinking the Legacy of Wilhelm Bleek. *History and African Studies Seminar Paper*, 1993.

Banks, Marcus and Richard Vokes, Introduction: Anthropology, Photography, and the Archive. *History and Anthropology*, 21, 2010: 337–49.

Barthes, Roland, The Rhetoric of the Image, In ibid., *Image, Music, Text*. New York, 1977, pp. 152–63.

Barthes, Roland, *Camera Lucida*. London, 1984.

Batchen, Geoffrey, *Burning with Desire: The Conception of Photography*. Cambridge, MA, 1997.

Baylis, G., A Few Too Many Photographs? Indexing Digital Histories. *History of Photography*, 38, 1, 2014: 3–20.

Bazin, André and Hugh Gray, The Ontology of the Photographic Image. *Film Quarterly*, 13, 4, 1960: 4–9.

Beck, Roger B., *The History of South Africa*. Santa Barbara, Denver, Oxford, 2014.

Becker, Peter, The Standardized Gaze: The Standardization of the Search Warrant in Nineteenth-Century Germany, in Jane Caplan and John Torpey (eds.), *Documenting Individual Identity: The Development of State Practices in the Modern World*. Princeton and Oxford, 2001, pp. 139–63.

Behrend, Heike, *Contesting Visibility: Photographic Practices on the East African Coast*. Bielefeld, 2013.

Beinart, William and Colin Bundy, State Intervention and Rural Resistance: The Transkei, 1900–1965, in Martin A. Klein (ed.), *Peasants in Africa*. Beverly Hills, 1980, pp. 271–315.

Beinart, William, Soil Erosion, Conservationism and Ideas about Development: A Southern African Exploration, 1900–1960. *Journal of Southern African Studies*, 11, 1, 1984: 52–83.

Beinart, William and Colin Bundy, *Hidden Struggles in Rural South Africa. Politics and Popular Movements in the Transkei and Eastern Cape 1890–1930*. Berkeley, Los Angeles, 1987.

Beinart, William and Saul Dubow (eds.), *Segregation and Apartheid in South Africa*. London, 1995.

Beinart, William and Saul Dubow, Introduction: The Historiography of Segregation and Apartheid, in ibid. (eds.), *Segregation and Apartheid in Twentieth Century South Africa*. London, New York, 1995, pp. 1–24.

Beinart, William, *The Rise of Conservation in South Africa: Settlers, Livestock, and the Environment 1770–1950*. Oxford, 2003.

Bell, Morag, Robin Butlin and Michael Heffernan (eds.), *Geography and Imperialism, 1820–1940*. Manchester and New York, 1995.

Benjamin, Walter, The Work of Art in the Age of its Mechanical Reproduction, in Hannah Arendt (ed.), *Illuminations*, New York, 1969, pp. 1–26.

Bennett, Tony, Anthropological Assemblages: Producing Culture as a Surface of Government. *CRESC Working Paper Series*, 52, 2008: 2–16.

Benson, Ed, Martin Guerre, The Historian and the Filmmakers: An Interview with Natalie Zemon Davis. *Film & History: An Interdisciplinary Journal of Film and Television Studies*, 13, 3, 1983: 49–65.

Bernault, Florence and Janet L. Roitman (eds.), *A History of Prison and Confinement in Africa*. Portsmouth, 2003.

Bernault, Florence, The Politics of Enclosure in Colonial and Postcolonial Africa, in Florence Bernault and Janet L. Roitman (eds.), *A History of Prison and Confinement in Africa*. Portsmouth, 2003, pp. 1–54.

Berner, Oskar T., *Die Schweizer in Südwestafrika*. Windhoek, 1998.

Betts, Melissa Jeanne, *Namibia's No Man's Land. Race, Space, and Identity in the History of Windhoek Coloureds under South African Rule 1915–1990*. Unpublished PhD, UCLA, 2009.

Bhabha, Homi K., The Other Question…Homi K Bhabha Reconsiders the Stereotype and Colonial Discourse. *Screen*, 24, 6, 1983: 18–36.

Bickford-Smith,V., *Ethnic Pride and Racial Prejudice in Victorian Cape Town: Group Identity and Social Practice, 1875–1902.* Cambridge, 1995.

Bickford-Smith, Vivian, South African Urban History, Racial Segregation and the Unique Case of Cape Town? *Journal of Southern African Studies*, 21, 1995: 53–78.

Bley, Helmut, *Kolonialherrschaft und Sozialstruktur in Deutsch-Südwestafrika 1894–1914.* Hamburg, 1968.

Bley, Helmut and Leonhard Harding (eds.), *Namibia under German Rule.* Münster, 1996, pp. 164–65.

Bogard, William, Surveillance Assemblages and Lines of Flight, in David Lyon (ed.), *Theorising Surveillance: The Panopticon and Beyond.* New York, 2006, pp. 97–122.

Bonner, Phil, Desirable or Undesirable Sotho Women? Liquor, Prostitution and the Migration of Sotho Women, in Cheryl Walker (ed.), *Women and Gender in Southern Africa to 1945.* London, 1990, pp. 221–51.

Botha, Christo, The Politics of Land Settlement in Namibia, 1890–1960. *South African Historical Journal*, 42, 2000: 232–76.

Bozzoli, Belinda, Marxism, Feminism, and South African Studies, in W. Beinart and S. Dubow (eds.), *Segregation and Apartheid*, 1995, pp. 118–44.

Bratu-Hansen, Miriam, Benjamin's Aura. *Critical Inquiry*, 34, 2008: 336–75.

Braun, Lindsay Frederick, *Colonial Survey and Native Landscapes in Rural South Africa, 1850–1913: The Politics of Divided Space in the Cape and Transvaal*, Leiden and Boston, 2015.

Breckenridge, Keith, Flesh Made Words: Fingerprinting and the Fantasy of Documentary Panopticism, 1900–1930. *History and African Studies Seminar*, 2, 2001: 76–96.

Breckenridge, Keith, Verwoerd's Bureau of Proof: Total Information in the Making of Apartheid. *History Workshop Journal*, 59, 2005: 83–108.

Breckenridge, Keith, Fighting for a White South Africa: White Working-Class Racism and the 1922 Rand Revolt. *South African Historical Journal,* 57, 2007: 228–43.

Breckenridge, Keith, Introduction: The Global Biometric Arena, in ibid., *Biometric State: The Global Politics of Identification and Surveillance in South Africa, 1850 to the Present.* Cambridge, 2014, pp. 1–26.

Brooks, Pamela E., *Boycotts, Buses, and Passes: Black Women's Resistance in the US South and South Africa.* Amherst, 2008.

Brückenhaus, Danile, Identifying Colonial Subjects. Fingerprinting in British Kenya, 1900–1960. *Geschichte und Gesellschaft,* 42, 2016: 60–85.

Buck-Morss, Susan, Aesthetics and Anaesthetics: Walter Benjamin's Artwork Essay Reconsidered, *October*, 62, 1992, 3–41.

Bundy, Colin, *The Rise and Fall of the South African Peasantry.* Berkeley, Los Angeles, 1979.

Bundy, Colin, Land and Liberation: The South African National Liberation Movements and the Agrarian Question, 1920s–1960s. *Review of African Political Economy*, 29, 1984: 14–29.

Bundy, C., Lessons on the Frontier: Aspects of Eastern Cape History. *Kronos*, 30, 2004: 9–21.

Bunting, B., *The Rise of the South African Reich.* London, 1964.

Buranello, Robert, Between Fact and Fiction: Italian Immigration to South Africa. *Altreitalie*, January–December, 2009: 23–44.

Burleigh, Peter, The Burden of the Moment: Photography's Inherent Monumentalizing Effect, in Ladina Bezzola Lambert and Andrea Ochsner (eds.), *Moment to Monument: The Making and Unmaking of Cultural Significance.* Bielefeld, 2009, pp. 185–95.

Burrows, E., *A History of Medicine in South Africa up to the End of the Nineteenth Century.* Cape Town, 1958.

250   *Bibliography*

Cadava, Eduardo, *Words of Light: Theses on the Photography of History.* Princeton, 1997.

Cadava, Eduardo, Of Veils and Mourning: Fazal Sheikh's Widowed Images, in Fundacion MAPFRE, *Fazal Sheikh.* Madrid, 2009 [exhibition catalogue].

Campbell, Courtney J., Space, Place, and Scale: Human Geography and Spatial History in Past and Present. *Past and Present,* 239, 1, 2016: e23–e45.

Campt, Tina M., *Listening to Images.* Durham and London, 2017.

Cape of Good Hope, *Report on the Management and Discipline of Convict Stations and Prisons for the Year 1895.* Cape Town, 1896.

Caplan, Jane and John Torpey (eds.), *Documenting Individual Identity: The Development of State Practices in the Modern World.* Princeton, 2001.

Capus, Alex, *Eduard Spelterini: Photographs of a Pioneer Balloonist.* Zürich, 2007.

Carabot, Philip, Yannis Hamilakis and Eleni Papargyriou (eds.), *Camera Graeca: Photographs, Narratives, Materialities.* London, 2016.

Caraffa, Costanza and Tiziana Serena, Photographs, Archives and the Discourse of Nation, in C. Caraffa and T. Serena (eds.), *Photo Archives and the Idea of Nation.* Berlin, Munich, Boston, 2015.

Chanock, Martin, Criminological Science and Criminal Law on the Colonial Periphery: Perception, Fantasy and Reality in South Africa, 1900–1930. *Law and Social Inquiry,* 20, 4, 1995: 911–39.

Chanock, Martin, *The Making of South African Legal Culture 1902–1936: Fear, Favour and Prejudice.* Cambridge, 2001.

Chakkalakal, Silvy, *Margaret Meads Anthropologie der Sinne: Ethnographie als ästhetische und aisthetische Praxis. Berliner Blätter,* 67, 2015: 14–28.

Chatterjee, Partha, *The Nation and Its Fragments: Colonial and Postcolonial Histories.* Princeton, 1993.

Chaudhary, Zahid R., *Afterimage of Empire.* Minneapolis, 2012.

Chaudhary, Zahid R., Subjects in Difference: Walter Benjamin, Frantz Fanon and Postcolonial Theory. *Differences,* 23, 2012: 151–83.

Christopher, A.J., Land Policy in Southern Africa in the 19th century. *Zambezia,* 2, ii, 1971: 1–9.

Christopher, A.J., "To Define the Indefinable": Population Classification and the Census in South Africa. *Area,* 34, 2002: 401–8.

Cohen, David William, *The Combing of History.* Chicago and London, 1994.

Cole, Simon, *A History of Fingerprinting and Criminal Identification.* Cambridge, MA, 2001.

Collier, Peter, The Impact on Topographic Mapping of Developments in Land and Air Survey, 1900–1939. *Cartography and Geographic Information Science,* 29, 3, 2002: 155–74.

Collier, Peter, The Colonial Survey Committee and the Mapping of Africa. Unpublished Paper presented at the *International Symposium "Old Worlds-New Worlds": The History of Colonial Cartography,* pp. 1750–950, Utrecht University, 21–23 August 2006.

Comaroff, Jean and John L. Comaroff, Criminal Obsessions, After Foucault: Postcoloniality, Policing, and the Metaphysics of Disorder. *Critical Inquiry,* 30, 4, 2004: 800–24.

Comaroff, Jean and John L. Comaroff, Introduction: The Portraits of an Ethnographer as a Young Man, in John L. Comaroff, Jean Comaroff and Deborah James (eds.), *Picturing a Colonial Past: The African Photographs of Isaac Schapera.* Chicago, London, 2007, pp. 1–18.

Coombes, Annie E., *History After Apartheid: Visual Culture and Public Memory in a Democratic South Africa.* Durham, 2003.

Cooper, Frederick, Introduction: Colonial Questions, Historical Trajectories, in ibid., *Colonialism in Question: Theory, Knowledge, History*. Berkeley, Los Angeles, London, 2005, pp. 3–32.

Cosgrove, Denis and William L. Fox, *Photography and Flight*. London, 2010.

Cox, Richard J., Secrecy, Archives, and the Archivist: A Review Essay (Sort Of). *The American Archivist*, 72, 2009: 214–31.

Crais, Clifton, *The Politics of Evil: Magic, State Power, and the Political Imagination in South Africa*. Cambridge, 2002.

Crane, Susan A., Of Photographs, Puns, and Presence, in R. Ghosh and E. Kleinberg (eds.), *Presence*, pp. 62–78.

Crush, Jonathan, Alan Jeeves and David Yudelman, *South Africa's Labour Empire: A History of Black Migrancy to the Gold Mines*. Cape Town, 1991.

Cuthbertson, Greg, Albert Grundlingh and Mary-Lynn Suttie (eds.), *Writing a Wider War: Rethinking Gender, Race and Identity in the South African War, 1899–1902*. Athens, 2002.

Dale, Richard, Reconfiguring White Ethnic Power in Colonial Africa: The German Community in Namibia, 1923–1950. *Nationalism and Ethnic Politics*, 7, 2, 2001: 75–94.

Dale, Richard, *The Namibian War of Independence, 1966–1989: Diplomatic, Economic, and Military Campaigns*. Jefferson, NC, 2014.

Dant, Tim and Graeme Willoch, Pictures of the Past. Benjamin and Barthes on photography and history. *European Journal of Cultural Studies*, 5, 1, 2002: 5–23.

Davenport, T.R.H., *The Beginnings of Urban Segregation in South Africa: The Natives (Urban Areas) Act of 1923 and Its Background*. Grahamstown, 1971.

Davie, Grace, *Poverty and Knowledge in South Africa: A Social History of Human Science, 1855–2005*. Cambridge, 2015.

Deacon, Harriet, *A History of the Breakwater Prison from 1859 to 1905*. Unpublished Honours Thesis, University of Cape Town, 1989.

Deacon, Harriet, Racial Segregation and Medical Discourse in 19th Century Cape Town. *Journal of Southern African Studies*, 22, 2, 1996: 287–308.

Deacon, Harriet (ed.), *The Island: A History of Robben Island, 1488–1990*. Cape Town, 1996.

Deacon, Harriet, Howard Phillips and Elizabeth van Heyningen (eds.), *The Cape Doctor in the Nineteenth Century*. Amsterdam, New York, 2004.

Dedering, Tilman, Air-power in South Africa, 1914–1939. *Journal of Southern African Studies*, 41, 3, 2015: 451–65.

Deflem, Mathieu, Law Enforcement in British Colonial Africa: A Comparative Analysis of Imperial Policing in Nyasaland, the Gold Coast, and Kenya. *Police Studies* 17, 1, 1994: 45–68.

Deleuze, Gilles and Félix Guattari, *A Thousand Plateaus: Capitalism and Schizophrenia*. Minneapolis and London, 1987.

Deriu, Davide, The Ascent of the Modern Planeur: Aerial Images and Urban Imaginary in the 1920s, in Christian Emden, Catherine Keen and David Midgley (eds.), *Imagining the City*. Oxford, 2006, pp. 189–211.

Derrida, Jacques, *Archive Fever: A Freudian Impression*. Chicago, 1996.

De Wet, Chris, Betterment Planning in South Africa: Some Thoughts on Its History, Feasibility, and Wider Policy Implications. *Journal of Contemporary African Studies*, 6, 1/2, 1987: 85–122.

Dhupelia-Mesthrie, Uma, *From Cane Fields to Freedom: A Chronicle of Indian South African Life*. Cape Town, 2000.

Dhupelia-Mesthrie, Uma, Producing Biographical Knowledge about Indians in the Cape: The State, the Archives and the Historian. Unpublished Inaugural Lecture, Department of History, Faculty of Arts, University of the Western Cape. Cape Town, 2009, pp. 9–10.

Dhupelia-Mesthrie, Uma, The Form, the Permit and the Photograph: An Archive of Mobility between South Africa and India. *Journal of Asian and African Studies*, 46, 2011: 650–62.

Didi-Huberman, Georges, *Confronting Images: Questioning the Ends of a Certain History of Art*. Pennsylvania, 2005.

Didi-Huberman, Georges, *Images in Spite of All*. Chicago and London, 2008.

Dietrich, Keith and Andrew Bank (eds.), *An Eloquent Picture Gallery: The South African Portrait Photographs of Gustav Theodor Fritsch, 1863–1865*. Johannesburg, 2008.

Dixon, Robert, *Prosthetic Gods: Travel, Representation and Colonial Governance*. St. Lucia, Brisbane, Queensland, 2001.

Dlamini, Jacob, *Native Nostalgia*. Johannesburg, 2009.

Dönges, T.E., *The New South African Citizenship*. London, 1949.

Domanska, Ewa, The Material Presence of the Past. *History and Theory*, 45, 2006: 337–48.

Drechsler, Horst, *Aufstände in Südwestafrika. Der Kampf der Herero und Nama 1904 bis 1907 gegen die deutsche Kolonialherrschaft*. Berlin, 1984.

Dube, Saurabh and Ishita Banerjee-Dube, Introduction: Critical Questions of Colonial Modernities, in ibid. (eds.), *Unbecoming Modern: Colonialism, Modernity, Colonial Modernities*. New Delhi, 2006, pp. 1–31.

Dubow, Saul, Holding "A Just Balance between White and Black": The Native Affairs Department in South Africa, ca. 1920–33. *Journal of Southern African Studies*, 12, 2, 1986: 217–39.

Dubow, Saul, Afrikaner Nationalism, Apartheid and the Conceptualization of "Race". *Journal of African History*, 33, 1992: 209–37.

Dubow, Saul, *Scientific Racism in Modern South Africa*. Cambridge, 1995.

Dubow, Saul, South Africa and South Africans: Nationality, Belonging, Citizenship, in Robert Ross, Anne Kelk Mager and Bill Nasson (eds.), *The Cambridge History of South Africa*. Cambridge, 2011, pp. 17–65.

Duggan-Cronin, Alfred M., *The Bantu Tribes of South Africa: Reproductions of Photographic Studies*. Vol. III, Section I: The Nguni. Cambridge and Kimberley, 1939.

Du Toit, Marijke, Blank Verbeeld, or the Incredible Whiteness of Being: Amateur Photography and Afrikaner Nationalist Historical Narrative. *Kronos*, 27, 2001: 77–113.

Du Toit, Marijke, The General View and Beyond: From Slum-yard to Township in Ellen Hellmann's Photographs of Women and the African Familial in the 1930s. *Gender & History*, 17, 3, 2005: 593–626, here pp. 612–13.

Du Toit, Marijke, "Binnelandse Reise" (Journey to the Interior): Photographs from the Carnegie Commission of Investigation into the Poor White Problem, 1929/32. *Kronos*, 32, 2006: 49–76.

Earf, Barny, *Time Space Compression: Historical Geographies*. Abingdon, 2008.

Eberhardt, M., *Zwischen Nationalsozialismus und Apartheid. Die deutsche Bevölkerungsgruppe Südwestafrikas 1915–1965*. Berlin, 2005.

Edwards, Elizabeth, Ordering Others: Photographies, Anthropologies, Taxonomies, in Chrissie Iles and Russel Roberts (eds.), *In Visible Light. Photography and Classification in Art, Science and the Everyday*. Oxford, 1997, pp. 54–68.

Edwards, Elizabeth, *Raw Histories: Photographs, Anthropology and Museums*. Oxford, New York, 2001.

Edwards, Elizabeth, Professor Huxley's "Well-Considered Plan", in Elizabeth Edwards (ed.), *Raw Histories*, pp. 131–56.

Edwards, Elizabeth and Janice Hart, Introduction. Photographs as Objects, in Elizabeth Edwards and Janice Hart (eds.), *Photographs Objects Histories: On the Materiality of Images*. New York and Oxford, 2004, pp. 1–15.

Edwards, Elizabeth, Thinking Photography Beyond the Visual? in J.J. Long, Andrea Noble and Edward Welch, *Photography: Theoretical Snapshots*. Abingdon, New York, 2009, pp. 31–48.

Edwards, Elizabeth, Photography and the Material Performance of the Past. *History and Theory* 48, 2009: 130–50.

Edwards, Elizabeth, *The Camera as Historian: Amateur Photographers and Historical Imagination, 1885–1918*. Durham, 2012.

Edwards, Elizabeth, Photographic Uncertainties: Between Evidence and Reassurance. *History and Anthropology*, 25, 2, 2014: 171–88.

Edwards, S., The Machine's Dialogue. *The Oxford Art Journal*, 13, 1, 1990: 63–76.

Ellenbogen, Josh, *Reasoned and Unreasoned Images: The Photography of Bertillon, Galton, and Marey*. Pennsylvania, 2008.

Elo, Mika, Walter Benjamin on Photography: Towards Elemental Politics. *Transformations*, 15, 2007: n.p.

Emmett, Tony, *Popular Resistance and the Roots of Nationalism in Namibia, 1915–66*. Basel, 1999.

Enwezor, Okwui, Archive Fever: Photography between History and the Monument, in Enwezor, Okwui (ed.), *Archive Fever: Uses of the Document in Contemporary Art*. New York, 2008, pp. 11–51.

Esposito, Roberto, The *Dispositif* of the Person. *Law, Culture and the Humanities*, 8, 1, 2012: 17–30.

Evans, Ivan, *Bureaucracy and Race: Native Administration in South Africa*. Berkeley, 1997.

Evans, I.L., *Native Policy in Southern Africa: An Outline*. Cambridge, 1934.

Feinstein, Charles H., *An Economic History of South Africa: Conquest, Discrimination and Development*. Cambridge, 2005.

Feyder, Sophie, Lounge Photography and the Politics of Township Interiors: The Representation of the Black South African Home in the Ngilima Photographic Collection, East Rand, 1950s. *Kronos*, Special Issue on Documentary Photography in South Africa, 38, 2012: 131–53.

Flournoy, Richard W., The New British Imperial Law of Nationality. *American Journal of International Law*, 9, 1915: 870–82.

Förster, Larissa, Dag Henrichsen and Michael Bollig (eds.), *Namibia-Deutschland. Eine geteilte Geschichte*. Köln, 2004.

Förster, Larissa and Holger Stoecker, *Haut, Haar und Knochen. Koloniale Spuren in naturkundlichen Sammlungen der Universität Jena*. Weimar, 2016.

Foote, Nicola, Rethinking Race, Gender and Citizenship: Black West Indian Women in Costa Rica, *c*.1920–1940. *Bulletin of Latin American Research*, 23, 2004: 198–212.

Forsythe, William James, *The Reform of Prisoners 1830–1900*. London, 1986.

Foster, Jeremy, "Land of Contrasts" or "Home We Have Always Known"? The SAR&H and the Imaginary Geography of White South African Nationhood, 1920–1930. *Journal of Southern African Studies*, 29, 3, 2003: 657–80.

Foucault, Michel, The Subject and Power. *Critical Inquiry*, 8, 4, 1982: 777–95.

Foucault, Michel, Of Other Spaces: Utopias and Heterotopias. *Architecture/Mouvement/Continuité*, October, 1984: 1–9.

Foucault, Michel, *Security, Territory, Population: Lectures at the Collège de France, 1977–8*. New York, 2007.

Foucault, Michel, *The Birth of Biopolitics: Lectures at the Collège de France, 1978–9*. New York, 2008.

Frankema, Ewout and Marlous van Waijenburg, Metropolitan Blueprints of Colonial Taxation? Lessons from Fiscal Capacity Building in British and French Africa, c. 1880–1940. *The Journal of African History*, 55, 3, 2014: 371–400.

Freund, Bill, Cities in Revolt: The Long-Term Crisis of South African Urbanism, in ibid., *The African City: A History*. Cambridge, 2007, pp. 107–43.

Friedrichsmeyer, Sara, Sara Lennox and Susanne Zantop (eds.), *The Imperialist Imagination: German Colonialism and Its Legacies*. Ann Arbor, 1998.

Fugard, Athol, *Township Plays*. Oxford, 2000.

Furlong, P.J., The National Party of South Africa: A Transnational Perspective, in M. Durham and M. Power (eds.), *New Perspectives on the Transnational Right*. New York, 2010.

Gabaccia, Donna R., *Italy's Many Diasporas*. Seattle, 2000.

Gadamer, Hans-Georg, The Continuity of History and the Existential Moment. *Philosophy Today*, 16, 3/4, 1972: 230–40.

Gandhi, Leela, *Postcolonial Theory: A Critical Introduction*. New York, 1998.

Gaupp, Robert, Über den heutigen Stand der Lehre vom "geborenen Verbrecher". *Monatsschrift für Kriminalpsychologie und Strafrechtsreform*, 1, 1904/05: 25–42.

Gavish, Dov, *The Survey of Palestine Under the British Mandate, 1920–48*. London and New York, 2005, pp. 167–68.

Gewald, Jan Bart, *Herero Heroes: A Socio-Political History of the Herero in Namibia 1890–1923*. Oxford, Cape Town, Athens, 1999.

Gewald, Jan-Bart, Missionaries, Hereros, and Motorcars: Mobility and the Impact of Motor Vehicles in Namibia before 1940. *The International Journal of African Historical Studies*, 35, 2/3, 2002: 257–85.

Gewald, Jan-Bart, Diluting Drinks and Deepening Discontent. Colonial Liquor Control and Public Resistance in Windhoek, Namibia, in D.F. Bryceson (ed.), *Alcohol in Africa: Mixing Business, Pleasure, and Politics*. Portsmouth, 2002, pp. 117–38.

Ghosh, Ranjan and Ethan Kleinberg (eds.), *Presence: Philosophy, History, and Cultural Theory for the Twenty-First Century*. Ithaca and London, 2013.

Gibson, Mary, Review Essay: Global Perspectives on the Birth of the Prison. *The American Historical Review*, 116, 4, 2011: 1040–63.

Giliomee, Hermann, The Making of the Apartheid Plan, 1929–48. *Journal of Southern African Studies*, 29, 2, 2003: 373–92.

Godby, M., Images of //Kabbo, in P. Skotnes (ed.), *Miscast: Negotiating the Presence of the Bushmen*. Cape Town, 1996, pp. 115–27.

Goodrich, Michael, The Theatre of Emblems: On the Optical Apparatus and the Investiture of the Person. *Law, Culture and the Humanities*, 8, 2012: 47–67.

Gordon, Robert J., The Impact of the Second World War on Namibia. *Journal of Southern African Studies*, 19, 1, Special Issue: Namibia: Africa's Youngest Nation, 1993: 147–65.

Gordon, Robert J., The Rise of the Bushman Penis: Germans, Genitalia, and Genocide. *African Studies*, 57, 1, 1998: 27–54.

Gordon, Robert J., Vagrancy, Law & "Shadow Knowledge", in Hayes et al. (eds.), *Namibia under South African Rule. Mobility and Containment, 1915–46*. Oxford, Windhoek, Athens, 1998, pp. 51–76.

Gordon, Robert J., Hiding in Full View. The "Forgotten" Bushman Genocides in Namibia. *Genocide Studies and Prevention*, 4, 1, 2009: 29–57.

Gottschalk, Keith, The Political Economy of Healthcare: Colonial Namibia 1915–1961. *Social Science and Medicine*, 25, 6, 1988: 577–82.

Graham, Ron and Alexander Koh, *Digital Aerial Survey: Theory and Practice*. Caithness and Boca Raton, 2000.

Grendon, Paul, Giorgio Miescher, Lorena Rizzo and Tina Smith, Usakos. *Photographs Beyond Ruins. The Old Location Albums, 1920s–1960s*. Basel, 2015.

Grundlingh, Albert, The King's Afrikaners? Enlistment and Ethnic Identity in the Union of South Africa's Defense Force During the Second World War, 1939–45. *Journal of African History*, 40, 1999: 351–65.

H.M. Stationary Office, *Colonial Reports – Annual. No. 1410 Northern Rhodesia. Report for 1927*. London, 1928.

Haffner, Jeanne, Historicizing the View from Below: Aerial Photography and the Emergence of a Social Conception of Space. *The Proceedings of Spaces of History / Histories of Space: Emerging Approaches to the Study of the Built Environment*. A Conference at the University of California, Berkeley, April 30 and May 1, 2010 [published online on eScholarship, University of California, 15 September 2010].

Haffner, Jeanne, *The View from Above: The Science of Social Space*. Cambridge, MA, 2013.

Hagemann, A., Nationalsozialismus, Afrikaaner Nationalismus, und die Entstehung der Apartheid in Südafrika. *Vierteljahrshefte für Zeitgeschichte*, 39, 3, 1991: 413–36.

Hamilton, Peter and Roger Hargreaves, *The Beautiful and the Damned: The Creation of Identity in 19th Century Photography*. London, 2001.

Hamilton, Carolyn, Verne Harris, Jane Taylor, Michele Pickover, Graeme Reid and Razia Saleh (eds.), *Refiguring the Archive*. Dordrecht, 2002.

Haney, Erin, *Photography and Africa*. London, 2010.

Hans, Anjeana K., *Gender and the Uncanny in Films of the Weimar Republic*. Detroit, 2014.

Harries, P., *Work, Culture and Identity: Migrant Laborers in Mozambique and South Africa, c. 1860s–1910*. Portsmouth, Johannesburg, London, 1994.

Hartmann, Wolfram (ed.), *Hues between Black and White. Historical Photography from Colonial Namibia, 1860s to 1915*. Windhoek, 2004.

Hayes, Patricia, Jeremy Silvester and Wolfram Hartmann, Photography, History and Memory, in Wolfram Hartmann, Jeremy Silvester and Patricia Hayes (eds.), *The Colonising Camera: Photographs in the Making of Namibian History*. Cape Town, Windhoek, Athens, 1998, pp. 2–9.

Hayes, Patricia, Jeremy Silvester, Marion Wallace and Wolfram Hartmann (eds.), *Namibia under South African Rule: Mobility and Containment, 1915–46*. Oxford, Windhoek, Athens, 1998.

Hayes, Patricia, Jeremy Silvester and Wolfram Hartmann, "Picturing the Past": The Visual Archive and Its Energies, in Carolyn Hamilton, Verne Harris, Jane Taylor, Michele Pickover, Graeme Reid and Razia Saleh (eds.), *Refiguring the Archive*. Dordrecht, 2002, pp. 103–33.

Hayes, Patricia, Introduction: Visual Genders. *Gender & History*, 17, 3, 2005: 519–37.

Hayes, Patricia, Power, Secrecy, Proximity: A Short History of South African Photography. *Kronos*, 33, 2007: 139–62.

Hayes, Patricia, Compound Nation: Migrant Worker Portraits in the Politics and Photography of 1980s Namibia, in Costanza Caraffa and Tiziana Serena (eds.), *Photo Archives and the Idea of the Nation*. Berlin, Munich, Boston, 2015, pp. 279–300.

Hayes, Patricia, The Production of Red: Aesthetics, Work, and Time. *Kronos*, 42, 1, 2016: 103–20.

Hebinck, Paul and Wim van Averbeke, Rural Transformation in the Eastern Cape, in Paulus Gerardus, Maria Hebinck and Peter C. Lent (eds.), *Livelihoods and Landscapes: The People of Guquka and Koloni and Their Resources*. Leiden, 2014, pp. 33–66.

Heidegger, Martin, *The Question Concerning Technology and Other Essays*. Translated and with an Introduction by William Lovitt. New York, London, Toronto, Sidney, 1977, pp. 3–35.

Hendrick, Fred T., Loose Planning and Rapid Resettlement: The Politics of Conservation and Control in Transkei, South Africa, 1950–1970. *Journal of Southern African Studies*, 15, 2, 1989: 306–25.

Henrichsen, Dag, Teilnachlass E.R. und A. Scherz im Personenarchiv der Basler Afrika Bibliographien. Internal library finding aid, Basel, 1990.

Henrichsen, Dag, "A Glance at Our Africa". The History and Contents of South West News, in ibid., *A Glance at Our Africa: Facsimile Reprint of South West News 1960*. Basel, 1997, pp. 13–44.

Henrichsen, Dag, Ozombambuse and Ovasolondate. Everyday Military Life and African Service Personnel in German South West Africa, in Wolfram Hartmann (ed.), *Hues between Black and White: Historical Photography from Colonial Namibia 1860s to 1915*. Windhoek, 2004, pp. 161–84.

Henrichsen, Dag, Naomi Jacobson and Karen Marshall (eds.), *Israel Goldblatt. Building Bridges. Namibian Nationalists Clemens Kapuuo, Hosea Kutako, Brendan Simbwaye, Samuel Witbooi*. Basel, 2010.

Henrichsen, Dag, Giorgio Miescher, Ciraj Rassool and Lorena Rizzo, Rethinking Empire in Southern Africa. *Journal of Southern African Studies*, 41, 3, 2015: 431–35.

Herwitz, Daniel, Monument, Ruin, and Redress in South African Heritage. *The Germanic Review: Literature, Culture, Theory*, 86, 4, 2011: 232–48.

Hight, Eleanor M. and Gary D. Sampson, Photography, "Race", and Postcolonial Theory, in Eleanor M. Hight and Gary D. Sampson (eds.), *Colonialist Photography: Imag(in)ing Race and Place*. New York, 2002, pp. 1–19.

Hirson, Baruch, The General Strike of 1922. *Searchlight South Africa*, 3, 3, 1993: 63–93.

Hofmann, Anette, Widerspenstige Stimmen – Unruly Voices. Gespenster – Spectres, in ibid. (ed.), *What We See. Reconsidering an Anthropometrical Collection from Southern Africa: Images, Voices, and Versioning*. Basel, 2009, pp. 23–57.

Hofmeyr, Isabel, The Spoken Word and the Barbed Wire. Oral Chiefdoms versus Literate Bureaucracies, in ibid., *"We Spend Our Years as a Tale That Is Told": Oral Historical Narrative in a South African Chiefdom*. Portsmouth, Johannesburg, London, 1993, pp. 59–77.

Hoogland, Renée C., *A Violent Embrace: Art and Aesthetics after Representation*. Lebanon, NH, 2014.

Hüppauf, Bernd, Experiences of Modern Warfare and the Crisis of Representation. *New German Critique*, 59, 1993, pp. 41–76.

Hüppauf, Bernd, The Emergence of Modern War Imagery in Early Photography. *History & Memory*, 5, 1, 1993: 131–51.

Hull, Matthew, *Government of Paper: The Materiality of Bureaucracy in Urban Pakistan*. Berkeley, 2012.

Hull, Matthew, Book Symposium. The Materiality of Indeterminacy…On Paper, At Least. *HAU: Journal of Ethnographic Theory*, 3, 3, 2013: 441–47.

Hungwe, Chipo, Putting Them in Their Place: "Respectable" and "Unrespectable" Women in Zimbabwean Gender Struggles. *Feminist Africa*, Issue on Subaltern Sexualities, 6, 2006: 33–46.

Hunt, Lynn, *Measuring Time, Making History*. Budapest, New York, 2008.

Hunt, Lynn and Vanessa R. Schwartz, Editorial. Capturing the Moment: Images and Eyewitnessing in History. *Journal of Visual Culture*, 9, 3, 2010: 259–71.

Hunt, Nancy Rose, *A Nervous State: Violence, Remedies, and Reverie in Colonial Congo*. Durham and London, 2016.

Hutcheon, Linda, *A Poetics of Postmodernism: History, Theory, Fiction*. New York and London, 2004.

Illsley, John, Seeing Our Land from Above: The First Decades. *PositionIT*, 2012: 22–26.

Ingold, Tim, The Temporality of the Landscape. *World Archaeology*, 25, 2, 1993: 152–74.

Jacobs, André and Hennie Smit, Topographic Mapping Support in the South African Military During the 20th Century. *Scientia Militaria*, 32, 1, 2004: 32–50.

Jacobs, Sean, Coloured Categories. Review of Mohamed Adhikari, Not White Enough, Not Black Enough: Racial Identity in the South African Coloured Community, H-South Africa, H-Net Review, May 2007.

Jäger, Jens, Photography: A Means of Surveillance? Judicial Photography, 1850–1900. *Crime, Histoire et Sociétés/Crime, History and Societies*, 5, 2001: 27–52.

Jäger, Jäger, Erkennungsdienstliche Behandlung. Zur Inszenierung polizeilicher Identifikationsmethoden um 1900, in Jürgen Martschukat and Steffen Patzold (eds.), *Geschichtswissenschaft und performativer turn. Ritual, Inszenierung und Performanz vom Mittelalter bis zur Neuzeit*. Köln, 2003, pp. 207–28.

Johnson, Peter, The Geographies of Heterotopia. *Geography Compass*, 7, 11, 2013: 790–803.

Johnston, John, Machinic Vision. *Critical Inquiry*, 26, 199: 27–48.

Kahn, Farieda, Rewriting South Africa's Conservation History – The Role of the Native Farmers Association. *Journal of Southern African Studies*, 20, 4, 1994: 499–516.

Karatani, Rieko, *Defining British Citizenship: Empire, Commonwealth and Modern Britain*. London, 2003.

Kaulich, Udo, *Die Geschichte der ehemaligen Kolonie Deutsch-Südwestafrika (1884–1914). Eine Gesamtdarstellung*. Frankfurt, 2001.

Keegan, Timothy, Gender, Degeneration and Sexual Danger: Imagining Race and Class in South Africa, c.1912. *Journal of Southern African Studies* Special Issue for Shula Marks, 27, 2001: 459–77.

Kennedy, Rosanne, Jonathon Zapasnik, Hannah McCann and Miranda Bruce, All Those Little Machines: Assemblage as Transformative Theory. *Australian Humanities Review*, 55, 2013: 45–6.

Kingwill, Rosalie, Papering over the Cracks: An Ethnography of Land Title in the Eastern Cape. *Kronos*, Special Issue on Paper Regimes, 40, 1, 2014: 241–68.

Kössler, Reinhart, *In Search of Survival and Dignity: Two Traditional Communities in Southern Namibia under South African Rule*. Windhoek, 2007.

Kössler, Reinhart, *Namibia and Germany: Negotiating the Past*. Windhoek, 2015.

Kondlo, Kwandiwe, *In the Twilight of the Revolution. The Pan-Africanist Congress of Azania (South Africa) 1959–1994*. Basel, 2009.

Kostka, Helga, *SeinerZeit. Redakteur Franz Seiner und seine Zeit*. Graz, 2007.

Kozol, W., Madonnas of the Fields: Photography, Gender, and 1930s Farm Relief. *Genders*, 2, 1988: 1–23.

Kracauer, Siegfried, *The Mass Ornament: Weimar Essays*. Edited by Thomas E. Levin. Cambridge, MA, London, 1995.

Krautwurst, Udo, The Joy of Looking. Early German Anthropology, Photography and Audience Formation. *Visual Anthropology Review*, 18, 1–2, 2002: 55–79.

Kreike, Emanuel, De-Globalisation and Deforestation in Colonial Africa: Closed Markets, the Cattle Complex and Environmental Change in North-Central Namibia, 1890–1990. *Journal of Southern African Studies*, 35, 1, 2009: 81–98.

Kunars, Andrea, Traditions of Collecting and Remembering: Gender, Class and the 19th Century Sentiment Album and Photographic Album. *Early Popular Visual Culture*, 4, 3, 2006: 227–43.

Kundrus, Birthe, From Herero to Holocaust? Some Remarks on the Current Debate. *Africa Spectrum*, 40, 2, 2005: 299–308.

Kynoch, Gary, Controlling the Coolies: Chinese Mine Workers and the Struggle for Labour in South Africa, 1904–10. *International Journal of African Historical Studies*, 36, 2002: 309–29.

La Capra, Dominick, Rethinking Intellectual History and Reading Texts. *History and Theory*, 19, 3, 1980: 245–76.

Langford, Martha, *Suspended Conversations: The Afterlife of Memory in Photographic Albums*. Montreal, Kingston, London, Ithaca, 2008.

Lau, Brigitte (ed.), *An Investigation of the Shooting at the Old Location on 10 December 1959*. Windhoek, 1995.

Lalu, Premesh, Medical Anthropology, Subaltern Traces, and the Making and Meaning of Western Medicine in South Africa, 1895–1899. *History in Africa*, 25, 1998: 133–59.

Lalu, Premesh, The Grammar of Domination and the Subjection of Agency: Colonial Texts and Modes of Evidence. *History and Theory*, 39, 4, Theme Issue "Not Telling": Secrecy, Lies, and History, 39, 2000: 45–68.

Lalu, Premesh, *The Deaths of Hintsa. Postapartheid South Africa and the Shape of Recurring Pasts*. Cape Town, 2002.

Landau, Paul and Deborah Kaspin (eds.), *Images and Empires: Visuality in Colonial and Postcolonial Africa*. Berkeley, Los Angeles, London, 2002.

Larkin, Brian, Infrastructure, the Colonial Sublime and Indirect Rule, in ibid., *Signal and Noise: Media, Infrastructure and Urban Culture in Nigeria*. Durham and London, 2008.

Latour, Bruno, Anti-zoom, in Michael T. Clarke and David Wittenberg (eds.), *Scale in Literature and Culture*. Cham, 2017, pp. 93–6.

Lefebvre, Henri, *The Production of Space*. Oxford and Cambridge, MA, 1991.

Lefebvre, Henri, Space. Social Product and Use Value, in ibid., *State, Space, World: Selected Essays*. Minneapolis, 2009.

Legassick, Martin, *The Struggle for the Eastern Cape 1800–1854: Subjugation and the Roots of South African Democracy*. Johannesburg, 2010.

Lehmuskallio, Asko and Edgar Gomez Cruz, Why Material Visual Practices? in Edgar Gomez Cruz and Asko Lehmuskallio (eds.), *Digital Photography and Everyday Life*. Abingdon, New York, 2016, pp. 1–16.

Lemke, Thomas, New Materialisms: Foucault and the "Government of Things". *Theory, Culture & Society*, 32, 4, 2015: 3–25.

Levine, Philippa, Sexuality, Gender, and Empire, in Phillipa Levine (ed.), *Gender and Empire*. Oxford, 2004, pp. 134–55.

Leys Stepan, Nancy, "Race, Gender, Science and Citizenship", in Catherine Hall (ed.), *Cultures of Empire: Colonizers in Britain and the Empire in the 19th and 20th Centuries*. Manchester, 2000.

Liebenberg, John and Patricia Hayes, *Bush of Ghosts: Life and War in Namibia, 1986–90.* Cape Town, 2010.

Likuwa, Kletus, Contract Labour System and Farm Labourers' Experiences in Pre-Independent Namibia: Historical Reflections, Perspectives and Lessons, *BAB Working Paper*, 2, 2014.

Lindner, Ulrike, Contested Concepts of "White"/"Native" and Mixed Marriages in German South-West Africa and the Cape Colony 1900–1914: A histoire croisée. *Journal of Namibian Studies*, 6, 2009: 57–79.

Lindner, Ulrike, *Koloniale Begegnungen. Deutschland und Grossbritannien als Imperialmächte in Afrika 1880–1914.* Frankfurt, New York, 2011.

Lüdtke, Alf, *The History of Everyday Life: Reconstructing Historical Experiences and Ways of Life.* Princeton, 1995.

Macdonald, Andrew, The Identity Thieves of the Indian Ocean: Forgery, Fraud and the Origins of South African Immigration Control, 1890s–1920s, in Keith Breckenridge and Simon Szreter (eds.), *Recognition and Registration: Documenting the Person in World History.* Oxford, 2012, pp. 390–428.

Mager, Anne K., "The People Get Fenced": Gender, Rehabilitation and African Nationalism in the Ciskei and Border Region, 1945–1955. *Journal of Southern African Studies*, 18, 4, 1992: 761–82.

Malherbe, Vertrees C., Family Law and the "Great Moral Public Interests" in Victorian Cape Town, ca. 1850–1902. *Kronos*, 36, 2010: 7–27.

Mamdani, Mahmood, *Citizen and Subject: Contemporary Africa and the Legacy of Late Colonialism.* Princeton, 1996.

Manicom, Linzi, Ruling Relations: Rethinking State and Gender in South African History. *Journal of African History*, 33, 1992: 441–65.

Marcus, George E. and Erkan Saka, Assemblage. *Theory, Culture & Society*, 23, 2–3, 2006: 101–109, here pp. 102–03.

Marks, Shula and Richard Rathbone (eds.), *Industrialization and Social Change in South Africa, 1870–1930.* London and New York, 1982.

Marston, Sallie A., John Paul Jones III and Keith Woodward, Human Geography without Scale. *Transactions of the Institute of British Geographers*, 30, 2005: 416–32.

Matera, Marc, *Black London: The Imperial Metropolis and Decolonisation in the Twentieth Century.* Oakland, 2015.

Maxwell, Anne, *Picture Imperfect: Photography and Eugenics 1870–1940.* East Sussex, 2008.

Maylam, Paul, Explaining the Apartheid City: 20 Years of South African Urban Historiography. *Journal of Southern African Studies*, 21, 1, 1995: 19–38.

Mbembe, Achille, The Power of the Archive and Its Limits, in Carolyn Hamilton, Verne Harris, Jane Taylor, Michele Pickover, Graeme Reid and Razia Saleh (eds.), *Refiguring the Archive.* Dordrecht, Boston, London, 2002, pp. 19–26.

McAllister, Patrick A., The Impact of Relocation on Social Relationships in a "Betterment" Area in the Transkei. *Development Southern Africa*, 3, 3, 1986: 467–78.

McAllister, Patrick A., Resistance to "Betterment" in the Transkei: A Case Study from Willowvale District. *Journal of Southern African Studies*, 15, 2, Special Issue on The Politics of Conservation in Southern Africa, January, 1989: 346–68.

McGarth, Roberta, Geographies of the Body and the Histories of Photography. *Camera Austria*, 51–52, 1995: 99–106.

McGerr, Michael, The Price of the "New Transnational History". *The American Historical Review*, 96, 4, 1991: 1056–67.

McKittrick, Meredith, The "Burden" of Young Men: Property and Generational Conflict in Namibia, 1880–1945. *African Economic History*, 24, 1996: 115–29.

Mehring, Christine, Siegfried Kracauer's Theories of Photography: From Weimar to New York. *History of Photography*, 21, 2, 1997: 129–36.

Melber, Henning, Revisiting the Windhoek Old Location. Unpublished paper presented at the 3rd Namibia Research Day organized by the Basler Afrika Bibliographien, Basel, 2016.

Meyer, Hans (ed.), *Das deutsche Kolonialreich; eine Länderkunde der deutschen Schutzgebiete. Unter Mitarbeit von Professor Dr Siegfried Passarge und Professor Dr Leonhard Schultze.* Band 2, Leipzig 1910/11.

Miescher, Giorgio and Lorena Rizzo, Popular Pictorial Constructions of Kaoko in the 20th Century, in Giorgio Miescher and Dag Henrichsen (eds.), *New Notes on Kaoko: The Northern Kunene Region (Namibia) in Texts and Photographs.* Basel, 2000, pp. 10–47.

Miescher, Giorgio, *Namibia's Red Line: The History of a Veterinary and Settlement Border.* New York, 2012.

Miescher, Giorgio, Facing Barbarians: A Narrative of Spatial Segregation in Colonial Namibia. *Journal of Southern African Studies*, 38, 4, 2012: 769–86.

Miescher, Giorgio, Usakos' Urban Past. Traces in the Archive, in Paul Grendon, Giorgio Miescher, Lorena Rizzo, and Tina Smith (eds.), *Usakos: Photographs beyond Ruins. The Old Location Albums, 1920s–1960s.* Basel, 2015, pp. 28–63.

Miescher, Giorgio, The NE51 Series Frontier: The Grand Narrative of Apartheid Planning and the Small Town. *Journal of Southern African Studies*, 41, 3, 2015: 561–80.

Miescher, Stephan F., Takyiwaa Manuh and Catherine M. Cole, When Was Gender? in Catherine M. Cole, Takyiwaa Manuh and Stephan F. Miescher (eds.), *Africa After Gender?* Bloomington, 2007, pp. 1–15.

Mignolo, Walter, Introduction. *Cultural Studies*, 21, 2–3, 2007: 155–67.

Minkley, Gary and Helena Pohlandt-McCormick, The Speaking Crow or "On a Clear Day You Can See the Class Struggle from Here"? (Career Girls 1997). *Parallax*, 22, 2, 2016: 183–202.

Minkley, Gary, How, in Heaven's Name, Are These People to Provide Photographs for Themselves? The Intimate Photographic Event, the Provision of Politics, and the Encounter of an "Empire of Love" in South Africa. Unpublished conference paper, n.d.

Mitchell, Timothy, *Rule of Experts: Egypt, Technopolitics, Modernity.* Berkeley, 2002.

Mitchell, W.T.J., *Picture Theory: Essays on Verbal and Visual Communication.* Chicago and London, 1995.

Mitchell, W.T.J., Interdisciplinarity and Visual Culture. *Art Bulletin*, 77, 4, 1995: 540–44.

Mitchell, W.T.J., What Do Pictures "Really" Want? *October*, 77, 1996: 71–82.

Mitchell, W.T.J., *Landscape and Power.* Chicago and London, 2002.

Mitchell, W.T.J., *What do Pictures Want? The Lives and Loves of Images.* Chicago, 2004.

Mitchell, W.T.J., *Seeing Through Race.* Cambridge, MA, 2012.

Mofokeng, Santu, The Black Photo Album, in Pascal Martin Saint Leon, N'Goné Fall and Jean Loup Pivin (eds.), *Anthology of African and Indian Ocean Photography.* Paris, 1998, pp. 68–75.

Moorsom, Richard, Underdevelopment, Contract Labour and Worker Consciousness in Namibia, 1915–72. *Journal of Southern African Studies*, 4, 1, 1977: 52–87.

Moorsom, Richard, The Formation of the Contract Labour System in Namibia, 1900–1926, in Abebe Zegeye and Shubi Ishemo, *Forced Labour and Migration: Patterns of Movement within Africa.* London, 1989, pp. 55–108.

Morrell, Robert, *White but Poor: Essays on the History of Poor Whites in Southern Africa.* Pretoria, 1992.

Morshed, Adnan, The Aesthetics of Ascension in Norman Bel Geddes's Futurama. *Journal of the Society of Architectural Historians*, 63, 1, 2004: 74–99.

Morton, Christopher and Elizabeth Edwards (eds.), *Photography, Anthropology and History: Expanding the Frame.* London, New York, 2009.

Morton, Christopher and Darren Newbury (eds.), *The African Photographic Archive: Research and Curatorial Strategies.* London, New Delhi, New York, Sidney, 2015.

Morton, Christopher, The Ancestral Image in the Present Tense. *Photographies*, 8, 3, 2015: 253–70.

Mülder-Bach, Inka, The Exile of Modernity. Kracauer's Figurations of the Stranger, in Johannes von Moltke and Gerd Gmünden (eds.), *Culture in the Anteroom: The Legacies of Siegfried Kracauer.* Ann Arbor, 2012, pp. 276–92.

Mukaiwa, Martha, Social Life in the 1950s. *The Villager*, 304, 2011 [n.p.].

Muschalek, Marie, Honourable Soldier-Bureaucrats: Formations of Violent Identities in the Colonial Police Force of German South West Africa, 1908–18. *The Journal of Imperial and Commonwealth History*, 41, 4, 2013: 584–99.

Namhila, Ellen Ndeshi, *Recordkeeping and Missing, Native Estate' Records in Namibia. An Investigation of Colonial Gaps in a Post-colonial National Archive.* Tampere, 2015.

Newbury, Darren, The Visibility of Poverty: A Rural Vision of Depression in the Photographs of the Farm Security Administration. *Visual Anthropology*, 8, 1996: 1–31.

Newbury, Darren, "Lest We Forget": Photography and the Presentation of History at the Apartheid Museum, Gold Reef City, and the Hector Pieterson Museum, Soweto. *Visual Communication*, 4, 3, 2005: 259–95.

Newbury, Darren, Photographs of Windermere: The Brian Heseltine Collection. *Photography and Culture*, 3, 2, 2010: 225–37.

Newbury, Darren, *Defiant Images: Photography and Apartheid South Africa.* Pretoria, 2009.

Ngcaba, Siyanda Vincent, The Decline of Agriculture in Rural Transkei: The case of Mission Location in Butterworth. Unpublished MA Thesis, Rhodes University, Grahamstown, 2002.

Noyes, John, *Colonial Space: Spatiality in the Discourse of German Southwest-Africa, 1884–1915.* Chur, 1992.

Nutz, Thomas, *Strafanstalt als Besserungsmaschine: Reformdiskurs und Gefängniswissenschaft 1775–1848.* Munich, 2001.

Olusoga, David and Casper W. Erichsen, *The Kaiser's Holocaust. Germany's Forgotten Genocide and the Colonial Roots of Nazism.* London, 2010.

Osborne, Peter (ed.), *Walter Benjamin: Critical Evaluations in Cultural Theory.* Vol. I Philosophy. London and New York, 2005.

Palmquist, Peter, Women in Photography – Archives and Resources for Second World War Women Photographers. *History of Photography*, 18, 3, 1994: 247–55.

Park, Yoon Jung, Sojourners to Settlers: Early Constructions of Chinese Identity in South Africa. *African Studies*, 65, 2006: 201–23.

Pasanen, Outi, Notes on the Augenblick in and around Jacques Derrida's Reading of Paul Celan "The Meridian". *Research in Phenomenology*, 36, 2006: 214–37.

Paschalidis, Gregory, Images of History and the Optical Unconscious. *Historein* 4, 2003: 33–44.

Passarge, Siegfried, Grundlinien im ethnographischen Bilde der Kalahari-Region. *Zeitschrift der Gesellschaft für Erdkunde*, 1905: 68–88.

Patton, Paul, *Deleuzian Concepts: Philosophy, Colonization, Politics.* Stanford, 2010.

262   Bibliography

Peberdy, Sally, *Selecting Immigrants: National Identity and South Africa's Immigration Policies 1910–2008.* Johannesburg, 2009.

Peffer, John, Vernacular Recollections and Popular Photography in South Africa, in Christopher Morton and Darren Newbury (eds.), *The African Photographic Archive: Research and Curatorial Strategies.* London, New Delhi, New York, Sidney, 2015, pp. 115–33.

Peires, Jeffrey B., *The House of Phalo: A History of the Xhosa People in the Days of Their Independence.* Berkeley, Los Angeles, London, 1982.

Penn, N., "Close and Merciful Watchfulness": John Montagu's Convict System in the Mid-Nineteenth-Century Cape Colony. *Cultural and Social History*, 5, 4, 2008: 465–80.

Petrie, G., A Short History of British Stereoplotting Instrument Design. *Photogrammetric Record*, 9, 50, 1977: 213–38.

Pierce, Steven and Anupama Rao, Discipline and the Other Body. Humanitarianism, Violence, and the Colonial Exception, in ibid. (eds.), *Discipline and the Other Body. Correction, Corporeality, Colonialism.* Durham, London, 2006, pp. 1–21.

Pinney, Christopher, *"Photos of the Gods": The Printed Image and Political Struggle in India.* London, 2004.

Pinney, Christopher, *The Coming of Photography in India.* London, 2008.

Poole, Deborah, An Excess of Description: Ethnography, Race, and Visual Technologies. *Annual Review of Anthropology*, 34, 2005: 159–79.

Posel, Deborah, *Influx Control and the Construction of Apartheid.* Oxford, 1987.

Povinelly, Elizabeth A., Notes on the Gridlock. Genealogy, Intimacy, Sexuality. *Public Culture*, 14, 2002: 215–38.

Rahn, Kathleen, Die Geburt des Gefängnisses in Deutsch-Südwestafrika. Freiheitsstrafe und Strafvollzug von 1884 bis 1914. *Jahrbuch für Überseeische Geschichte*, 14, 2014: 243–54.

Rajchman, J., Foucault's Art of Seeing. *October*, 44, 1988: 88–117.

Ramaswamy, Sumathi, Introduction: The Work of Vision in the Age of European Empires, in Martin Jay and Sumathi Ramaswamy (eds.), *Empires of Vision: A Reader.* Durham and London, 2014.

Rancière, Jacques, The Distribution of the Sensible: Politics and Aesthetics, in Jacques Rancière, *The Politics of Aesthetics.* London, 2004.

Rancière, Jacques, *Dissensus: On Politics and Aesthetics.* London, New Delhi, New York, Sydney, 2010.

Rassool, Ciraj and Sandra Prosalendis (eds.), *Recalling Community in Cape Town: Creating and Curating the District Six Museum.* Cape Town, 2001.

Rassool, Ciraj, Power, Knowledge and the Politics of Public Pasts. *African Studies*, 69, 2010.

Rassool, Ciraj, Human Remains, the Disciplines of the Dead, and the South African Memorial Complex, in Derek Peterson, Kodzo Gavua and Ciraj Rassool (eds.), *The Politics of Heritage in Africa: Economies, Histories, and Infrastructures.* Cambridge, 2015.

Reagin, Nancy, The Imagined *Hausfrau*: National Identity, Domesticity, and Colonialism in Imperial Germany. *Journal of Modern History*, 73, 2001: 54–86.

Regener, Susanne, *Fotografische Erfassung.* München, 1999.

Regener, Susanne, Criminological Museums and the Visualisation of Evil. *Crime, History, Society*, 7, 1, 2003: 43–56.

Ricoeur, Paul, Narrative Time. *Critical Inquiry*, 7, 1, 1980: 169–90.

Rizzo, Lorena, A Glance into the Camera. Gendered Visions of Historical Photographs in Kaoko (North-Western Namibia). *Gender & History*, 17, 3, 2005: 682–713.

Rizzo, Lorena, *Gender and Colonialism: A History of Kaoko in North-Western Namibia, 1870s–1950s*. Basel, 2012.

Rizzo, Lorena, Visual Aperture: Bureaucratic Systems of Identification, Photography and Personhood in Colonial Southern Africa. *History of Photography*, 37, 2013: 263–82.

Rizzo, Lorena, Between the Book and the Lamp – Interiors of Bureaucracy and the Materiality of Colonial Power. *African Historical Review*, 45, 2, 2013.

Rizzo, Lorena, Faszination Landschaft – Landschaftsphotographie in Namibia. *BAB Working Paper*, 1, 2014.

Rizzo, Lorena, Paul Grendon, Giorgio Miescher, and Tina Smith, Photographs beyond Ruins. The Usakos Old Location Albums, 1920s to 1960s, in Paul Grendon, Giorgio Miescher, Lorena Rizzo and Tina Smith (eds.), *Usakos Photographs Beyond Ruins: The Old Location Albums, 1920s–1960s*. Basel, 2015, pp. 7–25.

Roach Pierson, Ruth, Nations: Gendered, Racialised, Crossed with Empire, in Ida Blom, Karen Hagemann and Catherine Hall (eds.), *Gendered Nations: Nationalisms and Gender Order in the Long Nineteenth Century*. Oxford, 2000, pp. 41–62.

Roberts, John, Photography after the Photograph: Event, Archive, and the Non-symbolic. *Oxford Art Journal*, 32, 2, 2009: 281–98.

Roscher, Gustav, Bedürfnisse der modernen Kriminal-Polizei. *Archiv für Kriminal-anthropologie und Kriminalistik*, 1899: 244–58.

Roscher, Gustav, Die daktyloskopische Registratur. *Archiv für Kriminalanthropologie und Kriminalistik*, 1904: 129–41.

Roscher, Gustav, *Grossstadtpolizei. Ein praktisches Handbuch der deutschen Polizei*. Hamburg, 1912.

Rose, Gilian, Family Photographs and Domestic Spacings: A Case Study. *Transactions of the Institute of British Geographers*, 28, 2003: 5–18.

Rose, Gilian, *Doing Family Photography: The Domestic, the Public and the Politics of Sentiment*. Ashgate, 2010.

Runia, Eelco, Presence. *History and Theory*, 45, 2006: 1–29.

Runia, Eelco, *Moved by the Past: Discontinuity and Historical Mutation*. New York, 2014.

Ruppenthal, Jens, *Kolonialismus als Wissenschaft und Technik. Das Hamburgische Kolonialinstitut 1908 bis 1919*. Stuttgart, 2007.

Ryan, James, *Picturing Empire. Photography and the Visualisation of the British Empire*. London, 1997.

Saint, Lily, Reading Subjects: Passbooks, Literature and Apartheid. *Social Dynamics*, 38, 1, 2012: 117–33.

Sandler, W., Deutsche Heimat in Afrika: Colonial Revisionism and the Construction of Germanness through Photography. *Journal of Women's History*, 25, 1, 2013: 37–61.

Sawada, Nao, Sartre et la photographie: autour de la théorie de l'imaginaire. *Etudes Françaises*, 49, 2, 2013: 103–21.

Schoeman, Karel, *The Face of the Country: A South African Family Album 1860–1910*. Cape Town, 1996.

Schepp, Sven, *Unter dem Kreuz des Südens. Auf Spuren der Kaiserlichen Landespolizei von Deutsch Südwestafrika*. Schriftenreihe der Deutschen Gesellschaft für Polizeigeschichte Bd. 8. Frankfurt, 2009.

Schinkel, Anders, Imagination as a Category of History: An Essay Concerning Koselleck's Concepts of Erfahrungsraum and Erwartungshorizont. *History and Theory*, 44, 2005: 42–54.

Schlottau, Rolf, *Deutsche Kolonialrechtspflege. Strafrecht und Strafmacht in den deutschen Schutzgebieten 1884 bis 1914*. Frankfurt, 2007.

Schmidt-Lauber, Brigitta, *Die abhängigen Herren: Deutsche Identität in Namibia*. Münster und Hamburg, 1993.

Schmokel, Wolfe W., The Myth of the White Farmer: Commercial Agriculture in Namibia, 1900–1983. *The International Journal of African Historical Studies*, 18, 1, 1985: 93–108.

Schröder, Martin, *Prügelstrafe und Züchtigungsrecht in den deutschen Schutzgebieten Schwarzafrikas*. Münster, 1997.

Schultze Jena, Leonhardt, *Aus Namaland und Kalahari. Bericht an die Kaiserliche Preussische Akademie der Wissenschaften zu Berlin über eine Forschungsreise im westlichen und zentralen Südafrika, ausgeführt in den Jahren 1903–1905*. Jena, 1907.

Schultze Jena, Leonhardt, Zur Kenntnis des Körpers der Hottentotten und Buschmänner. In ibid., *Zoologische und anthropologische Ergebnisse einer Forschungsreise im westlichen und zentralen Südafrika ausgeführt in den Jahren 1903–1905 mit Unterstützung der Kgl. Preussischen Akademie der Wissenschaften zu Berlin*. Bd. 5: Systematik, Tiergeographie und Anthropologie. Jena, 1928, pp. 145–27.

Scott, James C., *Seeing Like a State: How Certain Schemes to Improve the Human Condition Have Failed*. New Haven, 1998.

Seekings, Jeremy, "Not a Single White Person Should Be Allowed to Go Under": *Swartgevaar* and the Origins of South Africa's Welfare State. *Journal of African History*, 48, 2007: 375–94.

Seekings, Jeremy, The Continuing Salience of Race: Discrimination and Diversity in South Africa. *Journal of Contemporary African Studies*, 26, 1, 2008: 1–25.

Seiner, Franz, Die Buschmänner des Okawango- und Sambesigebietes der Nord-Kalahari. *Globus. Illustrierte Zeitschrift für Länder- und Völkerkunde*, 1910.

Seiner, Franz, Beobachtungen und Messungen an Buschleuten. *Zeitschrift für Ethnologie, Sonderdruck aus Band 3, Heft 2*, 1912.

Seiner, Franz, Ergebnisse einer Bereisung der Omaheke in den Jahren 1910–1912. *Mitteilungen aus den deutschen Schutzgebieten*, 26, 3, 1912: 227–316.

Seiner, Franz, Beobachtungen an den Bastard-Buschleuten der Nord-Kalahari. *Mitteilungen der Anthropologischen Gesellschaft*, 1913.

Sekula, Allan, The Instrumental Image: Streichen at War. *Artforum*, 14, 4, 1975: 26–35.

Sekula, Allan, The Body and the Archive. *October*, 39, 1986: 3–64.

Shapera, Isaac, Review: Zur Kenntnis des Körpers der Hottentotten und Buschmänner (Zoologische und anthropologische Ergebnisse einer Forschungsreise im westlichen und zentralen Südafrika. Bd. V, Lfg. III) by Leonhard Schultze. *Africa: Journal of the International African Institute*, 2, 4, 1929: 433–34.

Shapiro, Gary, Nietzsche's Story of the Eye: Hyphenating the Augen-blick. *Journal of Nietzsche Studies*, 22, 2001: 17–35.

Shear, K., *Constituting a State in South Africa: The Dialectics of Policing, 1900–1939*. Unpublished PhD, Evanston, Illinois, Northwestern University, 1998.

Sher, Mark, From Dompas to Disc: The Legal Control of Migrant Labour, in Dennis Davis and Mana Slabbert (eds.), *Crime and Power in South Africa: Critical Studies in Criminology*. Cape Town, 1985, 72–89.

Shetty, Sandhya and Elizabeth Jane Bellamy, Postcolonialism's Archive Fever. *Diacritics*, 30, 1, 2000: 25–48.

Siiskonen, Harri, *Trade and Socioeconomic Change in Ovamboland, 1850–1906*. Helsinki, 1990.

Silvester, Jeremy, Marion Wallace and Patricia Hayes, "Trees Never Meet". Mobility & Containment: An Overview, 1915–1946, in Patricia Hayes, Jeremy Silvester, Marion Wallace and Wolfram Hartmann (eds.), *Namibia under South African Rule: Mobility & Containment 1915–1946*, Oxford, Windhoek, Athens, 1998, pp. 3–48.

Silvester, Jeremy, Beasts, Boundaries & Buildings. The Survival and Creation of Pastoral Economies in Southern Namibia, 1915–1935, in Patricia Hayes, Jeremy Silvester, Marion Wallace and Wolfram Hartmann (eds.), *Namibia Under South African Rule: Mobility & Containment 1915–1946*, Oxford, Windhoek, Athens, 1998, pp. 95–116.

Silvester, Jeremy, Patricia Hayes and Wolfram Hartmann, "This Ideal Conquest": Photography and Colonialism in Namibian History, in Wolfram Hartmann, Jeremy Silvester and Patricia Hayes (eds.), *The Colonising Camera: Photographs in the Making of Namibian History*. Cape Town, Windhoek, Athens, 1998, pp. 10–19.

Silvester, Jeremy, Your Space or Mine? The Photography of the Police Zone, in Wolfram Hartmann, Jeremy Silvester and Patricia Hayes (eds.), *The Colonising Camera: Photographs in the Making of Namibian History*. Cape Town, Windhoek, Athens, 1998, pp. 138–44.

Silvester, Jeremy and Jan Bart Gewald, *Words Cannot Be Found: German Colonial Rule in Namibia: An Annotated Reprint of the 1918 Blue Book*. Leiden, 2003.

Simbao, Ruth, Review of Figures & Fictions: Contemporary South African Photography by Tamar Garb. *Kronos*, 38, 2012: 272–75.

Simon, David (ed.), *South Africa in Southern Africa: Reconfiguring the Region*. Oxford, 1998.

Simson, H., *The Social Origins of Afrikaner Fascism and its Apartheid Policy*. Stockholm, 1980.

Singh, S., The Historical Development of Prisons in South Africa: A Penological Perspective. *New Contree*, 50, 2005: 15–28.

Sippel, Harald, Rechtspolitische Ansätze zur Vermeidung einer Mischlingsbevölkerung in Deutsch-Südwestafrika, in Frank Beker (ed.), *Rassenmischehen, Mischlinge, Rassentrennung. Zur Politik der Rasse im deutschen Kolonialreich*. Stuttgart, 2004, pp. 138–64.

Smith, Adam, *The Political Landscape: Constellations of Authority in Early Complex Polities*. Berkeley, 2003, pp. 48–49.

Sontag, Susan, *Regarding the Pain of Others*. New York, 2003.

Southall, Roger J., *South Africa's Transkei: The Political Economy of an Independent Bantustan*. New York, 1983.

Spivak, Gayatri Chakravorty, Can the Subaltern Speak? in Cary Nelson and Lawrence Grossberg (eds.), *Marxism and the Interpretation of Culture*. Urbana, 1988, pp. 271–313.

Spyer, Patricia, Photography's Framings and Unframings: A Review Article. *Society for Comparative Study of Society and History*, 43, 1, 2001: 181–92.

Stahr, H., *Fotojournalismus zwischen Exotismus und Rassissmus. Darstellungen von Schwarzen und Idianern in Foto-Text-Artikeln deutscher Wochenillustrierter 1919–1939*. Hamburg, 2004.

Steedman, Carolyn, *Dust: The Archive and Cultural History*. New Brunswick, 2002.

Steinberg, K., *Das Staatsangehörigkeitsrecht der Südafrikanischen Union (einschliesslich Südwest-Afrika)*. Frankfurt am Main, 1955.

Steiner, Shepherd, Reading in Benjamin's "Little History of Photography". *In Tensions*, 1, 2008: 1–20.

Steinmetz, George, The Uncontrollable Afterlives of Ethnography. Lessons from "Salvage Colonialism" in the German Overseas Empire. *Ethnography*, 5, 3, 2004: 251–88.

Steinmetz, George and Julia Hell, The Visual Archive of Colonialism: Germany and Namibia. *Public Culture*, 18, 1, 2005: 147–84.

Stoecker, Holger, Thomas Schnalke and Andreas Winkelmann (eds.), *Sammeln, Erforschen, Zurückgeben? Menschliche Gebeine aus der Kolonialzeit in akademischen und musealen Sammlungen*. Berlin, 2013.

Stoler, Ann L., Making Empire Respectable: The Politics of Race and Sexual Morality in 20th Century Colonial Cultures. *American Ethnologist*, 16, 1989: 634–60.

Stoler, Ann L., "In Cold Blood": Hierarchies of Credibility and the Politics of Colonial Narratives. *Representations*, 37, 1992: 151–89.

Stoler, A.L., Colonial Studies and the History of Sexuality, in ibid., *Race and the Education of Desire: Foucault's History of Sexuality and the Colonial Order of Things*. Durham, 1995, pp. 1–18.

Stoler, Ann L., and Frederick Cooper, Between Metropole and Colony: Rethinking a Research Agenda, in Ann L. Stoler and F. Cooper (eds.), *Tensions of Empire: Colonial Cultures in a Bourgeois World*. Berkeley, Los Angeles, 1997, pp. 1–41.

Stoler, Ann L., Colonial Archives and the Arts of Governance. *Archival Science*, 2, 2002: 87–109, here p. 90.

Stoler, Ann L., *Carnal Knowledge and Imperial Power: Race and the Intimate in Colonial Rule*. Berkeley, 2002.

Stoler, Ann L., Imperial Debris: Reflections on Ruins and Ruination. *Cultural Anthropology*, 23, 2, 2008: 191–219.

Stoler, Ann L., *Along the Archival Grain: Epistemic Anxieties and Colonial Common Sense*. Princeton, 2009.

Stone, Jeffrey C., Imperialism, Colonialism, and Cartography. *Transactions of the Institute of British Geographers*, 13, 1988: 57–64.

Struebel, H., Die Entwicklung des Nationalsozialismus in Südwestafrika. *Vierteljahrshefte für Zeitgeschichte*, 1, 2, 1953: 170–76.

Swanepoel, S. and S. Mngqolo, *Galeshewe, Champion of the People*. Kimberley, 2011.

Switzer, Les, *Power and Resistance in an African Society. The Ciskei Xhosa and the Making of South Africa*. Madison, 1993.

Switzer, L., *South Africa's Alternative Press. Voices of Protest and Resistance, 1880–1960*. Cambridge, 1997.

Sylvain, Renee, Bushmen, Boers and Baasskap: Patriarchy and Paternalism on Afrikaner Farms in the Omaheke Region, Namibia. *Journal of Southern African Studies*, 27, 4, 2001: 717–37.

Tagg, John, *The Burden of Representation: Essays on Photographies and Histories*. Minneapolis, 1988.

Tagg, John, A Democracy of the Image: Photographic Portraiture and Commodity Production, in John Tagg, *The Burden of Representation: Essays on Photographies and Histories*. Minneapolis, 1988, pp. 34–59.

Tagg, John, Evidence, Truth, Order: A Means of Surveillance, in Jessica Evans and Stuart Hall (eds.), *Visual Culture: The Reader*. London, Thousand Oaks, New Delhi, 1999, pp. 244–73.

Thomas, Julia Adeney, The Evidence of Sight, *History and Theory*, Theme Issue 48, (December) 2009: 151–68.

Thomas, Kylie and Louise Green, Stereoscopic Visions: Reading Colonial and Contemporary African Photography. *Social Dynamics*, 40, 1, 2014: 1–11.

Thomas, Lynn, The Modern Girl and Racial Respectability in 1930s South Africa. *Journal of African History*, 47, 2006: 461–90.

Thompson, Malcolm, Foucault, Fields of Governability, and the Population-Family-Economy Nexus in China. *History and Theory*, 51, 2012: 42–62.

Torpey, John, The Great War and the Birth of the Modern Passport System, in Jane Caplan and John Torpey (eds.), *Documenting Individual Identity*, pp. 256–70.

Tropp, Jacob, The Contested Nature of Colonial Landscapes: Historical Perspectives on Livestock and Environments in the Transkei. *Kronos*, 30, 2004: 118–37.

Tucker, Jennifer, in collaboration with Tina Campt, Entwined Practices: Engagements with Photography in Historical Inquiry. *History and Theory*, Theme Issue 48, 2009: 1–8.

Twomey, Christina, Framing Atrocity: Photography and Humanitarianism. *History of Photography*, 26, 3, 2012: 255–64.

Union of South Africa, *South West Africa and the Union of South Africa: The History of a Mandate*. (n.p.), 1947.

Van den Berghe, Pierre L., Miscegenation in South Africa. *Cahiers d'Etudes Africaines*, 1, 1960: 68–84.

Van Heyninge, E., Agents of Empire: The Medical Profession in the Cape Colony, 1880–1910. *Medical History*, 33, 1989: 450–71.

Van Niekerk, J.P., An Introduction to South African Law Reports and Reporters 1828 to 1910. *Fundamina: A Journal of Legal History*, 19, 1, 2013: 106–45.

Van Onselen, Charles, Crime and Total Institutions in the Making of Modern South Africa. *History Workshop Journal*, 1985.

Van Onselen, Charles, *The Fox and the Flies: The Secret Life of a Grotesque Master Criminal*. New York, 2007.

Van Onselen, Charles, Jewish Police Informers in the Atlantic World, 1880–1891. *The Historical Journal*, 50, 1, 2007: 119–44.

Vec, Milos, Die Spur des Täters. Bertillonage, Daktyloskopie und Jodogramm: Fortschritte und Versprechungen der naturwissenschaftlichen Kriminalistik um 1900. *Juridikum*, 2, 2001: 89–94.

Viditz-Ward, Vera, Photography in Sierra Leone, 1850–1918. *Africa: Journal of the International African Institute*, 57, 4, 1987: 510–18.

Virilio, Paul, *The Vision Machine*. Bloomington, 1994.

Viyas Mongia, Radhika, Race, Nationality, Mobility: A History of the Passport. *Public Culture*, 11, 1999: 527–56.

Vokes, Richard (ed.), *Photography in Africa: Ethnographic Perspectives*. Woodbridge, Rochester, 2012.

Wahab, Amar, Race, Gender, and Visuality: Regulating Indian Women Subjects in the Colonial Caribbean. *Caribbean Review of Gender Studies*, 2, 2008: 1–23.

Waits, Mira Rai, The Indexical Trace: A Visual Interpretation of the History of Fingerprinting in Colonial India. *Visual Culture in Britain*, 17, 1, 2016: 18–46.

Waldheim, Charles, Aerial Representation and the Recovery of Landscape, in James Corner (ed.), *Recovering Landscape: Essays in Contemporary Landscape Architecture*. Princeton, 1999, pp. 121–39.

Walker, C., The Limits to Land Reform: Reviewing "The Land Question". Unpublished paper presented at the African Studies/History seminar University of Natal, Durban 19 November 2003.

Wallace, Marion, *A History of Namibia: From the Beginning to 1990*. London, 2011.

Wallace, Marion, *Health, Power and Politics Windhoek, Namibia, 1915–45*. Basel, 2002.

Wallenstein, Sven-Olof, Introduction: Foucault, Biopolitics, and Governmentality, in Jakob Nilsson and Sven-Olof Wallenstein (eds.), *Foucault, Biopolitics, and Governmentality*. Stockholm, 2013, pp. 7–34.

Walther, Daniel Joseph, *Creating Germans Abroad: Cultural Policies and National Identities in Namibia*. Athens, 2002.

Ward, Koral, *Augenblick. The Concept of the "Decisive Moment" in 19th and 20th Century Western Philosophy*. Hampshire, 2009.

Webb, Denver A., Lords of All They Surveyed? The Royal Engineers, Surveying, Mapping and Development in South Africa's Eastern Cape. *African Historical Review*, 45, 1, 2013: 22–45.

Weil, Simone, Human Personality, *An Anthology*, edited by Siân Miles. London, 1986, pp. 49–78.

Wells, Julia C., *We Now Demand: The History of Women's Resistance to Pass Laws in South Africa*. Johannesburg, 1994.

Werner, Wolfgang, "Playing Soldiers": The Truppenspieler Movement among the Herero of Namibia, 1915 to ca. 1945. *Journal of Southern African Studies*, 16, 3, 1990: 476–502.

Werner, Wolfgang, A Brief History of Land Dispossession in Namibia. *Journal of Southern African Studies*, 19, 1, 1993: 135–46.

Werner, Wolfgang, *"No One Will Become Rich"*. *Economy and Society in the Herero Reserves in Namibia, 1915–1946*. Basel, 1998.

Wessler, Adelheid, Von Lebendabgüssen, Heimatmuseen und Cultural Villages. Museale Repräsentationen des Selbst und des Anderen im (De)Kolonisierungsprozess Namibias. Unpublished PhD thesis, Köln, 2007.

White, Hayden, The Question of Narrative in Contemporary Historical Theory. *History and Theory*, 23, 1984: 1–33.

Willoughby-Herard, T., *Waste of a White Skin: The Carnegie Corporation and the Racial Logic of White Vulnerability*. Berkeley, 2015.

Withers, Charles W.J., Place and the "Spatial Turn" in Geography and in History. *Journal of the History of Ideas*, 70, 4, 2009: 637–58.

Witz, Leslie, Gary Minkley and Ciraj Rassool, *Unsettled History: Making South African Public Pasts*. Ann Arbor, 2017.

Wonnacott, Richard, 90 Years of Surveying and Mapping. *PositionIT*, 2010: 26–32.

Woodward, Wendy, Patricia Hayes and Gary Minkley (eds.), *Deep HiStories: Gender and Colonialism in Southern Africa*. Amsterdam, 2002.

Worden, Nigel, Review of *Creating the Creole Island: Slavery in Eighteenth–Century Mauritius* by Megan Vaughan. *Journal of African History*, 47, 2006: 332–33.

Wu, Cynthia, Review of Tina Chen, Double Agency: Acts of Impersonation in Asian and American Literature and Culture. *Journal of Asian American Studies*, 9, 2, 2006: 209–12.

Yancy, George, *Black Bodies, White Gazes: The Continuing Significance of Race in America*. Lanham, Boulder, New York, London, 2016.

Yudelman, David and Alan Jeeves, New Labour Frontiers for Old: Black Migrants to the South African Gold Mines, 1920–85. *Journal of Southern African Studies*, 13, 1, 1986: 101–24.

Zeller, Joachim, "Wie Vieh wurden hunderte zu Tode getrieben und wie Vieh begraben". Fotodokumente aus dem deutschen Konzentrationslager in Swakopmund/Namibia 1904–1908. *Zeitschrift für Geschichtswissenschaft*, 3, 2001: 226–43.

Zeller, Joachim, Oorlog in Deutsch-Südwestafrika. Fotografien aus dem Kolonialkrieg 1904 bis 1907. *Fotogeschichte*, 85/86, 2002: 31–44.

Zeller, Joachim, "Images of the South West African War": Reflections of the 1904–1907 Colonial War in Contemporary Photo Reportage and Book Illustration, in Wolfram Hartmann (ed.), *Hues between Black and White: Historical Photography from Colonial Namibia 1860s–1915*. Windhoek, 2004, pp. 309–23.

Zeytlin, David, Redeeming Some Cameroonian Photographs: Reflections on Photographs and Representations, in C. Morton and D. Newbury (eds.), *The African Photographic Archive: Research and Curatorial Strategies*. London, New Delhi, New York, Sidney, 2015, pp. 61–76.

Zimmerer, Jürgen, *Deutsche Herrschaft über Afrikaner. Staatlicher Machtanspruch und Wirklichkeit im kolonialen Namibia.* Hamburg, 2001.

Zimmerling, Jürgen, *Die Entwicklung der Strafrechtspflege für Afrikaner in Deutsch-Südwest Afrika 1884–1914.* Eine juristisch/historische Untersuchung. Bochum, 1995.

Zollmann, Jakob, *Koloniale Herrschaft und ihre Grenzen. Die Kolonialpolizei in Deutsch Südwest Afrika, 1894–1915.* Göttingen, 2010.

Archival Sources

National Archives of Namibia

NAN BKE 62, Fahndungssachen.

NAN BKE 212 B II 66.0 1-3, Gefangenen Register, Auszüge *1898–1912.*

NAN BKE 237, UA 12/6, Suchregister *für entlaufene Eingeborene,* 1910–1915.

NAN BLU 265, Bezirksamt Lüderitz.

NAN BRE 27, Bezirksamt Rehoboth.

NAN BSW 29, Bezirksamt Swakopmund, Gefängnissachen

NAN BWI 254, Bezirksamt Windhoek., Sicherheitspolizei und Erkennungsdienst.

NAN BWI 435, Bezirksamt Windhoek. Eingeborenen Strafregister 1895–1907.

NAN, SWAA 422 A 50/34, Native Affairs. Passports for Natives.

NAN SWAA 1855 A 406 2, Magistrate's office Swakopmund.

NAN ZBU 637 F III e 2, Gefängniswesen.

NAN ZBU 751 G IIa 3, Fahndungsblätter.

NAN ZBU 751 II a 4, Verbrecheralbum, Fingerabdrücke, Bd 1.

NAN ZBU 751, Polizeiwesen.

NAN ZBU Pol/A. 737, Fotografie Album 1a Farbige.

NAN ZBU 2043 W II o 2, Bezirksamtmann Grootfontein.

Western Cape Archives and Records Service

KAB AG 1391 1461, Attorney General.

KAB AG 1419, Attorney General.

KAB AG 1738 8057, Attorney General.

KAB, CMT 3/1434 30 B, Vol. 1, Chief Magistrate Transkeian Territories.

KAB, CMT 3/1435 30B, Chief Magistrate Transkeian Territories.

KAB CO 2090 484, Colonial Office Records.

KAB CO 6978-6986 (Vol. 1–9), Breakwater Convict Albums.

KAB PIO 1 – Principal Immigration Officer.

KAB JUS 108 23029, Law Department.

KAB IRC – 1/2/4 73C, Immigration Papers.

KAB 1/ALC, Magistrate's Office Alice.

KAB, 1/ECO, Magistrate's Office Engcobo.

KAB, 2/KMN 22, Magistrate's Office Kuruman.

KAB, 1/KTN 127, Magistrate's Office Kentani.

KAB, 1/TSM, Magistrate's Office Tsomo.

KAB, 1/TSM 7/1/46 N1/23/2, The Director of the Registration Office Pretoria to the Magistrate Tsomo, 28 April 1960.

KAB 1/UTA, Magistrate's Office Mtata.

KAB, 1/XAA, Magistrate's Office Cala.

South African National Archives Pretoria

SAB LDB_2099/R3730, Vol. 1. Department of Agriculture. Aerial Photography. General Correspondence, 24.7.1930-24.10.1947
SAB_LTD_461/R3730, Vol. 1–3. Aerial Photography. General Correspondence, 1953–68.
SAB_NTS_8356 20/355, Vol. 1. Native Affairs Department, Survey of Native Allotments by Air photography. Aerial Survey.
SAB_NTS_8356 20/355, Vol. 2. Native Affairs Department, Survey of Native Allotments by Air photography. Aerial Survey.
SAB_NTS_8356 20/355, Vol. 3. Native Affairs Department. Survey of Native Allotments by Air Photography.

Deutsches Bundesarchiv

BArch R1001/5119, Reichskolonialamt, Gefängniswesen in Deustch-Südwestafrika.

Basler Afrika Bibliographien, Basel

BAB Scherz collection, I.A:3.2., E.R. Scherz, Fahrt nach Swakopmund. März 1942.

Interviews

Interview with Gisela Pieters and Olga//Garoës, Okombahe, 8 August 2014.
Interview with Cecilie//Geises, Usakos, 19 November 2012.
Interview with Cecilie//Geises, 11 August 2014.
Interview with Wilhelmine Katjimune, Usakos, 12 August 2014.

Websites

Hayden White in conversation with Ethan Kleinberg, Center for the Humanities, Wesleyan University, October 2013, www.youtube.com/watch?v=ViG30Fkz2cI.

List of Illustration

National Archives of Namibia

NAN ZBU Pol/A.737, Fotografie Album 1b, Farbige. [Figures 1.1 through 1.5; 1.8b]
NAN BWI 254 S 8 q, Kaiserliches Bezirksamt Windhoek, Sicherheitspolizei und Erkennungsdienst Band 1, 1.1.1911, Verzeichnis der im Gefängnis befindlichen Gef angenen [n.d.]. [Figures 1.6a and b; 1.7a and b]
NAN BRE 27, Das Kaiserliche Bezirksamt Windhuk an das Kaiserliche Bezirksamt Rehoboth, 13, Juni 1914. [Figure 1.8a]
NAN ZBU 751 G II a 4, Verbrecheralbum, Fingerabdrücke, Bd 1. Der Kaiserliche Gouverneur Seitz an das Bezirksamt Windhoek, Anschluss an die Verfügung vom 3.8.1911. [Figure 1.9a and b]

National Archives of Namibia (NAN), SWAA 422 A 50/34, Native Affairs. Passports for Natives. Magistrate Windhoek, Declaration to be made by Applicant for Passport, Windhoek, 20 September 1934. [Figure 2.1]

NAN SWAA 1855 A 406 2, passports issued to Augusta and Ella Dietrich by the German General Consul in Pretoria in 1924. [Figures 2.4 and 2.5]

Western Cape Archives and Records Service, Cape Town

KAB PIO 1 – 1 47 E, Principal Immigration Officer, Application by Marie Schiffer Lafite, Cape Town, 1914. [Figure 2.2]

KAB IRC, Immigration Papers, 1/2/4 73C Lai Wing. [Figure 2.3]

KAB 1/UTA 6/1/79, Magistrate Umtata, Dompas issued to Xalisile John Tiwani. [Figure 2.6]

KAB, 1/ECO 6/1/32 N1/23/2, Dompas Application submitted by Andile Pinkerton Booi, Engcobo, 1961. [Figures 2.7 and 2.8]

KAB, 1/TSM 7/1/46 N1/23/2, The Director of the Registration Office Pretoria to the Magistrate Tsomo, 28 April 1960, Photograph included in The Director of the Registration Office Pretoria to the Magistrate Tsomo, 28 April 1960. [Figure 2.9]

KAB, 2/KMN 22, N 1/23/2, Vol. 1, Identity card application, Martha Swarts van Wyk, 17 March 1956. [Figure 2.10]

KAB CO 6978–6986 (Vol. 1–9), Breakwater Convict Albums, CO 6982, Vol. 5, page 23, photographs of John Rizzo, convict number F9427, 17.8.[18]99. [Figure 5.3]

KAB CO 6978–6986 (Vol. 1–9), Breakwater Convict Albums, CO 6978, Vol. 1, page 3. [Figure 5.4]

KAB CO 6978–6986 (Vol. 1–9), Breakwater Convict Albums, CO 6980, Vol. 3, page 15. [Figure 5.5]

KAB CO 6978–6986 (Vol. 1–9), Breakwater Convict Albums, CO 6978, Vol. 1, detail from page 2. [Figure 5.6]

KAB CO 6978–6986 (Vol. 1–9), Breakwater Convict Albums CO 6982, Vol. 5, detail from page 25. [Figure 5.7]

South African National Archives, Pretoria

SAB_NTS_8356 20/355, Vol. 1. Native Affairs Department, Survey of Native Allotments by Air photography. Aerial Survey, Secretary for Lands to Secretary for Native Affairs, 18.9.1926. [Figure 4.4a and b]

SAB_NTS_8356 20/355, Vol. 2. Native Affairs Department, Survey of Native Allotments by Air photography. Aerial Survey, Plan No. 1651/45 – Portion of Transkei Covered by Aerial Photography and Division into Areas 1-6, no date, [1945]. [Figure 4.5]

SAB_NTS_8356 20/355, Vol. 2. Native Affairs Department, Survey of Native Allotments by Air photography. Aerial Survey, Secretary for Native Affairs to Chief Magistrate Umtata, 4.6.1945 [Figure 4.6]

National Geo-Spatial Information (NGI), Cape Town

Umtata, Flight job 132, Strip 001, Image Number 18174, 1938. [Figure 4.1]

Butterworth, Job 468, Strip 1, Image Number 8433, 1961. Total of photographs: 638, scale 1:36'000. [Figure 4.7]

Ditsong National Museum of Cultural History, Pretoria

SA_dnmch_grondsake 133, Union of South Africa, Department of Native Affairs, Projects [n.d.]; Image No. 2244b, "Fencing has been erected in the rural districts of the Eastern Cape. Development was undertaken by the South African Bantu Trust", p. 29. [Figure 4.8]

SA_dnmch_grondsake 133, Union of South Africa, Department of Native Affairs, Projects [n.d.], Image No. 2241h, "Social life in the rural districts of the Eastern Cape", p. 24. [Figure 4.9]

Museum Africa, Johannesburg

PH 2006_8907, Fordsburg 1922. [Figure 4.3]

Basler Afrika Bibliographien, Basel

Archival Collection, Album A03, Foto-Album Südwestafrika. [Figure 1.10a and b]

E.R. and A. Scherz Collection, S08_0097, untitled photograph. [Figure 3.1]

E.R. and A. Scherz Collection, S004_123, untitled photograph; from album Hochzeitsreise 1938. [Figure 3.2]

E.R. and A. Scherz Collection, S004_152, 148, 153, Hochzeitsreise 1938, "Boers on the move" series. [Figure 3.3a–c]

E.R. and A. Scherz Collection, S004_160, "Eingeborene in Haribes", Hochzeitsreise 1938. [Figure 3.4]

E.R. and A. Scherz Collection, S001_0026, untitled photograph, 1933-1938. [Figure 3.5]

Ethnographic Museum Berlin

EM-SMB/32/915 (357), Magoma as Prisoner, Robben Island, Table Bay, Photographer: Gustav Fritsch. [Figure 5.1]

Pitt Rivers Museum, Oxford

Photograph Nr. 1998.211.13.10: David Selkirk, 1871, Group of prisoners. [Figure 5.2]

Police Museum Hamburg

8G/III, Fingerprints of a Hottentott woman in Lüderitzbucht, n.d. [Figure 1.12a and b]

Digital Namibian Archives

NAN, Ottilie Nitzsche-Reiter Collection, image number 034486, Natives: Damaras. Usakos Location', n.d. [Figure 3.6]

Wilhelmine Katjimune Collection

Usakos Old Location; Wilhelmine Katjimune (in a white dress) at her first communion, with Sibilla (girl on the right, surname unknown), Petrus Chabagae and Maria
Schiefer (on the left), Gertrud Schiefer and Alex Hagendorn (on the right), names
of children unknown, late 1930s [11.5 × 8.5 cm]. [Figure 3.7]
Petrus Chabagae (left) and Mr. Reiter; photographer: C.F. Fenton, Walvis Bay
[8.5 × 13.5 cm]. [Figure 3.9]

Cecilie//Geises Collection

Cecilie Geises, Usakos Old Location, n.d. [8.5 × 14 cm] [Figure 3.8]

Gisela Pieters and Olga //Garoës Collection

Herodia Goreses (on the left) and Gisela Pieters, next to Olga//Garoës' house, Usakos
old location, ca. 1950s [11 × 6.5 cm]. [Figure 3.10]

Paul Grendon Collection

Paul Grendon, Old location showers, Usakos, 2013. [Figure 3.11]

Swiss National Library

Eduard Spelterini Collection, EAD-WEHR-32111-B, Johannesburg 1911. [Figure 4.2]

Reproductions from published sources

Schultze Jena, Leonhardt, Zur Kenntnis des Körpers der Hottentotten und Buschmänner.
In ibid., *Zoologische und anthropologische Ergebnisse einer Forschungsreise im westlichen
und zentralen Südafrika ausgeführt in den Jahren 1903-1905 mit Unterstützung der Kgl.
Preussischen Akademie der Wissenschaften zu Berlin.* Bd. 5: Systematik, Tiergeographie
und Anthropologie. Jena, 1928, pp. 145–127. Plate number VII, photograph number
45, *O:sob*, Keetmanshoop in 1905. [Figure 1.11]
Duggan-Cronin, Alfred, *The Bantu Tribes. Reproductions of Photographic Studies.* Vol. III,
Section I: The Nguni. Cambridge and Kimberley, 1939. Plate 22. [Figure 4.10]
Swanepoel, S. and S. Mngqolo, *Galeshewe, Champion of the People.* Kimberley, 2011,
p. 30. [Figure 5.8]

Index

Printed in the United States
By Bookmasters